International Migration

*Evolving Trends from the Early Twentieth
Century to the Present*

States have long been wary of putting international migration on the
global agenda. As an issue that defines sovereignty – that is, who enters
and remains on a state's territory – international migration has called
for protection of national prerogatives and unilateral actions. However,
since the end of World War I, governments have sought ways to address
various aspects of international migration in a collaborative manner.
This book examines how these efforts to increase international cooperation have evolved from the early twentieth century to the present.
The scope encompasses all of the components of international migration: labor migration, family reunification, refugees, human trafficking, and smuggling, as well as newly emerging forms of displacement
(including movements likely to result from global climate change). The
final chapter assesses the progress (and lack thereof) in developing an
international migration regime and makes recommendations toward
strengthening international cooperation in this area.

Susan F. Martin is the Donald G. Herzberg Professor of Interna-
tional Migration and serves as the Director of the Institute for the
Study of International Migration in the School of Foreign Service at
Georgetown University. Previously Dr. Martin served as the Execu-
tive Director of the Congressionally mandated U.S. Commission on
Immigration Reform and as Director of Research and Programs at the
Refugee Policy Group. Her recent publications include *A Nation of
Immigrants*; *The Migration-Displacement Nexus: Patterns, Processes
and Policies* (ed.); *Managing Migration: The Promise of Coopera-
tion*; *Mexico–U.S. Migration Management: A Binational Approach*
(ed.); and *The Uprooted: Challenges in Managing Forced Migration*.
Dr. Martin received her BA in History from Douglass College, Rutgers
University, and her MA and PhD in the History of American Civiliza-
tion from the University of Pennsylvania. She is a past president of the
International Association for the Study of Forced Migration and serves
on the U.S. Comptroller General's Advisory Board and the Boards of
the Advocacy Project and DARA USA.

International Migration

Evolving Trends from the Early Twentieth Century to the Present

SUSAN F. MARTIN
Georgetown University

CAMBRIDGE
UNIVERSITY PRESS

CAMBRIDGE
UNIVERSITY PRESS

32 Avenue of the Americas, New York, NY 10013-2473, USA

Cambridge University Press is part of the University of Cambridge.

It furthers the University's mission by disseminating knowledge in the pursuit of education, learning, and research at the highest international levels of excellence.

www.cambridge.org
Information on this title: www.cambridge.org/9781107691308

© Susan F. Martin 2014

This publication is in copyright. Subject to statutory exception and to the provisions of relevant collective licensing agreements, no reproduction of any part may take place without the written permission of Cambridge University Press.

First published 2014

Printed in the United States of America

A catalog record for this publication is available from the British Library.

Library of Congress Cataloging in Publication Data
Martin, Susan Forbes.
International migration : evolving trends from the early twentieth century to the present / Susan F. Martin, Georgetown University.
    pages cm
Includes bibliographical references and index.
ISBN 978-1-107-02458-8 (hardback) – ISBN 978-1-107-69130-8 (pbk.)
1. Emigration and immigration.   2. Emigration and immigration – History – 20th century.   3. Emigration and immigration – Government policy.   I. Title.
JV6021.M37   2014
304.8 – dc23   2013045302

ISBN 978-1-107-02458-8 Hardback
ISBN 978-1-107-69130-8 Paperback

Cambridge University Press has no responsibility for the persistence or accuracy of URLs for external or third-party Internet Web sites referred to in this publication and does not guarantee that any content on such Web sites is, or will remain, accurate or appropriate.

Contents

Foreword

Peter D. Sutherland

UN Secretary General's Special Representative on International Migration and Development

On October 3, 2013, the UN General Assembly convened to discuss international migration for only the second time in its history. As Secretary General Ban Ki-moon opened the meeting that morning, four thousand miles away, in the Mediterranean Sea, rescue crews were recovering the bodies of hundreds of migrants who had drowned the previous night in their desperate attempt to reach Europe. Human smugglers had packed them like lemmings into a rickety boat; more than 350 died. A few days later, another boat capsized; still more children, women, and men perished.

The juxtaposition between the formal setting of the General Assembly and the macabre one on the southern shores of Europe begged an obvious question: What precisely can we do to make it safer for migrants to cross international borders? How can we ensure that their determined, courageous, and often desperate pursuit of a better life pays dividends for them, for their families, and for receiving communities – rather than for those who exploit them?

The twenty-first-century scale and complexity of international migration far exceeds our current capacity to govern it well. To redress that imbalance we must first understand the recent history of human mobility. And there is no better place to start than with Susan Martin's masterful overview of how the international community has addressed the challenges of refugees and international migrants over the past century.

Today, migrants are coming from, and going to, more places than ever before. In less than a decade, membership in the International Organization for Migration has soared from 90 states to 154. The old paradigm of people moving from poor countries to a handful of richer ones – the United States, the countries of Europe, Canada, and Australia – has been shattered. Almost half of international migrants now head to developing countries. As a result, dozens of states with little prior experience of contending with migration are being forced to wrestle with it.

The political calculus of governing migration is maddeningly complex. It is where sovereignty, human rights, powerful economic interests, national identity, and the individual will for a better life all intersect. Since 9/11, security concerns have scrambled the calculus even further. Perhaps no other governance issue poses such challenges. National politicians tend to shrink from it, given how migration can damage poll numbers and careers. This neuralgia makes it even harder for policy makers to address migration in the context of international cooperation.

Yet cooperate we must. Our ability to contend with migration not only affects hundreds of millions of lives; it also stands as a test of whether we can effectively manage a globalized world, of which migrants are the human face. Our approach to migration will speak volumes about our ability to address a range of fundamental challenges: Do we know how to build truly diverse, well-functioning societies? Can we slay the monsters of discrimination and xenophobia? How do we address extreme inequality?

Above all, as it has been throughout history, migration remains the most effective strategy for people to lead safer, more fulfilling lives. John Kenneth Galbraith put this best. "Migration is the oldest action against poverty," he wrote. "It selects those who most want help. It is good for the country to which they go; it helps break the equilibrium of poverty in the country from which they come." This remains as true as ever – perhaps even more so in our era of extraordinary inequality.

Fortunately, we have seen important progress over the past decade. In 2006, Kofi Annan and I advocated for the creation of a Global Forum on Migration and Development. The Forum's design – it is linked to the UN but led by member states – allowed states to maintain their sovereignty while also fostering cooperation. In the seven years of its existence, the Forum has prompted not only a common understanding of migration among states and stakeholders but also a convergence in what they see as priorities for action.

In the outcome document of the October 2013 UN High-Level Dialogue on Migration and Development, member states unanimously acknowledged "that the Global Forum on Migration and Development has proved to be a valuable forum for holding frank and open discussions, and that it has helped to build trust among participating stakeholders through the exchange of experiences and good practices, and by virtue of its voluntary, informal State-led character." Secretary General Ban Ki-moon, noting the changed mood since 2006, underscored "this progress has been made possible by the climate of trust that we established in the Global Forum on Migration and Development."

Now we must move to action. In doing so, we would do well to focus on challenges where the interests of states clearly converge.

Broadly speaking, the first such area is where the rights of migrants are violated by bad actors – smugglers, traffickers, rapacious recruiters, unscrupulous employers. "Too often, migrants live in fear – of being victimized as the so-called 'other'; of having little recourse to justice; or of having their wages or passports withheld by an unscrupulous employer," Ban Ki-moon said at the 2013 High-Level Dialogue.

There are myriad ways in which we can protect migrant rights and reduce or eliminate discrimination against them in the workplace and in the neighborhoods in which they live. We already have made significant progress on several migration-related fronts – for example, in prosecuting human traffickers. Also, I have urged states to define how we can better protect migrants affected by humanitarian crises such as civil conflicts and natural and manmade disasters. The United States and the Philippines, working with international agencies and experts, have offered to lead an initiative to address this challenge. This kind of "mini-multilateralism" – whereby small groups of interested stakeholders work together closely and efficiently to develop innovative ideas that are then debated in more formal settings – can help propel cooperation and strengthen the international system from the bottom up.

The second realm for immediate action is in drawing out the development benefits from migration. In the autumn of 2013, the World Bank released its latest figures on remittances from migrants to developing countries. These are expected to total $414 billion in 2013 (up 6.3 percent over 2012), and $540 billion by 2016. Yet, about 9 percent of these funds get lost to wire transfer fees. If we could get this down to 5 percent, we would liberate an extra $20 billion annually for some of the world's neediest families and communities. (By way of comparison, in 2012, all overseas development assistance combined totaled just $133.5 billion.) Many billions more could be saved by reforms to how migrants are recruited.

Susan F. Martin is not content just with demystifying the history of how the international community has contended with refugees and international migrants over the past century. She also offers many smart ideas for how the international community might organize itself to address the twenty-first-century challenges and opportunities of migration. We have a long way to go to turn rhetoric into action and safer, better lives for migrants and our societies. Reading this book is an important first step in making that journey.

Acknowledgments

This book is the result of more than a decade of research and participant observation of various initiatives to improve mechanisms to promote international cooperation in the management of international migration. My thanks to the organizers of the Global Forum on Migration and Development, UN High-Level Dialogue on Migration and Development, International Organization for Migration's International Dialogue on Migration, the UN Department of Social and Economic Affair's Coordination Meeting on International Migration, and other events for inviting me to participate in these important venues.

I also thank Samantha Howland and Anamaria Trujillo, my research assistants at Georgetown University, for their invaluable research support. A special thanks to Shea Houlihan who provided excellent research support for the chapter on human trafficking. I am grateful to the John D. and Catherine T. MacArthur Foundation and, especially, John Slocum and Milena Novy-Marx for their generous support of this project.

My thanks also to Alexander Betts, Rey Koslowski, Randall Hansen, Jobst Koehler, and Jeannette Money for having invited me to participate in their projects on global migration governance. I learned much that I hope is reflected in this volume.

I am grateful to Wilma and Ray Harrison for their careful reading of the entire manuscript and marvelous copyediting. And, as always, my husband Michael provided emotional support, especially during the long days of writing and fretting that accompany any endeavor of this type.

Acronyms

American Relief Administration (ARA)
General Agreement on Trade in Services (GATS)
Global Commission for International Migration (GCIM)
Global Forum on Migration and Development (GFMD)
High-Level Dialogue on Migration and Development (HLD)
Intergovernmental Panel on Climate Change (IPCC)
International Committee on Refugees (ICR)
International Conference on Refugees in Africa (ICARA)
International Covenant on Civil and Political Rights (ICCPR)
International Covenant on Economic, Social and Cultural Rights (ICESCR)
International Criminal Police Organization (INTERPOL)
International Labour Organization (ILO)
International Migrants Bill of Rights (IMBR)
International Organization for Migration (IOM)
International Refugee Organisation (IRO)
League of Nations
Nansen Refugee Office
Office of Foreign Relief and Rehabilitation Operations (OFRRO)
Organization for Security and Co-operation in Europe (OSCE)
Organisation of African Unity/African Union (OAU)
Poverty Reduction and Economic Management, World Bank (PREM)
Provisional Intergovernmental Committee for the Movement of Migrants
    from Europe (PICMME)
Transfer of Knowledge through Expatriate Nationals (TOKTEN)
UN Convention against Transnational Organized Crime
UN Convention on the Rights of Migrant Workers and Members of Their
    Families
UN Convention on the Rights of the Child

UN Convention Relating to the Status of Refugees
UN Development Programme (UNDP)
UN Framework Convention on Climate Change (UNFCCC)
UN High Commissioner for Refugees (UNHCR)
UN Korean Rehabilitation Administration (UNKRA)
UN Office of the High Commissioner for Human Rights (UNHCHR)
UN Population Fund (UNFPA)
UN Special Committee on Palestine (UNSCOP)
UNAIDS
UNICEF
United Nations Conference on Trade and Development (UNCTAD)
United Nations Educational, Scientific and Cultural Organization (UNESCO)
United Nations Entity for Gender Equality and the Empowerment of
    Women (UN Women)
United Nations Global Initiative to Fight Human Trafficking (UN GIFT)
United Nations Office on Drugs and Crime (UNODC)
United Nations Relief and Rehabilitation Administration (UNRRA)
United Nations Relief and Works Agency for Palestine Refugees in the Near
    East (UNRWA)
United Nations Voluntary Trust Fund for Victims of Trafficking in Persons,
    Especially Women and Children
United Nations Working Group on Contemporary Forms of Slavery
Universal Declaration of Human Rights (UDHR)

Introduction

States have long been wary of putting international migration on the global agenda. As an issue that defines sovereignty – that is, who enters and remains on a state's territory – international migration has called for protection of national prerogatives and unilateral action. Only in the area of refugee movements, and more recently human smuggling and trafficking in persons, have many governments agreed to binding international laws and norms. Destination countries in particular have been reluctant to engage in multilateral discussions of labor migration, fearing that irreconcilable differences would develop between themselves and source countries, thereby inflaming tensions. Nor have they been willing to establish a single intergovernmental organization with responsibilities for labor migration within or associated with the UN structure.

This book examines the progress (or lack thereof) in developing an international migration "regime." It adopts the definition of international regimes as "principles, norms, rules, and decision-making procedures" that facilitate a convergence of expectations among states (Krasner 1983:1). As Krasner (1983:7) explains, "In a world of sovereign states the basic function of regimes is to coordinate state behavior to achieve desired outcomes in particular issue-areas." The book assesses two facets of international regimes: (1) mechanisms for interstate cooperation in responding to and managing an area of common interest, and (2) the emergence of international organizations to support state initiatives.

Unlike the systems in place for movements of capital (International Monetary Fund) or goods and services (World Trade Organization), there is a complex network of intergovernmental organizations within and outside of the United Nations that focus on international migration but little in the way of a coherent regime that meets Krasner's definition (except in the case of refugees). In recent years, however, there has been growing recognition that effective management of international migration and its impact defies unilateral action, even though the barriers are formidable. This is not a new concept. As early as 1945, Hutchinson and Moore (1945:170), writing of post–World War II migration, captured the dilemma:

> Agreement with respect to migration controls is perhaps less easily reached than agreement with respect to trade and exchange controls, for the power to determine who shall enter and leave is an essential attribute of national sovereignty, and no country would compromise this power in the absence of clear indications of national self-interest in doing so. Furthermore, a migrant is not a commodity to be sent abroad regardless of his preferences or those of the countries involved. But if the control of emigration and immigration must perforce reflect national and perhaps even individual interests, migration is also essentially an international problem and would seem to require attention as such.

By definition, movements of people across borders involve at least two states, and often three or more as migrants transit through countries in order to move from source to destination countries. Bilateral and regional consultation mechanisms have proliferated to help states address the need for cooperation in managing flows of people. But negotiating such agreements to manage movements of people is an inefficient, time-consuming way to address what increasingly are global problems and opportunities.

Most governments appear willing to discuss issues related to international migration, and even to consult in identifying effective policies and practices, as witnessed in the establishment of the Global Forum on Migration and Development in 2007. They have not, however, shown the desire or capacity to coordinate migration policies or to establish an institutional locus of responsibility for helping states manage movements of people. The UN system instead has focused on improving coordination among its agencies and the International Organization for Migration, through the Global Migration Group (GMG). It has also encouraged governments to collaborate more effectively. With this intent, the UN Secretary General has appointed a Special Representative on Migration and Development to consult with states on international migration issues and discussions.

By focusing on consultation and coordination among states and within the United Nations, rather than on decision making, these incipient regime-forming steps aim to build confidence on the part of member states. States remain ambivalent about the degree or form of collaboration that makes most sense in managing flows of people. Nor have they come to agreement on the goals of a migration regime. How to balance facilitation of movements and control of unwanted migration is no doubt on the minds of most governments. But just as clearly, they must recognize that, as human beings, migrants have fundamental rights that must be protected, and there is a role for the international community in seeking to ensure that states fulfill their obligations in this regard. Hence, unlike the regimes established to address movements of capital or goods, any global regime for managing movements of people must take into account the human dimension of mobility. This means finding appropriate ways to balance concerns for the rights of migrants with the interests of states in managing movements.

Any international organization that becomes the principal focus of international institutional responsibility on migration management would similarly need to balance dual responsibilities – toward states and toward migrants. Whether states will permit this to happen depends largely on the discussions taking place in regional and global forums to determine what forms of interstate cooperation are mutually beneficial to source and destination countries, as well as to the migrants themselves. If these forums lead to the conclusion that a more robust international regime would be beneficial to all parties, then states will need to spell out the norms, decision rules, procedures, and institutional arrangement (that is, what makes a regime) to support international cooperation. In so doing, the roles and relationships among the various components of a new migration regime would need to be clarified. How the more evolved forced migration (refugees/trafficking) and more newly emerging labor migration norms and institutions would develop and intersect must be determined.

States are taking very preliminary steps toward defining the nature and form of an international migration regime, and they are not doing so in a total vacuum. Rather, since the end of World War I, a number of international organizations have been established to address various aspects of international migration. Similarly, the international community has adopted a series of conventions and treaties that set out important rights of migrants and refugees. Understanding the future of international migration requires a firm understanding of the past. The following questions are relevant in this regard: (1) Why have states taken action on certain forms of migration and not on others? (2) Why have states ratified some conventions and not others? (3) Why have states ceded some authorities to international organizations, but not others?

This book examines the evolution of the international migration regime from the early twentieth century to the present. The final chapter makes recommendations for the future. The scope encompasses all of the components of international migration: labor migration, family reunification, refugees, trafficking, smuggling, and newly emerging forms of displacement (including movements likely to result from global climate change). The intersection of international and internal migration and the evolution of international responses to internal displacement resulting from conflict, human rights violations, natural disasters, and environmental factors also are discussed.

In each case, there is a presentation of existing and emerging legal norms. Norms are important not only in defining the nature of regimes but also because they affect state behavior. As Martha Finnemore (1996:2) observes, "State interests are defined in the context of internationally held norms and understandings about what is good and appropriate. That normative context influences the behavior of decision makers and of mass publics who may choose and constrain those decision makers."

The book also examines the evolution of the international organizations that form part of any migration regime-building process. Particular attention is given to the principal organizations that emerged during the twentieth century to manage migration, including the International Labor Organization (1919), the UN High Commissioner for Refugees (1950), and the Intergovernmental Committee for the Movement of Migrants from Europe, now known as the International Organization for Migration (1951). In addition, more recent initiatives to increase international cooperation, including the 2006 and 2013 UN High Level Dialogue on Migration and Development, the Global Forum on Migration and Development (a state-owned, informal consultative process), and the Global Migration Group, are assessed.

The book builds on a series of articles I have written on migration management, going beyond these pieces to provide a more comprehensive review of current and emerging modes of international cooperation. It includes new research into the origins of the principal international organizations with migration-related responsibilities, including contemporary accounts of their formation. It also benefits from the author's participant observation in a number of the organizations and mechanisms discussed in the book, including her role as an adviser to the Global Commission on International Migration, the Global Forum on Migration and Development, and the International Organization for Migration, as well as consultancies with the UN High Commissioner for Refugees, the International Organization for Migration, and other international organizations.

THEORETICAL UNDERPINNINGS

As previously stated, this book takes Krasner's concept of international regimes as its point of departure. Krasner, in his 1983 edited volume, posited regimes as encompassing norms, principles, rules, and decision-making procedures that enable convergence of views on issues in which divergence might otherwise predominate. Hasenclever et al. (1997:9) define these terms as follows: "Principles are beliefs of fact, causation, and rectitude. Norms and standards of behavior are defined in terms of rights and obligations. Rules are specific prescriptions or proscriptions for action. Decision-making procedures are prevailing practices for making and implementing collective choice." In Krasner's view, norms and principles are fundamental defining characteristics of regimes. By contrast, rules and procedures can be changed as long as they are consistent with the norms and principles.

At the risk of grossly oversimplifying his perspective on regimes, Krasner took a realist approach to the issue. He argued that states act on their own self-interest in establishing regimes and are willing, if necessary, to modify their behavior to the dictates of the regime, because the alternative may be far worse.

In effect, international regimes emerge in order to preserve the prerogatives of states, not to constrain them. This analytic framework helps explain the reasons that governments ratify international legal instruments that bind future policy makers to the norms and principles encompassed in them. They are willing to forgo short-term gains in operating independently for the long-term benefits that convergence in state behavior offers.

In analyzing the emergence of international regimes in the area of global migration, this book focuses on three defining characteristics of an international regime. The first are international conventions and treaties, as these are often the means through which states articulate the norms and principles that will govern their behavior and their relationship with other states. Equally important in an area such as migration, international conventions also establish the rights of individuals in relationship to state actors. Because of a paucity in well-ratified international law related to migration, the book focuses on nonbinding guidance as well on discussing the principles and norms that are widely accepted.

The emergence of international organizations with migration-related missions is a second element of regime formation. In some cases, institutional missions are mandated in international conventions, which tend to legitimate certain behavior but may constrain the organization from taking on new roles. In others, the missions arise to meet specific needs and solidify over time into a coherent program of activities. As discussed in greater depth, the UN High Commissioner for Refugees represents the former model and the International Organization for Migration the latter one.

The third aspect of regime formation to be discussed herein are models of interstate cooperation – that is, the mechanisms through which states come to agreement about the norms, principles, rules, and procedures. These models also determine which other actors will be permitted to join in the deliberations. These other actors include nongovernmental organizations, experts, the private sector, and international organizations.

The study of migration regimes has taken on new importance as international movements of people have increased. Several edited volumes have been published in just the past two years that have contribute greatly to our understanding of the processes and barriers to a single, coherent international migration regime with recognized norms, principles, rules, and procedures. Alexander Betts (2011:7) focuses on global governance, which "comprises a complex range of formal and informal institutions existing on a range of levels of governance and involving a host of states and non-state actors." Putting the analysis squarely within the context of globalization, he asks why what exists in terms of global migration governance is "fragmented and incoherent in comparison to most trans-boundary issue-areas" (Betts 2011:8). Betts makes a number of points in attempting to respond. He argues that states' interests in migration governance are significantly determined by intrastate politics. Finding consensus across states in an area so susceptible to highly emotional internal responses is exceptionally difficult. Moreover, powerful states (generally the destination countries of migrants) are able to define unilateral migration policies that are consistent with their own self-interest and often see little need to cooperate with countries of origin. As discussed in this book, and as Betts discusses as well, this conceptualization may be changing since irregular migration undermines the argument that destinations have full control over who enters their territory. A further contribution of Betts's analysis is his understanding that migration tends not be discussed on its own merits but usually in its relationship to other issue areas – development, security, the environment, and so forth. This is both a strength and a weakness in formulating a migration regime. The connections to these other issues make the need for international cooperation all the more essential, but they also complicate who should be at the table in formulating the norms, principles, rules, and procedures. Finally, Betts raises the serious question of the ideas that states hold about international migration. These are very much in flux at present. There is no overarching definition of what constitutes migration or its impact on source, transit, or destination countries.

Rey Koslowski (2011) takes a somewhat different approach in his volume on *Global Mobility Regimes*. As the title implies, Koslowski sees mobility as a more encompassing term than migration is. He posits three interacting regimes: "the established international refugee regime; a latent but strengthening international travel regime; and a nonexistent but potential international labor migration" (Koslowski 2011:xiii). Each of these regimes has its own normative frameworks, but some are more developed than others. They have their own institutions as well. Yet, as Koslowski acknowledges, one form of movement often morphs into another, so these ideal types are not necessarily consistent over time. The international traveler decides to stay and work in a new country. Plans to return home are thwarted by political events in the home country, and the labor migrant or traveler becomes a refugee. The refugee is resettled in a third country and becomes a permanent settler who joins the labor force.

Koslowski agrees with Betts that a principal barrier to strengthening these regimes is the reluctance of states to join together, particularly in facilitating labor migration. Destination countries "have little incentive to join such a regime because foreign labor, especially low-skilled labor, is in abundant supply" (Koslowski 2011:7). Koslowski (2011:7) also notes that "bargaining between states on labor migration is not inherently conditioned by reciprocity." This is in contrast to trade regimes, in which opening up markets to transfer of goods is seen as beneficial for all parties.

Koslowski points to the indifference of the United States, which has the largest migrant population in the world, as one of the principal barriers to a labor migration regime. In the absence of the leadership among powerful states to forge a regime, one is unlikely to occur. By contrast, the United States and other powerful actors have had substantial interest in ensuring that the international travel regime takes form because of the linkages between border security and international flow of terrorists. One could argue, as well, that the leadership of Western powers assured the establishment of the international refugee regime as a tool of Cold War foreign policy. Many refugees assisted and protected by the UN High Commissioner for Refugees during its first forty years had fled communist countries or superpower proxy wars, such as those in Southeast Asia, Afghanistan, Central America, and parts of Africa.

Hansen (2011) also seeks to explain the relative absence of an international migration regime compared to other issue areas in which cooperation is more commonplace. His starting point is rational choice theory, which assumes that policy makers are self-interested in determining whether and how to cooperate with others. He argues that international migration is not an area "in which there is a natural incentive to cooperate" (Hansen 2011:14). This is particularly the case in seeking global cooperation, as compared to bilateral or regional agreements. Hansen points out that "the sending state and the receiving state bear the benefits and costs, and other states are only indirectly affected" (Hansen 2011:17). Moreover, the interests of sending and receiving states often differ fundamentally, especially when source countries want to increase emigration and destination countries (particularly their publics) want to reduce immigration. Incentivizing cooperation is difficult at best. The linkages between migration and other issue areas, such as trade in which greater cooperation is seen as mutually beneficial, may be one way to overcome these constraints. Hansen concludes that the greatest scope for international cooperation is in mechanisms that are informal, regional, nonbinding, and "relatively closed to public scrutiny" (Hansen 2011:14).

Kunz, Lavenex, and Panizzon (2011) lend further perspective on international migration governance by seeking to explain what they call the multilayered governance system that has arisen. The authors note that "legal norms relating to international migration today are dispersed over a variety of multilateral regimes, regional and trans-regional treaties as well as bilateral arrangements" (Kunz et al. 2011:6). An architecture for cooperation has developed, although the authors refer to it as occurring in a "very fragmented, overlapping and sometimes inchoate manner" (Kunz et al. 2011:6). The focus is on the partnerships that states have established in managing movements of people. Like Hansen, Kunz and her coauthors see regional processes as important mechanisms in the quest for greater international cooperation. They are effective in building trust, exchanging information, increasing government capacity, and promoting open dialogue. The authors suggest that these regional processes provide "fertile ground for more far-reaching and legally binding commitments" but they caution that these so-called partnerships "mask the profound asymmetry of interaction between the receiving and the sending and transit countries" (Kunz et al. 2011:17). They remark as well on the reframing of international migration as mobility, with a preference for circulation rather than permanent settlement. This formulation is consistent with the ways in which labor migration is treated in trade agreements, and it seeks to show the parallels between mobility of goods and mobility of people.

All of these works seek to place into an international relations framework the rather tentative steps being taken in the twenty-first century toward greater international cooperation on migration. All recognize that the reality of cooperation lags well behind the rhetoric that assumes that migration, as a transnational issue, requires greater collaboration among states if it is to be addressed in a more coherent manner. This is not to say that the field is without global governance. All four works describe modes of cooperation that vary depending on forms of migration, for example, forced versus voluntary, the linkages to other issue areas (e.g., trade or development), and the unit of cooperation (bilateral, regional, or global). What is missing – and all the authors are skeptical about it soon coming into play – is a single regime that would pull all of these threads together.

What Jagdish Bhagwati (2003) referred to as a World Migration Organization is unlikely in the near future. Nevertheless, the reasons he called for its formation remain: "The world badly needs enlightened immigration policies and best practices to be spread and codified. A World Migration Organization would begin to do that by juxtaposing each nation's entry, exit, and residence policies toward migrants, whether legal or illegal, economic or political, skilled or unskilled" (Bhagwati 2003:104).

The emerging literature on migration and the international political economy (IPE) helps explain the gap between rhetoric and reality. Hollifield describes IPE theorists as "interested in the connections between domestic/comparative and international politics. In addition to focusing on domestic interests, they also stress the importance of institutions in determining policy outcomes" (Hollifield and Brettell 2000:206). Yet Phillips points out that it is "striking and curious that the field of international political economy should have so neglected the study of global migration" (Phillips 2011:1), especially given that migration helps shape labor markets in a globalized economy. Hollifield explains, however, that despite the strong political-economic dimension to international migration, "until recently there was little demand for international cooperation (or policy) in the area of migration, with the major exception of managing refugee flows" (Hollifield and Brettell 2000:207).

Geddes's (2011) work on borders and migration in the EU is illustrative of an IPE approach to regime formation. If any regional entity could readily harmonize labor migration policies across its members, it would be the EU. It is composed of like-minded states with similar democratic forms of government and market economies. The EU has made substantial progress in pulling down barriers to mobility across member states and forging agreement on asylum policy. Yet a fully harmonized immigration policy framework has been elusive because, as Geddes (2011:206) describes, "member states have been reluctant to cede competence to the European Union." He attributes the reluctance to the multiple meaning of borders, not only as territorial ones but also as "organizational borders of work and welfare and conceptual borders of belonging, entitlement and identity" (Geddes 2011:207). How these borders are understood determine whether migration is seen "as a benefit, a threat, an opportunity, a risk, a danger, an asset and so on" (Geddes 2011:208). These definitions also inform the linkages between migration and broader economic and political policy debates, in this case economic reform, security, and the international identity of the EU. Geddes points out that in the political economy of the EU, labor migration is part of all of these debates and it in turn influences their ultimate outcomes. As a result, harmonization of labor migration policies can proceed only very slowly (Geddes 2011).

This book shares the skepticism that a single international migration regime will take form in the near future. With my coauthors, Philip Martin and Patrick Weill (Martin et al. 2006), I have argued that a bottom-up approach to building international cooperation on migration is preferable to a top-down one. Even if states decided to establish a World Migration Organization, there is serious doubt that they would cede any significant authorities over admission of immigrants to it. When we took this perspective, the High Level Dialogue on Migration and Development had not yet taken place. The Global Commission on International Migration was still deliberating, and the Global Forum on Migration and Development and the Global Migration Group were not on anyone's agenda. In the intervening six years, there has been a proliferation of informal consultative processes aimed at building trust and exploring modes of greater collaboration among states. The need to build a stronger normative and institutional base for managing international migration is better understood now than it was just a few years ago.

I also share with the others who have been examining the global governance of migration that much currently exists on which to build a stronger international migration regime with agreed upon norms, principles, rules, and procedures. This book takes an historical approach to these issues. I argue that the building blocks of an international migration regime were formed in the early twentieth century. In the aftermath of World War I, the interconnections among migration, economic reconstruction, and security led to the creation of new institutions, treaties, and processes under the general framework of the League of Nations. As with most of the League's apparatus, these nascent steps did not survive the advent of fascism and the outbreak of World War II. After the conflict ended with the Allied victory, norm and institution building resumed, largely to address the ways in which mass displacement affected economic recovery and international security. These soon were caught in the Cold War conflict and remained rather dormant, with the exception of the largely Western-supported refugee regime, until the breakup of the Soviet Union. It should not be surprising then that new attention has been paid to issues of international cooperation in the post–Cold War era. Examining closely the regimes that tried or succeeded in emerging in these earlier periods helps to frame the way in which international migration governance is being approached today.

Before turning to the past, however, the remainder of this chapter sets out the contemporary nature of international migration and the argument for enhancing international cooperation.

INTERNATIONAL MIGRATION: THE TWENTY-FIRST CENTURY ISSUE

There are good reasons to believe that international migration will be a defining issue of the twenty-first century. More than 200 million persons now live outside of their home country. International migrants come from all parts of the world and go to all parts of the world. In fact, few countries are unaffected by international migration. Many countries are sources of international flows, while others are net receivers, and still others are transit countries through which migrants reach receiving countries.

Every major period of globalization has seen rapid increases in international migration. The sixteenth- and seventeenth-century mercantile revolution prompted an age of exploration that in turn led to the colonization of the Americas, Africa, and Asia. The industrial revolution of the nineteenth and early twentieth centuries set off the first age of mass migration, when 55 to 60 million Europeans migrated to the Americas. Many of the migrants who were birds of passage seeking higher wages to finance upward mobility at home settled in the New World (Priore 1979). A combination of rapid population growth and displacement from agricultural areas in Europe, a need for labor in the New World, and the evolution of networks linking settled immigrants abroad to their communities of origin facilitated transatlantic migration.

The next age of mass migration began during and after World War II. In Europe, the Iron Curtain limited migration from the east, but labor-hungry Western Europe launched guest worker programs, bringing migrants from southern Europe and North Africa, some of whom settled and unified their families. Canada and the United States in the mid-1960s switched from selecting immigrants on the basis of their countries of origin to giving preference to relatives seeking family reunification. They also opened admission categories for foreigners requested by employers and for refugees resettled away from governments that were persecuting them. The result was a change in the origins of immigrants from Europe to Latin America, Asia, North Africa, and more recently, sub-Saharan Africa.

It is important to keep in mind, however, that international migration remains the exception, not the rule. Most people do not want to leave family and friends for another country. In the absence of compelling reasons at home and opportunities abroad, moving to another country is not worth even the temporary loss of these connections. Moreover, migration is very costly to migrants and their families and to countries trying to control movements. Migrants often bear the costs of recruitment fees, training for new jobs, health exams, language training, transportation to the new destination, return to their home countries, and the everyday costs of living abroad while still supporting families at home. There are additional costs of smuggling fees when the migrants are moving illegally. While they can recoup these costs because of the higher wages paid in destination locations, having access to the initial resources needed for migration separates many aspiring migrants from those who actually move.

Another reason migration remains the exception in a globalizing world is that economic growth in source countries can narrow wage differences, thereby reducing the motivation to move. The migration transition that takes a country from a net emigration area to a net immigration area occurred in southern European nations such as Italy and Spain in the 1960s and 1970s and in Asian nations such as Korea in the 1980s. The challenge is to ensure that the globalization reflected in rising flows of goods and people across national borders leads to beneficial economic and political convergence rather than the converse.

Inertia, costs, and development factors have thus reduced the differences that motivate migration in some areas. In other respects, however, the differences have been widening. Increasing differences in demographics, economics, and security between wealthier and poorer countries have created pressures toward increased migration. At the same time, revolutions in communications, transportation, and rights facilitate movement over borders. Migration networks transmit information and advice about opportunities abroad and they often provide funds to migrate as well as shelter and jobs for new arrivals. Growing differences between nations and stronger transnational networks means there are more reasons and additional means to cross borders. This promises greater levels of international migration, as discussed later in this chapter.

Demographic Factors

While population growth has slowed in many parts of the world, the momentum from past and present fertility rates means that the world's population will continue to grow even as future fertility falls. More than 80 percent of the world's population – 7.1 billion in mid-2010 – is in the developing world (Population Reference Bureau 2012). Fertility rates in developing countries have decreased to 2.5 children per woman, but fertility in the least developed countries remains high at more than 5 children per woman (UN Population Division 2013). Fertility in wealthier countries is much lower. No developed country has fertility levels that are above replacement (i.e., 2.1 children per woman); half of all developed countries have fertility rates that are below 1.4 children per woman (ibid.). Without immigration, these very different fertility patterns mean that the population shares of the world's countries will change radically during the next decades. Africa is expected to grow the fastest (more than doubling) by 2050 whereas Europe is expected to remain at current population levels or decline (Population Reference Bureau 2012).

In 2000, the UN Population Division issued a controversial report, *Replacement Migration: Is it A Solution to Declining and Ageing Population?* The report notes, "replacement migration refers to the international migration that would be needed to offset declines in the size of population, the declines in the population of working age, as well as to offset the overall ageing of a population" (UN Population Division 2000:1). Noting extremely low fertility and increased longevity in many developed countries, the report cites immigration as the principal contributor to any population increase. In the absence of immigration, most of these countries would experience population decline.

Population decline and particularly aging would in turn pose challenges for governments in terms of maintaining a tax base to support already stretched pension and medical systems. Population aging likely will lead to gaps in the labor force, particularly in sectors older workers are unlikely to fill (e.g., construction). Growth is also projected in the demand for services aimed particularly at elderly populations, including geriatricians, nurses, home health aides, and other caregivers. Immigrants already represent large shares of the workforces in these sectors. With population ageing, immigration may well be an important avenue for meeting increased labor demand in countries with low levels of population growth.

The UN report reinforced for many academics and some policy makers (especially in Europe) that international migration must be an important part of any strategy to combat population decline and aging. However, as the report pointed out, "maintaining potential support ratios at current levels through replacement migration alone seems out of reach, because of the extraordinarily large numbers of migrants that would be required" (United Nations Population Division 2000:4). The report advised governments to reassess policies and programs relating to admission of foreign workers and the integration of large numbers of recent migrants and their descendants.

While it is a fact that population decline in developed regions has been slowed by positive net immigration (UN Population Division 2000), the debate continues about what role immigration can and should play in addressing demographic changes in the future. Opposition to immigration remains strong in many countries, and public opinion may well restrict any policy options that require substantial increases in admission. During the past decade, however, even countries with little tradition of immigration have acknowledged that they have sizeable immigrant populations and are likely to continue to admit immigrants.

Economic Factors

Economic differences between nation states are widening, increasing the motivation for economically motivated migration. The world's GDP was $1.3 trillion (U.S. trillion) in 1960 and expanded to almost $70 trillion in 2011. Overall, per capita income (in constant USD) grew from about $2,400 in 1960 to just over $6,000 in 2011. Variation among countries is extremely large, however. Per capita income (taking into account parity in purchasing power – PPP) in Qatar, for example, was more than $104,300 in 2011 whereas it was only $400 in the Democratic Republic of Congo (CIA 2012).

Most migrants are young people seeking work. According to the ILO, "In 2011, 74.8 million youth aged 15–24 were unemployed, an increase of more than 4 million since 2007. The global youth unemployment rate, at 12.7 per cent, remains a full percentage point higher than the pre-crisis level. Globally, young people are nearly three times as likely as adults to be unemployed" (ILO 2012:9). Young people are also more likely to be underemployed or in jobs that are highly vulnerable to frequent periods of unemployment. This situation has been exacerbated by the global economic crisis that began in 2007, which has increased both unemployment and poverty: "Out of a global labour force of 3.3 billion [in 2011], 200 million are unemployed and a further 900 million are living with their families below the US$2 a day poverty line" (ILO 2012:31).

Another dimension of increasing economic differences between countries adds to international migration. In 2011, about 35 percent of the world's workers were employed in agriculture, down from 40 percent in 2000. In South Asia and sub-Saharan Africa, more than 50 percent of workers are in agriculture. By contrast, less than 4 percent of workers in developed countries are employed in that sector. In the poorest countries, those employed in agriculture are usually small farmers or hired workers. Farmers in these countries generally have lower-than-average incomes.

Such migration from rural areas has implications for international labor migration. First, ex-farmers everywhere are most likely to accept so-called 3-D (dirty, dangerous, difficult) jobs in urban areas, either inside their countries or abroad. Second, rural to urban migration within a country can serve as a step-stone to international migration. Ex-farmers who must find new jobs often make physical as well as cultural transitions when they move to cities. Some may find adaptation in a foreign city as easy as integration in larger cities within their home countries. This is particularly the case if past migration from their areas of origin has resulted in settled friends and relatives abroad. International migration is also less expensive for those already living in urban areas of their own countries because they are physically closer to transportation hubs and to government agencies that provide passports and visas.

Human Security

Rising demographic and economic differences combine with a third major difference among countries: human security. After the global conflict between capitalism and communism ended in the early 1990s, local conflicts erupted in many areas, leading to physical and political instability, separatist movements, new nations, and more migrants. In addition, failed states, ethnic cleansing, and genocide produced millions of refugees and displaced persons who were unable to remain safely in their home communities. Violence, kidnappings, rapes, and other manifestations of insecure societies induced still more people to migrate in search of safety.

The 1990s saw a proliferation of new states formed from the breakup of countries with artificial borders and surging nationalism within sub-regions. Creating new nations is usually accompanied by migration, as populations are reshuffled so that the "right" people are inside the "right" borders.[1] Finally, with more nations, there are more borders to cross. There were 191 generally recognized nation-states in 2000, up from 43 in 1900. A growth in state-lessness also resulted from the changing borders, with some persons having neither the citizenship of the state in which they resided nor the state of their origin.

Changing Gender Roles

Women represent a growing share of migrants, as economies of destination countries offer more service jobs and barriers to migration erode for women in sending countries. Today, about 49 percent of the world's migrants are women, up only modestly from 47 percent in 1960 (UN Division for the Advancement of Women 2004). The proportion of migrants who are women has grown to 51.5 percent in developed regions. The highest proportions of migrant women are in Europe and the lowest proportions are in northern Africa.

During the past few decades, there has been an increase in the absolute and proportional number of women migrating as primary wage earners within their families. Here again, differences between source and destination countries explain some of the trends. Overseas domestic service is a common occupation for migrant women. As women in developed countries enter the labor force in increasingly greater numbers, the demand for migrant women to perform domestic work and child and elder care services has also been increasing. Women may migrate through official contract labor programs that match workers and employers, or they may obtain such employment after migrating, often through informal networks.

Networks and Facilitators of Migration

Differences encourage migration, but it takes links between sending and receiving areas for people to move over borders. Demographic, economic, gender, and security differences are sometimes likened to negative and positive battery poles, and networks to the links that enable a current to flow. Migration

---

[1] Governments have in the past sometimes sent migrants to areas that later broke away and formed a new nation, and these internal migrants and their descendants can become international migrants without moving again, as with Russians in the newly independent Baltic States or Indonesians in East Timor.

networks are a broad concept, and include factors that enable people to learn about opportunities abroad as well as the migration infrastructure that enables migrants to cross national borders and remain abroad (Massey et al. 1993). Migration networks have been shaped and strengthened by four major revolutions in the past half-century: global economic integration, communications, transportation, and rights.

The growing integration of the world's economies is the other side of the growing economic differentials discussed previously. Economic trends facilitate international movements of people in a number of ways. The growth in multinational corporations, for example, has put pressure on governments to facilitate the inter-country movements of executives, managers, and other personnel. Similarly, corporations use contingent labor and contract out assignments at an unprecedented rate. In manufacturing, it is common for components of a single product to be made in several different countries. The corporate interest in moving its labor force to meet the demands of this type of scheduling often runs into conflict with immigration policies.

Bilateral, regional and international trade regimes are beginning to have a profound effect on migration. The European Union's evolution of a harmonized migration regime to serve as a counterpart to its customs union is but one example. The North American Free Trade Agreement (NAFTA) includes migration-related provisions permitting freer movement of professionals, executives, and others providing international services from signatory countries. The General Agreement on Trade in Services (GATS) is another example, with trade in services often requiring greater freedom for service providers to move internationally.

The communications revolution helps potential migrants to learn about opportunities abroad, and often provides both the motivation and the funds that encourage and enable people to move over national borders. The best information about opportunities abroad comes from migrants already in the destination, since they can inform family and friends at home in a context both understand. Those without family and friends abroad may see movies and TV shows produced in high-income countries that make recruiters' stories about the riches attainable abroad seem plausible.

The transportation revolution highlights the declining cost of long-distance travel. British migrants unable to pay passage to the colonies in the eighteenth century often indentured themselves, promising to work for three to six years to repay one-way transportation costs to the Americas. Migrants would sign contracts before departure, and settlers looking for workers would meet arriving ships, pay the fare, and obtain a worker who was obliged to stay with the master to pay off the transportation debt. Transportation costs today are far less. Studies suggest the times necessary for migrants to repay these costs are much shorter than in previous historic periods, so that even migrants who pay high smuggling fees can usually repay them within two or three years (Kyle and Koslowski 2001).

Through the revolution in individual human rights, many irregular migrants are allowed to stay abroad. Many countries have ratified UN human rights conventions that commit them to providing all persons with basic rights such as due process. As a result, in many countries, migrants without legal status can nevertheless stay several years by applying for various forms of relief from deportation. They may have been smuggled into a country, work in the underground economy, and apply for relief only when apprehended. Most industrial countries extend eligibility for at least some basic services to all residents, regardless of legal status, making it easier for migrants to survive while trying to establish a foothold.

Ensuring respect for human rights is especially important in the context of forced migration. Unfortunately, a large segment of migration is by dire necessity, not choice – to escape life-threatening situations. Forced migration has many causes and takes many forms. People leave because of persecution, human rights violations, repression, conflict, natural and human-made disasters, and environmental degradation that destroys livelihoods in addition to habitat. Many depart on their own initiative to escape these life-threatening situations. In a growing number of cases, however, people are driven from their homes by governments and insurgent groups intent on depopulating or shifting the ethnic, religious, or other composition of an area. Most of those who are forced to migrate for these reasons are internally displaced but an unknown number cross international borders in search of refuge.[2] Although policies tend to distinguish between forced and voluntary migration, there are many instances of mixed migration. For example, people may have been forced to leave their home countries but have chosen their country of destination, often because of family ties or greater economic opportunities.

NEED FOR INTERNATIONAL COOPERATION

As international migration has indeed become a global phenomenon, the limitations of unilateral approaches to migration have also emerged. A number of trends portend the need for enhanced international cooperation:

Growing economic integration means that multinational corporations want governments to facilitate the movements of their executives, managers, and other key personnel from their offices in one country to those in another. When labor shortages appear in such sectors as information technology or seasonal agriculture, companies also seek to import foreign workers to fill these positions. The rules for admission of foreign workers are largely governed by national legislation. However, such regional and international treaties as

---

[2] While there are good estimates from the UN High Commissioner and others on the numbers of refugees fleeing persecution and conflict, there is no consensus on the number of those migrating because of natural disasters or environmental harm.

NAFTA and the General Agreement on Trade in Services now include provisions for admission of foreign executives, managers, and professionals.

Changing geo-political and security interests view international mobility as problematic although necessary for commerce and economic growth. Balancing the competing interests of facilitation and security in an age of terrorism poses challenges to all governments. It requires cooperation in information sharing to prevent the movement of those who pose security threats while maintaining opportunities for legitimate forms of transnational mobility.

Increasing transnationalism allows migrants to maintain strong ties in two or more countries. Money transferred between immigrants and those who remain at home is an important aspect of transnationalism, as is the growing acceptance of multiple-nationality by both source and destination countries of immigrants.

Technological innovation supports migration, as discussed, but also calls for increased cooperation. The communications, information, and transportation revolutions transforming society make travel and telecommunications cheaper and easier than ever before. This increases the likelihood that migrants can move far distances. At the same time, the communications revolution has transformed the ways in which governments manage migration and share information.

Growing reliance on smugglers and traffickers has transformed international migration into a security issue linked to control of transnational organized crime. Human smuggling and trafficking in persons have become lucrative criminal enterprises. As the smugglers and traffickers organize themselves to circumvent immigration laws and policies, governments are finding it necessary to organize themselves to fight this criminal activity. The international Protocols on Smuggling and Trafficking quickly received sufficient ratifications to go into force with large numbers of state parties. This reflects the growing recognition that cooperation is needed in this particular area of migration management.

New challenges, including climate change, may prompt large-scale migration within and across borders if the worst case scenarios of rising sea levels and intensified desertification prove to be a reality. As the environment is a global issue that defies unilateral solutions, so too will be the potential migration that occurs if the impact of climate change worsens.

To some extent, these issues can be addressed through bilateral and regional mechanisms. The complexity of migration today, however, is such that migrants often transit several countries between departure from their home countries and arrival in their destination countries. In some cases, the same source countries produce migrants to multiple destination countries in different regions. These situations call for global responses. Negotiating bilateral and regional agreements to manage movements of people is an inefficient, time consuming way to address what are increasingly global problems and global opportunities.

FORMS OF MIGRATION

The people who share the migrant label differ considerably. Most move across borders for greater economic opportunity while others are joining family members settled abroad. Still others are fleeing persecution and violence. The principal forms of international migration correspond with the reasons people migrate: family formation and reunification; labor migration; and refugees and other forced migrants. Each of these categories includes individuals who migrate legally and others who migrate through irregular channels or overstay their legal authorization.

Family Formation and Reunification

Family formation and reunification are significant reasons for moving internationally. Upon marriage, one or both spouses generally move from the family home to a new residence. Usually, this move occurs within the same country, but it can involve relocation to a new country. A spouse may also move internationally for work purposes and then bring family members to reunify in the new area. In some instances, a foreign worker or student who marries a citizen of the destination country may remain there as a permanent resident.

Governments often permit close family members of those already in the country to enter through legal channels, although this policy is found more frequently in the traditional immigration countries than in those only authorizing contract laborers. The anchor relative in the host country may have been married and had children at the time of arrival but left his or her family members behind. Having determined to remain in the host country, he or she petitions for family reunification. Alternatively, a citizen or international migrant already living in the host country marries a foreign national and seeks his or her admission.

Family reunification and formation programs can invite various abuses unless managed well. Fraud may result if marriage to a citizen or permanent resident is the only or principal route to admission. Companies recruiting mail-order brides tend to be highly successful in countries with poor economies and few economic opportunities for women. While many companies have a legitimate interest in matching spouses, some of these businesses use the lure of immigration as a pretext for trafficking the women into prostitution. To combat the potential for fraud, the United States, for example, offers conditional status to the immigrating spouse in recent marriages and reviews the cases after one year to make sure that the marriage is valid before granting permanent status. The United States also provides means by which women and children who are victims of domestic abuse may become permanent residents without the permission of or remaining with the abusive husband/father.

Family reunion is often seen to be a consequence of labor migration. For example, in the years after guest worker programs ended in Europe, most officially sanctioned international migration consisted of family reunion as former guest workers brought relatives to join them. Similarly, a substantial share of the migration into the United States in the past decade has been family members of unauthorized migrants who gained legal status through the Immigration Reform and Control Act of 1986.

Family reunion is also a cause of still further migration. Many would-be labor migrants learn of employment prospects through their family members in other countries and then seek authorized or, in some cases, unauthorized entry to take the jobs. Moreover, once family members obtain residence status in a new country, they are often able to bring in additional relatives through family reunification programs. This process is called chain migration. Few countries permit legal immigration of extended family members but such movements can still take place. As an example, an international migrant with long-term residence sponsors his new spouse for admission. They then sponsor each of their parents, who in turn, sponsor their other children who enter with their spouses, who in turn sponsor their parents. In this way, the chain continues.

Eligibility for family reunification is not universal. Many contract labor arrangements preclude admission of family members. Admission rules often restrict family reunification for asylum seekers and those granted temporary protection, even in traditional immigration countries.

Migrating spouses are more likely to be women than men. In the United States, for example, almost twice as many women immigrate as the spouses of U.S. citizens and permanent residents. These figures are not surprising because family reunification often follows male-dominated labor migration. In the years after guest worker programs ended in Europe, most officially sanctioned international migration consisted of family reunion as former guest workers brought their spouses and children to join them. A distinct minority of contract workers were female. The majority comprised men who then sought the admission of their female spouses and children. Similarly, the wives and dependent children of male unauthorized migrants who gained legal status through the Immigration Reform and Control Act of 1986 constitute a substantial share of the migration into the United States in the past decade.

Labor Migration and Education

Labor migration is a significant part of voluntary movements. Migration for study purposes is also common. These occur as individuals seek improved economic opportunities away from their home communities. Migrants may move through legal, registered channels or they may move without authorization by government authorities. Migration can be temporary (individuals move for a short period and then return to their home communities), circular (individuals move back and forth between home and work communities), or permanent (individuals relocate themselves and, possibly, their families). Furthermore, some individuals move from being one type of migrant to another. For example, workers may intend initially to remain only temporarily or to circulate but then become permanent residents.

Several distinct categories of people migrate for work purposes, differentiated by their skills, the permanence of their residence in the host country, and their legal status. At the lower end of the skills spectrum, migrants pick fruits and vegetables, manufacture garments and other items, process meat and poultry, work as nursing home and hospital aides, clean restaurants and hotels, and provide multitude of other services. Overseas domestic service is a common occupation for migrant women.

At the higher end of the skill spectrum, migrants engage in equally diverse activities. They fill jobs requiring specialized skills, run multinational corporations, teach in universities, supply research and development expertise to industry and academia, and design, build, and program computers, to name only a few activities. Sizeable numbers of migrants are in the health professions, particularly nursing and physical therapy. They are found in such occupations throughout the world.

In most countries, international migrants are admitted as temporary workers and they are granted work authorization for specified periods. They have no right to remain in the destination country beyond the period of authorized employment. This is particularly true in the Persian Gulf states and East and Southeast Asia. In some cases, particularly in Europe, if a permit is renewed several times, the international migrant is allowed to remain indefinitely. The traditional immigration destination countries – the United States, Canada, and Australia – also have mechanisms for direct admission of foreign workers for permanent settlement.

While many people migrate through legal work programs, unauthorized workers can be found in almost as diverse a range of jobs and industries as authorized workers. Agricultural and food processing jobs, light manufacturing, and service jobs are the most common types of employment. In many cases, the jobs are highly exploitative and the migrants have little recourse but to accept low wages and highly undesirable working conditions.

Refugees and Displaced Persons

Refugees have a special status in international law. A refugee is defined by the 1951 UN Convention Relating to the Status of Refugees as: "a person who, owing to well-founded fear of being persecuted for reasons of race, religion, nationality, membership of a particular social group or political opinion, is outside the country of his nationality and is unable or, owing to such fear, is unwilling to avail himself of the protection of that country" (UN Convention 1951). Refugee status has been applied more broadly, however, to include other persons who are outside their country of origin because of armed conflict, generalized violence, foreign aggression, or other circumstances which have seriously disturbed public order and therefore require international protection.

By most estimates, 70–75 percent of the world's refugee and displaced population is composed of women and their dependent children (Martin 2003). Children account for about half of all refugees, with adult women often outnumbering adult men. This picture varies, however, by countries of origin and refuge. It is particularly true when refugees flee conflict in one developing country and take refuge in another, usually neighboring country. This distribution does not generally hold for asylum-seekers who seek admission to more developed countries in North America, Europe, and Oceania. A higher proportion of male applicants can be found making their way to these more distant places.

Refugees present many challenges to the international community. Foremost are their special needs for legal and physical protection. Civilians are increasingly the targets of attacks in civil conflicts, including rape and sexual violence that is now a recognized war crime. Assault also occurs during flight at the hands of border guards, government and rebel military units, bandits, and others. Refugee safety may be no more ensured once in camps or settlements. For example, refugee and displaced women have faced serious threat of rape when they seek firewood, often the only source of heating and cooking fuel. Refugees have been forced to provide sexual favors in exchange for obtaining food rations for themselves and their families.

Some refugees are unable to return home or to remain in countries of first asylum. They may be candidates for resettlement to a third country. Resettlement in third countries is generally considered to be the least desirable solution for refugees because it moves them further from their own countries and cultures. In many situations, however, resettlement is the best solution for the individuals and groups involved, particularly when needed to provide protection or durable solutions.

Migration versus Trafficking

A particularly troubling trend in recent years has been the emergence of professional trafficking operations that exploit primarily women and children. Trafficking is defined as: "the recruitment, transportation, transfer, harboring or receipt of persons, by means of the threat or use of force or other forms of coercion, of abduction, of fraud, of deception, of the abuse of power or of a position of vulnerability or of the giving or receiving of payments or benefits to achieve the consent of a person having control over another person, for the purpose of exploitation."[3] The trafficking of people for prostitution and forced labor is one of the fastest growing areas of international criminal activity and one that is of increasing concern to the international community.

Generally, trafficking moves people from less developed countries to industrialized nations or toward neighboring countries with marginally higher

---

[3] Protocol to Prevent, Suppress and Punish Trafficking in Persons, Especially Women and Children, Supplementing the United Nations Convention Against Transnational Organized Crime.

standards of living. Since trafficking is an underground criminal enterprise, there are no precise statistics on the extent of the problem. However, even conservative estimates suggest the problem is serious. Trafficking in persons is now considered the third largest source of profits for organized crime, behind only drugs and guns. It generates billions of dollars annually.

Recognizing the growth of trafficking operations, states agreed to a UN Protocol to Prevent, Suppress and Punish Trafficking in Persons, Especially Women and Children. This instrument, in combination with its companion protocol on human smuggling, requires international cooperation in combating smuggling and trafficking and encourages states to pass measures for the prevention of those who have been trafficked. The Trafficking Protocol entered into force on December 31, 2003, and the Smuggling Protocol entered into force on January 28, 2004. They filled a void by laying out a mechanism to enable governments to cooperate in prohibiting and prosecuting smugglers and traffickers of humans.

POLICY IMPLICATIONS

Given the large and growing movements of people across international borders, policy makers at the national, regional, and global levels face many challenges. Five areas stand out:

Managing Flows of People

The most controversial forms of migration are those that occur outside of legal channels. Reducing irregular migration is a difficult process that requires a complex set of policy options, including enforcement at borders and in the interior, detention and removal of persons who pose security risks, and regularization of those who are unlikely to be removed and who perform needed services. Steps to address the root causes at home are needed as well.

Managing migration also requires an effective and efficient system for legal admissions. Included are programs to address labor market needs, facilitate family reunification, and respond to humanitarian needs for admission. Many countries have legal immigration systems that fall well short of meeting the demand for workers or their humanitarian obligations.

Integrating Newcomers and Second Generation

The impact of immigration (particularly permanent migration) will largely be determined by the extent to which international migrants successfully integrate into their new countries. Integration is often described as a two-way street. It involves the adaptation of immigrants to a new economy, society, and culture, as well as adaptations made by the destination country to the presence and participation of the newcomers. Measures of integration include economic ones (employment, earnings, etc.), host country language acquisition, residential integration/segregation, naturalization, and civic participation. Even when immigrants appear to be integrated economically, they may face discrimination and marginalization.

Reducing Forced Migration

With millions displaced within and across borders for reasons beyond their control, policy makers are searching for new approaches to providing assistance and protection to today's forced migrants and finding solutions to even greater displacement in the future. As will be discussed in this book, the best developed international regime for addressing forced migration pertains to refugees who are covered under the well-ratified Refugee Convention served by the UN High Commissioner for Refugees. The policies for addressing displacement from other crises, such as acute natural disasters, nuclear and industrial accidents, or pandemics are far less developed at the national, regional, and international levels. The looming problems of climate change and the potential for displacement of millions from slow-onset situations, such as rising sea levels and persistent drought, place further pressure on policy makers to take proactive actions to help people adapt, in some cases, through migration.

Promoting Migration-Related Development

Migration has an impact on both sources and destinations of migrants. The migration-development nexus has two components: the effects of development (and underdevelopment) on migration and the effects of migration on development. Economists posit a migration hump – meaning that, paradoxically, in the short- to medium-term, greater economic development at home increases international migration until wages and income between source and destination begin to equalize. At that point, a formerly emigration country may well become an immigration country. In the meantime, much attention has been put on the remittances that migrants send to their home countries, which may exceed foreign trade, foreign investment, and official development assistance. Other contributions of migrants, including their social remittances – that is, the values, norms and ideas they bring home – are receiving new attention.

Improving International Cooperation

This last issue is the aim of this book – steps that can be taken to build greater collaboration among and between governments, civil society, and the private sector to manage a transnational issue that affects all of these parties while retaining the rights and responsibilities of individual nations to determine who will become their new citizens.

ORGANIZATION OF THE BOOK

This book is organized both chronologically and topically. Chapter 1 reviews the origins of current organizational and conceptual models of international cooperation in the aftermath of World War I. It focuses on successes and failures in three principal areas: the development of the International Labor Organization (ILO) and its migration functions; efforts to harmonize passport standards to provide uniform documentation for travel purposes; and the establishment of international responsibility within the League of Nations for addressing the problem of refugees.

Chapter 2 addresses refugee policies in the post-World War II era, when the UN High Commissioner for Refugees was founded and the 1951 Refugee Convention was promulgated. It discusses the evolution of the refugee regime during the past sixty years and concludes with analysis of its strengths and weaknesses in addressing forced migration today.

In Chapter 3, there is a return to issues of labor migration. In the aftermath of World War II, the ILO drafted the first binding convention on cooperation between states in managing migration for employment. Building on an abortive effort in 1939, the convention delineated rights of migrant workers and responsibilities of states. The chapter explores ILO's continuing role in helping states address labor migration issues, as well as efforts to forge a Migrant Workers Convention in the United Nations.

Chapter 4 examines the evolution of the only international organization with an explicit migration management mandate – the International Organization for Migration (IOM). IOM had its origins in the post–World War II era, mostly to facilitate the resettlement of displaced persons. Over the past sixty years, its program has grown in scale and complexity. It stands outside of the UN and to date its member states prefer its flexibility and reliance on direct programmatic government support. Unlike the other two organizations discussed, IOM's work is not tied to a specific set of conventions; nor does it have independent authority to monitor the way in which governments carry out their responsibilities toward migrants.

The next four chapters focus on international responses to issues on the current policy agenda. Chapter 5 examines responses to trafficking in persons. The chapter explores the reasons that trafficking has long been seen as an area for international cooperation and the steps taken in the past decade to address the problems associated with this issue.

Chapter 6 discusses the interconnections between migration and security. Arguing that the securitization of the migration discourse began well before the September 11 terrorist attacks, the chapter examines in detail the ways in which terrorist threats have helped shaped areas of intergovernmental cooperation. It also addresses issues related to human smuggling as a manifestation of transnational organized crime.

Chapter 7 addresses issues related to anticipatory and forced migration related to environmental change. It explains the interconnections between environmental pressures and migration, displacement, and planned relocation of populations in the context of climate change. The chapter explores developments within the UN Framework for the Climate Change Convention to address these issues under the rubric of climate change adaptation. It also covers ways in which discussion of climate change related displacement has led to a reexamination of policies and legal frameworks for addressing forced migration.

In Chapter 8, the focus is on the interconnections between migration and development. The chapter examines the shifting frameworks for international consultations from a formal decision-making conference that focused primarily on ways to reduce emigration pressures to a hybrid system of informal consultations within the UN and in state-led processes at the regional and global level.

Chapter 9 looks toward the future at the two principal ways in which the migration regime has been developing. These include efforts to establish and coordinate international institutions to respond to the growing challenges of international migration, and efforts to establish mechanisms for intergovernmental exchange of information, consultation, and (most elusively) action in addressing one of the great transnational issues of today.

I

Early Roots

This chapter explores the origins of international efforts to manage movements of people, focusing on developments in the early twentieth century. After briefly discussing the rather open system that prevailed in the nineteenth century and the closing of that system as World War I approached, the chapter discusses patterns of migration that affected these developments. Specifically, new challenges are addressed, such as the advent of immigration quotas, passports, and visas as mechanisms to balance perceived concerns about security with the desire to facilitate beneficial mobility. This chapter also discusses the ways in which growing nationalism in Europe in the pre-World War I period heralded an era in which mass displacement became the norm as new states emerged from the revolution and the break up of the Hapsburg, Ottoman, and German empires.

The Treaty of Versailles created the first international organization that addressed issues related to migration of workers – the International Labor Organization (ILO). The ILO's constitution was drafted between January and April 1919 by a commission chaired by Samuel Gompers. It included representatives from Belgium, Cuba, Czechoslovakia, France, Italy, Japan, Poland, the United Kingdom, and the United States. The constitution created a tripartite organization, including representatives of governments, employers, and workers in its executive bodies. The preamble to the constitution listed a number of areas in which the ILO could make improvements, including "protection of the interests of workers when employed in countries other than their own." Some of the earliest conventions adopted by the ILO pertained to employment of seafarers – an appropriate area of international attention since much of their work involved moving from country to country outside the jurisdiction of any one government. For the most part, however, the ILO's attempts to promulgate standards on migrant workers did not yield positive effects in the subsequent intra-war period. Negotiations took place on such issues as inspection of migrant workers on ships, pension rights of migrant workers, and migration for employment, but these conventions were shelved or withdrawn. It was not until 1949 that the Convention on Migration for Employment was adopted, and it did not come into force until 1952 (and even then with relatively few state parties).

As early as 1920, the newly formed League of Nations convened an international conference on the subject of passports and customs controls. The conference sought consistency in passport standards. It recommended uniform provisions for their layout, content, validity, and for issuing fees. For example, the conferees determined that all passports should be in French (considered a universal language of diplomacy) in addition to the language(s) of the issuing country. Countries that were not members of the League, such as the United States, nevertheless adopted the standards.

The most difficult migration issue for the League was what to do about the millions of refugees in Europe. In 1919, the League appointed Fridtjof Nansen as High Commissioner for Refugees and charged him with finding solutions for Russian refugees. His mandate expanded over the next decade as new groups became displaced. In 1922, the high commissioner introduced what is now called the Nansen passport for refugees who had no country that could or would issue them documentation. Nansen passports became internationally recognized travel documents that gave their bearers a measure of mobility.

The League's refugee organizations had some success in addressing the problems arising from refugees created by the Russian Revolution and the Greco-Turkish population exchanges after the Treaty of Lausanne. They failed miserably, however, in finding solutions for refugees from Nazi Germany and its conquered areas. This chapter ends with a discussion of the Evian conference, convened in 1938, during which only one of the assembled government representatives offered to resettle the refugees. Instead, it recommended a committee to continue to study the problem and try to find resettlement opportunities. The failure to save refugees from Nazi Germany provided the context for development of the international refugee regime, described in Chapter 2.

CHANGING IMMIGRATION POLICIES AND CONTEXTS IN THE EARLY TWENTIETH CENTURY

The nineteenth century and the first decade of the twentieth were periods of mass international migration. The principal countries attracting permanent immigration – the United States, Canada, Australia, South Africa, and a number of Latin American countries – had few restrictions on immigration. Rather, they welcomed millions of newcomers, largely from Europe, to build nations that were predicated on the admission and integration of immigrants. Timothy Hatton and Jeffrey Williamson's seminal study, *The Age of Mass Migration: Causes and Economic Impact*, on European migration from 1850–1914, explains:

The story begins with two economic shocks of enormous proportions: a resource discovery in the New World and an industrial revolution in the Old World.... The two shocks produced a profound labor market disequilibrium early in the century. Wage gaps between the labor-scarce New World and the labor-abundant Old World reached huge dimensions.... But these two shocks also produced the means by which global labor market integration could, at least eventually, be achieved. (Hatton and Williamson 1998:250)

The same process was unfolding within Europe as people migrated from rural to urban areas and from agrarian to industrial countries. The nineteenth and early twentieth centuries saw growth in physical mobility within Europe as many countries eliminated restrictions on travel within their territories and allowed commerce across newly emerging national borders. Passport requirements that had been imposed largely to restrict internal migration and regulate emigration were loosened considerably as feudalism ended and the dictates of mercantilism and industrialization encouraged freer movement of goods and labor.[1]

The primary economic activity that would draw immigrants in the nineteenth century was occurring in industrializing cities. Calavita (1984:3) describes this period in the United States (but equally applicable to the other countries) as dominated by capitalist immigration, which had the following characteristics: "1) the complete separation of the work force from the means of production; 2) relations of production that are based on free contract and bargaining, not outright force; and 3) an insatiable drive for increasing levels of surplus labor and surplus value." New technologies linked markets throughout the world, and immigration was but one manifestation of this era of globalization.

Initially, much of the migration from and within Europe came from Britain, Ireland, Germany, and Scandinavia. By the 1880s, however, wages in the principal northern and western European emigration countries had increased significantly enough to offer economic rewards to those who remained at home. Emigration from Europe did not stop, however. The new source countries were largely in southern and eastern Europe. Lagging behind the now industrializing northern and western European countries, the Mediterranean countries and the peripheral areas of the Austro-Hungarian and Russian empires (e.g., Italy, Greece, Poland) became new sources of immigrants. Wages and living

---

[1] An exception to this pattern was Italy, which passed legislation in 1901 requiring that "transoceanic travelers be in possession of a passport before purchasing their steamer tickets." Rather than seeking to restrict emigration, the new passport was said to be needed because too many Italians were denied admission when they arrived in the United States (Torpey 2000: 103). The requirement would ensure that would-be emigrants received appropriate advice and information from the Italian government to help them qualify for admission, while providing the destination countries proof of the immigrants' identities. An outlier of the opposite type was Russia, which continued to require passports that restricted both internal travel and emigration (except for Jews who were required to live in specific areas or exit the country) well into the twentieth century.

standards remained far lower in these countries than could be found in North America or in Western Europe. Moreover, the cost of transport and the time needed to reach destination countries had fallen dramatically with the advent of steam powered ships and the proliferation of railroads across Europe.

These lower financial and other costs of migration had profound implications for the type of migration that emerged in the late nineteenth century, with a significant portion of the migrants seeking temporary work options. No longer was the cost of return migration prohibitive for many Europeans who sought higher wages in the New World. Between 1908 and 1910, 2.297 million immigrants were admitted to the United States alone and 713,356 departed (Immigration Commission 1911:41).

Not all migration of this period was motivated solely by economic interests and certainly, temporary migration was not the norm for many of the arriving immigrants. Jewish immigration was seen at the time as an exception to the largely economic motivation of other immigrant groups.[2] In 1882, Russian Jews were required to move from rural areas and villages into small towns (shtetls) within the Pale of Settlement. In 1891–1892, even more restrictive measures were introduced, including the expulsion of Jews from eastern Russia into the Pale, including 30,000 from Moscow, 20,000 from St. Petersburg, and still more from villages throughout the Pale. The growing number and changing characteristic of the attacks on Jews (pogroms) that began after Czar Alexander II's assassination in 1881 and the ascension of Alexander III to the throne also stimulated emigration. The pogroms of 1903–1905 were particularly devastating and led to the highest rates of Jewish emigration – some 125,000 emigrated in 1905–1906 alone.

Concerns about the new immigrants and their impact soon arose and contributed to efforts to restrict admissions. A leading proponent of restriction in the United States concluded that the new immigrants "are beaten men from beaten races, representing the worst failures in the struggle for existence" (Walker 1896).[3] In Canada, a socialist leader described immigrants from eastern and southern Europe as "poor, illiterate, and with a code of morals none too high" and "a most undesirable class" who "lie most naturally and by preference (quoted in Kelley and Trebilcock 1998:137)."

These concerns led to a series of bills in the traditional immigration destination countries designed to shift the *nature* of immigration but not yet its scale. Those who were barred from admission to the United States included prostitutes and convicts (1875), persons likely to become a public charge (1882), migrants brought in under contract for the performance of labor or services of any kind (1885), and persons suffering from certain contagious disease, felons,

---

[2] More recent historiography on Jewish immigration emphasizes the economic roots. See, for example, Hertzberg (1998).

[3] Francis A. Walker (1896). "Restriction of Immigration," *Atlantic Monthly*. Available online at http://www.theatlantic.com/magazine/archive/1896/06/restriction-of-immigration/306011/.

individuals convicted of other crimes or misdemeanors, polygamists, and immigrants whose passage was paid by other persons (1891). After several failed attempts, legislation imposing literacy requirements on admission to the United States was adopted over President Wilson's veto in 1917. Australia adopted similar types of restrictions when the federal government gained control over immigration policy in 1901. For example, the Immigration Restriction Act of 1901 included bars on admission related to infectious or communicable diseases, mental illness, and a range of chronic, noncommunicable diseases, such as chronic alcoholism, paralysis, cancer, and chronic rheumatism (Bashford and Howard 2004).

The United States, Canada, and Australia made special efforts to restrict immigration from Asia after an initial phase of welcoming workers to build their railroads and undertake other backbreaking work. U.S. legislation in 1882 barred admission of Chinese workers, although it allowed those who were already in the country to leave and reenter if they obtained proper documentation of their status prior to departure (a harbinger of later passport and visa documentation requirements) (Torpey 2000). Canadian legislation in 1885 deterred Chinese arrivals through a prohibitively expensive head tax. In the 1887 Alien Labour Act, Canada enacted restrictions on the arrival of contract workers to bar entry of Indians and Japanese, by specifying that those who came to Canada had to embark on a "continuous journey" from their countries of origin (Kelley and Trebilcock 1998:149). Since no shipping company provided direct service from India to Canada, and Japanese had to transit Hawaii to get there, this regulation served to ban immigration from these countries. Australia had adopted what is often described as the "White Australia" policies beginning in 1901 with passage of the Immigration Restriction Act. It "enabled the government to exclude any person who 'when asked to do so by an officer fails to write out at dictation and sign in the presence of the officer, a passage of 50 words in length in a European language directed by the officer"[4]

MIGRATION TRENDS AND POLICIES DURING WORLD WAR I

Within Europe, in the words of John Torpey (2000:111), "The booming of the guns of August 1914 brought to a sudden close the era during which governments viewed foreigners without 'suspicion and mistrust' and they were free to traverse borders relatively unmolested." The restrictions during World War I took two forms: imposition of passport and other documentation requirements on foreigners, especially those from enemy states, and the passage of legislation to restrict movements of foreigners into and within the territory of a given country.

---

[4] See "Home." Museum of Australian Democracy at Old Parliament House. Available at http://moadoph.gov.au/.

As an example, in France, identification cards became mandatory for all foreigners older than fifteen. The cards showed the nationality, civil status, occupation, photograph, and signature of foreign nationals, as well as a code demonstrating whether they worked in agriculture or industry. The UK Aliens Restriction Act of 1914 put the responsibility on foreigners to demonstrate their identity and nationality. While not explicitly requiring passports or identity cards, the provision effectively necessitated that foreigners obtain documents to prove their nationality. The legislation also allowed the government to prohibit foreigners from living in certain areas and required foreigners to register their place of domicile and movement within the UK with government authorities. Germany required anyone, including German citizens, who wished to enter or leave its territory to be in possession of a passport and visa with a personal description, photograph, and signature of the bearer (Torpey 2000). The United States also enacted wartime controls, passing the Entry and Departure Controls Act in 1918. The legislation authorized the president to control entry and departure in times of war or national emergency of any alien whose presence was deemed contrary to public safety.

Governments initially justified the new requirements as temporary exigencies of conflict. The requirement to show documentation when exiting the country was often aimed at reducing the likelihood that those subject to military service would leave without permission. Passport and visa requirements on foreigners as well as limits on their freedom of movement were justified as appropriate security measures to ensure that the nationals of enemy states did not infiltrate or cause harm. When the war came to an end, however, passport requirements were retained. Peace and security seemed shaky, particularly in light of new conflicts arising in the Balkans, the Bolshevist threat in Russia, and the rise of fascism. Torpey adds, however, that the imposition of documentation requirements distinguishing between citizens and foreigners was also a natural bureaucratic response to the needs of the nation-state and was particularly strong in democracies: "The tighter connection between citizens and states as a result of democratization led to an intensified preoccupation with determining who is 'in' and who is 'out' when it came to enjoying the benefits – both political and economic – of membership in those states" (Torpey 2000:121).

Although immigration decreased somewhat during and immediately after World War I, it resumed as soon as conditions in Europe permitted. Believing that the qualitative restrictions were inadequate to stem the tide, those favoring reduction in immigration turned to quantitative restrictions. The resulting National Origins quotas established in the Immigration Acts of 1921 and 1924 accomplished these aims. They led to substantial reductions in numbers of immigrants, with severe limitations on immigration from eastern and southern Europe and bars on almost all Asian migration. Migration within the western hemisphere remained without numerical quotas but was subject to the various grounds of exclusion already discussed. By 1926, Canada had also adopted a mixed immigration system, with what were essentially bars on migration from

Asia, Africa, and the Caribbean (even from British colonies) and restrictions on immigration from southern and eastern Europe, but a rather open system for migration from Britain and the United States. Australia maintained its "White Australia" policies into the 1960s.

The immigration policy changes initially restricted and then effectively eliminated migration to the New World as a safety valve for the unemployed and the oppressed of eastern and southern Europe, Asia, and Africa. Over time, they also required those who wished to emigrate to gain permission from the receiving country prior to embarking on the journey, whether they were intending to settle or to visit. Documentation became increasingly more important as a way to demonstrate who had permission to enter and who did not.

These restrictions in immigration policies were occurring just as migration emerged as a major issue in postwar Europe. Three factors caused people to be on the move. First, the war itself displaced millions of people. In Europe, about 10 million were displaced between 1914 and 1918. As Proctor described, World War I ushered in a new era in conflict that had grave consequences for civilian populations: "The 1914–1918 conflict witnessed the first aerial bombing of civil populations, the first widespread concentration camps for the internment of enemy alien civilians, and an unprecedented use of civilian labor and resources for the war efforts" (Proctor 2010:3). Each of these resulted in mass displacement. Many were internally displaced, but others fled across borders or were deported to forced labor camps. An estimated 1.5 million Belgians alone fled the fighting in their country (Proctor 2010). By January 1917, more than 4 million Russians had been displaced (Gatrell 1997). Several hundred thousand Jews fled or were deported from Latvia and Galicia at the hands of Russian troops (Proctor 2010).

The second cause of large-scale migration was the Russian Revolution and subsequent civil war. Williams (1997) estimates that there were between 2 and 3 million refugees in the early 1920s. They included a range of ethnic groups, including ethnic Russians, Poles, Jews, and others. Most were characterized by their opposition to the Bolshevist regime. Many were described as "White Russians," referring to a movement that took that name in fighting the Soviet army during the civil war. They took refuge in France, Germany, Czechoslovakia, the Balkans, Poland, the Baltic States, Turkey, and China (Williams 1997). Some found their way to the United States, Canada, and Australia.

The third factor influencing displacement in the early twentieth century was the growth of extreme nationalism as the Austro-Hungarian and, especially, the Ottoman empire disintegrated. The collapse of the Ottoman Empire began prior to World War I. In 1908, as the Ottomans were responding to internal dissent from what was termed the "Young Turks," the Hapsburg Austro-Hungarian Empire annexed Bosnia–Herzegovina. The Balkan Wars of 1912 and 1913 resulted in the Ottoman withdrawal from much of the remaining territory it held in Europe, ceding that territory to Serbia, Greece, and Bulgaria. Approximately 800,000 people were displaced by the fighting,

Armenian Genocide
↓

including 400,000 Muslims who left the Balkan states, fearing retribution (Zürcher 2003). The treaties ending the Balkan Wars left "a large Muslim majority, in Greek hands and Eastern Thrace, which was two thirds Greek and Bulgarian, in Ottoman hands" (Zürcher 2003:2). The second Balkan War resulted in an agreement between Bulgaria and the Ottomans for voluntary population exchange, but it was not carried out because of the intervention of World War I. The model reemerged, however, in the 1920s.

In 1915, a much bloodier uprooting occurred, resulting in large-scale deportations and mass killings. The Turkish authorities argued that the deportations were merely legitimate wartime relocations to guard against Armenian complicity with invading Russian forces. Historians have generally questioned this assertion, however, because of the scope of the deportations (which included whole communities of men, women, and children who had remained loyal to the Ottoman Empire and lived far from border areas) and the ruthlessness with which they were carried out. As Walker (2004:248) describes, "In the burning summer heat, they were driven on and on, by gendarmes who completely dehumanized them, along designated routes, until they collapsed and died by the wayside. No mercy was shown for pregnant women or nursing mothers. If they would not go on, they were killed." As the deportations and killings proceeded, Muslim refugees from the Balkan Wars were resettled in the Armenian refugees' homes (Walker 2004:249). Estimates of the number of Armenians who were deported and how many survived vary, but indicate that about 1.5 million were deported from their villages and towns, out of 2 million in the empire, and between 800,000 and 1 million were killed. Those who survived fled to the then Czarist Empire, with smaller numbers going to Syria, and even fewer to Egypt. An estimated 200,000 ethnic Armenians took refuge in the Russian trans-Caucusus to escape Turkish attacks in 1915 (Proctor 2010).

THE TREATY OF VERSAILLES

The end of World War I marked a decisive shift in international relations, and the beginnings of new approaches to the governance of international migration. Most notable were the establishment of the League of Nations and the incorporation of labor issues into the Treaty of Versailles, which decreed establishment of the ILO. Although neither of these steps focused directly on immigration, the League of Nations and the ILO began to engage these issues.

League of Nations

With the end of the war, President Wilson tried to impose his views of democracy on the peace process through promulgation of his fourteen points that emphasized transparency in foreign relations, free trade, democracy, and self-determination. While Wilson did not achieve adoption of all of his points, the Treaty of Versailles (1919) did lay out his vision of a League of Nations that would resolve future tensions before they resulted in open hostilities. Article 10 committed members of the League to "undertake to respect and preserve as against external aggression the territorial integrity and existing political independence of all Members of the League."[5] Article 11 held that "Any war or threat of war, whether immediately affecting any of the Members of the League or not, is hereby declared a matter of concern to the whole League, and the League shall take any action that may be deemed wise and effectual to safeguard the peace of nations."

Steps deemed necessary to safeguard the peace were broadly interpreted. In Article 23, the covenant set out principles to which its members should adhere:

Subject to and in accordance with the provisions of international conventions existing or hereafter to be agreed upon, the Members of the League:

(a) Will endeavour to secure and maintain fair and humane conditions of labour for men, women, and children, both in their own countries and in all countries to which their commercial and industrial relations extend, and for that purpose will establish and maintain the necessary international organisations;

(b) Undertake to secure just treatment of the native inhabitants of territories under their control;

(c) Will entrust the League with the general supervision over the execution of agreements with regard to the traffic in women and children, and the traffic in opium and other dangerous drugs;

(d) Will entrust the League with the general supervision of the trade in arms and ammunition with the countries in which the control of this traffic is necessary in the common interest;

(e) Will make provision to secure and maintain freedom of communications and of transit and equitable treatment for the commerce of all Members of the League. In this connection, the special necessities of the regions devastated during the war of 1914–1918 shall be borne in mind; and

(f) Will endeavour to take steps in matters of international concern for the prevention and control of disease.

In notable contrast to the charter of its successor, the United Nations, the covenant did not set out the rights of individuals but focused on the responsibilities of states towards each other. Nevertheless, its members were exhorted to take steps to secure fair, humane, and just treatment of people, not only in their own countries but throughout the world. The covenant also gave the League itself special responsibilities in protecting especially vulnerable populations, such as those who have been trafficked. The role of the League and its subsidiary bodies with regard to trafficking is discussed more fully in Chapter 5.

---

[5] All quotes are from the version of the Treaty of Versailles found at: http://avalon.law.yale.edu/subject_menus/versailles_menu.asp.

The covenant envisioned the League as the natural host for existing organizations or commissions established under international treaties as well as the venue for future such offices:

> There shall be placed under the direction of the League all international bureaux already established by general treaties if the parties to such treaties consent. All such international bureaux and all commissions for the regulation of matters of international interest hereafter constituted shall be placed under the direction of the League. In all matters of international interest which are regulated by general conventions but which are not placed under the control of international bureaux or commissions, the Secretariat of the League shall, subject to the consent of the Council and if desired by the parties, collect and distribute all relevant information and shall render any other assistance which may be necessary or desirable. (Article 24)

Article 24 also gave the council the authority to include as part of the expenses of the secretariat the expenses of any bureau or commission which is placed under the direction of the League. Interestingly, offices established by the League under other auspices (which was the case of the Nansen Refugee Office discussed later in this chapter) would need to raise external funds.

Labor Issues

Part XIII of the Treaty of Versailles focused exclusively on labor issues and became the basis for the League's involvement in many migration issues. Consideration of labor matters as a pivotal concern in securing the peace was a novelty of the treaty. The preamble to Part XIII explains the linkages that the negotiators made:

> Whereas the League of Nations has for its object the establishment of universal peace, and such a peace can be established only if it is based upon social justice;

> And whereas conditions of labour exist involving such injustice, hardship, and privation to large numbers of people as to produce unrest so great that the peace and harmony of the world are imperilled; and an improvement of those conditions is urgently required . . . ;

> Whereas also the failure of any nation to adopt humane conditions of labour is an obstacle in the way of other nations which desire to improve the conditions in their own countries;

> The HIGH CONTRACTING PARTIES, moved by sentiments of justice and humanity as well as by the desire to secure the permanent peace of the world, agree to [establish a permanent labor organization].

The preamble also set out the types of labor arrangements that would reduce injustice, hardship, and privation:

- the regulation of the hours of work, including the establishment of a maximum working day and week,
- the regulation of the labour supply,
- the prevention of unemployment,
- the provision of an adequate living wage,
- the protection of the worker against sickness, disease and injury arising out of his employment,
- the protection of children, young persons and women,
- provision for old age and injury,
- *protection of the interests of workers when employed in countries other than their own*,
- recognition of the principle of freedom of association, and
- the organisation of vocational and technical education. (emphasis added)

Labor issues found a place in the treaty because of a confluence of interests. The idea that labor standards should be internationalized emerged in the nineteenth century. In accepting the 1969 Nobel Peace Prize, ILO Secretary General David Morse acknowledged this pioneering work:

> As early as the 1830's and the 1840's, such humanitarian industrialists as Charles Hindley in England and Daniel Le Grand in France had proposed that coordinated action should be taken at an international level to regulate conditions of labor in order to ensure that no country which provided its workers with improved conditions would be at a competitive disadvantage in the international market.[6]

International labor conferences had been held in Berlin in 1890, London in 1896, and Zurich and Brussels in 1897. In 1901, the International Association for Labor Legislation was formed and its 1912 conference in Berne, which attracted participation from twenty-two government delegations, helped prepare the way for the negotiations over the Treaty of Versailles.

Labor issues would not have reached the agenda of the peace negotiations, however, if they had not been at the forefront of policy makers' concerns for other reasons – stability most importantly. In summarizing the origins of the ILO, Wubnig explained: "Labor unrest was running up a fast crescendo throughout the countries of the world; Communism was taking hold in Russia; there were dangers elsewhere in Europe of a proletarian revolution from below. By bending before the wind, the Allied Powers diminished the possibilities of being broken by it" (Wubnig 1935:246).

The Paris peace negotiations established a Commission on International Labor Legislation, headed by Samuel Gompers, the president of the American Federation of Labor. The commission was charged with making recommendations for language to be included in the treaty on labor issues. The commission report was submitted in March 1919 and was adopted with some revision of

---

[6] http://www.nobelprize.org/nobel_prizes/peace/laureates/1969/labour-lecture.html.

the language included in the Labor Charter the following month (Josephson 1974). The main point of contention had been whether a new labor organization would impose binding laws on its members or would draft conventions and make recommendations that would be referred to national governments. The U.S. delegation argued strongly against the former since regulation of labor standards was largely a state-level responsibility. This position was largely adopted.

The Treaty of Versailles established that the ILO would consist of a General Conference of Representatives of the Members, a Governing Body, and an International Labor Office. The General Conference made decisions regarding conventions and recommendations to be transmitted to states. The Governing Body appointed the director of the International Labor Office and oversaw its work and budget. The Office had two principal divisions: diplomatic and scientific. The former was responsible for negotiating with governments, employers' organizations, and trade unions to obtain the ratification of the conventions adopted by the International Labor Conferences. The scientific division collected information on social and economic problems and prepared publications. There were also seven technical sections, one of which addressed emigration issues (Gregory 1921).

The ILO governance system contained some important differences from other international bodies. Most important was the composition of the General Conference. Each member state would have four delegates, "of whom two shall be Government Delegates and the two others shall be Delegates representing respectively the employers and the workpeople of each of the Members" (Article 389). Each delegate had a separate vote. A contemporary account concluded:

> This is a principle entirely new to international bodies which include government representatives. The employers' and workers' delegates from each state are, strictly speaking, nominated by their respective governments, but the governments undertake in so doing that the delegates shall be "chosen in agreement with the industrial organizations, if such organizations exist, which are most representative of employers or work people." (Sumner 1924)

The Governing Board also reflected the tripartite composition. The twenty-four members would include "twelve persons representing the Governments; six persons elected by the Delegates to the Conference representing the employers; and six persons elected by the Delegates to the Conference representing the workers" (Article 393). The government representatives would be apportioned to ensure that eight of the twelve were officials of countries of "the chief industrial importance" (Article 393). Sumner observed that unlike other international bodies, there was often less disagreement among the government officials of different countries than among the three sectors represented in the General Conference and Governing Board.

A second innovation of the ILO was the formal incorporation of experts into the discussions and deliberations of the organization. Each delegate to the General Conference could be accompanied by no more than two advisers for discussion of each item on the agenda of the meeting. The delegate could give the adviser the authority to speak and vote. The articles of the ILO also specified that when questions specially affecting women were to be considered, at least one of the advisers should be a woman.

Commissions and committees became important mechanisms through which the ILO operated. A contemporary assessment emphasized how crucial these bodies were to the work of the organization:

> [A]n increasing share in this work is now being done by the various commissions set up under the control of the Conference and the Governing Body, e.g., on agriculture, maritime questions, industrial hygiene, anthrax, emigration, statistics, war disablement. These commissions are essentially meetings of experts, but, with a few exceptions, they are also formed on the same root principle as the Conference and the Governing Body – the principle of bringing together government, employers', and workers' representatives so that from their common deliberations sound working proposals can be formulated, based on the special knowledge thus made available and on the special requirements thus brought to light. (Sumner 1924)

One such commission focused on emigration, to be discussed in greater detail in the next section.

ILO ROLE IN MIGRATION

When discussion first took place in the Commission on International Labor Legislation regarding the Labor Charter, a statement on foreign workers was not included. The U.S. and British delegations, which took the lead in developing language for the charter, had not seen it as an appropriate or necessary issue for discussion. Böhning, who had been chief of the International Migration for Employment branch of ILO, argues in his history of ILO and international migration that neither country wanted interference by outsiders in their immigration policies. The United States had already developed an extensive body of immigration legislation. For Britain, migration was primarily a matter of imperial policy as subjects of the crown moved within the mother country and its overseas dominions and colonies.

Gompers's own opposition to immigration may also have been a factor. He headed a federation of unions that organized skilled workers who felt threatened by immigrants. Gompers himself had argued that the new immigrants "could not be taught to render the same intelligent service as was supplied by American workers" (Calavita 1984, quoting Karson: 111). As early as 1919, the AFL began to advocate that U.S. immigration be restricted in numbers and only the immediate dependent relatives of foreigners already in the United States should be permitted to enter. He was especially opposed to labor migration, given high levels of unemployment in the United States and what he saw as millions of Europeans who were desperate to leave their countries.

Some Continental European delegations considered international migration to be a priority and introduced language to be incorporated into the treaty. Two conferences had taken place during the war that set the stage for their proposals. The Allied Trade Unions had met in Leeds in July 1917 to discuss a range of labor issues and the rights of foreign workers were prominently on the agenda. A second conference was held in Bern in October 1917, organized by the International Trade Union Conference and the International Socialist Conference.

The Leeds conference emphasized equality of treatment between foreign and native workers: "no alien workman should be paid a lower rate of wages than the normal or prevailing rate of wages, or be made to work under worse conditions than those prevailing in the same locality or district for workers of the same trade or the same specialty."[7] With regard to admissions, the conference recommended that "emigration of workmen shall be organized and based on national labor exchanges" (Bauer 1919). It also urged every country to establish a special commission on emigration and immigration, consisting of representatives of government, employers, and workers. These commissions would determine if there was need for recruitment of foreign workers and whether the labor contracts were in conformity with labor standards otherwise enunciated in the statement.

The Bern conference – which included more radical labor advocates – agreed on the need for equality of treatment but it categorically opposed restrictions on exit and entry except in highly defined situations. Its equal treatment of foreign and native workers included a provision that immigrant workmen "shall without consideration of the probable duration of their sojourn in the foreign country have the same status as to rights and duties in all branches of social insurance as native workers" (Bauer 1919). The resolution barred states from enacting prohibitions on emigration and barred general prohibitions on immigration. Temporary restrictions on immigration were permissible during economic depressions, and governments retained the right to control and restrict immigration to protect the national health. Perhaps in recognition of the recent passage of the U.S. literacy requirement, the resolution stated that such provisions could be enacted to protect national culture and the efficient enforcement of labor laws. The resolution called on signatory states to prohibit the hiring of contract labor from abroad, as well as employment bureaus operated for profit.

---

[7] These quotes are taken from Stephen Bauer, *International Labor Legislation and Society of Nations*. Washington, DC: Government Printing Office.

The draft Labor Charter that was eventually submitted to the Versailles conference included nineteen planks, of which two focused specifically on migration:

6) The principle that in all matters concerning the rights of workpeople, working conditions and social insurance, foreign workmen and their families should be treated on the same footing as the nationals of the country in which they reside, and that they may not be subject as such to any special taxation.

10) The principle of freedom of migration, subject to the consent of the Governments and Trade Unions of the countries directly concerned. (Official Bulletin 1919:192).

The draft was criticized as including both too many and too few provisions and for going too far and not far enough in establishing the rights of workers. As to the migration-related principles, discussions in the next session of the commission led to revision in point six, with reference to taxes taken out and the language changed to: "In all matters concerning their status as workers and social insurance foreign workmen lawfully admitted to any country and their families should be ensured the same treatment as the nationals of that country" (Official Bulletin 1919:205). France continued to press for greater adherence to the equality principle, recommending that the First General Conference "Prepare for signature Conventions for equality of wages and working conditions (hours of work, provision of rest, health, safety) between foreign and native workers" (Official Bulletin 1919:235). Representatives of Italy, which was a major emigration country and had recently signed a labor migration agreement with France, wanted the charter to press for legislation in support of several principles, including:

(a) Equality of status as regards social and labour legislation, and equality of economic treatment, as between foreign workmen and their families on the one hand and native workers and their families on the other.
(b) Exemption from all taxation in the country of immigration which affects the foreign workmen as such.
(c) The principle that any State shall have the right to send special officials to assist in any way and to protect its own emigrant and that any State to which they emigrated shall be obliged to admit such officials and to assist them in the performance of their duties. (Official Bulletin 1919:241)

The traditional immigration destination countries – Canada, Australia, and the United States, supported by Britain – opposed including specific language on the rights of foreign workers and equality of treatment between foreign and native workers. The British delegation, after consulting with its dominions, proposed what became the language in the preamble: "protection of the interests of workers when employed in countries other than their own." Although much vaguer than the provisions proposed by the French and Italians, the language satisfied those who opposed any reference and was included in the commission's report and appeared in the preamble to Part XIII of the treaty. None of the French or Italian proposals were included in the Labor Charter, however. Instead, the closest thing to equality between foreign and native workers is the eighth principle in the charter: "The standard set by law in each country with respect to the conditions of labour should have due regard to the equitable economic treatment of all workers lawfully resident therein" (Article 427).

The first meeting of the General Conference, which took place in Washington in 1919, took up a number of the points made by the French and Italian delegations and included recommendations that were consistent with their suggestions. A first order of business was drafting a convention on unemployment, which was adopted at the Washington meeting. It included the concept of reciprocity in setting out principles regarding migrant workers with regard to systems of unemployment insurance: "workers belonging to one Member and working in the territory of another shall be admitted to the same rates of benefits . . . as those which obtain for the workers belonging to the latter" (Article 3). The General Conference also issued recommendations to be taken up by national governments (unlike conventions, recommendations are nonbinding) specifying a wider range of issues to be addressed in a reciprocal fashion:

> The General Conference recommends that each Member of the International Labour Organization shall, on condition of reciprocity and upon terms to he agreed between the countries concerned, admit the foreign workers (together with their families) employed within its territory, to the benefit of its laws and regulations for the protection of its own workers, as well as to the right of lawful organization as enjoyed by its own workers. (Official Bulletin 1919:421)

Recognizing that additional migration issues needed to be addressed, the General Conference also agreed to the establishment of two bodies within the ILO. The first was a special section in the International Labor Office, which was charged with consideration of all questions concerning the migration of workers and the condition of foreign wage earners. The second was an international commission, which would consider and report on measures to regulate the migration of workers and to protect the interests of wage earners residing in states other than their own. The commission was to present its report at the meeting of the General Conference in 1920.

The International Emigration Commission came fully into operation in August 1921. Its membership was balanced between immigration and emigration countries (Bohning nd). The chair was British and the vice chair was Italian. The commission was created by the Governing Board and reported to it. It did not have the same status, however, as formal committees of the board. As such, the commission "floated somewhere between a technical meeting of experts and an international conference of political representatives" (Bohning nd:10). Debate over whether to make the commission into a permanent committee proved acrimonious and failed by a split vote of nine for and nine against (Bohning nd). The Governing Board concluded that there was no reason to change its status. Initially, the work of the commission was modest. The technical section within the International Labor Office was no more ambitious in its aims. Mostly, the section collected and distributed information in support of the commission's work and supported academic research on such topics as the rights of emigration and immigration (Bohning nd).

One of the earliest accomplishments of the commission and technical office was adoption of a recommendation to governments on migration statistics. The resolution stated that:

> Members of the International Labour Organisation should communicate to the International Labour Office at intervals as short as possible, and not exceeding three months, all available information, legislative, statistical or otherwise, concerning emigration, immigration, the repatriation and transit of emigrants, including reports on measures taken or contemplated in respect of these questions. (Official Bulletin 1922:410–11)

Having a common database for analysis of immigration and emigration trends was seen as an essential prerequisite for cooperation in regulating movements. In a concern that is still commonly heard regarding migration statistics, the issue of whether the consistency of data was adequate was raised in the deliberations on the recommendation:

> The statistics of different countries often relate to different things, and fundamental differences exist between them which could only be eliminated by changes in legislation and administrative practice. Comparison is also rendered difficult by differences in regard to the manner of presentation, owing to the variety of methods employed in the analysis and classification of returns. Statistics do not even invariably distinguish emigrants according to sex, the methods of classification according to age vary considerably from country to country, and difficulties are also encountered in any attempt to classify emigrants according to occupation. It is only occasionally that indications are available regarding such details as the month or season of migration, whether it is a first or subsequent migration. (Official Bulletin 1922:412–13)

The discussion focused especially on gaining uniformity in the definitions of the terms "emigrant" and "immigrant." Analysis of questionnaires submitted to governments about statistics concluded:

> the word "emigration" is not employed in the same sense in all national statistical systems, and the definition of "immigrant" in one country does not always correspond with the definition of the word "emigrant" accepted in the country from which the "immigrant" comes, with the result that it is impossible to arrive at an exact balance between emigration and immigration statistics. It would appear, therefore, most desirable to arrive at a uniform definition of these terms. (Official Bulletin 1922:416)

The countries of emigration – disappointed at the slow progress of the commission and the unwillingness of the General Conference to take action on the broader agenda issues that were raised during the Treaty of Versailles negotiations – determined to bring these issues to international attention through an alternative route. In 1924, Italy convened an intergovernmental conference on emigration. Although the ILO was invited to attend and provide documentation, the conference was not held under its auspices (Bohning nd). The director-general of the Office ascribed the separate process to the failure to establish the commission as a permanent committee (Bohning nd). Despite continued opposition from Britain and its dominions, the Governing Board followed his advice and set up a Permanent Emigration Committee. Countries designated experts to serve on the committee. In all, ninety-nine experts joined, seemingly a testament to the interest of states in having a role in the committee, even when they did not have substantial expertise on the issues (Bohning nd). In the spring of 1929, the committee was reconstituted and became the Migration Committee, with twelve members and five outside experts. Despite these steps, a parallel system of state-led conferences and ILO deliberations continued, with Cuba hosting a successor meeting to the Rome conference in 1928 (Bohning nd).

The Rome conference touched on four broad sets of issues: health, protection of migrants, international cooperation, and proposals for new laws or conventions. The focus was primarily on emigration. It generally did not touch on the admission policies of destination countries, except in the context of cooperative actions that could be taken by emigration and immigration countries to regulate movements. These included exchange of information, suppression of clandestine emigration and immigration, uniformity and simplification of passports and consular visas, exchange of skilled laborers, emigration of intellectual workers, and principles relating to the establishment and the performance of labor contracts.

Implementation of the recommendations of the Rome conference was a subject of debate. Countries that were members of the ILO and the League generally preferred to refer the resolutions to those bodies, whereas countries that were not members (particularly, the United States) preferred more ad hoc arrangements. The role and perceptions of the U.S. delegation were especially interesting because they were a harbinger of concerns that have recurred through the years regarding international cooperation on migration matters. The head of the U.S. delegation, Assistant Secretary of Labor Arthur Hennings, wrote a lengthy summary of the deliberations. He explained the U.S. opposition to the participation of international organizations in the conference, noting that the United States was a member of neither the League nor the ILO, and had attended the conference expressly because only governments would be attending. He explained that the United States could not vote for many of the resolutions because the areas of competence did not belong to the federal government (a repetition of the position at the Paris peace conference that labor was a matter of state competence). He also stated that the issues were a domestic matter of the United States and not appropriate for international action. In some cases, U.S. legislation already covered the issue. In others, the resolution in question could be determined only in accordance with the U.S. Constitution. In reference to this latter point, the U.S. delegation explained that the Egyptian proposal for a resolution on recognition or tolerance of religious practices of immigrant workers was unnecessary in the United States because constitutional protection of freedom of religion would prohibit adoption of any legislation on that matter (U.S. Department of Labor 1924).

An output of the Rome conference was the 1926 Inspection of Emigrants Convention (subsequently shelved), which included provisions that had been long championed by Italy. It allowed for placing representatives of source countries on ships to accompany its emigrants. In 1929, the conference adopted two resolutions offered by the Chinese delegation to consider taking action on recruitment of foreign workers and equality of treatment. These matters were referred to the Immigration Committee for study.

By then, however, the political and economic situation had begun to shift with the emergence of Mussolini's fascist government in Italy and then the Great Depression. Mussolini's views on emigration changed considerably during his term in office. When he came to power, he advocated a higher quota for Italian immigration to the United States. He was rebuffed, however, in the legislative negotiations over the 1924 Immigration Act. By 1926, he had come to see large-scale emigration as a violation of the fascist ideal and began to make emigration more difficult (Finkelstein 1988). Over time, restrictions were placed on issuance of passports and it became harder to receive permission to exit the country. With regard to the ILO, Italy ceased to be a voice for increased cooperation on migration matters when it withdrew from the organization in 1937.

Nevertheless, the 1930s did see the first attempt to negotiate a convention on migration for employment. In 1939, the General Conference of the ILO negotiated a convention concerning the recruitment, placing, and conditions of labor of migrants for employment. It also issued a recommendation on cooperation between states related to these issues. Notably, the convention used the term migrant, as compared to the League's tendency to refer to such individuals as "workers employed in countries other than their own." Although the convention never went into force amid the outbreak of World War II, it outlined important principles. Parties to the convention would need to regulate recruitment agencies, restricting them to public agencies, private not-for-profit organizations, and other organizations established through international instruments that would operate under the supervision of competent authorities of the state. Parties would also need to maintain a system of supervision over the contracts between an employer or his representative and the migrant. Contracts would be drawn up or be translated into a language understood by the migrant. They should include information on duration, where the migrant would be working, the date on which to report, the method of meeting travel expenses, and the members of the family authorized to travel with or join the migrant. In addition, the contracts should specify any deductions which the employer may make from remuneration in accordance with the law or agreements between countries of emigration and immigration, housing conditions, and any arrangements to ensure the maintenance of the migrant's family in the country of origin.

In keeping with previous discussions, the convention included a number of provisions related to equality of treatment, using language that "Parties to the Convention" will apply to foreigners treatment no less favorable than that which it applies to its own nationals, with respect to conditions of work, remuneration, the right to join a trade union, employment taxes, and legal proceedings related to contracts of employment. The terms of the convention did not apply to migration within the territory of the ratifying party or from one territory of a party to another territory of the same party; frontier workers living in one state and working in another; or seamen or indigenous workers defined by the 1936 Recruiting of Indigenous Workers Convention.

The recommendation on international cooperation addressed situations in which the volume of migration is "fairly considerable." It urged states to conclude bilateral or multilateral agreements to repress illegal and misleading propaganda. The recommendation also advocated agreements on the issuance of identification documents; methods of recruitment; ways to prevent the separation of families or the desertion of their families by migrants; transfer of earnings and savings to the country of origin; repatriation; and the settlement of pension rights.

INTERNATIONAL STANDARDS FOR PASSPORTS

The League's role in the harmonization of passport standards derived from a different part of the Treaty of Versailles than that of the ILO. The treaty gave jurisdiction to the League over provisions "to secure and maintain freedom of communications and of transit and equitable treatment for the commerce of all Members of the League (Article 23 (e))." The issue of passports was assigned to the Committee on Communications and Transit, reflecting the understanding that documentation for travel within and across borders had become an essential component of communications and transit.

The concept of uniformity in passport requirements was not a new idea. In his comprehensive treatise on the history of the passport, Torpey noted that "a 'Pass-Card Treaty' (Passkartenvertrag) of 18 October 1850 among 'all the German states' except the Netherlands, Denmark, Hessen-Homburg, and Liechtenstein loosened passport requirements for travelers among them" (Torpey 2000:76). The treaty simplified and standardized the information that was to be included in pass-cards: "the coat-of-arms of the issuing state; signature and seal or stamp of the issuing authority; name, status, and residence of the bearer; pass register number, and the bearer's description – age, 'characteristics' (Natur), hair color, and distinguishing marks" (76).

In 1920, the League convened an International Conference on Passports, Customs Formalities, and Through Tickets to discuss harmonization. The deliberations leading up to and at the conference showed basic ambivalences about passports. On the one hand, the League was committed to reducing barriers to transit and generally recognized the value of free movement. On the other hand, the member states were still concerned with the security ramifications of unfettered migration and saw the imposition of documentation requirements as essential to maintaining public order.

The recommendations of the 1920 conference and its successors in 1925 and 1929 tried to balance these concerns in the form of a resolution that was forwarded to governments by the League. The 1920 preamble began: "Convinced that many difficulties affecting personal relations between the peoples of various countries constitute a serious obstacle to the resumption of normal intercourse and to the economic recovery of the world" (quoted in Salter 2003:78). The resolution also recognized "that the legitimate concern of every Government for the safeguarding of its security and rights prohibits, for the time being, the total abolition of restrictions" (78–79). Balancing these two perspectives, the conference acknowledged that passports would continue to be used by governments to regulate movement and recommended harmonization of standards for their production and use.

Initially, the League conceived of the passport as valid for a single journey but subsequently shifted toward a specified duration. In 1920, the duration was set at two years or the duration of the journey. The conference proposed that the passport take the form of a booklet, setting in place the format that has persisted.

> The passport is to contain 32 pages. The first four pages only are reproduced herewith.
>
> The other 28 pages should all be numbered and should contain the visas of the countries for which the passport is valid.
>
> The passport should be drawn up in at least two languages, *i.e.*, in the national language and in French.
>
> The passport must be bound in cardboard, bearing on the top the name and in the centre the coat-of-arms of the country, and at the bottom the word "Passport," with the addition, according to the desire of the various Governments, of any practical information concerning the regime of passports.
>
> Any passport of which the pages are entirely filled must be replaced by a fresh passport. (League of Nations 1920)

The conference discussed modes of identification of the bearer and determined that a photograph would be incorporated into the passport. Proposals to increase the biometric information and include fingerprints were defeated as too intrusive and inefficient.

Following the 1920 resolution, governments were asked to fill out a questionnaire about their implementation. The request summarized the most important elements of the resolution with regard to standards, fees, and duration of passports and visas. While there was general agreement on the benefits of establishing uniform standards, some reservations were expressed regarding the specific recommendations. Several governments believed that each nation should set the maximum fees for the passport and visa based on its own assessment of costs. Others mentioned that reciprocity would govern their fees. Some took exception to the recommendation that the passport be issued for at least two years. For example, Finland thought the period was too long and presented a potential security risk "in view of the difficulties which might arise if a foreigner who had been granted a visa and who had originally justified the confidence thus placed in him was later found undesirable" (League of Nations 1922:24). Italy's objection to the two-year passport was consistent with its position on regulation of emigration:

> The passport is the only effective means at the disposal of the Government for regulating emigration, and preventing immigration into countries where it is impossible to procure work; if extended from one to two years, the duration of the validity of the passport will diminish the effectiveness of this control, which is necessary, not only in the interest of Italy, but also in the interest of the countries of destination (35).

More specific concerns were raised about the degree of flexibility each state should have in determining the paper, ink, watermarks, and other distinguishing characteristics of the passports. Some governments preferred to keep their existing format. The Chinese government noted the differences between their alphabet and the French one and indicated that this would present difficulties in producing a useful document.

The balancing of facilitation issues and security concerns continued throughout the decade. A passport of lengthier duration was becoming the norm. In 1926, the League recommended "minimum validity of two years, and, if possible, validity approaching five years" for passports (League of Nations 1926). The League also recommended that visas be issued for a two-year period, but specified that states could limit the duration of individual stays to whatever period was appropriate for the purpose of the visit (League of Nations 1926).

At the same time, the League showed concern about fraudulent use of passports. In 1926, the conference observed that the British passport was "perfection itself [in guarding against fraud], but is so expensive that many countries might be unable to adopt it." The passports issued by France, Germany, and Austria were "cheaper, afford all necessary safeguards, and might be taken as models. The paper employed is such as to obviate all risks of erasures or falsifications of the writing by the use of chemicals" (League of Nations 1926). The technical subcommittee preparing for the conference recommended that police stations issue the passports to ensure that criminals would not receive passports and use them to cross frontiers. This proposal was rejected (Salter 2003). The alternative – that post offices be the places in which applicants could apply for passports – was seen as more fitting given the role of passports in regulating commerce and communications as well as transit. Governments continued to try to straddle two differing objectives – providing passports to facilitate lawful travel (even abolishing passport requirements among like-minded states) while ensuring that mobility for unlawful purposes was blocked.

REFUGEES

The population displacement caused by the rising nationalist tensions before and during World War I was a harbinger of still larger movements to come. In entering World War I, U.S. President Woodrow Wilson had pledged to fight

> for the things which we have always carried nearest our hearts – for democracy, for the right of those who submit to authority to have a voice in their own governments, for the rights and liberties of small nations, for a universal dominion of right by such a concert of free peoples as shall bring peace and safety to all nations and make the world itself at last free. (Wilson 1917b)

A key concept of the treaties that ended World War I was national self-determination, defined as "the belief that each nation has a right to constitute an independent state and determine its own government" (Cobban 1945:4). That concept had profound implications as new states emerged but their governments did not regard all residents as legitimate citizens. Those who fell outside of the system of self-determination often became refugees. This issue became the third major issue on the League's agenda. It also caused the eruption of new conflicts, particularly as nationalists contested borders derived from the same territory (an example being the establishment of a new Poland out of territory formerly part of the Austro-Hungarian, German, and Russian empires).

The challenge of self-determination was in defining what a nation was and who belonged to it. Wilson had in mind the American civic nation of multiple ethnicities, which he saw as a model for others. "For Wilson self-determination meant the right of communities to self-government. It had nothing to do with the tradition of collective or ethnic nationalism, in which the principal agent was the nation as distinct from the individuals constituting the nation" (Lynch 2002:424). For many of those seeking self-determination in Europe and the Middle East, however, the notion was quite different. They equated the nation-state they sought with a specific ethnicity, language, or religion. Richmond explains the lure of self determination based on ethnicity: "'Location' and 'sovereignty' constitute the key to ethnic survival; freedom from interference in a defensible territory is seen as vital to ensuring the survival of distinct communities. Consequently, what matters to an ethnie [sic] is the possession or association with a physical 'homeland'" (Richmond 2002:393). The peace treaties generally included provisions for protection of minorities, with the expectation that the new nations would ensure the rights of those not of the dominant ethnicity. As will be discussed, these protections too often failed.

In the immediate aftermath of the war, as the new national boundaries were set, millions relocated to live in the territory they (or others) considered to be their own. Some moved voluntarily while others were expelled. Marrus's seminal work on refugees between the two World Wars described the impact on Germany:

> The humiliated Weimar Republic, for example, received close to a million refugees. Germans poured across the new frontiers from Alsace-Lorraine, now attached to France; from northern Schleswig, which went to Denmark; from Eupen and Malmedy, now joined to Belgium. From the east, nationalism and the turmoil of postwar politics forced about half a million Germans to move. (Marrus 2002:71)

The new state of Hungary received about 230,000 ethnic Hungarians from what became the states of Romania, Czechoslovakia, and Yugoslavia – all of which had been part of the Austro-Hungarian Empire.

At the same time, more traditional reasons for displacement continued as repressive governments acted to quell opposition. The situation in the Soviet Union continued to deteriorate for many critics of the Bolshevist system. Complicating the situation were the hundreds of thousands of prisoners of war and interred German civilians who remained in the Soviet Union after the end of hostilities and the million plus Russians who had been in German camps. At first, the Allied command considered keeping the prisoners of war in place as a potential bulwark against Bolshevism but by the end of 1919, the Allies decided that repatriation should commence (Marrus 2002). Negotiating such a project, particularly given the poor relations between the Bolshevik government and the West, was a formidable task.

The Allies turned to Fridtjof Nansen, a Norwegian explorer whose attempt to reach the North Pole had generated worldwide acclaim. Writing in 1897, his biographer J. Arthur Bain captured his reputation: "No explorer of the Arctic regions since Franklin, no traveller indeed save Columbus, has gained so great a hold upon the imagination of his contemporaries" (Bain 1897:vi). Nansen was also a consummate diplomat. He operated outside of the political offices of the League, using an organization he designated as Nansen Help (Marrus 2002). The League provided administrative assistance, nongovernmental organizations (NGOs) provided support, and the International Committee of the Red Cross organized the actual transfers. In two years, Nansen's operations allowed more than 400,000 prisoners of war of twenty nationalities to return to their homes (Marrus 2002). He made clear, however, that repatriation was to be voluntary and he arranged for many Russian prisoners to remain in the West.

This collaboration with NGOs and the Red Cross movement built on the important role that these agencies were already playing in providing relief to many of the world's refugees. Both secular and religious organizations, along with the Red Cross, had already been providing care to civilians displaced by the fighting. They provided food, shelter, and health care to millions and were credited with saving numerous lives during the winter of 1918–1919 when freezing weather, starvation, and influenza resulted in enormous numbers of deaths. The late entry of the United States into the war enabled U.S. NGOs to operate throughout the theater of conflict. The Armenian Relief Committee, for example, provided aid to the survivors of the genocide who remained in Turkey. It morphed into the American Committee for Relief in the Near East. This organization operated in twelve countries in the Balkans, Asia Minor, and the Middle East, and brought together the efforts of the U.S. and British governments, a Canadian fund, the Red Cross, and others.

The scale of relief needed in Europe and the Middle East dwarfed the capacity of the private agencies. By 1918, it became apparent to the U.S. government that a different level of assistance was needed and preparations should be made for post-conflict relief when peace was achieved. President Wilson asked Herbert Hoover, who had directed the Belgian Relief Commission, to launch a new relief program. The aim was "delivery of nearly one billion dollars' worth of goods to twenty-two countries in the nine months following the 1918 armistice" (Marrus 2002:85). Dubbed the American Relief Administration (ARA), the initiative had a staff of four thousand. Hoover proposed extending the relief to the Soviet Union. The widely respected Nansen was asked to chair a neutral relief committee that would organize the aid. The Soviet authorities would not cooperate while the civil war raged but when they were more confident of victory, they finally agreed to the relief effort. Nansen's International Committee for Russian Relief, funded by the ARA, delivered food and other items to an estimated 10 million Russians who would otherwise have died of famine (Marrus 2002).

In 1921, growing concern about refugees led the International Red Cross to recommend that the League establish a High Commission for Refugees to coordinate assistance to Russian refugees – that is, those who were outside of the Soviet Union. Nansen was asked once more to assume responsibility. The high commissioner's mandate was to provide material assistance and legal and political protection.[8] The high commissioner had very limited scope, however. His mandate extended only to Russian refugees. Government funds could be used for administrative costs of the office, but separate funding had to be raised for any relief activities. Since the office was seen as a temporary expedient, the funding was both ad hoc and limited (Loescher 2001).

---

[8] For fuller discussions of the interwar refugee regime, see Claudena Skran (1995), *Refugees in Inter-War Europe: The Emergence of a Regime*, Oxford: Clarendon Press; Michael Marrus (2002), *The Unwanted: European Refugees from the First World War Through the Cold War*, Philadelphia: Temple University Press; and Gil Loescher (1993), *Beyond Charity: International Cooperation and the Global Refugee Crisis*, Oxford: Oxford University Press.

Nansen's principal achievement is often described as the Nansen passport. He recognized that one of the main constraints in finding solutions for the Russian refugees was their inability to cross borders in search of better opportunities because they lacked what had become the essential tool of mobility – a national passport. Refugees were unable to request a passport from the Soviet Union, which generally considered them to have renounced their citizenship, and unable to obtain passports from the countries in which they had taken refuge because they were not citizens of that territory. These refugees were without the legal protection that the new passport system dictated for those hoping to migrate.

Nansen's solution was a passport to be issued by the League of Nations in lieu of a willing government. A resolution (Arrangement with Regard to the Issue of Certificates of Identity to Russian Refugees) was adopted on July 5, 1922. The group covered under the passport was defined later to include: "any person of Russian origin who does not enjoy the protection of the Government of the Union of Soviet Socialist Republics and who has not acquired any other nationality" (Kaprielian-Churchill 1994: League of Nations A.48.1927 VIII). Nansen negotiated acceptance of the Nansen passport by more than fifty governments, although recognition of the passport did not mean its holders had an automatic right to enter their territory. In fact, most refugees found themselves unable to avail themselves of the opportunity to travel because they could not obtain a visa. In American parlance, they would be considered "intending immigrants" who would likely overstay their visas.[9] Canada, as a member of the League, took a harder line on the Nansen passports because of such concerns. The Canadian government would not recognize them since the holders could not be returned to their country of nationality or previous residence even if they committed crimes (Kaprielian-Churchill 1994).

The League tried to address these concerns in 1926 at a conference to resolve issues related to the passport. The resolution stated that return visas should be included on the passports, known as identity certificates, but gave governments the authority to make exceptions to the principle (Marrus 2002). Several governments agreed to issue one-year return visas on the passports to address the concerns of countries admitting refugees with Nansen passports. Canada cited situations in which deportation could be ordered up to five years after

---

[9] The United States accepted Nansen passports even though it was not a party to the agreements negotiated by the League. The State Department explained: "For entry into the United States, alien immigrants are required to present an immigration visa issued by the appropriate American consul. The American consuls will accept from aliens unable to present passports in connection with their applications for immigration visas appropriate documents of identity in lieu of passports. The Nansen certificates issued to Russian refugees have been considered to fall within the category of documents in lieu of passports" quoted in "Certificates of Identity for Refugees," *Advocate of Peace through Justice*, 86. 11:597–598. Nevertheless, all other immigration criteria (such as proving one would not be a public charge) applied, limiting the number of refugees who qualified for admission.

admitting an immigrant for permanent residence and indicated that without guarantees that countries would accept return of the passport bearers within that time frame, it would not accept the passports. Contemporary observers noted that applying this standard to refugees – who by definition could not be returned to their country of origin – defeated the purpose of the Nansen passports.

Even with limitations on its use, the Nansen passport established an important principle that has become the cornerstone of the international refugee regime. As Holborn describes, "Through it, refugees of specific categories become the recipients of a legal and juridical status. The refugee who is de facto stateless and has neither protection nor representation from his state is provided with both by the High Commissioner for Refugees" (Holborn 1939:126). Hence, in the absence of state protection of the rights of its citizens, refugees could call upon international protection – in this case in the form of a passport. Since passports had become the principal way in which governments identified their nationals, access to an internationally ordained document meant that refugees would not be totally without an identity or sense of belonging. Nevertheless, what remained unresolved and would continue to cause problems for refugees was the extent to which they should be subject to different international standards regarding admission than those applied to immigrants who were moving in search of work.

Nansen also implemented what Housden (2010:523) referred to as "the first properly organized, modern repatriation initiative: one which did its best to take seriously the lasting safety of returnees." The initiative was designed to repatriate Russian refugees through a program negotiated with the Soviet government. A fully voluntary program, it allowed staff from Nansen's office to monitor the conditions of return and investigate reports of violations against the returnees. Although the program returned only a few thousand out of the much larger number of Russian refugees, it established the principle of voluntary repatriation with international monitoring and involvement.

Nansen's role as high commissioner soon expanded to cover assistance needed in resettling millions of Greeks and Turks. Tensions between Greece and Turkey recurred almost immediately after the conclusion of World War I. In May 1919, the Greek army occupied Smyrna and large numbers of ethnic Greeks who had been displaced by the earlier fighting returned to their homes. The Treaty of Sevres, which was to end formal hostilities between the Allied Forces and the Ottoman Empire, was negotiated the following year. Greek forces broadened their occupation, moving into Anatolia in 1920. In the meantime, however, the Turkish nationalist movement under Kemal Ataturk, which repudiated the terms of the Treaty of Sevres, was gaining power. Seeking the establishment of a Turkish republic, the nationalist movement fought the Greek occupation, routing Greek forces from Anatolia and in 1922 retaking Smyrna. An estimated 400,000–500,000 ethnic Greek civilians were evacuated by ship. As the nationalist forces took control, another quarter of a million ethnic Greeks fled Eastern Thrace for Greece (Zurcher 2003).

The Allied powers agreed to renegotiate the terms of the peace agreement, meeting in Lausanne, Switzerland, in 1923. During the protracted negotiations, in which a newly declared Turkish state played a dominant role, the issue of a more formal resettlement program to redistribute the populations of Greece and Turkey was raised by Nansen. This concept was included in the negotiations of the Treaty of Lausanne and went into force shortly after the treaty was signed. Under the arrangement, about 1.25 million ethnic Greeks living in Asia Minor and about 500,000 ethnic Turks living in Greece were required to relocate to the other country. This included large numbers who did not speak the language of what was now considered to be their homeland and who had no family living in these countries. Since the number of ethnic Turks was much smaller, they generally had no problems with shelter, taking the homes that the ethnic Greeks had been forced to leave. Greece, however, did not have sufficient shelter for all of those who were resettled. Moreover, the rapidity of the movements meant that there was little time to prepare.

Nansen's work kept expanding and encompassed a growing number of refugees. In 1925, he turned attention to the continued plight of survivors of the Armenian genocide. His office succeeded in constructing villages to house upwards of 40,000 Armenians in Syria and Lebanon and the resettlement of another 10,000 in Erivan. A much larger plan to resettle Armenians in the Soviet republic of Armenia failed, however, because of lack of funding. Nansen did succeed in negotiating an agreement to allow Armenian refugees to obtain the Nansen passport. He was cautious, however, about investing too much in relocation of refugees, fearing that it would undermine the responsibilities of the European countries that were already hosting them.

Since many of the refugees' immediate needs were economic, Nansen argued that his office should be moved into the International Labor Organization. The transfer was logical: "Since technical questions like employment, emigration, and settlement were the means whereby solution had to be sought, Nansen proposed transference of these aspects of the work to the International Labor Office, as they fell within the scope of its activity" (Holborn 1939:129). In January 1925, the International Labor Office took on responsibility for the administrative and financial support of the high commissioner's office. It remained within the administration of the ILO until 1929. Nansen retained his role as negotiator, but with the office no longer reporting directly to the secretary general, it lost some of its authority. Nansen's main aim in moving the refugee function into the ILO failed; the Governing Board of the League would not agree to set up a long-term fund to support solutions for refugees. Nevertheless, the ILO refugee office could report some success. In 1928 it confirmed that "the number of unemployed refugees had been reduced from approximately 400,000 to about 200,000. The Office claimed direct credit for over 50,000 of these" (Holborn 1939:131).

In 1928, Nansen described his role at the League of Nations:

> For nearly eight years now it has been my task for the League of Nations to
> investigate the hideous aftermath which war leaves behind. I have had to spend
> my life with prisoners of war, in famines, with flying, panic-stricken refugees,
> with the tragedy of old men and women and tiny children, left by the chance of
> war alone, forlorn, robbed, destitute of everything of value in the world. (Nansen
> 1928:493)

These horrors, he noted, were "but little compared with the horrors of the
sufferings of the Armenian people. There is certainly no people in the world
which has suffered so much and been so badly treated" (496).

Nansen did not live to see the even greater calamity that came about with
the Holocaust, nor the failures of the system he created to save the lives of the
many refugees of Nazi persecution. After Nansen's death in 1930, the office of
the high commissioner ceased to exist and instead, the Nansen International
Office for Refugees, an autonomous body working under the authority of the
League of Nations, was established. Holborn described the structure:

> The post of High Commissioner was abolished. The supreme authority in the
> Nansen Office was to be exercised by a Governing Body of which the President
> was to be nominated by the League Assembly. The League voted grants for
> administrative expenses on a scale progressively diminishing to the date of the
> final liquidation. (Holborn 1939:131)

It was conceived as having a temporary mandate. Before his death, Nansen
himself had said in exploring options for the future of his office that the refugee
problem would be solved in ten years.

The office had responsibility for the service functions of the high commission
but never had sufficient resources to function effectively, relying primarily
on fees paid for Nansen passports. Nevertheless, the League office provided
material, legal, and financial help to about 800,000 refugees. Its ability to find
long-term solutions was further eroded by the economic crisis that caused high
levels of unemployment, and by the unsettling political developments in the
1930s with the rise of fascism.

The political and legal aspects of the high commissioner's office were
retained by the Secretariat of the League. In 1933, an intergovernmental conference, with fourteen states participating, adopted a convention on refugees
to set out in a more binding fashion the arrangements that had been negotiated
by Nansen for Russian refugees. The aim was a convention that would survive
after the Nansen office was abolished. The convention

> improved the Nansen certificate system in regard to the period of validity as well as
> the right to return to the hospitable country, restricted the practice of expulsion,
> insured the enjoyment of civil rights, and secured most favorable treatment in
> respect to labor, welfare, relief, and taxation. (Holborn 1939:132)

It applied only to refugees then under the mandate of the Nansen office.

Later in the 1930s, with fascism and Nazism producing massive new refugee flows, the League established a High Commissioner for Refugees from Germany, outside of the League's authority, which also gained a mandate to assist and protect refugees from Austria and the Sudetenland. Even this step was controversial because the League hoped at the time to reverse Germany's decision to leave the organization (Heim 2010). The funding of the new office was to come solely from private contributions (Holborn 1939). Since the 1933 convention applied only to refugees then under the Nansen office's authority, a new convention was negotiated in 1938, which gave

> German refugees certain privileges of sojourn and residence in signatory states; provided for a travel and identity document; gave a certain amount of protection against forcible return to Germany; and in general repeated the provisions of the 1933 convention with respect to legal status, labor conditions, and social welfare. (Holborn 1939:133)

It soon became evident that despite these efforts, few countries were willing to provide refuge to the German refugees, particularly those facing growing persecution because they were Jewish. Once the large-scale persecution of Jews began under the Nuremberg Laws that essentially made the German Jews stateless, the reception in Europe of refugees took a decided turn for the worse. As the numbers of Jewish refugees from countries now under German domination increased, particularly after 1938, they increasingly found a closed door. Sir John Hope Simpson, in a report issued early in 1938, tried to make the case that the numbers were actually quite small, relative to the much larger population exchanges that Europe had seen in the 1920s. Estimating that there were no more than 150,000 refugees from Germany, and that all but about 30,000 were settled in new countries, Hope Simpson argued that this was a manageable problem (Marrus 2002:167). With the German annexation of Austria, however, the situation became notably worse for larger numbers of Jews. In the early months after the *Anschluss*, about 30,000 Austrian Jews joined their German coreligionists in fleeing the country.

In July 1938, an international conference attended by representatives from thirty-two nations convened in Evian to discuss the problem of Jewish refugees. In calling for the conference, however, U.S. President Franklin Roosevelt made it clear that he was not asking any country, including the United States, to change its refugee policy. The Evian conference was a total failure, with no government pledging to resettle significant numbers of the Jewish refugees (except for the Dominican Republic's rather vague offer). From the beginning it was clear that not much would happen at the conference. Some delegates spent far more time enjoying the Alps than they did discussing the plight of the refugees.

Although many words of sympathy for the refugees were heard, few concrete proposals came out of the conference, except for establishment of the International Committee on Refugees (ICR). The ICR had a dual mandate – to

encourage countries to resettle refugees and to persuade Germany to establish
an orderly emigration process. Hence, the refugees under its authority were
defined as:

> (1) persons who have not already left their country of' origin (Germany, including
> Austria), but who must emigrate on account of their political opinions, religious
> beliefs or racial origin and (2) persons as defined in (1) who have already left
> their country of origin and who have not yet established themselves permanently
> elsewhere. (Jaeger 1978)

If Evian and the ICR failed in its first mission, to find refuge for the Jews, it failed
more spectacularly in its second. Germany responded in November 1938 with
Kristallnacht, a massive countrywide attack on Jewish businesses and syna-
gogues that was reminiscent of the Russian pogroms. When the war started,
mass incarceration of Jews and others in concentration camps increased, and
Hitler launched the Final Solution of genocide in the knowledge that other
countries would do little to rescue the European Jews.

At the end of 1938, the Nansen Office and the High Commissioner for
Refugees from Germany merged and moved their offices to London. The
new organization was known as the Office of the High Commissioner for
All Refugees under League of Nations Protection. It had as little success in
assisting and protecting the vast majority of Jews and others who were facing
Nazi persecution as had its predecessor.

CONCLUSION

The interwar period ushered in an era of both successes and failures in defining
international responsibilities for migrants. Progress was made in establishing
the need for harmonization of passport standards and principles related to
labor migration. The ILO assumed responsibilities for working with governments in the development of labor standards for migrants. Its work introduced
important principles related to the equal treatment of natives and migrants and
the value of reciprocity in managing labor migration programs. Moreover, the
1939 convention incorporated these principles into binding law, although its
implementation failed.

Initially, the League's actions regarding refugees were very promising. The
High Commissioner for Refugees established the core principle of international
responsibility for persons who were not under the protection of their own
governments. Its manifestation in the Nansen passport might appear to be
inconsequential compared to the great suffering of refugees, but as this chapter
has shown, governments had begun to identify their nationals through this form
of documentation. Without an internationally recognized passport, refugees
would be even more vulnerable. Nansen also put in place the institutional
collaboration that has come to dominate humanitarian assistance for refugees,
in setting out roles for governments, the League, NGOs, and the Red Cross.

Some of his concepts, however, have proven to have pernicious conse-quences. The population exchange he negotiated between Greece and Turkey would today be called "ethnic cleansing." Most importantly, the fledging inter-national arrangements were dependent on his strong character, reputation, and considerable diplomatic capabilities. Whether Nansen would have had greater success than his successors in the context of Nazi aggression and the antipathy of receiving countries to admit refugees, especially during the Great Depres-sion, is questionable. But, having negotiated with the Bolsheviks, he may have found "out of the box" solutions, at least for those who managed to escape persecution. Without a strong and permanent institutional base, his succes-sors had the backing of neither governments nor League leadership in taking strong action. In sum, the experience of the 1930s demonstrated a weakness that would continue to bedevil efforts to protect refugees – that is, the lack of political will to challenge countries, such as Nazi Germany, which have no regard for human life but are seen as formidable powers.

2

"The Problem of Refugees"

The title of this chapter is drawn from the 1951 UN Convention Relating to the Status of Refugees. The preamble to the convention expresses "the wish that all States, recognizing the social and humanitarian nature of the problem of refugees, will do everything within their power to prevent this problem from becoming a cause of tension between States" (UN Convention 1951). Adopted in the early days of the Cold War, with the memory of the Holocaust and the reality of hundreds of thousands still displaced by World War II, the convention provided normative underpinnings to the work of the UN High Commissioner for Refugees (UNHCR), established in 1950 to protect and find solutions to the problem of European refugees.

At its core, the Refugee Convention substitutes the protection of the international community (in the form of a host government) for that of an unable or unwilling sovereign state. In effect, the UNHCR was to provide alternative protection for those who had been persecuted by their own states, or who could not claim the protection of their states because of a well-founded fear of future persecution. This reasoning is based on the understanding that states produce refugees because they are unwilling or unable to protect their citizens from persecution. In the words of Charles Keely (1996:1057), the international refugee regime is designed to protect the "international system of states that is threatened when states fail to fulfill their proper roles."

This chapter discusses the evolution of the refugee regime from the 1950s through the present.[1] It examines the gradual expansion of the UNHCR's role as well as the scope of the norms underpinning the regime. The 1951 convention had geographic and time limitations; it covered European refugees

---

[1] This chapter focuses principally on persons who are outside of their own countries, but it will also discuss the evolving regime for those who are internally displaced for reasons that would have merited their consideration as refugees had they crossed an international border.

displaced by events that occurred prior to 1951. During the 1950s, however, the high commissioner used his "good offices" to assist refugees from the failed Hungarian revolution and then the colonial wars in Algeria. The work of the UNHCR in Africa and Asia in assisting and protecting refugees from other conflicts eventually led to adoption of the 1967 Protocol to the Convention. This agreement eliminated geographic and time restrictions, creating a universal refugee regime. The role of the UNHCR expanded rapidly in the 1970s and 1980s to address the situation of the millions displaced by surrogate Cold War conflicts in places such as Indochina, the Horn of Africa, Southern Africa, Afghanistan, and Central America. This chapter examines this evolution, as well as the role of the UNHCR in the post–Cold War era when new exigencies arose, particularly in the context of genocide and rabid nationalism in places like Rwanda and Bosnia.

At the same time, the scope of the refugee regime's normative framework also evolved. Regional conventions and agreements in Africa and Latin America expanded the definition of "refugee" to include persons fleeing from conflict and political instability, not only from persecution. In the 1990s, efforts began to expand the understanding of what constituted persecution. For example, rape, female genital mutilation, and certain forms of gender-based violence were newly understood to be instruments of persecution.[2] The concept of "agents of persecution" expanded as well to include insurgents, militias, gangs, and even family members as well as governments. When governments failed to protect those persecuted by "non-state actors," the victims could be considered refugees.

This chapter concludes with discussion of what is often referred to as mixed motive migration. It focuses on two aspects of the problem. The first deals with mixed flows – that is, situations in which refugees use the same mechanisms to enter countries as do those who have no claim to international protection. How governments differentiate between bona fide refugees and "illegal aliens" who are coming primarily for work purposes is the issue of paramount concern in this context. The second aspect of the problem deals with individuals who themselves have mixed reasons for migrating. They may have left their home countries because of conflict or persecution, but they have chosen a destination country because of the economic opportunities it affords. They may well fit the refugee definition and cannot be returned home. However, governments fearing mass influx have devised ways to exclude bona fide refugees, such as agreements that require return of asylum seekers to countries of first asylum (those through which refugees initially transit). This chapter will discuss evolving norms and institutional arrangements in this area.

---

[2] The convention refers to race, religion, nationality, political opinion, and membership in a particular social group as reasons individuals may be persecuted. Gender is not included in the definition, but many governments now include women as a particular social group when the claims to asylum are based on gender.

UN RELIEF AND REHABILITATION ADMINISTRATION   post WWII

The tragic ramifications of the failure of the international community to come to the aid of refugees became clear with the liberation of the concentration camps. The camp survivors joined millions of people uprooted by the conflict itself. During the 1940s, a number of distinct organizations were tasked with addressing the problem of refugees and displaced persons in Europe. The High Commissioner for Refugees from Germany and the International Committee on Refugees (ICR), which emerged from the Evian conference, continued to operate during the war. At a conference in Bermuda in 1943, the ICR's mandate was expanded to include all persons who, as a result of events in Europe, had to leave their countries of residence because of danger to their lives or liberties on account of their race, religion, or political beliefs (U.S. State Department 1943). This expansion allowed the organization to assist a broader range of minorities and political dissidents but it was adopted, in part, to avoid taking specific action on Jewish refugees (ibid.).

Tragically, the Bermuda conference failed to take any actions that might have prevented the Holocaust. In fact, the UK delegation noted as a complicating factor in devising new policies on refugees that "[t]here is a possibility that the Germans or their satellites may change over from the policy of extermination to one of extrusion, and aim as they did before the war at embarrassing other countries by flooding them with alien immigrants" (US State Department 1943:134). The Bermuda conference dismissed what were described by U.S. diplomats as "more radical proposals," including "negotiations with Germany for the release of the Jewish population . . . and the proposal to lift the blockade to allow departure of persecuted people of Europe" (ibid.:155). In setting out the criteria for making recommendations, the conference communiqué made clear that no actions would be taken on behalf of refugees that "interfered with or delayed the war efforts of the United Nations" (ibid.:174).

At the same time, the Allied powers were establishing their own mechanisms to address war-related displacement. In 1942, President Roosevelt established the Office of Foreign Relief and Rehabilitation Operations (OFRRO). Herbert Lehman, founder of Lehman Brothers and former Governor of New York, was tasked with organizing U.S. activities related to civilians in war zones (Holborn 1965). OFRRO cooperated with the British Middle East Relief and Refugee Administration (MERRA), which cared for those who had fled countries in North Africa as well as Greeks and Yugoslavs displaced by fighting in their home countries. These government agencies worked closely with a number of NGOs and the Red Cross in these activities.

In 1943, the Allied forces set up a new organization to address wider relief issues that were likely to emerge during the planned offensive and expected counteroffensive against Germany and Japan. Representatives of the forty-four United and Associated Nations signed the agreement to establish the United Nations Relief and Rehabilitation Administration (UNRRA) at a White

House conference. Under the agreement, there would be a legislative and policy-making council made up of all members, a central committee with limited executive powers that included China, the United States, the Soviet Union, and Great Britain, and a secretariat headed by a director-general (Sumberg 1945). Lehman was appointed to lead the organization.

UNRRA was to give aid to areas liberated from the Axis powers. It began operations during the war and continued in its immediate aftermath. UNRRA acted in conjunction with the military authorities and local officials in providing relief to civilians, including those who had been displaced. Its scope of operation in Europe was Austria, Germany, Italy, and certain areas in Africa and the Near East. It was also responsible for relief in China and other areas occupied by Japan. Other liberated countries, including France, Belgium, Holland, and Norway, did not request UNRRA's assistance. The Soviet military barred it from the areas under its occupation (Arnold-Forster 1946).

There was general acknowledgement that while the conflict continued, the military would have the principal responsibility for providing relief to civilians in areas of liberation. But there was also agreement that military relief operations were not a long-term solution: "the military is not geared to take permanent responsibility for the relief and rehabilitation of any one area, far less all of Europe. First and last, the Army's job is to defeat the enemy and move on" (Taylor 1945:41).

In addition to providing relief, UNRRA was charged with rehabilitation of agricultural and industrial production and restoring social infrastructure in liberated areas (Loescher 2001). Sounding a note similar to that which led to the inclusion of labor issues in the League, a contemporary account described the logic:

> Nor will the economies of the rest of the world be safe if the victimized nations are not given a chance to get back on their feet. Prosperity is just as indivisible as peace. In lands where a scorched-earth policy and wanton enemy destruction have devastated entire farming areas and every urban factory and public utility, agricultural and industrial rehabilitation must be made available to allow economies to begin again. Otherwise, unemployment and lower standards of living will be the lot of men in every country, with economic and political consequences of unforeseen peril. (Taylor 1945:40)

UNRRA never fully took on this long-term role because of funding issues, the continued dominance of the military in providing aid, and emerging tensions between East and West. It mostly functioned as a service agency working with the military authorities. All of the forty-four member states were to contribute to the administrative costs of the organization, but funding for actual services would be on a voluntary contribution basis. The states that had not been under enemy control were expected to shoulder the largest burden of these costs. A fixed quota was assigned to the payment of administrative costs: the "United States pays 40 per cent, Great Britain and Russia 15 (Russia later 10) per cent each, China 5 per cent, France 4 per cent, and 0.5 per cent for fifteen smaller countries" (Sumberg 1945:702). The service costs were not allocated on that basis but left to the states the decision on how much each would contribute to the budget (Sumberg 1945).

The funding of UNRRA began slowly (Dennett 1945), partly because of delays in gaining approval of the agreement from national governments, but accelerated as the demand increased. Similar to the situation of the ARA of World War I, UNRRA eventually was well funded by its member states in comparison to the experiences of the League offices. "From its inception in November 1943 until its disbandment in June 1947, UNRRA expended nearly $3.4 billion – of which the United States contributed $2.8 billion – and at the peak of its activity it employed 27,800 people" (Loescher 2001:35).

UNRRA also had to overcome political tensions in the countries in which it operated, particularly in the aftermath of the war and the growing dominance of the Soviet Union in Eastern Europe. Persuading receiving governments that the aid was without political strings proved to be difficult but surmountable. One analysis of its operations in Yugoslavia reported: "It was not until a detailed agreement had been signed in March 1945, in which responsibility for distribution of supplies was definitely assigned to the Government and a Russian Chief of Mission had been appointed that this mistrust was removed" (D.W. 1946). Drawing on the experiences of the League, Lehman required that all staff sign a loyalty statement attesting that their actions would reflect the organization's needs, not that of their countries:

> I solemnly undertake to exercise in all loyalty, discretion and conscience the functions entrusted to me as an (officer or employee) of the administration, to discharge my functions and regulate my conduct with its interests alone in view, and not to seek or receive from any government or authority external to the Administration any instructions controlling me in my performance of my official duties. (Lehman 1945:99)

His aim was to build a credible public international administration that would operate independent of the politics of the situation.

A contemporary assessment of UNRRA described its successes and failures. Its successes were in its relief activities; its failures in rehabilitation "Although the rehabilitation originally envisaged could not be carried out, U.N.R.R.A. supplies have enabled the devastated countries of the United Nations to scrape through the past two years free from starvation – though by a small margin in many cases – and miraculously free from major epidemics" (JR 1945:371).

From the beginning, UNRRA knew that displacement would be an important issue. Two studies prepared for UNRRA estimated that between 22 and 30 million displaced persons were in need of relief. Displaced people were divided into four categories. First were war refugees (civilians, war prisoners, and civilian internees). Second were those who suffered persecution for political, religious, or racial reasons and were effectively stateless (they were the responsibility of ICR). Third were those laborers who were forcibly taken to

Germany. The last category was ethnic Germans who were scattered throughout Europe. All of these groups, except for war prisoners and persons of ex-enemy nationalities, were to be cared for by UNRRA (Holborn 1965).

UNRRA's principal responsibilities were for the care and maintenance of the displaced persons awaiting repatriation in reception centers. UNRRA had no authority to resettle refugees to third countries, only to help the displaced with relief and, where possible, to facilitate return to their home communities. The preamble to the agreement that brought about UNRRA stated that "preparations and arrangements shall be made for the return of prisoners and exiles to their homes."[3] The military imperative was clear, as described in a 1946 article by W. Arnold-Forster, a former UNRRA official who had trained staff working with displaced persons:

> The armies worked on the assumption that there must at first be a standstill policy and that movement of displaced persons must be controlled. It followed that shelter, food and protection must be supplied and organized; repatriation must be arranged through collecting points, transit points and assembly centres in Germany, with reception centres in the countries of destination. (Arnold-Forster 1946:7)

By the end of May 1945, some 3.5 million displaced persons had been liberated. Repatriation westward proceeded quickly, with about 850,000 returned home (Arnold-Forster 1946:8). Repatriation to the Soviet Union also began in May under the terms of the Agreement Relating to Prisoners of War and Civilians Liberated by Forces Operating Under Soviet Command and Forces Operating Under United States of America Command, signed on February 11, 1945, during the negotiations in Yalta. The United States and the USSR agreed:

> All Soviet citizens liberated by the forces operating under United States command and all United States citizens liberated by the forces operating under Soviet command will, without delay after their liberation, be separated from enemy prisoners of war and will be maintained separately from them in camps or points of concentration until they have been handed over to the Soviet or United States authorities, as the case may be, at places agreed upon between those authorities.[4]

A similar agreement was made with the British.

By September, all but about 40,000 of the estimated 2 million Soviet citizens in the Western zones had been repatriated (Arnold-Forster 1946). The Yalta agreement did not specify the terms under which Soviet citizens would be repatriated, but some military commanders interpreted them to permit forcible return of those who would have preferred to remain outside of the Soviet Union (Plokhy 2010). The most controversial return was that of Cossacks who had fought against the Bolsheviks during the civil war and were under German orders and protection in southern Austria. When the British liberated the area around Linz, they forcibly repatriated about 40,000 Cossacks. These included

---

[3] Agreement for UNRRA reprinted at http://www.ibiblio.org/pha/policy/1943/431109a.html.
[4] Agreement reprinted at http://www.fordham.edu/halsall/mod/1945YALTA.html.

women, children, and elderly Cossacks and prewar refugees who were exempt from the Yalta Agreement (Sword, quoted in Cohen 1995).

By November, 5.2 million displaced persons had been repatriated from the areas of Western Germany occupied by U.S., British, and French forces with the assistance of UNRRA; approximately 1.1 million remained displaced. The largest number of returnees repatriated to the Soviet Union and France. The largest numbers of those who were still displaced were Poles (almost 720,000) (Arnold-Forster 1946).[5] With regard to its refugee work throughout Europe, another assessment concluded: "The number of refugees has been reduced by repatriation, absorption, and resettlement from 11 million at the end of the war to 3 million in May, 1947. In tackling the refugee problem U.N.R.R.A. has been careful to steer clear of international politics and to maintain its status as a super-national authority" (JR 1945:372).

Throughout the repatriation operations, UNRRA had emphasized the importance of ensuring that all returns were voluntary, but contemporary accounts questioned whether it achieved those aims. Note has already been made of the returns of the Cossacks. Commenting on a lecture by a former UNRRA official, the chairman of the UNRRA Board of Selection for Belgium and Holland raised the issue as a growing problem: "Recently, from camps in the charge of U.N.R.R.A., many truckloads of unfortunate individuals had been sent back to Eastern Europe against their supplications; that was a matter which should be included in the lecturer's category of things which must be attended to now" (Arnold-Forster 1946:13). Whether UNRRA was obligated to provide assistance to those who refused to return home was a further area of debate (Loescher 2001). The Western governments generally preferred to maintain support, whereas the Soviet Union and its allies wanted UNRRA's funds to be used only for those who repatriated. A compromise allowed aid to continue but, the Western governments framed it as transitional aid within the context of potential future returns.

INTERNATIONAL REFUGEE ORGANIZATION

It would be the new United Nations that would have to address these thorny issues, as it dealt with the transition from the League's refugee offices to new UN ones. Parallel to UNRRA, the League's offices continued to function during the war, but with the end of hostilities and formation of the UN, the dissolution of the League and the transfer of its responsibilities became an issue for debate. At the same time, the United States, as the largest donor country, had become disillusioned with UNRRA, much of whose work was now focused on

---

[5] Arnold-Forster, using data provided by the European Regional Office of UNRRA, notes that these are estimates and are low in comparison to the numbers of citizens of some of these countries who were believed to have been held by Germany during the war. Whether this was because they had been killed was unknown at the time.

repatriation and assistance to Eastern Europe. In effect, U.S. taxpayer funds were going toward aiding the return of refugees to countries under the Soviet sphere of interest – a situation not in keeping with the emerging Cold War hostile environmental.

The General Assembly of the UN considered further steps. "After a sharp debate on 'genuine refugees and displaced persons' the General Assembly adopted a resolution of February 12, 1946, calling upon the Economic and Social Council to appoint a special committee to report on the matter" (Myers 1948:345). The fault lines that emerged were between the West – which wanted to expand the options for displaced persons from repatriation to a broader set of solutions, including resettlement in third countries – and the Soviet bloc, which wanted to renew UNRRA's mandate or, at least, ensure that a new organization gave priority to repatriation to the East.

There was general agreement that if UNRRA and the ICR's mandates expired before these issues were resolved, large numbers of refugees and displaced persons would be in jeopardy. The constitution of the International Refugee Organization (IRO) was approved by the General Assembly on December 15, 1946. A piecemeal process paved the way for the organization to come into being. On January 1, 1947, the responsibilities and funding of the League High Commissioner for Refugees were transferred to the ICR "with regard to refugees from Germany and the Saar and the remaining Russian and Armenian refugees then under his jurisdiction, the funds transferred amounting to 287,164.47 Swiss francs" (Myers 1948:345). The ICR, in turn, transferred its funds and activities to the IRO on July 1, 1947 (345). In the meantime, a Preparatory Commission of the International Refugee Organization was put in place to serve as a transitional body until enough countries signed the IRO convention and authorized funding. Fifteen countries would have to ratify the constitution and 75 percent of the administrative funding be secured for the institution to begin its work.

The new organization came into being as the United Nations was negotiating the Universal Declaration of Human Rights (UDHR). Although not a binding document, the UDHR nevertheless was one of the most important, albeit ambiguous, developments in setting out the rights of refugees and the responsibilities of states. Its greatest achievement was establishing core political, civil, economic, and social rights that everyone should enjoy, regardless of where they resided. From the vantage point of refugees, the enunciation of these rights is important because their abuse is fundamental to the inability of refugees to return home.

The UDHR's more specific treatment of migration is where the ambiguity ensues. Article 13 of the UDHR established the individual right to move and reside freely within one's own country. That article also set out the right to leave any country (including one's own) and to return to one's own country. Guarantee of that right was more difficult, however, than merely stating it. To be able to leave one's own country, an individual must enter another one.

Member states differed considerably on how to resolve this issue. Some supported a right to asylum, but others, including the U.S. delegation led by Eleanor Roosevelt, preferred to limit state obligations with regard to refugees. Article 14 of the UDHR sought compromise language and affirms only a "right to *seek* and to *enjoy* in other countries asylum from persecution."[6] In a very close vote, states rejected any obligation on the part of states to *grant* asylum. As a result, the right of exit was not accompanied, in effect, by a right of entry, even for those who were escaping life-threatening situations. Nor did the UDHR clearly set out the terms under which the flip side of the right to reenter one's country – that is, the right to refuse to reenter – would be handled. The right to asylum has to this date not been enshrined in any convention, but the United Nations took up the issue of forcible return in the 1951 Refugee Convention, discussed in a later section of this chapter.

The refugees in Europe at the time of the IRO's formation included several distinct groups. First were prewar refugees who were still uprooted, including those under Nansen's original mandate (Russians and Armenians), refugees from the Spanish Civil War, and refugees from Nazi Germany. The second set included those displaced by the war itself, many of whom had already repatriated, and including others who refused to return. The third were the victims of anti-Semitic persecution, including concentration camp survivors. In addition, the Kielce pogrom in Poland – in which forty Jews were killed after rumors of ritual killings, kidnappings, and political agitation had inflamed mob violence – convinced about 60,000 Jews who had survived the Holocaust to leave Poland and effectively ended any prospects of repatriation for those already displaced (Szaynok 1997). The final group included those who left Soviet-occupied territories because of their opposition to the communist regimes that had taken control.

Not all of these groups were specified in the IRO's constitution as coming under its authority. Annex I stated:

The term "refugee" applies to a person who has left, or who is outside of, his country of nationality or of former habitual residence, and who, whether or not he had retained his nationality, belongs in one of the following categories:

(a) victims of the Nazi or fascist regimes or of regimes which took part on their side in the Second World War, or of the quisling[7] or similar regimes which assisted them against the United Nations, whether enjoying international status as refugees or not;

(b) Spanish Republicans and other victims of the Falangist regime in Spain, whether enjoying international status as refugees or not;

---

[6] http://www.un.org/en/documents/udhr/.

[7] The use of the term "quisling" is ironic since Vidkyn Quisling, the Nazi collaborator in Norway after whom the term is coined, was Nansen's deputy in both the Russian famine and Armenian refugee operations of the League.

(c) persons who were considered "refugees" before the outbreak of the second world war, for reasons of race, religion, nationality or political opinion.[8]

Those who persecuted others or who collaborated with enemy forces would not qualify as refugees.

The IRO's constitution recognized the new realities of the emerging Cold War – that not all refugees would return home. The preamble stated that "genuine refugees and displaced persons should be assisted by international action, either to return to their countries of nationality or former habitual residence, or to find new homes elsewhere". The functions of the IRO were specified to include "encouraging and assisting in every way possible the early return to their country of nationality, or former habitual residence, of those persons who are the concern of the Organization". But, it also gave the organization authority to work with those who did not repatriate to facilitate

(i) their re-establishment in countries of temporary residence; (ii) the emigration to, re-settlement and re-establishment in other countries of individuals or family units; and (iii) as may be necessary and practicable, within available resources and subject to the relevant financial regulations, the investigation, promotion or execution of projects of group re-settlement or large-scale re-settlement.

The IRO was established as an autonomous organization that had a "relationship" to the UN spelled out in a memorandum of understanding. Membership was open to UN members and other "peace-loving" states. The structure included a General Council, an Executive Committee, and a secretariat. The General Council was the decision-making body and would meet once per year (twice per year during the first three years). The Executive Committee could make decisions between sessions of the General Council in case of emergencies. The Executive Committee nominated the director-general of the Secretariat, who was to be approved by the General Council. The budget was to have three components: administrative expenses, operational expenses, and the costs of large-scale resettlement programs. The first two would be allocated among member states on a basis determined by the constitution and then updated by the General Council. Costs for resettlement would be raised through voluntary contributions. A majority of the allocated costs for administration and operations would be covered by the United States (40 percent and 45 percent, respectively) and the United Kingdom (11.5 percent and 15 percent).

When UNRRA was dissolved, the IRO constitution had not yet been ratified by enough countries to come into effect. Instead, the Preparatory Commission received funds to work through the transition period. In August 1948, Denmark became the fifteenth country to ratify the constitution without reservations and sufficient resources were secured for the IRO to be launched (Holborn 1965).

[8] All quotes are from the version of the Constitution found at http://www.refworld.org/docid/3ae6b37810.html.

During its years of operation, the IRO assisted more than 1.6 million refugees. Early in its existence, the agency conducted a census and categorized the refugees into three groups. Some needed care and maintenance, others received aid in resettlement or repatriation, and the rest needed only legal assistance (Holborn 1965). Most refugees were determined to be employable. According to the census, 38.6 percent of the refugees showed potential for skilled labor, and 22.3 percent had agricultural skills. However, most of the refugees did not have authorization to work in the local economies, although many of these restrictions were reduced in later years.

Refugees were registered to determine if they were, in fact, refugees in one of the categories eligible for IRO assistance. The decision for eligibility was made by an IRO eligibility officer after a private interview with the applicant or after the officer had reviewed the applicant's information. Adverse decisions could be appealed to the Review Board for Eligibility Appeals. The board was composed of Mr. de Baer, former Justice of Appeal in Brussels, and twenty-eight other persons. The board members traveled around Europe to hear those refugees who were appealing to be received by the IRO. Its standards of eligibility were the same as those of the eligibility officer (Holborn 1965).

Half a million refugees lived outside of the camps mixed in with local communities. In some locations, tensions erupted between locals and refugees. Some local authorities feared that the refugees were spies or security risks. About 700,000 refugees lived in displaced persons camps – called "assembly centers" at the time. There were three types of centers: long-term residences, transit centers for those to be resettled, and reception centers for those who were repatriating.

The long-term residence centers were divided by nationality. Jewish refugees tended to be in centers separate from those of others from the same country, not surprising given the high degree of complicity in many occupied countries with the Nazi extermination of Jews. The centers had a high degree of autonomy in their operations. The refugees often ran their own medical centers, schools, arts centers, and newspapers. They also established administrative centers in their communities with training from UNRRA and the military authorities. The centers distributed welfare, helped refugees find jobs, and dealt with health issues, recreational activities, and other matters (Holborn 1965). Over time, a sense of camaraderie emerged in many of the centers, prompting the refugees to request to be resettled in the same locations.

As with UNRRA, the IRO was highly dependent on the military for gaining access to refugees and displaced persons in territories still under occupation. The arrangements differed to some extent, depending on the occupied country and the occupying country. In U.S. zones, the military provided logistics but the IRO had substantial autonomy in conducting operations. In British and French zones, the military was responsible for operations, with the IRO's supervision (Holborn 1965). Initially, the Austrian government had more autonomy than the German government in approving arrangements for refugees. The

German government, however, took full responsibility for the largest number of displaced persons in its territory – ethnic Germans who had been expelled from Eastern European countries and were granted German citizenship. By 1950, both governments were playing an important role in decisions regarding refugees and displaced persons in their territories (Holborn 1965). In countries that had full sovereignty over their territories, the IRO negotiated agreements setting out its role and relationship to the government.

The IRO was also dependent on NGOs, which provided much of the material support that went to refugees and displaced persons. Holborn estimates that NGOs covered about 90 percent of all cash, goods, and personnel placed at the disposal of refugees. Many of these groups had a denominational identity, including Catholic (Catholic Immigrant Aid Society of Canada, Caritas Internationalis, and Pax Romana), Protestant (Refugee Commission of the World Council of Churches, the refugee assistance branch of the Lutheran World Federation, Church World Service, Mennonite Central Committee, American Friends Service Committee, the YMCA/YWCA, and the Unitarian Service Committee), and Jewish (American Joint Distribution Committee, Hebrew Immigrant Aid Society, Jewish Relief Board Committee for Relief Abroad, and Vaad Hatzala). Secular organizations included the Scout Movement, International Social Services, World Student Relief, International Rescue and Relief Committee (which became the International Rescue Committee), and the U.S. Committee for the Care of European Children. Former emigrants in Canada and the United States also contributed relief through the American Committee for Resettlement of Polish Displaced Persons, American Fund for Czechs Refugees, American National Committee to Aid Homeless Armenians, American Polish War Relief, Tolstoy Foundation, United Lithuanian Relief Fund of America, United Ukrainian American Relief Committee, and the Ukrainian Canadian Relief Fund. Adding to these organizations were many small organizations based within the affected countries that collaborated with the IRO locally (Holborn 1965).

The IRO established a Department of Voluntary Services to help coordinate its activities with those of these private actors. The relationship was symbiotic. The IRO gained resources and support in seeking funding from governments. The IRO in return gave the organizations status, granted them facilities, and represented them in negotiations for permission to work with the occupation authorities and national governments. In exchange, the agencies had to guarantee that they would not take political action antithetical to the IRO's constitution.

By the time the IRO closed its doors, it had assisted in the resettlement of about 1 million refugees. This number was in sharp contrast to the 54,000 who repatriated during the same period. As the Cold War intensified, many Western European countries closed the repatriation offices established by the Eastern European countries that were by then under communist control (Loescher 2001). Meanwhile, the traditional immigration countries overcame their resistance to expanding immigration and enacted policies that facilitated resettlement. The United States received 31.7 percent of the resettled; Australia 17.5 percent, the new state of Israel 12.7 percent, Canada 11.9 percent, the UK 8.3 percent, the rest of Western Europe 6.8 percent, and Latin America 6.5 percent (Loescher 2001:40). Most of the countries were selective in their admissions criteria, wanting (or rejecting) specific nationalities or religious groups and preferring those who were younger and more employable. At the end of the period, about 400,000, many old and infirm, remained in displaced persons camps.

That such large-scale resettlement occurred to the United States, in particular, was testament to the importance of the refugee issues to U.S. foreign policy. As discussed in Chapter 1, the United States had adopted immigration legislation in 1924 that severely restricted the access of would-be immigrants from Eastern Europe. The national origins quotas were reaffirmed in legislation enacted in 1952, showing that overall attitudes about immigration had not changed significantly. Immediately after the war, President Harry S. Truman signed a directive that outlined new administrative procedures to facilitate the admission of war victims into the United States. The refugees were to be admitted under the existing quotas with efforts to give them priority, to the extent possible under existing immigration law. The president directed his administration to enlist the help of voluntary agencies to ensure that the public charge requirement did not impede admissions:

> With respect to the requirement of law that visas may not be issued to applicants likely to become public charges after admission to the United States, the Secretary of State shall co-operate with the Immigration and Naturalization Service in perfecting appropriate arrangements with welfare organizations in the United States which may be prepared to guarantee financial support to successful applicants. This may be accomplished by corporate affidavit or by any means deemed appropriate and practicable. (Truman 1945)

The president's directive program succeeded in paving the way for the admission of 40,000 displaced persons. In 1947, with the support of the Truman administration, new legislation was introduced to permit the entry of 220,000 displaced persons. They were to be admitted within existing quotas, so as not to raise questions about the underlying law, but provisions were made to borrow, or mortgage, up to 50 percent of a country's annual numbers to facilitate the additional admissions. Up to 3,000 orphans under the age of sixteen could also be admitted outside of the immigration quotas. The bill pertained to those who entered displaced persons camps no later than 1945, with the exception of 2,000 Czechs who left their country following the communist takeover. It also gave priority to persons displaced from the Baltic States. The 1950 amendments to the Displaced Persons Act increased the numbers to be admitted to 415,000 but maintained the mortgaging provisions. It also allowed admission to those who had entered displaced persons camps after 1945.

Despite the success of the IRO's resettlement operations, by 1950 its principal donors were considering discontinuation of its operations. The annual costs of the organization seemed very high (Loescher 1993). U.S. Congress made clear that it did not intend to continue to fund the IRO and expected the European countries to assume the costs of the residual population. Marshall Plan funds could be used to shore up their capacities to accomplish this goal, with help from a smaller, less expensive international office that could succeed the IRO.

REFUGEES FROM OUTSIDE OF EUROPE

Europe was not the only area experiencing large-scale displacement in the post–World War II era. In another wave of violence and ethnic cleansing after new states were formed, one of the largest displacements in human history took place in 1947–1948 as a result of the partition of India. The Indian Independence Act of 1947, passed by the UK Parliament, partitioned British India into the two new independent dominions of Pakistan and India. The two new countries came into being on August 14 and 15, respectively. The scale of the displacement was immense: "It may be estimated that about five and half million people travelled each way across the new India-Pakistan border in Punjab. In addition about 400,000 Hindus migrated from Sind and well over a million moved from East Pakistan to West Bengal" (Nag 2001:4755). The large numbers mask differences in experiences. Many moved in crisis conditions out of fear of violence or actual attacks, and others had time to plan their movements. Some were able to exchange their land with a displaced family from the other country or were coming to join the new government bureaucracies of India and Pakistan (Rahman and van Schendel 2003).

Displacement because of ethnic violence was not new to the subcontinent. As it became clear that independence would be forthcoming, however, the levels of violence accelerated. An estimated 20,000–60,000 fled their homes from violence prior to partition (Oberoi 2005). The much larger-scale migration after partition was unexpected. The leaderships of the two countries did not expect to form religiously homogeneous nations and, in fact, India remained highly diverse in its population composition. As a result, neither country was prepared for the mass movements that took place within a relatively short period.

The flow of refugees after partition was different in a number of respects from the post–World War I population exchanges discussed in Chapter 1. First, as noted, the population exchanges were not a planned part of a peace negotiation. Rather, the movements were spontaneous, although each country did evacuate coreligionists who were in particularly threatening situations. The scale of the movements was not welcomed by the leadership, however, which tried to negotiate a halt to the exodus from each side (Oberoi 2005). Second, and more pertinent for the purposes of this book, they occurred with almost no international response in the form of relief or rehabilitation despite the appeals for assistance from India and Pakistan. Western powers held that the displaced/evacuees were not refugees because they would be settled in the country of their destination and have its citizenship (Oberoi 2005). This also could have been said about the Greeks and Turks relocated in the 1920s, but in 1947 the international community argued that only those without the protection of their own states needed international protection. Interestingly, as will be seen, the same might have been said of Korean refugees who did receive international attention. The absence of a strong tie to the Cold War may have had a greater impact, however, than did the principle behind international protection (Zolberg et al. 1989). The little assistance that was forthcoming from the UN was delivered by the World Health Organization and UNICEF, not the IRO, which was responsible only in Europe. Faced with this situation, India and Pakistan established their own offices to assist the new arrivals until housing and employment could be found for them.

The next major challenge to the evolving refugee regime occurred in 1948 with the partition of Palestine into Israel and Jordan, and the resulting conflict between Arabs and Jews. Unlike the Indian subcontinent, the Palestine partition was by UN action, not an act of parliament. As early as 1917, in the Balfour Declaration, the British had expressed support for "the establishment in Palestine of a national home for the Jewish people."[9] To gain Arab support in the fight against the Ottomans during World War I, the British had also given assurances to Arab leaders that they would gain control over their lands. After the war, the Treaty of Sevres gave Britain mandate authority over Palestine, meaning that Britain would control that territory until it was "ready" for national self-determination. The Peel Commission in 1937 explored the nature of that independence. The commission proposed that Palestine be divided into two entities – one to become a Jewish state and the other to become part of Jordan, with population transfers to accomplish the goal. Both Arab and Zionist leaders rejected the plan initially, although the Zionist leaders agreed in principle that it could serve as a blueprint for negotiations. Arab violence against British rule and Jewish immigration escalated significantly in the aftermath of the commission's proposal, leading to armed rebellion. Although the revolt was repressed by the British authorities, the British government made changes in its policies to address the concerns of the Arabs. Its 1939 White Paper backed off the Peel Commission recommendations, stating a preference for a single state with powers apportioned between Jews and Arabs. In the White Paper, the British also curtailed Jewish immigration into Palestine to about 75,000 immigrants over five years. The White Paper decreed that after five years, no further Jewish immigration would be permitted unless the Palestinian Arabs agreed to it.[10]

---

[9] What is generally referred to as the Balfour Declaration was a very brief letter from Arthur James Balfour to Lord Rothschild on November 2, 1917. The version cited herein is available at http://avalon.law.yale.edu/20th_century/balfour.asp.

[10] http://avalon.law.yale.edu/20th_century/brwh1939.asp.

In the ensuing years, and in the context of the loss of 6 million Jews in the Holocaust, the intent of Jewish nationalists to form a Jewish state hardened and became more militant, as did the Arab opposition. The Alexandria Protocol that established the League of Arab Nations in 1944 concluded:

> The Committee also declares that it is second to none in regretting the woes which have been inflicted upon the Jews of Europe by European dictatorial states. But the question of these Jews should not be confused with Zionism, for there can be no greater injustice and aggression than solving the problem of the Jews of Europe by another injustice, i.e., by inflicting injustice on the Arabs of Palestine of various religions and denominations.[11]

When World War II ended, the British continued to implement the terms of the 1939 White Paper and refused entreaties from President Truman and others to admit 100,000 Jewish displaced persons into Palestine. The government also ramped up its efforts to prevent illegal immigration into the territory under its mandate, at one point refusing to allow the passengers on a ship renamed *Exodus* to come into port, instead returning them to displaced persons camps.

The British had seen the UN as the appropriate body to determine the fate of its mandate territory. Unlike India, Palestine was not considered to be an integral part of the British Empire, so resolution of the situation did not call for an act of parliament. Britain brought the issue to the attention of the General Assembly in its first meeting. As a result, the eleven-member UN Special Committee on Palestine (UNSCOP) was formed in April 1947.

> The majority of the committee members recommended that Palestine be partitioned into an Arab State and a Jewish State, with a special international status for the city of Jerusalem under the administrative authority of the United Nations. The three entities were to be linked in an economic union. The minority plan called for an independent federal structure comprising an Arab State and a Jewish State, with Jerusalem as the capital of the federation. (United Nations 2008)

Although the Jewish leadership in Palestine cooperated with UNSCOP, the Arab leadership refused, saying that the UN had not separated the problem of Jewish refugees from the right of Arabs to an independent state in Palestine. Jewish leaders argued that the two issues were inseparable.

The future of Palestine came to a vote in November 1947. The operative chapters of General Assembly Resolution 181 were:

- The Mandate for Palestine shall terminate as soon as possible but in any case not later than 1 August 1948.
- The armed forces of the mandatory Power shall be progressively withdrawn from Palestine, the withdrawal to be completed as soon as possible but in any case not later than 1 August 1948.

[11] http://avalon.law.yale.edu/20th_century/alex.asp.

- Independent Arab and Jewish States and the Special International Regime for the City of Jerusalem, set forth in Part III of this Plan, shall come into existence in Palestine two months after the evacuation of the armed forces of the mandatory Power has been completed but in any case not later than 1 October 1948.[12]

After months of escalating violence, on May 14, 1948, the UK relinquished its mandate over Palestine and disengaged its forces. On the same day, Israel declared its independence. Troops from neighboring Arab states invaded on May 15. Fighting ensued, punctuated by UN efforts to bring about cession of hostilities. By the time the final armistice was signed between Israel and its opposing forces in July 1949, the boundaries had changed from those determined in Resolution 181. Israel had incorporated a larger portion of the territory, including the western part of Jerusalem; Jordan had taken over responsibility for the West Bank of Palestine, and Egypt for Gaza.

There were humanitarian consequences of the conflict as well – notably, the displacement of some 600,000 Arabs, most as refugees into neighboring countries or the West Bank and Gaza. Subsequently, a comparable number of Jews fled or were expelled from Arab countries that opposed the creation of the State of Israel. More than 600,000 arrived in Israel and more than 250,000 went to other countries (Basri 2003). In Israel, Jews had automatic access to citizenship. As in the case of the India and Pakistan situation, the Jewish refugees from Arab lands in Israel were not considered to be refugees by the international community. Many arrived destitute because of actions taken by the Arab countries to limit the property that they could take out of the country. Iraq, for example, adopted legislation in 1950 that required those who planned to emigrate to forfeit their citizenship. In 1951, the country passed legislation that deprived now stateless Jews of their property (Basri 2003). External funding to assist their integration in Israel came mostly from bilateral sources – Jewish organizations and individuals in the diaspora and national governments such as that of the United States.[13]

A complex set of factors caused the large-scale movements of Palestinians and the failure of the international community to resolve their situation to this day. Some left voluntarily, believing that the Arab states would quickly defeat the Israeli military and they would return to an independent Palestine. Others fled the conflict, seeking safety in neighboring countries. Still others were expelled from their homes as a matter of military exigencies. Whatever the cause of their initial displacement, they found themselves in Jordan, the West Bank, Gaza, Lebanon, and Syria, unable or unwilling to return to Israel.

---

[12] Resolution 181 is at http://www.yale.edu/lawweb/avalon/un/res181.htm.

[13] The issue of compensation for the Jews who lost their property has recurred in peace negotiations between Israel and the Palestinian Authority. After the failure to reach agreement in 2000, U.S. President Bill Clinton noted that progress had been made in conceiving a compensation mechanism that would have applied to both Jewish and Palestinian refugees (Basri 2003).

The host countries made clear that they did not intend to allow the Palestinians to settle permanently on their territory.

The UN established two agencies to respond to the situation of the Palestinian refugees. General Assembly Resolution 194, adopted on December 11, 1948, established a Conciliation Commission to take over the responsibilities of the UN mediator on Palestine. Although largely responsible for political matters, among its duties was the responsibility "to facilitate the repatriation, resettlement and economic and social rehabilitation of the refugees and the payment of compensation."[14] This role was consequent to the resolution's crucial statement that

> the refugees wishing to return to their homes and live at peace with their neighbors should be permitted to do so at the earliest practicable date, and that compensation should be paid for the property of those choosing not to return and for loss of or damage to property which, under principles of international law or in equity, should be made good by the Governments or authorities responsible.

The commission launched an economic survey mission, charged with examining the economic situation in the host countries of the Palestinian refugees. One of its preliminary findings – on the need to shift from a pure relief paradigm to one that would "increase the practical alternatives available to refugees" – led to discussion of a new agency to take over from the UN Relief for Palestine Refugees (Forsythe 1983:92). The following year, the UN Relief and Works Agency for Palestinian Refugees in the Near East (UNRWA) was established to provide assistance and employment opportunities. Until then, most aid was provided by the Red Cross and the American Friends Service Committee.

UNRWA was specifically asked to take on two tasks. First, it was to carry out the direct relief and works programs recommended by the economic survey mission, and second, it was to consult with the host countries on measures to reduce the need for international assistance. These two tasks were consistent with the sense of the General Assembly, expressed in the resolution, that

> continued assistance for the relief of the Palestine refugees is necessary to prevent conditions of starvation and distress among them and to further conditions of peace and stability, and that constructive measures should be undertaken at an early date with a view to the termination of international assistance for relief.[15]
> (United Nations 1949)

Although the first task continues to occupy UNRWA's attention, the second objective – to end international assistance – never came to pass. In 1950, a new resolution was adopted that extended UNRWA's operation. Still with hope for an end to the need for international relief, the resolution emphasized the need for economic "reintegration of the refugees into the economic life of the

---

[14] All quotes from Resolution 194 are at http://avalon.law.yale.edu/20th_century/decad171.asp.
[15] Resolution 302 at http://unispal.un.org/UNISPAL.NSF/0/AF5F909791DE7FB0852560E500687282.

Near East, either by repatriation or resettlement, is essential in preparation for the time when international assistance is no longer available, and for the realization of conditions of peace and stability in the area."[16]

In the meantime, the Conciliation Commission was undertaking its responsibilities to resolve the refugee situation. The commission undertook "shuttle diplomacy," going to each country in the region seeking the views of both the Arab states and Israel about implementing Resolution 194. The Arab states most involved in the refugee situation – Egypt, Jordan, Lebanon, and Syria – also had secret bilateral talks with Israel (Forsythe 1983). The Arab states held the position that they were not prepared to enter into peace negotiations with Israel until the refugee question had been settled, and Israel would not agree to any agreement regarding the Palestinian refugees outside of a general settlement of hostilities (UNCCP 1950).

Although the two sides seemed deadlocked, the commission invited the governments to convene on neutral territory to continue the discussions. These occurred in Lausanne during the summer of 1949. Each side presented proposals through the commission, with no direct communications between the Arab and Israeli negotiators. A compromise was reached as to the order of discussion – refugees or general peace terms – when the Israeli delegation agreed that the problem of refugees should be the first item on the agenda of joint discussions of a general peace settlement.

After some back and forth discussions through the commission, Israel proposed that it would accept the return to Israel of 100,000 refugees beyond the total Arab population existing at the end of the hostilities. The commission deemed the proposal to be insufficient, but it informally conveyed the terms to the Arab countries. They in turn unofficially rejected the proposal, arguing that no numerical limits should be imposed.

The commission then developed its own resolution to the problem in the form of a declaration to be signed by all parties. It included repatriation of some Palestinian refugees who would become citizens of Israel, and settlement of others in Arab countries or in the area of Palestine not under Israeli control (that is, the territory controlled by Jordan and Egypt). Both sides accepted elements of the overall framework in principle, but it was clear that they had different assumptions about the relative numbers to be repatriated or resettled. Israel wanted it made clear that the majority would be resettled. The Arab countries, particularly Egypt and Lebanon, pointed out the difficulties of resettling large numbers given their population density and poor economic situations.

Having received the commission's report of its progress, in 1952 the General Assembly expressed its "appreciation to the Conciliation Commission for Palestine for its efforts to assist the parties to reach agreement on their outstanding differences" but noted "with regret that . . . the Commission has been

---

[16] Report of the Interim Director of UNRWA at http://unispal.un.org/UNISPAL.NSF/0/EC8DE 7912121FCE5052565B1006B5152.

unable to fulfill its mandate under the resolutions of the General Assembly."[17] The General Assembly directed UNRWA "to pursue its program for the relief and rehabilitation of refugees" and requested it to continue to consult with the Conciliation Commission.[18] However, the Conciliation Commission had ceased to be an active participant in negotiating a resolution to the refugee situation or the conflict more generally. It continued to maintain land and property records that would be useful if a compensation agreement would ever be reached.[19]

UNRWA, for its part, continues to function throughout the West Bank and Gaza, Jordan, Syria, and Lebanon. Its current mandate has been extended until June 30, 2014. Under UNRWA's operational definition, Palestinian refugees are "people whose normal place of residence was Palestine between June 1946 and May 1948, who lost both their homes and means of livelihood as a result of the 1948 Arab-Israeli conflict."[20] UNRWA also provides services to refugees and people displaced by the 1967 Arab-Israeli conflict.

UNRWA's services are available to all those living in its area of operations – Jordan, Syria, Lebanon, West Bank, and Gaza – who meet this definition, who are registered with the agency, and who need assistance. The descendants of the original refugees are also eligible for services. UNRWA estimates a total of about 5 million Palestinian refugees with eligibility for its services today, with 1.4 million refugees living in fifty-eight recognized camps. The remainder are mixed in with host country communities. Under the 1954 Jordanian Citizenship Law, most Palestinian refugees on Jordanian territory were granted citizenship. In Syria and Lebanon, they have long-term residency but not full citizenship rights (for example, to employment in all sectors). UNRWA provides health and education services as well as relief when such assistance is needed. More than half of its budget each year is spent on education; about 20 percent goes to health services and 10 percent to relief and social services. UNRWA's biennial budget for 2011–2012 stands at $1.3 billion, but the full budget is seldom funded by donors. The growth in allocated funds has not kept pace with the growth in population. According to the agency, "average annual spending per refugee has fallen from about $200 in 1975 to around $110 today."[21]

Unlike the refugee agencies discussed so far, or the UNHCR to come, UNRWA does not have a protection mandate in the sense of having the authority to seek solutions for refugees. The Conciliation Commission had been given that role, and when it ceased to function in that capacity, finding solutions was left wholly to governments. Yet, UNRWA has increasingly taken on a

---

[17] Resolution 512 at http://unispal.un.org/UNISPAL.NSF/0/AFDEF7B30101C6A2852560EB006 DB365.

[18] Resolution 916 at http://avalon.law.yale.edu/20th_century/mid021.asp.

[19] See Fischbach (2002) for a fuller discussion of the commission's activities related to compensation.

[20] http://unrwa.org/etemplate.php?id=86.

[21] http://unrwa.org/etemplate.php?id=87.

protection role on behalf of Palestinian refugees. It cites itself as having a relief, protection, and human development mandate. A major part of its role is advocating with governments the need for political action to resolve the situation of Palestinian refugees. UNRWA's presence in the field is another aspect of its protection function. Its staff is the eyes and ears of the international community, observing and bringing attention to rights violations with the aim of reducing their occurrence.

The third specialized organization created to address refugee issues outside of Europe was the UN Korean Rehabilitation Administration (UNKRA). UNKRA was established by the General Assembly on December 1, 1950, as a "special authority with broad powers to plan and supervise rehabilitation and relief" (Lyons 1958:181). According to a contemporary analysis, the United States was the leading proponent of the new organization and based its support on three principal assumptions:

> First, the establishment of the agency was predicated on military success and an early cessation of hostilities.... Second, military success offered the prospect of creating a unified Korea under international auspices, an aim toward which United States policy had been directed since the liberation of the peninsula from Japanese control in 1945. And third, a unified Korea, striving for independence under the heavy burdens of military destruction, would require large sums of money in economic aid which the United States would be obliged to supply or risk losing Korea after winning the war. (182)

As a multilateral agency, organized in the context of the UN, UNKRA would help to ensure that the costs of this endeavor would be shared with other countries.

The first two assumptions proved more elusive than anticipated and the third was harder to achieve in the absence of an end to hostilities. With China's intervention on behalf of North Korea, the conflict persisted for another two years. As occurred during World War II, the military forces led by the United States retained broad authority over the relief operations occurring within their theater of activities. Even after the truce ending the hostilities was signed, raising funds for UNKRA was difficult because other countries saw South Korea as being within the U.S. sphere of interest. As such, the expectation was that the United States would fund the recovery.

Nevertheless, in 1952 UNKRA began operations with a budget of $71 million. One of its areas of concern was the integration of refugees from North Korea. Estimates at the time put the number of refugees from 1 million (Robbins 1956) to about 3 million (Rucker 1954). The principal need was addressing the shortage and poor quality of housing available for settling the refugees given the large-scale destruction of Korea's infrastructure. UNKRA activities on behalf of refugees occurred in the context of its broader mission to aid South Korean recovery and reconstruction. It was not mandated to protect the refugees, as this was seen as a responsibility of the South Korean government. Refugee experts at the time indicated some concerns with this perspective because of the authoritarian nature of the government in control of South Korea (Robbins 1956). There was broad agreement, however, that the refugees would be integrated, which obviated the need for an international agency to arrange for either return to North Korea or resettlement elsewhere. An exception was UNKRA's responsibility for a small number of refugee orphans who were eligible for resettlement in other countries (Robbins 1956). Notably, the fact that the refugees from North Korea had automatic citizenship in South Korea did not impede UNKRA's ability to provide assistance to them via its broader reconstruction efforts.

UNHCR AND THE UN REFUGEE CONVENTION

Within only a year of creating UNRWA, states returned to the situation of European refugees and displaced persons. As discussed, donors considered the IRO to have been too expensive an operation and were looking for a structure that would wind down the problem of refugees. Numbers seemed manageable; as compared to the millions displaced immediately after the war, only 400,000 people were still displaced by 1950. Moreover, concerns about immigration still persisted in the United States and other resettlement countries. U.S. Senator McCarran had already made it clear that his committee would not support the admission of displaced persons for much longer. He was already working on legislation that reaffirmed the national origins quotas.

Beyond concerns about financing and immigration policy were the Cold War foreign policy realities emerging by 1950. Gordenker captured the prevailing view in the West:

> However comprehensive IRO may have been, its supporting governments sought less, not better, involvement with refugee issues. Consequently, they pushed aside the opportunity offered by IRO's demise to incorporate its experience in a permanent, central, operating institution. Instead, using the machinery of the United Nations, they rescued some bits and pieces of IRO practice while allowing others to disappear. (Gordenker 1987:27)

The United States and its allies found it more efficient and less risky, given the Soviet role in the UN, to rely on their own resettlement programs rather than on an international agency. As will be discussed in Chapter 4, they created an organization outside of the UN system to help with the logistics. Nevertheless, they also recognized the need for an international body to affirm the legal status of refugees awaiting resettlement.

The organization that came out of this reassessment was the UN High Commissioner for Refugees. The first high commissioner, writing in a journal published by the Royal Institute of International Affairs, using just his initials, summarized the state of his organization: "This office, that of the United Nations High

Commissioner for Refugees, with a mandate for three years only, and with Dr. G. J. van Heuven Goedhart, of the Netherlands, at its head, has more restricted powers and a much smaller budget than I.R.O." (GJ v HG 1952:324).

UNHCR was created under General Assembly Resolution 428 (V) of December 14, 1950. Chapter 1 of its statute described its purposes:

> The United Nations High Commissioner for Refugees, acting under the authority of the General Assembly, shall assume the function of providing international protection, under the auspices of the United Nations, to refugees who fall within the scope of the present Statute and of seeking permanent solutions for the problem of refugees by assisting Governments and, subject to the approval of the Governments concerned, private organizations to facilitate the voluntary repatriation of such refugees, or their assimilation within new national communities.[22]

Like its League predecessors, UNHCR was tasked to protect refugees and identify solutions. The earlier concept – that the high commissioner would serve in lieu of a government in protecting those who were unable to return home – passed down to UNHCR.

The statute specified that the high commissioner would provide for the protection of refugees falling under the competence of his office by:

(a) Promoting the conclusion and ratification of international conventions for the protection of refugees, supervising their application and proposing amendments thereto;

(b) Promoting through special agreements with Governments the execution of any measures calculated to improve the situation of refugees and to reduce the number requiring protection;

(c) Assisting governmental and private efforts to promote voluntary repatriation or assimilation within new national communities;

(d) Promoting the admission of refugees, not excluding those in the most destitute categories, to the territories of States;

(e) Endeavoring to obtain permission for refugees to transfer their assets and especially those necessary for their resettlement;

(f) Obtaining from Governments information concerning the number and conditions of refugees in their territories and the laws and regulations concerning them;

(g) Keeping in close touch with the Governments and inter-governmental organizations concerned;

(h) Establishing contact in such manner as he may think best with private organizations dealing with refugee questions;

(i) Facilitating the co-ordination of the efforts of private organizations concerned with the welfare of refugees.

[22] All quotes are from the version of the Statute of the UNHCR found at http://www.unhcr.org/4d944e589.pdf.

Most of these activities require suasion, not direct action, in maintaining the intent to keep the organization small and inexpensive.

The high commissioner was responsible for refugees who had been under League and IRO mandates as well as a broader category of people who were unwilling or unable to return to their home countries because of a well-founded fear persecution in the country of origin. Using language similar to what would be adopted in the 1951 Refugee Convention, the statute specified race, religion, nationality, and political opinion as the bases upon which one might fear persecution. Article 6.A applies the definition to those whose fear is the result of events occurring before January 1, 1951, when the resolution went into effect. Article 6.B is broader, including "any other person who is outside the country of his nationality who has a well-founded fear of persecution." Hence, although set up as a time-limited, small, and underfunded organization to protect and find solutions for Europe's displaced, the statute gave it far broader authority that would open the way for UNHCR to address a much wider population.

UNHCR was not responsible for anyone who is "recognized by the competent authorities of the country in which he has taken residence as having the rights and obligations which are attached to the possession of the nationality of that country." This is consistent with earlier practice in applying international protection only when national protection is lacking (and unlike the operational definition of a refugee under UNRWA's authority). Moreover, UNHCR was not responsible for a refugee "who continues to receive from other organs or agencies of the United Nations protection or assistance." Since the IRO was going out of existence, this meant that Palestinian refugees and Koreans receiving aid from UNKRA were not eligible to receive the protection of UNHCR.

There was recognition that UNHCR might have to provide aid to selective categories of refugees (the elderly, for example) but the funds for such assistance would be a matter of negotiation between it and donors. The statute stipulates:

> The Office of the High Commissioner shall be financed under the budget of the United Nations. Unless the General Assembly subsequently decides otherwise, no expenditure other than administrative expenditures relating to the functioning of the Office of the High Commissioner shall be borne on the budget of the United Nations and all other expenditures relating to the activities of the High Commissioner shall be financed by voluntary contributions.

Funding was an acute problem in the early days. With the United States staunchly opposed to UNHCR having any type of operational role, it blocked an attempt by the high commissioner to establish a UN Refugee Emergency Fund, although the General Assembly authorized him in 1952 to raise $3 million for such a fund. Even that authorization was for new emergencies, not to support the refugees already under his mandate – many of whom were ineligible for resettlement and in dire need of relief. The United States argued that the Marshall Plan and its own refugee programs – which increasingly focused on escapees from communist countries – more than met the existing needs of refugees and host countries (Loescher 1993).

U.S. opposition to UNHCR was partly a reflection of broader concerns about multilateralism in the context of the Cold War. This is not a full explanation, however, since the United States continued to provide substantial funding to UNRWA and UNKRA. UN High Commissioner van Heuven Goedhart had been appointed over U.S. objections, which may have contributed to U.S. reluctance to support the organization he directed (Loescher 1993). Suffice it to say, in the absence of the largest donor of the UN and the largest resettlement country, UNHCR had a monumental task.

In 1951, the General Assembly took up the issue of a convention that would set out the rights of refugees and the responsibilities of states toward them. Paul Weiss, legal officer in the UNHCR in the 1950s, described the origins of the convention as follows:

> The Convention Relating to the Status of Refugees, adopted in Geneva on July 28, 1951, by the United Nations Conference of Plenipotentiaries, is designed to consolidate existing international instruments relating to refugees and to extend their scope to further groups of refugees. It aims at regulating their legal status in far greater detail than previous instruments, and thus should establish within the contracting states a uniform legal status for the existing groups of "United Nations protected persons." (Weiss 1954:194)

The convention was not a universal instrument. It applied only to those displaced prior to its adoption. Article 1 specifies that the term "refugee" applies to any person who:

> As a result of events occurring before 1 January 1951 and owing to well-founded fear of being persecuted for reasons of race, religion, nationality, membership of a particular social group or political opinion, is outside the country of his nationality and is unable or, owing to such fear, is unwilling to avail himself of the protection of that country; or who, not having a nationality and being outside the country of his former habitual residence as a result of such events, is unable or, owing to such fear, is unwilling to return to it.[23]

The convention also applied to those who had refugee status under the League and IRO mandates. It utilized the language of the statute and exempted refugees receiving aid or protection from other UN bodies.

Keely (1996:1057) argues that the international refugee regime is "not based primarily on humanitarian feelings." Rather, the refugee regime is designed to protect the "international system of states that is threatened when states fail to fulfill their proper roles" (1057). Article 35 specifies that

> The Contracting States undertake to co-operate with the Office of the United Nations High Commissioner for Refugees, or any other agency of the United

---

[23] All quotes are from the version of the Convention Relating to the Status of Refugees found at http://www.unhcr.org/3b66c2aa10.html.

Nations which may succeed it, in the exercise of its functions, and shall in particular facilitate its duty of supervising the application of the provisions of this Convention.

Weiss explains the importance of this linkage in that it gives UNHCR the authority to intervene with governments when the protection of refugees is at risk. He notes: "The international protection of refugees purports to remedy the situation created by the fact that they lack the protection which is usually afforded to nationals abroad by the state of nationality.... In exercising the international protection of refugees, an international agency asserts the rights of the refugees" (Weiss 1954:219). He acknowledges that the international organization, UNHCR in this case, has to use "amicable means," asserting its "moral responsibility" (219). Nevertheless, its actions on behalf of refugee protection have political and legal ramifications.

The convention is principally state-centric in establishing the responsibilities of state parties. The principal obligation of states is to refrain from *refouling* (that is, forcibly returning) refugees to countries in which they would face persecution (Article 33 of the convention). States do not have the obligation to provide asylum or admit refugees for permanent settlement, and they may relocate refugees in safe third countries that are willing to accept them. The convention has been interpreted to require states to undertake status determinations for asylum applicants at their frontiers or inside their territories to determine if they have valid claims to refugee protection. While the only obligation of states toward refugees is non-*refoulement*, in practice this has often meant admission and asylum in the host country.

The convention also enumerates the rights of refugees who have been admitted unto the territory of another country. Fundamental human rights such as freedom of religion and access to courts should be at least equal to those accorded to the citizens of the state hosting the refugee. Refugees lawfully residing in a host country are also to be guaranteed public relief that is granted to citizens. Rights regarding employment, property, elementary public education, and housing are to be accorded to refugees in a manner no less favorable than those accorded to citizens of other countries. The provisions of the convention are not to be applied in a discriminatory way regarding race, religion, or country of origin.

Expansion of UNHCR's Role

Funding continued to plague UNHCR and limit its role. The United States provided no resources toward the Refugee Emergency Fund and no other donors filled the vacuum sufficiently to allow UNHCR to respond to what it saw as growing need for assistance, not just protection. With the U.S. government largely out of the picture, U.S. foundations stepped in to provide what turned out to be critical funding. First, the Rockefeller Foundation funded a study of the economic situation of refugees in Europe, demonstrating the gap between need for material assistance and available aid. Then, in 1952, the Ford Foundation provided a grant of $2.9 million that allowed UNHCR to administer assistance to refugees in Western Europe (Loescher 1993).[24] In a critical use of these funds, UNHCR provided housing to refugees from East Germany who crossed by the tens of thousands into West Berlin amid the uncertainty in Eastern Europe after Stalin's death in March 1953 (Loescher 1993). Although the East Germans were not strictly within UNHCR's mandate, particularly since they were eligible for West German citizenship, this was clearly a humanitarian crisis. The availability of private funds became the justification for UNHCR taking on this unusual activity. These activities in turn helped convince the United States of UNHCR's value. In 1955, the United States made its first contribution to the Refugee Emergency Fund.

A far larger expansion of UNHCR's role in dealing with refugee issues came in 1956 with the Hungarian Revolution and the flight of Hungarian refugees into Western Europe. Although its mandate limited UNHCR's responsibility to those displaced prior to 1951, the UNHCR offered its good services to find solutions for the Hungarian refugees, generally via resettlement to the traditional immigration destination countries – the United States, Canada, and Australia. Then, in 1957, UNHCR was called upon to respond to the refugee crises generated by the Algerian conflict and the continuing flow of people from mainland China into Hong Kong. These were both sensitive situations, as the interests of the permanent members of the Security Council were implicated – France in Algeria and China (at that time the government in Taiwan held the seat) and Britain in Hong Kong. Labeling the refugees as coming under the protection of UNHCR in a legal sense (that is, as victims of persecution) was problematic for legal reasons as well as political ones. A contemporary account explained the legal problem for the Chinese:

> Should the Chinese refugees be considered citizens of communist China (for the sake of argument), the Nationalist Government would resent the implications that it had not sovereignty and that she cannot take care of "her own" nationals. Since the majority of the refugees consider themselves citizens of Nationalist China, they were not political refugees in the fullest legal sense. (Hambro 1957:75)

In any case, although UNHCR could respond to a broader set of refugees through its statute, the convention did not apply because neither of these

[24] Foundations continued to play an important role in assisting and protecting refugees. In 1981, when the capacity of the refugee system was sorely tasked with crises in Southeast Asia, South Asia, Africa, and Central America, the Ford Foundation launched an initiative to buttress the capacity of the operational refugee agencies. The foundation provided critical support to improve public education and information, policy analysis, education and training of refugee professionals, and assessment of service delivery. A number of organizations were either newly established or developed new capacities under this funding, including the Refugee Studies Center at Oxford University, the Refugee Policy Group (where I served as director of research and programs), the U.S. Committee for Refugees, and the Indochinese Resource Action Center. Subsequently, the Mellon Foundation launched a refugee program that further enhanced the education, training, and research that could be used to professionalize the field.

situations occurred in Europe. The compromise was to label the refugees as "de facto" refugees who were in need of international assistance. The refugees would be treated on a group basis without doing a status determination to assess whether they met the convention definition. The General Assembly resolution on the issue of Chinese refugees pointedly asked the high commissioner to use "his good offices" in coordinating aid, not referencing the convention.

In the 1960s, a further expansion occurred as UNHCR was asked to assist and protect refugees in Africa and Asia who were displaced by various wars of liberation. As the numbers of refugees grew and solutions were elusive, more and more of the resources of a growing regime were spent on care and maintenance of large numbers of refugees who were forced out of their homes because of conflict, and were living in refugee camps with international assistance.

In recognition of the nature of the forced movements occurring regularly in Africa, the Organization of African Unity (OAU) adopted the Convention Governing the Specific Aspects of Refugee Problems in Africa in 1969. While acknowledging the UN Refugee Convention as the basic and universal instrument regarding the protection of refugees, the OAU Convention broadened the definition and set out other important protection provisions. The expanded definition includes those who, "owing to external aggression, occupation, foreign domination or events seriously disturbing public order in either part or the whole of his country of origin or nationality, is compelled to leave his place of habitual residence in order to seek refuge in another place outside his country of origin or nationality."[25]

The OAU explicitly forbids states from rejecting asylum seekers at the frontier. The grant of asylum is declared to be a peaceful and humanitarian act, not to be regarded as unfriendly by other states. The convention also establishes the importance of settling refugees at a reasonable distance from the frontier of their country of origin for security reasons. This regional treaty also states that no refugee shall be repatriated against his will. Most African states are parties to the OAU Convention.

In a similar vein, the Cartagena Declaration on Refugees expands the definition of protected refugees in the Latin American region. Like the OAU definition, it supports the 1951 convention and adds protection to those who have fled their country "because their lives, safety or freedom have been threatened by generalized violence, foreign aggression, internal conflicts, massive violation of human rights or other circumstances which have seriously disturbed public order."[26] It emphasizes that repatriation of refugees must be voluntary, and embodies principles for their protection, assistance, and reintegration.

---

[25] Organization of African Unity Convention Governing the Specific Aspects of Refugee Problems in Africa, adopted by the Assembly of Heads of State and Government at its Sixth Ordinary Session, Addis-Ababa, Ethiopia, September 10, 1969.

[26] Cartagena Declaration on Refugees, adopted by the Colloquium on the International Protection of Refugees in Central America, Mexico, and Panama, Cartagena de Indias, Colombia, November 22, 1984.

Although a non-binding instrument, the declaration has been endorsed by the General Assembly of the Organization of American States and some states in the region have incorporated this definition into their own national legislation.

The OAU/Cartagena definition increasingly characterized the population of concern to UNHCR wherever in the world they were located. UNHCR and most countries of asylum made no attempt to determine which among the large number of persons who fled conflict also had a well-founded fear of persecution, instead treating those escaping conflict as prima facie refugees. For much of the 1980s, UNHCR focused its programs on refugees from surrogate Cold War conflicts, in which the United States or the Soviet Union supported or intervened on behalf of one side or the other. UNHCR had a significant presence in addressing large-scale refugee movements from such places as Vietnam, Cambodia, Laos, Afghanistan, Ethiopia, Somalia, Sudan, Angola, Mozambique, Nicaragua, El Salvador, and Guatemala.

Western states were more than willing to fund UNHCR's operations when the conflicts served their foreign policy goals, often referring to refugees as those who "voted with their feet" in escaping from communist countries. Refugee camps in Pakistan, Thailand, Honduras, and elsewhere became safe zones for the families of military forces fighting against the regimes in Afghanistan, Cambodia, and Nicaragua, respectively. At the same time, bipartisan political coalitions and important domestic constituencies in donor countries generally supported expenditure of resources on refugees. In the United States, for example, many veterans of the Vietnam conflict as well as religious and humanitarian organizations threw their support behind resettlement of refugees from Indochina. Although the Soviet bloc countries had not ratified the Refugee Convention or formally supported UNHCR, the agency served a purpose for them as well in limiting the human costs of conflicts that might otherwise spin out of control.

In 1990, with the collapse of the Soviet Union and the end of many of the surrogate Cold War conflicts, there was a major rethinking within the international humanitarian regime of how to deal with refugee issues. No longer was there a strong foreign policy rationale for a refugee regime that would support the civilian families of those fighting communist governments. As many of the conflicts of the 1970s and 1980s ended, refugees began returning to their home countries in record numbers. The UNHCR adapted, and in 1990, High Commissioner Sadako Ogata declared the 1990s to be the decade of repatriation.

At the same time, however, new refugee movements received international attention. They often occurred as the result of nationalist or ethnic conflicts, which were usually internal in nature and difficult for Western powers to understand fully. Examples are Bosnia, Kosovo, and Rwanda. When the Rwandan refugee camps in Zaire (present-day Democratic Republic of Congo) were used as staging areas to launch genocidal attacks against the Rwandan government,

Rwanda case

new attention was paid to the militarization of refugee aid – previously tolerated and even encouraged but now seen as being in violation of core humanitarian principles. Instead, humanitarian agencies were entreated to ensure that in providing aid, they "do no harm," as cautioned in a well-regarded book of that name by Mary Anderson.

Complicating the situation, many of the peace agreements that ended the Cold War conflicts were very fragile, and they did not necessarily take into account the fact that there were deep-seated internal problems that could lead to the resumption of fighting. Refugees who repatriated during the 1990s often returned home to high levels of insecurity. In some places, civil war recurred or highly repressive regimes (such as the Taliban in Afghanistan) took control. Some Afghan refugees who had repatriated returned to Pakistan, while others sought safety in cities away from their original areas of residence. In many countries, returnees found their lands inundated by landmines or discovered that their homes had been occupied by others during their long displacement. In places like Bosnia, peace agreements froze the conflicts, designating territories as coming under the control of the warring party that had occupied them. People found they would now be a minority in a community dominated by a different ethnic or religious group and chose to relocate rather than risk violence at home. Out of this complex picture came a new appreciation of the millions who were internally displaced by conflict and violence. Soon, data assembled by NGOs showed that internally displaced persons outnumbered refugees (those outside of their own country).

Addressing Internal Displacement

From at least the 1970s, UNHCR has aided persons still within their home countries. Implementing programs for returning refugees often prompted UNHCR to offer its good offices to internally displaced persons (IDPs) as well. This was the case in southern Sudan in the early 1970s when UNHCR assisted about 180,000 returnees and about 500,000 IDPs (Holborn et al. 1975). The UNHCR also assisted IDPs in Cyprus, in this case acting as the Secretary General's Special Representative and Coordinator for United Nations Humanitarian Assistance for Cyprus.

Although UNHCR had exercised its mandate on behalf of IDPs, the agency had considerable discretion in determining if and when to do so unless specifically requested by the General Assembly. In March 2000, UNHCR issued a position paper clarifying its relationship to IDPs. The agency made it clear that its interest in this population arises from its humanitarian mandate on behalf of persons displaced by persecution, situations of general violence, conflict, or massive violations of human rights. This mandate places upon UNHCR "a responsibility to advocate on behalf of the internally displaced; mobilize support for them; strengthen its capacity to respond to their problems; and take the lead to protect and assist them in certain situations" (UNHCR 2000:1).

Stopping short of asserting an operational responsibility for all IDPs, UNHCR set out six requirements for its involvement:

> a request or authorization from the Secretary General or a competent principal organ of the UN; consent of the state concerned, and where applicable, other entities in a conflict; access to the affected population; adequate security for staff of UNHCR and implementing partners; clear lines of responsibility and accountability with the ability to intervene directly on protection matters; and adequate resources and capacity. (2)

The policy paper specified that UNHCR would be ready to take the lead where its protection and solutions expertise was particularly relevant, or where involvement with IDPs was closely linked to the voluntary repatriation and reintegration of refugees. Recognition was given to the fact that the linkages between refugees and IDPs could be complicated:

> Countries of asylum may be more inclined to maintain their asylum policies if something is done to alleviate the suffering of the internally displaced, reduce their compulsion to seek asylum and create conditions conducive to return. On the other hand, UNHCR's activities for the internally displaced may be (mis)interpreted as obviating the need for international protection and asylum. (UNHCR 2000:7–8)

Gaps continued to persist in establishing responsibility for IDPs. After trying what it called a collaborative approach that failed to fill the gaps, the UN shifted to what it now calls the cluster leadership approach, in which a single UN agency is responsible for coordinating activities in a particular sector. UNHCR has taken on responsibility for the protection cluster (focusing on conflict-induced displacement) as well as the emergency shelter and camp management clusters.[27]

The Interagency Standing Committee (IASC) Guidance Note on Using the Cluster Approach explains:

> the role of sector leads at the country level is to facilitate a process aimed at ensuring well-coordinated and effective humanitarian responses in the sector or area of activity concerned. Sector leads themselves are not expected to carry out all the necessary activities within the sector or area of activity concerned. They are required, however, to commit to being the 'provider of last resort' where this is necessary and where access, security and availability of resources make this possible. (IASC 2006:7)

The Guidance Note also recognizes that "The 'provider of last resort' concept is critical to the cluster approach, and without it the element of predictability is lost" (10). For agencies with technical leads (e.g., health, nutrition, water, and

---

[27] The International Organization for Migration has responsibility for camp management in the context of natural disasters.

sanitation), the ability of the lead agency to take on responsibility is straight-forward. However, the Guidance Note is more circumspect regarding the leadership for crosscutting areas such as protection, early recovery, and camp coordination: "The concept of 'provider of last resort' will need to be applied in a differentiated manner. In all cases, however, sector leads are responsible for ensuring that wherever there are significant gaps in the humanitarian response they continue advocacy efforts and explain the constraints to stakeholders" (10–11).

UNHCR's 2007 policy on internal displacement went significantly further than its 2000 policy in specifying the circumstances under which the agency would assume responsibility:

> UNHCR stands ready to contribute to the inter-agency response in situations of internal displacement in any conflict-affected country where the presence and programmes of the Office have the consent of the authorities, where the humanitarian activities of UNHCR and its partners are free from undue political or military interference, and where the security environment enables its personnel to function within acceptable levels of risk. (UNHCR 2007b:3)

Although still constrained in terms of sovereignty and security, and limited to conflict-affected countries, the 2007 policy represented a major shift from earlier policies that severely limited UNHCR's involvement with IDPs. UNHCR reported in 2002 that 4.6 million conflict IDPs fell under its mandate (UNHCR 2002). In 2012, it reported assisting 17.7 million IDPs (UNHCR 2012).

The expansion of UNHCR's operations when it comes to conflict IDPs has not been without debate. Governments on the Executive Committee of the UNHCR have been supportive of the agency's initiatives on behalf of IDPs uprooted by conflict, but they have also cautioned the high commissioner that UNHCR was not the "IDP agency." A number of governments expressed concern in the 2007 Executive Committee session that "UNHCR's work with IDPs should not come at the expense of its protection of refugees" (UNHCR 2007c:21). The agency was also encouraged to develop exit strategies for internal displacement situations. Responding to such concerns, UNHCR incorporated "When Displacement Ends: A Framework for Durable Solutions," developed by the Brookings-Bern Project on Internal Displacement and Georgetown University, into its Handbook on Internal Displacement (UNHCR 2007a).

Within the academic community, the debate about the expansion of the refugee regime to include internally displaced persons has been particularly pointed. In a keynote speech to the International Association for the Study of Forced Migration, James Hathaway, a law professor at the University of Michigan, raised the alarm about a shift in focus from refugees to forced migrants. He argued that refugees have a special place in international law, whereas others who migrate or are displaced do not have an explicit status. Interestingly, Hathaway argues for the special treatment of refugees because they "are seriously at risk because of who they are or what they believe."

Constructing a human rights argument, he asserts that refugees are "doubly-deserving" of international protection having fled "profoundly serious" risks because of unchangeable and/or fundamental characteristics (Hathaway 2007).

Adelman and McGrath (2007), in their responses to Hathaway, point out that most refugees under UNHCR's mandate are not covered under the Refugee Convention because they have fled conflict, not persecution. UNHCR's mandate had already evolved, as it used its good offices to provide assistance and protection to millions of refugees because of the humanitarian, not legal imperative to act. To the extent that IDPs meet the same criteria, there would be no reason to treat them in an essentially different manner. Cohen (2007) argues further that widespread acceptance of the Guiding Principles on Internal Displacement, as well as the "Responsibility to Protect" doctrine espoused in the Millennium Summit, demonstrate acknowledgement by states that there is an international responsibility to protect and assist IDPs. In similar terms, Martin (2010) makes the case that the refugee regime, from its beginnings, has focused on persons who do not receive protection from a national government and hence require international protection. In that sense, it would be fully consistent with UNHCR's history to offer protection to those who are internally displaced by conflict or serious human rights violations and whose governments are unable or unwilling to protect them.

Non-Conflict Displacement

In recent years, UNHCR also began responding, albeit in an ad hoc way, to forced migration stemming from causes other than persecution or conflict. Although UNHCR has limited its cluster leadership to conflict-induced internal displacement, it has nevertheless been drawn into providing assistance during several notable natural disasters. In *State of the World's Refugees*, UNHCR explained its involvement in tsunami relief:

> The sheer scale of the destruction and the fact that many of affected populations were of concern to the organization prompted the move. Responding to requests from the UN Secretary-General and UN Country Teams, UNHCR concentrated on providing shelter and non-food relief. In Sri Lanka, UNHCR's presence in the country prior to the tsunami allowed for a comparatively swift and sustained humanitarian intervention – including efforts focused on the protection of internally displaced persons. (UNHCR 2006)

UNHCR also assisted tsunami victims in Somalia and Aceh, Indonesia, pointing out:

> The protection of displaced populations was especially urgent in areas of protracted conflict and internal displacement in Aceh, Somalia and Sri Lanka. Furthermore, there was concern for some affected populations whose governments declined offers of international aid, such as the Dalits (formerly known as untouchables) of India and Burmese migrant workers in Thailand; it was feared

they might be discriminated against and their protection needs compromised. (UNHCR 2006:21)

More recently, UNHCR has become involved in the international response to Cyclone Nargis in Burma and the earthquake in China, providing shelter and supplies, but not protection.

The potential for mass displacement from climate change (discussed in Chapter 7), natural disasters, and other humanitarian crises is an issue that has increasingly occupied the high commissioner's attention. Beyond the organizational challenges to the refugee regime are legal ones pertaining to those who cross international borders as well as those who are internally displaced for reasons unrelated to persecution. At present, there are no binding instruments and little in the way of national law to address the situation of forced migrants who do not fall within the Refugee Convention definitions. Although UNHCR has been innovative in finding ways to assist many of them, governments have no clear legal obligations in determining when and whether to accept persons fleeing or anticipating the need to flee life-threatening situations that do not involve persecution. These gaps will be discussed in greater detail in Chapter 7.

The capacity of UNHCR to take on new roles is limited by its budgetary authority. Currently made up of eighty-seven members, UNHCR's governing Executive Committee meets in Geneva annually to review and approve the agency's program and budget. In 2011, for example, the Executive Committee approved a budget of almost $3.8 billion. The budget is presented in four parts: Global Refugee Program (75 percent of total), Global Stateless Program (2 percent) Global Reintegration Projects (1 percent) and Global Internally Displaced Persons (IDP) Projects (16 percent). The budget for the refugee program is significantly higher than for IDPs even though the number of IDPs assisted by UNHCR is larger. This is in part because UNHCR is mandated to protect refugees but provides assistance and protection to IDPs as part of its good offices. UNHCR also allocates funding in accordance with broad sectors, budgeting about 44 percent of its costs to cover basic needs (food, shelter, etc.), 19 percent to protection, and 11 percent to durable solutions (repatriation, local integration, and resettlement), with the remainder going to coordination, logistics, partnerships, and headquarters costs. As conditions change during the course of a year and new emergencies occur, UNHCR will generally revise its budget and ask for supplementary authority to respond to the new demands.

UNHCR receives only a fraction of its budget from the UN, with the vast majority coming from contributions from states and other sources. An enduring challenge is to broaden the sources of support since funding is heavily dependent on the European Union, its members and other European countries, Japan, and the United States. UNHCR has made only partially successful efforts to increase funding from non-traditional donors (for example, the oil-wealthy Gulf Cooperation Council, GCC, countries and the private sector). Only Saudi

Arabia is within the top twenty government donors among the GCC countries, and all private contributions combined amounted to less than $70 million.

In an important change to the budgeting process made in 2010, UNHCR's biennial program budget is based on an assessment of needs rather than on the expected availability of funds. This means that the resources provided may not meet the needs that are identified in the budget request. In fact, the 2011 budget document indicates that the gap has been growing and can be substantial. As an indication, "For 2010, the total expenditure amounted to $1,878.2 million against funds available of $2,112.5 million and a final budget of $3,288.7 million" (UNHCR 2011). Expenditure as a percentage of the budget varies by region, with a high of 61 percent funded in Asia and the Pacific and a low of 28 percent in the Americas. Activities in Africa and the Middle East and North Africa received 55 percent and 51 percent of budgeted requests, respectively. European programs were funded at 49 percent of requests (UNHCR 2011).

CONCLUSION

Many of the characteristics of the current refugee regime emerged in the inter-war period, as discussed in Chapter 1. The failures of the League system, however, significantly influenced the refugee system that came out of World War II. Although many governments hoped that the "problem of refugees" would disappear within a few years, it has remained a persistent part of international relations and an enduring challenge to humanitarian values. The UNHCR, envisioned as a temporary agency that would advocate but not assist refugees, proved more resilient than expected. During the past sixty years, it has shown a capacity to respond to new situations while retaining its original mandate as the provider of international protection to those whose governments had forsaken them. Today, the UNHCR and its member states face new challenges emerging from the highly complex world in which many forms of migration abound. Options for addressing these challenges will be discussed in Chapter 9.

3

Labor Mobility

There are good reasons to believe that international labor migration will be a defining issue of the twenty-first century. Most of the more than 230 million people who live outside of their home countries fit the labor migration category. International labor migrants come from all parts of the world and they go to all parts of the world. In fact, few countries are unaffected by such movements. Many countries are sources of international labor flows, while others are net receivers, and still others are transit countries through which migrants seeking work reach receiving countries.

As discussed in the Introduction, it is highly likely that international labor migration will increase still further in the future, due to demographic, economic, and security trends. Migration occurs when there are economic disparities between source and receiving countries, and when individuals have the capacity to move from poorer and less secure places to wealthier and more secure countries with greater economic opportunities. These disparities are increasing, particularly with the demographic trends toward an aging developed world and a still-growing developing one. At the same time, globalization gives more people the knowledge and resources needed to find work in other countries.

It would be difficult to characterize the institutional response to labor migration as a regime. It has few norms, decision rules, or procedures that facilitate cooperation. Rather, there are a range of conventions and organizations that address various aspects of international migration, with more or less success and credibility. This chapter discusses the evolution of the International Labor Organization from the post–World War II period to the present. It examines the role of the ILO today regarding labor migration, discussing its role as an arbiter of standards and provider of technical assistance to governments. Particular attention is given to the ILO's efforts to place the treatment of migrant workers within the context of its broader program to ensure decent work opportunities for all.

This chapter will review the legal frameworks for international cooperation on labor migration. None of the international conventions on labor migration are well ratified. Included will be the reasons it has been so difficult to establish a legal regime comparable to that created for addressing refugee movements. In addition, the various ILO conventions that have been adopted – with particular focus on Convention 97 of 1949 (C97) concerning Migration for Employment and Convention 143 of 1975 (C143) concerning Migrations in Abusive Conditions and the Promotion of Equality of Opportunity and Treatment of Migrant Workers – will be addressed.

Full attention is given to the 1990 UN Convention on the Rights of All Migrant Workers and Members of their Families, discussing its provisions as well as the reluctance of major destination countries (the United States, Canada, Australia, European Union members, Gulf Cooperation Council members) to ratify it. This analysis underscores the practical and political barriers to establishing broad normative frameworks governing the management of international migration, despite most of the treaty's provisions being drawn from more widely ratified human rights instruments. The opposition to the migrant workers convention has less to do with specific norms, and more with concerns about state sovereignty regarding the rights of foreigners, especially those who are working illegally in the territory of the destination country.

The chapter then discusses the interconnection between labor migration and trade, and in particular the integration of labor mobility into trade agreements. Focusing on the General Agreement on Trade in Services (Mode 4), the chapter examines provisions in the Uruguay round of trade negotiations that include mechanisms to increase free movement of managers, executives, and certain professionals. Also covered are the difficulties in making progress toward freeing the movements of lesser-skilled service providers, a subject in the Doha round of negotiations.

Finally, there will be discussion of the challenges in moving toward a labor migration regime. The contrasts between the elements that enabled development of the refugee regime and those that would be required in building a labor migration regime will be presented.

THE INTERNATIONAL LABOR ORGANIZATION

The Great Depression, the rise of fascism, and then World War II hampered the work of the ILO for years. Yet even during the war, the organization began considering the implications of mass displacement on its work. In 1943, the Montreal office of the ILO published *The Displacement of Population in Europe* by Eugene Kulischer, a well-regarded Russian-American demographer who had himself been displaced first by the Russian Revolution and then the war. Viewing the situation as more than a humanitarian issue, the ILO preface to Kulischer's work saw the resolution of displacement as critical to achieving political, economic, and social reconciliation when the war ended:

> Political reconstruction requires that the nationals of each country shall be able to return within their own frontiers. Economic reconstruction depends not only on the re-equipment of industry and agriculture and on restocking with raw materials and seed, but also on the rebuilding of the labour force of each country. Lastly, social reconstruction is only possible if families are reunited and those who have been uprooted are resettled in their old homes or in new homes. (Kulischer 1943)

Kulischer (1943) classified the displaced population into three categories: migration of German peoples within territory occupied by Germany, displacement of non-Germans by German forces, and mobilization of foreign labor by Germany. A contemporary account of the report summarized the importance of Kulischer's focus:

> The immediate postwar problem of the relocation and readjustment of displaced peoples on a basis consistent with humanitarian ideals thus merges into the broader problem of the place of international migration in the creation and maintenance of a political and economic order that will permit continued full employment and increasing levels of living. ("Displacement of People" 1943)

Kulischer concluded that some degree of migration would be needed after the war, not just repatriation, but was skeptical that there would be a return to what he called the unregulated migration of the pre–World War I era. Rather, he declared, the revitalization of migration "will depend in future on the existence of an international organisation capable of co-ordinating the interests of the countries of emigration and immigration and of making available the capital necessary to enable the labour of the former countries to be used to develop the natural resources of the latter" (Kulischer 1943:170). Other migration experts expressed similar views, including Edward Hutchinson, director of research for the U.S. Immigration and Naturalization Service, and his coauthor Wilbert Moore of the Office of Population Studies at Princeton University: "an international authority, even if unable to secure a general lowering of migration barriers, could greatly facilitate international movements of population through the provision of information, technical advice, and financial support" (Hutchinson and Moore 1945:174).

ILO and the Cold War

The ILO sought to be such an organization. Discussions of the ILO's role in the new world order had already begun in the 1944 Philadelphia conference, at which the ILO's relationship to the emerging UN was discussed (Price 1945). The declaration emerging from the conference acknowledged that the ILO would need to develop linkages with any new international organization: "the Conference pledges the full cooperation of the International Labour Organization with such international bodies as may be entrusted with a share of the responsibility for this great task and for the promotion of the health, education and well-being of all peoples."[1] Discussions about the structure of the new UN indicated it was likely to have an Economic and Social Council (ECOSOC) that would complement the work of the Security Council. The issue was the likely division of responsibilities between ILO as an operational agency and ECOSOC as a more deliberative one.

The Philadelphia declaration reaffirmed that the ILO's agenda would focus on a broad range of issues, many similar to those enumerated in its 1919 constitution. These included:

(a) full employment and the raising of standards of living;
(b) the employment of workers in the occupations in which they can have the satisfaction of giving the fullest measure of their skill and attainments and make their greatest contribution to the common well-being;
(c) the provision, as a means to the attainment of this end and under adequate guarantees for all concerned, of facilities for training and the transfer of labour, including migration for employment and settlement;
(d) policies in regard to wages and earnings, hours and other conditions of work calculated to ensure a just share of the fruits of progress to all, and a minimum living wage to all employed and in need of such protection;
(e) the effective recognition of the right of collective bargaining, the cooperation of management and labour in the continuous improvement of productive efficiency, and the collaboration of workers and employers in the preparation and application of social and economic measures;
(f) the extension of social security measures to provide a basic income to all in need of such protection and comprehensive medical care;
(g) adequate protection for the life and health of workers in all occupations;
(h) provision for child welfare and maternity protection;
(i) the provision of adequate nutrition, housing and facilities for recreation and culture; and
(j) the assurance of equality of educational and vocational opportunity.

Subsection (c) specifies that the ILO would continue to have a role with regard to migration for employment and settlement.

In 1944, the Governing Board reconstituted the Permanent Emigration Committee as a technical advisory body composed of government experts. It met in August 1946 and again in 1948 and 1949. One of its first tasks was to reach an agreement with the UN, particularly ECOSOC, on the allocation of functions between the two bodies. An agreement was reached in 1947. The ILO was to be responsible for setting standards for "recruitment selection, vocational training, care during transport, employment, working conditions, social insurance

---

[1] The Declaration concerning the aims and purposes of the International Labour Organisation was adopted by the General Conference of the International Labour Organization, meeting in its Twenty-sixth Session in Philadelphia, on May 10, 1944 is found at http://www.ilocarib.org .tt/cariblex/pdfs/ILO_dec_philadelphia.pdf.

and formalities connected with departure from the country of residence and admission to the country of destination" (Alcock 1971:222). The UN would be responsible for the economic, demographic and legal aspects, including conditions of residence, expulsion, deportation, repatriation and naturalization (Alcock 1971).

The ILO was committed to viewing migration as an important component of its overall manpower program. Director General David Morse, formerly U.S. Assistant Secretary of Labor, outlined ILO's priorities in 1948, to include job training, the training of supervisors, and preparation of large scale movements of workers from labor surplus to labor shortage areas ("International Labor Organization" February 1949). The ILO also began to collect data on manpower needs and surpluses, using questionnaires sent to governments at three-month intervals (International Labor Organization February 1949). Migration from Europe to Latin America was given particular focus, with the topic prominently on the agenda at the Fourth Labor Conference of American States Members of the ILO in Montevideo in the spring of 1949 ("International Labor Organization" February 1949).

The ILO also launched programs with the International Refugee Organization and other international organizations. In 1949, for example, ILO, IRO, and UNESCO

> announced a campaign to speed up the migration for employment of 26,000 professional, scientific and artistic workers among the displaced persons receiving care from IRO. ILO sent a letter and questionnaire to each of its member governments asking for their help and that of worker, employer and professional organizations in finding employment for these people. ("International Labor Organization" November 1949)

The ILO Preliminary Migration Conference that convened in Geneva on April 25, 1950, "reviewed the present migration situation, discussed the administrative organization of migration, and considered economic development in relation to migration" ("International Labor Organization" 1950). The aim of the meeting was "to find a solution for the difficulties now restricting the movement of people from European countries which are over-populated in terms of present-day economic development to countries outside and inside Europe which urgently need manpower for their own development" (ibid.). The conference came to agreement on ways to reduce obstacles to migration, including "simplification of passport procedures and formalities, elimination of long delays at points of embarkation, abolition of customs fees on tools and personal effects, better distribution of information concerning emigrants and immigration opportunities, and better placement, settlement, and housing of immigrants" (ibid.). The conference requested ILO to "intensify its current activities in the field of migration, to study the best forms of international cooperation in the field, and to consult with interested governments in the drafting of specific proposals for international cooperation" (ibid.).

At first, it appeared that the major donors would support these types of activities. The foreign ministers of France, the UK, and the United States endorsed the recommendations of the Preliminary Conference. As part of the Marshall Plan, the United States offered $1 million to support the ILO's operational program on migration and promised more to come (Bohning n.d.). There was even interest in considering the ILO as the successor to the IRO (ibid.).

The support quickly dissipated, however, as Cold War tensions escalated. In October 1951, the U.S. House of Representatives passed legislation to finance a fund to resettle refugees and migrants from Europe with restrictions that effectively precluded the ILO from receiving money for this purpose. The legislation specified that "none of the fund made available... should be allocated to any international organization which has in its membership any communist, communist-dominated or communist-controlled country, to any subsidiary thereof or to any agency created by or stemming from such organization" (quoted in Bohning nd:17). Since Czechoslovakia and Poland were members of the ILO, the organization came under this restriction. Added to the concern about infiltration by communists into migration programs run by international organizations with communist state members were continuing concerns among the principal destination countries about interference with their sovereign right to manage migration as they saw fit. Policies such as "White Australia" and U.S. national origins quotas may not have passed muster in an organization whose principal convention called for an end to discrimination on the basis of race and nationality.

A migration conference in Naples was to have confirmed the plans for the migration operations but owing to the shift in funding, Director-General Morse chose not to attend or press for endorsement. Governments praised the plan but there was no substantive discussion of its implementation (Bohning nd). Although the need for an international operational organization remained, the United States and its allies pressed for an autonomous agency under their direct control. A subsequent conference in Brussels paved the way for the establishment of the Provisional Intergovernmental Committee for the Movement of Migrants from Europe (PICMME), which will be discussed in Chapter 4.

Norm-Setting

Even before its hopes of a larger operational role were dashed, the ILO had turned to the legal framework for migrant workers. In 1947, ECOSOC encouraged the ILO to revisit the aborted convention that had been adopted in 1939 (Bohning nd). Passed just a few months before the outbreak of hostilities, the convention had not been ratified by any governments. Rather than push for ratification of the existing document, the ILO determined to update it. As Bohning (nd:15) has described, "the resulting Migration for Employment Convention (Revised) (No. 97), was an early manifestation of European social-democratic views of how societies should handle migrant workers as well as of notions of manpower planning." The initial draft, in the form of a substitute amend-ment to the proposal of the Permanent Migration Commission, was offered by the United States and Canada (ibid.). Both countries signed the convention, although neither ratified it. Most of the ratifications in the early 1950s were by what were then source countries – for example, the United Kingdom (1951) and Italy (1952). While some destination countries – New Zealand (1950), Israel (1953), France and Uruguay (1954) – ratified it, for the most part, the convention suffered from what Bohning calls "a ratification deficit." To this day, only forty-nine countries have ratified the convention.

The 1949 Migration for Employment Convention defined a migrant for employment to be a person who migrates from one country to another with a view to being employed otherwise than on his own account. Frontier workers, seamen, and short-term entry of professionals and artists were not covered. The convention went well beyond the 1939 convention in its protection of the rights of migrant workers. Article 6 binds parties to the convention to apply to immigrants lawfully within its territory, treatment no less favorable than that which applies to its own nationals in respect to remuneration, hours of work, overtime arrangements, paid leave, restrictions on home work, minimum age for employment, membership in trade unions and enjoyment of benefits of collective bargaining, accommodation, social security, employment taxes, dues or contributions, and legal proceedings relating to the matters in the convention. It also specified that these were to apply without discrimination in respect to nationality, race, religion, or sex.

Annexes to the convention set out agreements related to recruitment, placing, and conditions of labor of migrants. The annexes restricted the recruitment agencies to public employment offices or other public bodies and those estab-lished in accordance with the terms of an international instrument. When national laws or a bilateral arrangement permitted, these functions could be undertaken by the prospective employer or a private agency. Recruitment and placement services rendered by employment services should be provided with-out charge to the migrants. In cases of migration as group transfers, rather than individual movements, if a migrant should fail to secure employment through no fault of his or her own, efforts should be made to find suitable employ-ment for the worker. If no suitable employment is available, the costs of return should not fall upon the migrant. If the migrant is a refugee or a displaced person, the government should take steps to ensure his maintenance pending suitable employment or resettlement. The annexes spell out the requirements related to contracts in terms that are similar to those adopted in 1939. They also specify that "any person who promotes clandestine or illegal immigration shall be subject to appropriate penalties."[2]

---

[2] All quotes from ILO Convention 97 are from the text at http://www.ilo.org/dyn/normlex/en/f?p=1000:12100:0::NO::P12100_ILO_CODE:C097.

The convention built on the work that preceded World War II but demonstrated the sensitivities of the post-conflict era. In 1949, the drafters were more detailed in specifying the areas in which migrants should be treated in the same manner as citizens. In addition, the 1949 convention is more cognizant of the potential for discrimination against migrant workers on the basis of nationality, race, religion, and sex. In fact, the ILO was attuned to gender abuse well before other institutions. Notably, the UNHCR statute and the Refugee Convention did not include sex among the reasons someone might be persecuted.

The convention itself was not well ratified, but the accompanying Model Agreement on Temporary and Permanent Migration for Employment, including Migration of Refugees and Displaced Persons, proved to be useful to member states. The Model Agreement largely assumes a bilateral agreement. Details such as the nature of medical examinations, vocational qualifications, measures to promote rapid adaptation, information and assistance to migrants, and education and vocational training are included. Also covered are conditions of transport, travel, and maintenance expenses, transfer of funds between the countries, supervision of living and working conditions, settlement of disputes between migrants and employers, and how to apply the standards related to equality of treatment. According to Bohning (nd:15), the Model Agreement "has inspired many countries at both ends of the migration chain."

In 1955, the agency returned to norm-setting in the context of a Recommendation on the Protection of Migrant Workers in Underdeveloped Countries. Rather than focusing on European countries, which had been its primary clients and supporters, the ILO addressed the needs of

> countries and territories in which the evolution from a subsistence form of economy towards more advanced forms of economy, based on wage earning and entailing sporadic and scattered development of industrial and agricultural centres, brings with it appreciable migratory movements of workers and sometimes their families.[3]

The recommendation also applied to source and transit countries if "existing arrangements...taken as a whole, afford less protection to the persons concerned during their journeys."

With regard to protection of migrants during their journey, the ILO recommended making available mechanized means of transport where physically possible, and providing rest camps with lodging, food, water, and first aid. They recommended placing on recruiters and employers the obligation to pay traveling expenses, or, if there is no labor contract, making provision for reducing traveling expenses to a minimum. Governments were encouraged to provide free medical examinations, especially if migrants came from regions

---

[3] All quotes from the Recommendation on the protection of migrant workers in underdeveloped countries are found at http://www.ilo.org/dyn/normlex/en/f?p=NORMLEXPUB:12100:0::NO: 12100:P12100_ILO_CODE:R100.

where there are communicable or endemic diseases. The recommendation also addressed the desirability of providing a period of acclimatization when the migrant arrived if needed because of health concerns. Arrangements for return of migrants were included as well. It set out specific recommendations about the protection of migrant workers during their employment, including provisions related to housing, fixing of minimum wage rates, supply of consumer goods, social security, and industrial safety and hygiene.

Issues seen as particularly relevant to developing country workers were elaborated on in greater depth than they had been in the 1939 or 1949 conventions. The recommendation addressed issues related to the "moral welfare" of workers, including arrangements to encourage voluntary forms of thrift, protect the workers against usury, and provide facilities for migrant workers to satisfy their intellectual and religious aspirations. Governments were also encouraged to have welfare officers familiar with the languages and customs of the migrants. Finally, the recommendation addressed the relations of migrant workers to their areas of origin, specifying that arrangements should be made for them to maintain contact with their families and remit their earnings.

Interestingly, in a recommendation that largely addressed what happened after the decision to migrate was made, another provision indicated the "general policy should be to discourage migration of workers when considered undesirable in the interest of the migrant workers and of the communities and countries of their origin." The recommendation urged measures designed to improve conditions of life and to raise standards of living in origin communities. The ILO specifically recommended economic development and vocational training programs to create new jobs and sources of income for workers who would otherwise be inclined to migrate. Governments were informed they could also limit recruitment in "regions where the withdrawal of labour might have untoward effects on the social and economic organization, and the health, welfare and development of the population concerned."

The timing of the recommendations proved useful, as many of the European countries that had heretofore been emigration nations transformed into immigration ones. Much of the initial migration was within the context of colonial movements from the periphery to the center and from one part of an empire to another. Independence sometimes merely accelerated the movements, as was the case in migration from the Indian subcontinent and the English-speaking Caribbean to the United Kingdom and from the Maghreb to France. As the economies of Western Europe improved, countries such as Germany became major importers of foreign labor. At the same time, increased migration took place from Haiti to the Dominican Republic, Ghana to Nigeria, Mali to Cote d'Ivoire, Indonesia to Malaysia, and much of southern Africa to South Africa. Whether countries had ratified or even read conventions and recommendations, they were developing formal and informal bilateral agreements to regulate many of these movements. Nevertheless, a significant amount of migration for employment and for family reunification was occurring outside of these agreements.

The guest worker programs of the United States and Europe are a case in point. The United States had signed a bilateral agreement with Mexico in 1943 for the admission of Mexican workers to fill labor shortages caused by the massive war effort. Mexicans picked fruits and vegetables and worked at industrial tasks under an agreement that set out the terms of employment. A commission that investigated labor standards in agriculture in the 1950s found that the workers who entered under the agreement (often called Braceros) had the best wages and working conditions in the sector. They also found, though, that a large segment of the agricultural workforce was undocumented, entering the country illegally, and had the poorest wages and working conditions. Employers preferred the undocumented workers to avoid fulfilling the terms of the legal contracts. In the 1950s, massive enforcement led to the deportation of hundreds of thousands of undocumented workers (and some citizens unable to prove their citizenship). The bilateral agreement was not renewed in its previous form and employers received concessions on hiring practices, including the right to veto the return of workers who complained about their situation. The changes enticed employers to join or rejoin the temporary work program. The Bracero system persisted until its demise in 1964 when, in the context of the civil rights movement, the United States made major reforms in immigration policy. The legacy of the Bracero program was the resumption of large-scale undocumented migration, as employers continued to hire Mexican workers who were not legally present.

Germany epitomized the European guest worker schemes. As economist Philip Martin describes:

> By 1960 there were more job vacancies registered with the Employment Service than there were unemployed workers. Employers asked for permission to recruit guest workers, and the government complied, reasoning that the guests would work for one or two years in Germany, and then return to Italy, Yugoslavia, or Turkey with their savings and skills in a mutually beneficial labor exchange. (Martin 2001)

The recruitment began slowly but accelerated with further improvements in the economy and the development of effective recruitment networks. The assumption had been that the migrants would come on a rotation base:

> Guestworkers in West Germany were recruited for a specific period of time, usually two or three years, and often not permitted to bring in family members, with the expectation that they would return to their country of origin after their employment contract expired. When the movements first started, the intention of migrants largely paralleled the expectations of employers and governments of the migrant-receiving countries. They intended to stay for a few years to save enough money to accomplish their financial goals at home. (Icduygu 2008:2)

Neither migrants nor employers stayed committed to the principle or reality of rotation. Many migrants developed ties in Germany and the other destination countries with guest worker programs, or they were unable to accomplish their financial goals. Many employers were satisfied with the workers that they hired and preferred to stay with a known entity rather than risk recruiting new workers who might prove inadequate. Conditions in countries of origin often became barriers to return. For millions of guest workers, remaining in Europe and bringing their families to join them was preferable. When the 1973 oil crisis led to high levels of unemployment, the European countries closed their guest worker programs, but by then many of their guests had become permanent residents. Governments slowly responded to these realities and opened up legal channels for family reunification, which resulted in overall growth in the foreign-born populations in many Western European countries.

By the early 1970s, conditions were ripe for consideration of a new ILO convention to address some of these developments. Representatives of workers in the tripartite system had been pressing for action by the ILO on migration issues. In 1971, the ILO conference adopted a resolution raising the issue of equality of migrant workers in all social and labor matters (Bohning nd). The Governing Board commissioned a comprehensive study of labor migration and determined that migrant workers would be an issue for discussion at the 1974 conference. By the time the conference met, many of the European countries had dismantled their migrant worker programs. The policy debate shifted from legal work programs to irregular migration, as well as family reunification and integration of the remaining guest workers.

Emanating from these concerns came an unwieldy convention that attempted to address both sets of issues. Convention 143, adopted in 1975, focused on Migrations in Abusive Conditions and the Promotion of Equality of Opportunity and Treatment of Migrant Workers. With regard to migrations in abusive conditions, Article 1 specified that "each member for which this Convention is in force undertakes to respect the basic human rights of all migrant workers."[4] The remaining articles focus on actions that governments should take alone or in cooperation with others to curb clandestine movements of migrants seeking employment and the illegal employment of migrants in the workforce. In keeping with the tripartite nature of the organization, governments are encouraged to consult representative organizations of employers and workers on these measures. Exchange of information among states about the extent and forms of clandestine migration was another focus of the convention.

The convention specifies that provision should be made under national laws and regulations for the detection of illegal employment of migrant workers, with appropriate administrative, civil, and penal sanctions for violations. A

---

[4] All quotes from Convention 143 are found at http://www.ilo.org/dyn/normlex/en/f?p=NORM LEXPUB:12100:0::NO:12100:P12100_ILO_CODE:C143.

good faith defense by employers found to have engaged in illegal employment (for example, not having known that the employee was illegally in the country) should be incorporated into the policies. The worker should also retain rights arising out of past employment with regard to remuneration, social security, and other benefits. If the worker and his or her family are expelled from the country after presenting their case to a competent body, the workers should not bear the costs of the removal. The convention further specifies that "nothing in this Convention shall prevent Members from giving persons who are illegally residing or working within the country the right to stay and to take up legal employment."

Part II of the convention focuses on equality of opportunity and treatment in respect to employment and occupation, social security, trade union, and cultural rights. In addition, it deals with individual and collective freedoms for workers and their families. Education is a large part of the convention, with members agreeing to "enact such legislation and promote such educational programs as may be calculated to secure the acceptance and observance of the policy" and "encourage education programs ... aimed at acquainting migrant workers ... with their rights and obligations." Parties to the convention shall guarantee equality of treatment with regard to working conditions for all migrant workers who perform the same activity. They also shall take steps "to assist and encourage the efforts of migrant workers and their families to preserve their national and ethnic identity and their cultural ties with their country of origin, including the possibility for children to be given some knowledge of their mother tongue."

The convention also addressed issues of family reunification. Using a weak formulation, it states that parties to the convention may – not should – take steps to facilitate it. A 1973 ILO report had set out the importance of family reunification:

> Uniting migrant workers with their families living in the countries of origin is recognised to be essential for the migrants' well-being and their social adaptation to the receiving country. Prolonged separation and isolation lead to hardships and stress situations affecting both the migrants and the families left behind and prevent them from leading a normal life. The large numbers of migrant workers cut off from social relations and living on the fringe of the receiving community create many well known social and psychological problems that, in turn, largely determine community attitudes towards migrant workers. (quoted in Cholewinski 1994:568)

Language on free choice of employment is also weak, using *may* rather than *should*. It also applied only to those who had been in the country for a prescribed period not to exceed two years.

A recommendation issued at the same time elaborated on the issue of equality of opportunity and treatment with nationals. It specified areas in which the principle should apply, including access to vocational guidance and placement services; access to vocational training and employment on the basis of individual suitability for such training or employment; and advancement in accordance with the workers' individual character, experience, ability, and diligence. It also urged providing security of employment, the provision of alternative employment, and relief work and retraining; remuneration for work of equal value; conditions of work; membership in trade unions; rights of full membership in any form of cooperative; and conditions of life, including housing and the benefits of social services and educational and health facilities.

Perhaps not surprisingly, C143 was ratified by fewer states than its 1949 predecessor. Part of the reticence was related to the attempt to address both illegal immigration and work and equality of treatment. The principal destination countries, particularly in developed regions, remained unwilling to cede any authority over decisions on treatment of foreign nationals to an international process even though the convention had many escape clauses in establishing that actions should generally be in accordance with "national conditions and practice." Representatives of some source countries, as well as those of trade unions, expressed concern over the provisions on illegal immigration, although they might have supported those on equality of treatment.

Some economists have argued that resistance to ratifying conventions is related to tensions between the rights afforded migrant workers and the numbers who are likely to be admitted. Ruhs and Martin (2008:253) state:

> Our basic argument is that there is a trade-off, i.e., an inverse relationship between the number and rights of migrants employed in low-skilled jobs in high-income countries. The primary reason for this trade-off is that employer demand for labor is negatively sloped with respect to labor costs, and that more rights for migrants typically means higher costs. The result is that more migrants tend to be associated with fewer rights for migrants, and vice versa.[5]

The argument, in effect, is that employers want foreign workers precisely because they can be treated differently than native workers. If migrant workers were to have exactly the same rights as native workers, particularly with regard to wages and working conditions, there would be no economic advantage to hiring them. For their part, migrants assess the desirability of employment from the vantage point of the wages and working conditions available in their home countries. They often view wages considered low in the destination country as quite desirable. At least initially, they are less concerned with achieving equality of treatment with citizens of the destination country than with improvement of their income compared to home standards. To the extent that the demand is related to shortages of workers, rather than desire for lower costs, this

---

[5] Matthew Cummins and Francisco Rodríguez counter the argument using data on migrant integration, accessibility to services, and several other variables and find that, the GCC aside (where there are very large numbers of migrants and few rights), they found no correlation. The authors caution, however, that measures of migrant integration (which they use as a proxy for rights) are at a nascent stage.

argument may not apply. Often, however, there is a supply of native workers who would accept the jobs if wages were higher and working conditions improved.

Improving Knowledge and Technical Skills

After 1975, the ILO focused primarily on research, technical cooperation, and meetings on international migration. A 2004 review of the ILO's activities showed them to fall into six categories:

- Building a global knowledge base on labor migration through research and the International Labour Migration (ILM) database. A research program was undertaken initially within the context of the World Employment Program (WEP), which received resources to engage a migration expert. ILO had two main series of publications: *International Migration Papers* series, with the results of empirical studies on a broad range of issues, and *Perspectives on Labour Migration* series, which disseminated the exchange of specialist views on selected migration policy issues (ILO 2004). The ILM database provides online data on labor migration patterns and characteristics, and NATLEX is a database on labor legislation, which includes relevant migration laws.
- Promotion and supervision of relevant ILO norms. ILO continued to promote ratification of its own migration related conventions and was part of initiatives to encourage ratification of the Migrant Workers Convention. A fundamental mandate was to assist governments in their efforts to incorporate these norms into national law.
- Promoting and strengthening social dialogue on migration and integration questions. ILO organized conferences and other opportunities for the tripartite partnership of governments, trade unions and employers to discuss migration issues and forge common understandings.
- Technical cooperation and capacity building to assist governments and social partners in improving their capabilities for policy-making and administration. These activities are carried out at the national and regional levels. As described in the 2004 report to the International Conference, "Regional technical cooperation projects carried out in Asia, North Africa, and in Central and Eastern Europe, for example, have enabled the Office to meet in a cost-effective manner countries' common needs for information and training in the management of labour migration. They supported the establishment of networks among labour ministries which continued long after the externally funded projects had ended. Through technical cooperation the Office has assisted governments in developing a firm base for national policies by grounding them on conditions in national and international labour markets, by harmonizing national with international normative standards, and by broadening support for policy through social dialogue" (ibid.: 40).

- Special action programs to combat trafficking and forced labor of children and adults, to protect groups at risk, especially from HIV/AIDS, and to promote integration and non-discrimination.
- Building an international framework for cooperation on migration. (ILO 2004)

The ILO engaged in some operational activities, particularly related to migrant workers who were precipitously expelled or forced to leave receiving countries. Expulsions of Tunisian and Egyptian workers from Libya in 1985 and Senegalese from Mauritania in 1989 led to negotiations to ensure that the migrants received compensation for work they had done. The mass exodus of migrant workers after the Iraqi invasion of Kuwait led to an even more operational role for the ILO, which was involved in registering and documenting the wage and other losses of many of the migrant workers. When the UN Compensation Commission was established to distribute a portion of Iraq's oil exports to compensate victims, the ILO data proved useful in ensuring payment to the migrant workers. Individual migrants received $4,000 and families received $8,000 if they claimed no loss other than compensation for lost work. For other losses, they received $2,500 ($5,000 for families) pending adjudication. The ILO's director general successfully advocated with the secretary general and the Security Council that the migrant claims should be given priority for resolution before those of governments and corporations (Bohning 2001).

A Fair Deal on Migrant Workers

In 1999, a report of the Committee of Experts on the Application of Conventions and Recommendations raised significant questions about the status quo, particularly related to norm-setting. Noting the small number of ratifications, the committee found that the ILO had two options – to continue the unsatisfactory status quo or to revise the conventions significantly.[6] The 2004 international conference chose a third approach, tasking the organization with developing "a non-binding multilateral framework for a rights-based approach to labor migration which takes account of labor market needs, proposing guidelines and principles for policies based on best practices and international standards" ("Proceedings" 2004). Preparations for the 2004 conference included a report entitled "Towards a Fair Deal for Migrant Workers in the Global Economy," which had spelled out the realities of international migration, the work of the ILO to date, and the results of a survey of governments about their labor migration policies. The report concluded:

---

[6] The report of th committee can be found at http://www.ilo.org/public/english/standards/relm/ilc/ilc87/r3-1b.htm.

A rights-based international regime for managing migration must rest on a framework of principles of good governance developed and implemented by the international community that will be acceptable to all and suitable as a basis for
cooperative multilateral action. Existing international instruments defining the
rights of migrant workers provide many of the necessary principles, but a sound
framework would have to include principles on how to organize more orderly
forms of migration that benefit all. (ILO 2004:139)

To prepare the actual framework, the ILO convened a tripartite meeting
of experts, which met in Geneva from October 31 to November 2, 2005.
They debated and adopted the "ILO Multilateral Framework on Labour
Migration: Non-binding principles and guidelines for a rights-based approach
to labour migration." The ILO Governing Body at its 295th Session in
March 2006 decided that the "Framework" should be published and disseminated.

The "Framework" was developed in the context of the ILO's more general commitment to decent work: "access for all to freely chosen employment,
the recognition of fundamental rights at work, an income to enable people
to meet their basic economic, social and family needs and responsibilities and
an adequate level of social protection for the workers and family members"
(ILO 2006:5). The framework also promoted the organization's preference
for tripartite agreement, specifying that "Governments, in consultation with
employers' and workers' organizations, should engage in international cooperation to promote managed migration for employment purposes" (7). While
recognizing the sovereign authority of states to enact and implement their own
immigration policies, the "Framework" encouraged them to give "international
labor standards and other international instruments, as well as guidelines, as
appropriate . . . an important role to make these policies coherent, effective and
fair" (11).

States were encouraged to consider expanding avenues for regular labor
migration, "taking into account labor market needs and demographic trends"
(ibid.:12). A proper knowledge base and consultation with stakeholders would
improve policy making. The "Framework" also encouraged consideration of
all stages of migration, including planning and preparing for labor migration,
transit, arrival and reception, return, and reintegration (ibid.:23)."

With regard to the treatment of migrant workers, states were reminded that
"the human rights of all migrant workers, regardless of their status, should be
promoted and protected" (ibid.:15). Accordingly, national laws should seek to
conform to international standards. The "Framework" further called attention
to the need to prevent abusive practices, referencing measures to terminate
migrant smuggling and trafficking in persons. States should strive to prevent
irregular labor migration (ibid.). Governments and social partners should also
"promote social integration and inclusion, while respecting cultural diversity,
preventing discrimination against migrant workers and taking measures to

combat racism and xenophobia" (ibid.:27). Each of these major objectives included more specific guidance as to how to achieve the aims.

THE CONVENTION ON MIGRANT WORKER RIGHTS

States possess broad authority to regulate the movement of foreign nationals across their borders, although these powers are not absolute. States exercise their sovereign powers to determine who will be admitted and for what period, but their authority is limited by certain rights accorded foreign nationals in international law. Non-nationals have all of the unalienable rights applicable in international law. The International Covenant on Civil and Political Rights (ICCPR) defines such basic rights of all persons as: the right to life, liberty and security; the right not to be held in slavery or servitude; the right not to be subjected to torture or to cruel, inhuman, or degrading treatment or punishment; the right not to be subjected to arbitrary arrest, detention or exile; the right to marry and to found a family. Additional rights are conveyed by the International Covenant on Economic, Social, and Cultural Rights (ICESCR), the Convention on the Elimination of All Forms of Discrimination against Women (CEDAW), the International Convention on the Elimination of All Forms of Racial Discrimination, the Convention against Torture, and the Convention on the Rights of the Child (CRC).[7] Most of these conventions have been ratified by a wide range of states.[8]

After passage of the 1975 ILO convention, discussions began with regard to an additional convention that would focus specifically on the rights of migrant workers and their families. These discussions were testimony to the growth in international migration as well as increasing concerns about the situation of migrants throughout the world. In 1978, the UN General Assembly noted the need for improvements in the status of migrant workers. In addition to calling upon states to ratify the ILO conventions, the resolution recommended that the UN Commission on Human Rights and the Economic and Social Council consider further the situation of migrant workers. The secretary general followed up on these recommendations, issuing a report on migrant workers and their families (Nafziger and Bartel 1991). The report "highlighted the particular problems migrant workers often experience in having to adjust to urban life in a new culture. It identified special problems women and children face

---

[7] The Refugee Convention is also a core human rights instrument; its provisions were discussed previously.

[8] Notable in not having ratified several of these instruments, including ICESCR, CEDAW, and CRC, is the United States. In addition to Congressional reluctance to enter into multilateral conventions, issues of federalism in terms of the relative powers of the federal and state governments have been raised in relationship to ratification. U.S. unwillingness to enter into such agreements is especially noteworthy regarding the CRC, which has been ratified by all countries except the United States, Somalia, and South Sudan.

and the limited access migrant workers may have to social services" (Nafziger and Bartel 1991).

The General Assembly resolved in 1979 to establish a working group to elaborate a general convention on migrant workers and members of their families. Meeting for the first time in Mexico in 1980, the working group subsequently held semi-annual sessions. An early decision was made to draft a convention that would apply to all migrant workers. It was also decided to assess the applicability of the full range of rights articulated in the core human rights conventions, including both civil and political rights as well as social, economic, and cultural ones. A contemporary account described the working group's approach as ad hoc, rather than systematic – meaning that the articles of the convention considered were not necessarily in the order in which they would finally appear (Lillich 1984).

It is important to assess what the International Convention on the Rights of Migrant Workers and Members of their Families does not embrace. It includes no obligations on states to admit migrant workers; nor does it include barriers to state removal of migrant workers who violate immigration laws. There are no provisions for amnesties or legalization of irregular migrants.

Decisions on admission and removal thus remain firmly within the sovereign authority of states (Cassel 2005). Bosniak and Zolberg (1991) note that the convention defers throughout to state sovereignty:

> One key article reaffirms states' authority to pursue the immigration control and admission policies they see fit (Article 79); another requires them to undertake control measures to end the process of clandestine migration and the presence and employment of irregular migrants including, "whenever appropriate," employer sanctions (Articles 68 and 69). Another provision explicitly emphasizes that states are not obliged to regularize the status of irregular migrant workers or members of their families in their territories (Article 35), even if they are required to extend to them the panoply of rights previously mentioned. Yet another underlines that migrants are not exempt from "the obligation to comply with the laws and regulations of . . . the State of employment" (Article 34), including, by implication, states' laws against unauthorized entry, employment or residence.

What does the convention accomplish? Basically, it reaffirms core human rights norms and embodies them in an instrument applicable to migrant workers and their families. The convention builds on the ILO conventions previously discussed (Hasenau 1991). The underlying goal of the convention is to guarantee minimum rights for migrant workers and their families who are in legal or irregular status. The convention brings together provisions that are dispersed in other instruments, establishing a clearer normative framework (Ghosh 2003). In fact, the preliminary working draft of the convention, presented to the working group in 1981, was little more than a laundry list of protections drawn from other instruments (Nafziger and Bartel 1991).

The convention defines the rights of migrant workers under two main headings: "The human rights of migrant workers and members of their families" (Part III of the convention), which reaffirms the human rights of all migrants regardless of their legal status, and "Other rights of migrant workers" (Part IV of the convention) which sets out additional rights applicable only to migrant workers in a regular situation. A migrant worker is defined as a "person who is to be engaged, is engaged or has been engaged in a remunerated activity in a State of which he or she is not a national" (Article 2 of the convention).[9] This broad definition refers not only to those currently working but those who intend to work or have worked previously even if they entered the country for other purposes (Bosniak 1991). Documented migrants are defined as those "authorized to enter, to stay and engage in a remunerated activity in the State of employment pursuant to the law of that State and to international agreements to which that State is a party" (Article 5). Those who do not comply with those conditions are classified as undocumented.

Many of the provisions also relate to family members. The drafting working group had considered different standards to use in defining family for purposes of the convention. A contemporary observer noted that the major point of disagreement was between delegations that would restrict definition of "members of the family" to the "nuclear family" and those who argued for a broader definition of marriage and family (Hune 1987). The definition chosen for the convention was a compromise, allowing for consideration of dependence on the wage-earner. The convention includes persons married to migrant workers or having with them a relationship which, according to applicable law, produces effects equivalent to marriage. It also covers dependent children and other dependent persons who are recognized as members of the family by applicable legislation or applicable bilateral or multilateral agreements. Notably, the convention leaves it to states to make the final decision about the extended family.

Article 6 specifies persons to whom the convention does not apply. These include:

(a) Persons sent or employed by international organizations and agencies or persons sent or employed by a State outside its territory to perform official functions, whose admission and status are regulated by general international law or by specific international agreements or conventions;
(b) Persons sent or employed by a State or on its behalf outside its territory who participate in development programmes and other co-operation programmes, whose admission and status are regulated by agreement with

---

[9] All quotes from the International Convention on the Protection of the Rights of All Migrant Workers and Members of Their Families are taken from http://www2.ohchr.org/english/bodies/cmw/cmw.htm.

the State of employment and who, in accordance with that agreement, are not considered migrant workers;

(c) Persons taking up residence in a State different from their State of origin as investors;

(d) Refugees and stateless persons, unless such application is provided for in the relevant national legislation of, or international instruments in force for, the State Party concerned;

(e) Students and trainees;

(f) Seafarers and workers on an offshore installation who have not been admitted to take up residence and engage in a remunerated activity in the State of employment.

The convention specifies the right of migrant workers, regardless of documented status, to protection from violence and attacks. Article 10 prohibits torture or cruel, inhuman, or degrading treatment or punishment. Article 11 prohibits slavery or servitude and forced or compulsory labor. Article 14 prohibits arbitrary or unlawful interference with privacy or attacks on honor and reputation. Article 16 entitles migrants "to effective protection by the State against violence, physical injury, threats, and intimidation, whether by public officials or by private individuals, groups or institutions."

A number of other articles focus on the social and economic status of migrants. Article 64 (paragraph 2) states that "due regard shall be paid not only to labour needs and resources, but also to the social, economic, cultural and other needs of migrant workers and members of their families involved, as well as to the consequences of such migration for the communities concerned." Article 70 guarantees "working conditions . . . in keeping with the standards of fitness, safety, health, and principles of human dignity." Article 43 provides equal treatment of documented migrants with nationals with respect to access to education, vocational training, housing, and health services. Article 45 confers the same rights for members of families. Article 50 provides that in case of death or dissolution of marriage, the state shall favorably consider granting authorization to stay to the families of documented migrants.

Although the rights provided by the convention apply to both men and women migrants and Article 45 specifically addresses the equality of rights, the convention does not expressly address many needs that are particular to women. Many migrant women work in non-regulated sectors of the economy, including domestic work, which leaves them vulnerable to exploitation and abuse. Guaranteeing equal treatment with nationals does not help migrant workers in such situations because the regulatory structure is weak for both populations (Hune 1991; Cholewinski 1997).

The Migrant Workers Convention establishes a Committee on the Protection of Rights of All Migrant Workers and Members of Their Families, consisting of fourteen experts of "high moral standing, impartiality and recognized competence in the field covered by the convention." Committee members are elected from a list of nominees. States parties (only those who have ratified the convention) may nominate one person from their own nationals. Elections are by secret ballot. The convention reflects an intention that there be geographic diversity as well as diversity between source and receiving states.

Article 73 requires State parties to the convention submit "for consideration by the committee a report on the legislative, judicial, administrative and other measures they have taken to give effect to the provisions of the . . . convention" within one year after entry into force and every five years thereafter. The committee will examine the reports and will transmit comments to the state. The committee may invite the specialized agencies and organs of the UN as well as intergovernmental organizations and "other concerned bodies" to submit written information on matters that fall within the convention's scope for the committee's consideration.

Article 76 sets forth a process for states that have ratified the convention to complain about another state's failure to fulfil its obligations. Only states that are parties to the convention and that have declared that they recognize the competence of the committee may make complaints to the committee. Article 77 provides that individuals of states parties may bring complaints against states parties only under certain circumstances: namely, they are not involved in some other international settlement mechanism; they have exhausted domestic remedies; the states party against which the complaint has been made has recognized the competence of the committee to hear individual complaints; and ten states parties declare that they recognize the competence of the committee to receive and consider communications from or on behalf of individuals.

Why have states been reluctant to ratify the convention? The obstacles are both practical and political.[10] On the practical side, Nafziger and Bartel (1991:784) observed soon after the convention was signed: "Although the Convention brings together a welter of protections for migrant workers in a single document, its vocabulary and complexity do not augur well for quick ratification or accession by states." The convention is extensive in its coverage of migrant rights issues, raising technical questions as well as financial obligations on states parties. For example, Article 65 of the convention requires states parties "to maintain appropriate services to deal with questions concerning international migration of workers and members of their families. Their functions shall include, inter alia:

(a) The formulation and implementation of policies regarding such migration;
(b) An exchange of information, consultation and co-operation with the competent authorities of other States parties involved in such migration;

---

[10] For a fuller discussion of the barriers to ratification, see de Guchteneire et al. 2009, which provides a detailed analysis of attitudes towards ratification in Asia, South Africa, Canada, the United Kingdom, France, Italy, Germany, and other countries of the EU.

(c) The provision of appropriate information, particularly to employers, workers and their organizations on policies, laws and regulations relating to migration and employment, on agreements concluded with other States concerning migration and on other relevant matters;

(d) The provision of information and appropriate assistance to migrant workers and members of their families regarding requisite authorizations and formalities and arrangements for departure, travel, arrival, stay, remunerated activities, exit and return, as well as on conditions of work and life in the State of employment and on customs, currency, tax and other relevant laws and regulations.

Almost all states have some emigration and immigration but countries with relatively low levels of migration may find no particular reasons to ratify the convention, particularly given the practical hurdles.

On the political level, the convention raises basic questions about state sovereignty, particularly regarding the capacity of states to deter irregular migration. The convention requires states parties to cooperate in curbing irregular migration and returning those without authorization to remain in a destination state. Many receiving countries are concerned, however, that the rights granted to irregular migrants will hinder their ability to control such movements. Some states are concerned that specifying the rights of irregular migrants will serve as a magnet, drawing them to their territory. A Dutch government paper on the convention explains the reluctance of the Netherlands to ratify: "The granting of certain social and economic rights on the part of the state is considered to be more of an encouragement for illegal residence and employment than a deterrent" (Government of the Netherlands 2005:3). As Bosniak and Zolberg (2004) notes:

> However much actual effort a state expends on immigration control measures, "illegal aliens," as they are often called, are treated as symbols of the state's violated sovereignty. It is one thing to require that these migrants be provided with basic procedural protections in the deportation context, and to ensure that they are protected by those limited rights recognized as customary under international law. But can the Convention's supporters hope to require that states provide undocumented immigrants with guarantees to extensive labor rights and to civil and cultural rights while purporting to acknowledge the states' vital interests in territorial integrity? As a political matter, the answer to this question is almost certainly "no."

With regard to documented migrants, "the Convention's central concept of non-discrimination interferes with explorations of other forms of temporary immigration in which this principle would not be fully abided by" (Bosniak and Zolberg 2004). As discussed in relationship to the ILO conventions, states often see a trade-off between the number of migrants admitted and the generosity of rights bestowed upon them. Providing rights equivalent to those held by nationals, particularly when such rights entail financial obligations on the part of receiving states, may severely limit the number of migrants to be admitted. Otherwise, states fear, there will be a public backlash against migrants who are perceived as being a costly burden on taxpayers. Even when there is little factual basis to such charges, and migrants can be seen to be contributing to the economy, public opinion may view migrants to be competitors for limited jobs and resources.

Some states recognize no need to ratify the convention, claiming that other human rights instruments already provide protection to any person of the most fundamental rights outlined in the Migrant Workers Convention. Alternatively, they state national laws provide adequate protection. Canada, for example, emphasizes that the Charter of Rights and Freedoms protects migrants, regardless of legal status (Piche et al. 2009). Moreover, the Canadian government notes that the convention's focus on temporary workers contradicts and is more limiting than Canada's preference for settlement of migrants as permanent residents and eventually citizens (ibid.).

Other states, however, view the convention as promoting rights not specified elsewhere and not necessarily in their national interest. The Dutch paper, discussed above, holds that the convention "contains a number of new provisions that were not previously included in broadly ratified treaties" (Government of the Netherlands 2005). In particular, the Dutch paper points out that the convention grants a right to family reunification to both legally and illegally resident migrants (ibid.).

The convention took effect in 2003 when it received its twentieth ratification. At present, forty-seven countries have ratified the convention (Mozambique joined in August 2013). In comparison, 145 countries have ratified the Refugee Convention. To date, none of the traditional countries of permanent immigration (the United States, Canada, Australia, or New Zealand) or members of the European Union (EU) have ratified the instrument. Nor has any member of the GCC or any of the immigrant receiving countries in East Asia. Among Arab states, Libya and Syria (net receivers) have ratified, along with Egypt and Morocco (net sources). The largest number of ratifications (fifteen, plus one signatory who has not ratified) have come from Latin America, where countries experiencing immigration, such as Chile and Argentina, have ratified it along with emigration countries in Central and South America. An almost equal number of ratifications have been made by sub-Saharan African countries. Countries in South and Southeast Asia with large numbers of emigrants (Philippines, Indonesia, Bangladesh, and Sri Lanka) have ratified, whereas others (India and Pakistan) have not. Eastern and Central Asian source countries, including Albania, Azerbaijan, Bosnia and Herzegovina, Kyrgyzstan, and Tajikistan, have ratified, as has Turkey.

At present, there are two UN human rights bodies that monitor the situation of migrant workers. When the Migrant Workers Convention went into force, the Committee on the Protection of the Rights of All Migrant Workers and Members of their Families was established. Under the terms of the Migrant

Workers Convention, all state parties are obliged to submit regular reports to the committee on how the rights enshrined in the convention are being implemented. The committee examines the reports and conveys its concerns and recommendations. The committee also must take complaints and communications from individuals and states regarding potential violations of the convention. An analysis of the reports submitted by parties to the convention demonstrates great inconsistencies in adherence. Some countries have submitted no reports. Some of those that have been submitted are quite short, but Mexico's was described as voluminous. They differ as well in level of detail and input from nongovernmental sources (Edelenbos 2009). The resulting comments by the committee have been equally varied.

The committee also issues General Comments on topics of broad concern. Its first comment was issued in 2010 on the issue of domestic workers (Committee on Migrant Workers 2010). In preparation for issuing the comment, the committee hosted a meeting in 2009 to explore the issues in greater detail. The timing coincided with consideration of a convention on domestic workers at the ILO. The comment made clear that foreign nationals working in private residences were covered by the Migrant Workers Convention. It also outlined the legal and practical gaps that often placed domestic workers in a tenuous situation, not least of which was the privacy of their workplace. The comment concluded specific recommendations of steps that states could take to protect the rights of migrant domestic workers. As of September 2012, the committee was at work on a second General Comment on migrants in an irregular status.

In 1999, the UN Commission on Human Rights established a Special Rapporteur on the Human Rights of Migrants who now reports to the Human Rights Council. The special rapporteur's mandate covers all states, not just those that have ratified the Migrant Workers Convention. Reports are based on communications from individuals and official visits to selected countries. The visits are with the agreement of the designated countries. Since 2000, the special rapporteurs have averaged about two to three fact-finding visits per year. They have visited destination countries (e.g., South Africa, Japan, United Kingdom, United States, South Korea, Italy, and Canada), source countries (Senegal, Guatemala, Mexico, Indonesia, Burkina Faso, Morocco, Philippines, and Ecuador), and transit zones (U.S.–Mexico border). The reports of these missions are submitted to the Human Rights Council and published on the special rapporteur's website for more general access. The special rapporteur also submits an annual report on his or her findings. The Human Rights Council also asks the special rapporteur to report on specific issues. A 2008 resolution asked the special rapporteur to examine "arbitrary detention of migrants, particularly of migrant children and adolescents."[11]

---

[11] Resolution 9/5. Human rights of migrants. Available at http://imprasc.net:29572/Basededatos legal/DerechoInternacional/Documents/Resoluciones/057.pdf.

TRADE AND MIGRATION

While the UN was paying attention to protecting the rights of labor migrants, issues regarding economically motivated movements of people were being addressed in a different context – trade agreements. Migration, as such, was generally not a part of the negotiations over these treaties. Particularly in the context of trade in services, however, barriers to the mobility of people were increasingly seen as impediments that needed to be addressed. Yet, policy makers responsible for trade – an emblematic part of the global economy – generally had little understanding of or interest in knowing more about migration processes or impacts; similarly, immigration policy makers were largely ignorant of what was happening in the trade arena.[12]

This situation began to change in the 1990s. The development of a single European market contributed to the shift, when a core part of the project was the opening of borders and the free movement of people along with goods within the EU. The 1992 Single European Act's intent was "to formulate a European market within which the free movement of people, services, goods and capital would be assured" (Geddes 2011:204). In pursuit of this goal, the 1997 Amsterdam Treaty defined Europe as "an area of freedom, security and justice" and "formulated positions on free movement, migration and asylum" (Geddes 2011:204). Previously, the Schengen Agreement – a voluntary agreement among a subset of European countries – had eliminated border controls within the common territory of parties to the agreement. The concept was extended to the rest of the EU (with an opt-out provision that some states took). With elimination of internal borders, policing the external border of the Schengen zone became a shared responsibility.

Interestingly, this agreement did not extend to shared responsibility for admission of labor migrants from outside of Europe or for free movement of third country nationals admitted to work in one state to be able to cross the borders into another state. A summit in Tampere in 1999 spelled out, however, the areas in which a common EU approach would be useful: partnership with countries of origin, a common asylum system, fair treatment for third country nationals, and management of migration flows (Geddes 2011). Some progress was subsequently made in developing a common migration policy, particularly in introduction of the blue card scheme for skilled workers. However, the EU has still not achieved full harmonization of its immigration policies. Any examination of the difficulties encountered among like-minded countries with

---

[12] My own situation in government is a case in point. When I was serving as the executive director of the U.S. Commission on Immigration Reform, I was called in to meet with a senior official in the office of the U.S. trade representative who was worried that an immigration reform proposal we were considering would have put the United States out of compliance with one of our trade commitments. I was unaware that the United States had made any immigration-related commitments and inquiries to other senior immigration officials showed I was not alone.

similar economies highlights the challenges that harmonization would create among nations with highly divergent economies and forms of government.

A second notable attempt in the 1990s to link migration and trade came in the Americas with negotiation of the North American Free Trade Agreement (NAFTA). Unlike the discussions in Europe, negotiators never intended to create a free mobility zone. In fact, Carla Hills, the U.S. trade negotiator, had been explicit that including migration too explicitly in any agreement would spell its death in the U.S. Congress. Speaking a decade after NAFTA went into force, Hills argued: "Given the enormous income disparity between Mexico on the one hand and the United States and Canada on the other, a common market would create a politically untenable incentive for northward migration."[13] Rather than liberalizing Mexico–U.S. migration within the agreement, the supporters asserted instead that NAFTA would help curtail emigration pressures by providing economic opportunities at home. President Salinas of Mexico famously said that Mexico would prefer to export its tomatoes rather than its tomato pickers.

The political concerns were about what was seen as the dominant form of Mexican migration – low-skilled, low-wage workers. NAFTA did include provisions that liberalized mostly high-skilled migration among the three countries. Within the context of trade in services, the provisions focused on the temporary admissions of business persons, investors, intra-company transfers, and certain professionals. The agreement defined who was covered by each of these terms. For example, professional services were defined as those "which require specialized post-secondary education, or equivalent training or experience, and for which the right to practice is granted or restricted by a Party."[14] The parties agreed in an annex on a list of such professionals and the level of education required of those providing such services. Under the agreement, the three countries could not impose conditions for temporary entry that would require prior approval procedures, petitions, labor certification tests, or other procedures of similar effect. Nor could the countries impose or maintain any numerical restrictions relating to temporary entry, except for a pre-approved imposition of a quota of 5,500 visas per year on Mexican professionals during a transition period that has since expired. Article 1201 of the agreement made clear, though, that "Nothing in this Chapter shall be construed to impose any obligation on a Party with respect to a national of another Party seeking access to its employment market, or employed on a permanent basis in its territory, or to confer any right on that national with respect to that access or employment."

The Uruguay round of negotiations that led to the General Agreement on Trade in Services (GATS) was occurring as the same time as the events in the

---

[13] Taken from transcript of panel presentation, NAFTA:10 Years On, at the Council on Foreign Relations. Available at http://www.cfr.org/trade/nafta--ten-years/p6802.

[14] Quotes from the North American Free Trade Agreement are taken from http://www.nafta-sec-alena.org/Default.aspx?tabid=97&language=en-US.

EU and North America. The issue of mobility soon became an area of debate. GATS does not refer specifically to migration but rather to movements of "natural persons," as distinct from corporations. Natural persons are defined in Mode 4 of the agreement as "individuals travelling from their own country to supply services in another."[15] GATS has three components: general obligations, annexes dealing with rules for specific sectors, and individual countries' specific commitments to provide access to their markets. The first component includes obligations that all parties are required to make, the second focuses on specific sectors (e.g., movement of natural persons), and the third includes commitments on the part of individual countries to liberalize trade in services. The annex on natural persons specifies:

- The Agreement shall not apply to measures affecting natural persons seeking access to the employment market of a Member, nor shall it apply to measures regarding citizenship, residence or employment on a permanent basis.
- Members may negotiate specific commitments applying to the movement of all categories of natural persons supplying services under the Agreement. Natural persons covered by a specific commitment shall be allowed to supply the service in accordance with the terms of that commitment.
- The Agreement shall not prevent a Member from applying measures to regulate the entry of natural persons into, or their temporary stay in, its territory, including those measures necessary to protect the integrity of, and to ensure the orderly movement of natural persons across, its borders, provided that such measures are not applied in such a manner as to nullify or impair the benefits accruing to any Member under the terms of a specific commitment.[16]

Specific commitments on Mode 4 varied. Some preferences clearly emerged, however. Generally, countries were more comfortable with liberalizing admission of "persons linked to a commercial presence (e.g. intra-corporate transferees) and highly skilled persons (managers, executives and specialists)."[17] Other restrictions were clearly drawn from immigration policies: "defined duration of stay; quotas, including on the number or proportion of foreigners employed; 'economic needs tests' (a test that conditions market access upon the fulfilment of certain economic criteria) or 'labour market tests,' generally inscribed without any indication of the criteria of application; pre-employment conditions; residency and training requirements."[18] Although there was interest in moving beyond these agreements in the subsequent Doha round of negotiations,

---

[15] http://www.wto.org/english/thewto_e/whatis_e/tif_e/agrm6_e.htm.
[16] XXXV. Annex on Movement of Natural Persons Supplying Services Under the Agreement Available at http://www.wto.org/english/res_e/booksp_e/analytic_index_e/gats_03_e.htm#move.
[17] http://www.wto.org/english/tratop_e/serv_e/mouvement_persons_e/mouvement_persons_e.htm.
[18] http://www.wto.org/english/tratop_e/serv_e/mouvement_persons_e/mouvement_persons_e.htm.

TABLE 3.1. *Ratification of Core Human Rights Conventions*

No. of Ratifications	Name of Treaty
142	Convention on the Prevention and Punishment of the Crime of Genocide
145	Convention Relating to the Status of Refugees
175	International Convention on the Elimination of All Forms of Racial Discrimination
160	International Covenant on Economic, Social and Cultural Rights
167	International Covenant on Civil and Political Rights
187	Convention on the Elimination of All Forms of Discrimination against Women
150	Convention against Torture and Other Cruel, Inhuman or Degrading Treatment or Punishment
193	Convention on the Rights of the Child
46	International Convention on the Protection of the Rights of All Migrant Workers and Members of their Families
115	Convention on the Rights of Persons with Disabilities

little agreement was reached on further liberalization, especially with regard to providers of less-skilled services.

THE LABOR MIGRATION REGIME AT PRESENT

This chapter began with the observation that it would be difficult to characterize what exists today for the management of labor migration as a regime. As the chapter has shown, it is not for lack of trying to develop the norms, decision rules, and institutions that generally characterize a regime. Since the League of Nations established the ILO, and especially since the end of World War II, there have been repeated attempts to develop a binding normative framework that would set out the rights of migrant workers and the obligations of states toward them and each other. There is currently a significant set of conventions that apply to migrant workers and their families promulgated by the ILO and, more recently, the United Nations. Yet, these are among the least ratified of all major conventions. Table 3.1 shows that a minimum of 115 states have ratified the other major UN treaties. The smaller number for the disabilities convention is understandable because it has only been open for ratification since 2006.

The number of countries ratifying the ILO migrant workers conventions is not inconsistent with ratifications of other technical conventions, but approximately 175 countries have ratified what are termed "fundamental conventions," such as those that pertain to forced and child labor.

Financial support for migration-related activities within ILO is also well below that provided for other labor issues. In the budget for 2012–2013, the

ILO includes resources to accomplish its migration related goal: More migrant workers are protected and more migrant workers have access to productive employment and decent work. The agency requests $14.9 million in regular budgetary authority, plus $11.5 million in anticipated extra budgetary expenditures, up from $12.2 and $7.7 million in 2010 and 2011, respectively. The 2012–2013 request for migration compares to requests of $42 million in regular authority for activities related to social security, $39 million for occupational safety and health, and $25 million for working conditions within the same strategic objective: enhanced coverage and effectiveness of social protection for all. ILO's migration funding serves three purposes: "(1) upgrading the knowledge base; (2) strengthening services to Members, in particular through products that cut across relevant outcome areas and the Office's administrative boundaries; and (3) improving coordination and collaboration with major external agents" (ILO 2011).

States clearly view migrant workers and their families differently from comparable populations of potentially vulnerable populations – refugees, children, victims of torture or forced labor, persons with disabilities, or those discriminated against on the basis of race or gender. Of course, migrants fit into all of these categories and may be afforded protection as such, but when they are viewed merely as workers, they are seen as a matter of national rather than international policy importance. Governments are far from willing to cede any of their sovereignty when it comes to determining the appropriate admissions policies, treatment after entry, or deportation of migrant workers.

This is in sharp distinction from refugees, who have been afforded a high degree of international protection. As discussed in Chapter 2, refugees are essentially a threat to the nation-state system, in a way that labor migrants are not. Refugees are without protection of their home countries and often unwanted by their receiving countries – which makes them of concern to the international community. By contrast, labor migrants – without other justification – cannot claim that their home countries are unwilling or unable to protect them if they remained at home or returned. In fact, in the context of bilateral agreements, countries of origin generally are negotiating terms of admission and treatment on behalf of their citizens – thus, playing their role as responsible sovereign. Similarly, the receiving state retains the authority, indeed the responsibility, to determine who can enter its territory and the duration of stay. It may prefer to do so in a cooperative manner, but this will generally be for efficiency, not from any obligation to the country of origin or the migrant. For this reason and from an international relations perspective, there appears to be little motivation for states to intercede in these matters through conventions or other means.

Of course, the reality is much more complicated. Labor migrants often fall through the cracks of the nation-state system. They belong fully to neither their home nor their receiving state. Many destination countries do not afford even long-term migrants the opportunity to settle permanently and citizenship is totally beyond their grasp. Yet, the reasons that caused them to migrate in the first place may not permit their return home. The situation of migrant workers during conflicts in the past decade in Libya, Cote d'Ivoire, and Lebanon are cases that highlight the vulnerability of this group. Even when their home countries tried to evacuate them, the capacity to do so was often lacking and international assistance was essential to safely rescue the migrant workers.

Many labor migrants are indeed vulnerable populations unable to protect themselves during key stages of their migration experience – as they are leaving their countries, are in transit, or are foreign nationals in lands in which they have access to few legal or practical measures for protection of their rights or even their safety. These rights issues implicate at least two countries (source and destination), but often more depending on the transit route. Ensuring that their rights are upheld at each of these stages cannot be readily accomplished through unilateral policies alone.

Governments have ceded some of their authorities regarding vulnerable populations who never cross international borders – for example, the robust ratification of the Convention on the Rights of the Child. States that find it appropriate to agree to a set of international obligations to children could logically apply the same attention to migrant workers in their midst. What is often lacking is the political will to do so.

A major reason that international consensus on labor migration makes sense is that migrant workers are an essential part of the global economy – much as the movement of capital, goods, and services. Trade in services is often dependent on the ability of service providers to move freely from one country to another. There is general agreement that it is in every country's best interest to regulate the movement of capital and goods at the international level in order to ensure efficiency and to prevent unfair competition. The difficulties in negotiating agreement on movement of "natural persons" via Mode 4 of the General Agreement on Trade in Services indicates that governments have not fully embraced that logic when it comes to the movement of service providers. Governments are even less committed to the concept that liberalization of labor flows (i.e., labor migration) would be beneficial to all parties. The World Bank and other institutions are developing a body of research to prove the value of migration liberalization but it has not yet (and may never) become conventional wisdom.[19] Scholars have also been considering the nature of an organization that would complement the World Trade Organization and the International Monetary Fund – dubbed by economist Jagdish Bhagwati (2003) as the "World Migration Organization." Trachtman (2011) has advanced the concept by suggesting the features of such an organization. It would include a secretariat that would facilitate negotiations among nations in regards to liberalization of migration agreements and dispute resolution.

---

[19] Also see Pecaud and de Guchteneire (2007), which attempts to assess the extent to which greater freedom of movement would be desirable and feasible.

In the event that governments do agree on the wisdom of liberalization of labor movements on an economic basis, it is not clear that the general public would agree. After all, people are not tomatoes, to return to President Salinas' statement regarding NAFTA. Tomatoes (or dollars) do not care where they are moved and under what conditions, but people certainly do. And, it is not just the workers who care. So do the communities they leave and those that they enter. A regime on labor migration cannot make its agreements on a purely economic level (Pecoud and de Guchteneire 2007). It must also take into account the human costs and benefits of labor migration. We will return to this issue in the concluding chapter.

4

Orderly and Humane Migration Management

This chapter focuses on the International Organization for Migration (IOM), the successor to PICMME. A full chapter on IOM is warranted because the agency, although outside of the UN system, has the strongest capabilities to take on the range of activities needed if an international migration regime were to be adopted. The chapter discusses IOM's history and current role. The title is taken from its designated strategic mission "to facilitate the orderly and humane management of international migration" (IOM 2007).

IOM has 155 member states and 11 state observers, and operates in 470 field locations in more than 100 countries. The agency works in four broad areas of migration management that correspond to the agendas of many states: (1) migration and development; (2) facilitating migration; (3) regulating migration; and (4) addressing forced migration. IOM activities that intersect these areas include the promotion of international migration law, policy debate and guidance, protection of migrants' rights, migration health, and the gender dimension of migration. IOM provides a range of services related to building the capacity of states to manage migration, migrant health, migration and development, return assistance, and counter-trafficking. The organization also serves as secretariat to many regional consultation mechanisms and houses a light support structure for the Global Forum on Migration and Development.

What is not included in IOM's mission is an explicit mandate to protect the rights of migrants. That responsibility rests with states, most of which have not signed any of the international conventions related specifically to migrant worker rights. Yet, over the past sixty years, IOM has come to see protection falling within its mandate, although others might contest the extent of the agency's commitment to protection principles.

This chapter examines IOM's relationships with governments and with civil society. IOM is often described by state representatives as a lean, efficient organization that has greater capacity than the UN to respond quickly to the needs of states. The absence of a mandated obligation to protect migrant rights is actually seen as the organization's strength, although IOM itself argues that ensuring migrant rights is essential to effective migration management and is integral to its entire mission. Many civil society organizations in turn criticize IOM as yielding to the agenda of states, particularly wealthier destination countries, with too little regard for migrants.

IOM's current role in developing frameworks for international cooperation on migration is also discussed. The chapter explores its relationships with the other organizations that now make up the Global Migration Group, which was established in 2006 as a successor to the Geneva Migration Group, to help coordinate the work of the multiple organizations within and associated with the UN that have some responsibilities regarding migration. IOM's role as secretariat to numerous regional consultative mechanisms and its support for interstate dialogue on migration is also reviewed. The chapter concludes by assessing the prospects of IOM evolving into the institutional base for a new international migration regime. At the heart of the analysis is the extent to which the organization can balance the twin obligations discussed in the Introduction – to assist governments in managing migration while helping to protect the rights of the migrants.

COLD WAR ANTECEDENTS

As Cold War tensions heightened and Western governments, led by the United States, looked toward new institutional arrangements that would preclude communist countries from membership, discussion turned to a new migration organization. Toward the end of 1951, at the urging of the United States, the Belgian government hosted a conference in Brussels to discuss the successor to IRO's more operational activities, including the transport of displaced persons to their new home countries. As discussed, UNHCR was tasked with the legal protection of refugees, but it was given no resources or mandate to take on large-scale operations. The ILO's goal of developing an operational program in this area was thwarted by U.S. Congress' restrictions in funding organizations with communist member countries.

The Brussels conference was tasked with trying "to find some way of moving the large number of persons who remain homeless, dispossessed, and disinherited," as described by a contemporary observer ("Brussels Migration Conference" 1952). The framework for discussion, however, went well beyond the needs of refugees and displaced persons. An overarching theme was referred to as Europe's surplus population. This topic had already been discussed by the Council of Europe. A meeting of Experts on Refugees and Surplus Population, which included member states, ILO, IRO, UNHCR, the International Bank for Reconstruction and Development, and the U.S. State Department had gathered to discuss settlement in and outside Europe ("Council of Europe" 1953). It was agreed that some countries had too many workers and too few jobs, whereas others had a deficit of workers for the available employment. Matching willing workers with job prospects would be of benefit to both the source and the destination countries. In some cases, the surplus of workers seemed to be systemic, as in Italy and Greece, which had long exported labor. In other cases, countries were struggling with emergency conditions, such as the large numbers of ethnic German workers who had entered West Germany after the war and the Dutch citizens who had returned to the Netherlands after its colonies gained independence. In all of these cases, it was believed, the countries would not soon create enough jobs to employ all of those seeking financial security. The Council of Europe experts concluded that there were in Europe "some 4.5 million refugees who have neither finally nor temporarily been absorbed into the economy of their country of residence" and it estimated "that the surplus population in certain European countries amounts to several million workers" (Marks 1957). The situation of unemployed refugee youth was of particular concern ("Council of Europe" 1953). Attention was paid to the traditional immigration countries that sought to increase their populations – Canada, Australia, and New Zealand – as well as countries in Latin America and Africa that needed skilled workers to help them improve their economies.

The Brussels conference brought together representatives of twenty-three countries, which Edward O'Connor (1952), head of the U.S. Displaced Persons Commission, divided into four categories: (1) countries of emigration (e.g., Germany, Italy, Netherlands, Austria, and Greece); (2) countries of immigration (e.g., Canada, Australia, Brazil, Chile, and Bolivia); (3) interested countries (neither emigration nor immigration) that recognized the seriousness of the problem (e.g., France, Belgium, Switzerland, Turkey, and Luxembourg); and (4) the United States, which had agreed to fund much of the initial budget of any new organization. Some countries attended but had to defer their participation in the outcomes of the conference until their parliaments took action; the United Kingdom was in this category.

The conference reached agreement on a number of points, including the need for a new organization. First, the scope of the problem was larger than the "problem of refugees." Many of those who had interest in migrating and would be valued in a receiving country were citizens of the Western European countries in which they resided. Although some had been displaced earlier, their need to migrate did not stem from their experiences as refugees or displaced persons but rather from the economic difficulties of their home countries. The conferees did not underestimate the large number of refugees still in need of resettlement, but they understood that not only refugees would be in the migrant pool.

They also were wary of the terminology used previously in describing Europe's surplus population. As referenced by O'Connor (1952), the conferees believed that such terms as surplus population or overpopulation "might lead people to think this meant those who were misfits, or undesirables, or the unwanted." Not only would that make it more difficult to find immigration opportunities, but it would also obfuscate the true nature of the population: those with "useful talents and services to give but for whom there was no opportunity to contribute their full worth to society" (ibid.).

The conference focused primarily on migration for settlement in new countries (ibid.). This formulation raised the gap already developing in the international system; UNHCR focused on asylum and ILO on temporary labor migration, but there was no international body addressing the permanent relocation of migrants from one country to another. Since the focus was on settlement, the conferees framed the issues in terms of planning for relocation in a manner that would enhance the potential for integration into the new country. In the conferees' view, "Without such planning, the dangers to the welfare of the settlers, as well as to the economy of the receiving country, were apparent" (ibid.). Some of the immigration countries were less developed economically than others, so there was a need to build their capacity to successfully settle migrants. There was also a need to prepare the migrants for what they would experience in their new homes. Family union would play an important role in this type of immigration.

The conferees agreed that migration was not only a humanitarian gesture to help the unfortunate but also an economically shrewd policy to match supply of workers with the demand for their services. A French delegate in Brussels had noted: "one of the lessons to be learnt from our predecessors is that one of the greatest difficulties in the way of unified international action in this field is to find, in the midst of a welter of conflicting interests, a core of interests that are common to all, a common denominator for an international program" (quoted in Perruchoud 1989:504). The "desire to improve the lot of human beings," as the French delegate described it, would be one such common denominator, but the conferees also saw the economic benefits to emigration and immigration countries.

As a final decision, the conferees resolved to establish PICMME. Sixteen of the twenty-three participating countries approved the organization immediately and the others said they would consider membership in the near future. As participants such as O'Connor readily admitted, the new organization was intended to buttress the interests of the democracies that participated against the interests of the communist world. Only countries that believed in freedom of movement for their citizens could become members, which meant that communist governments that restricted departures could not join. This provision not only complied with the U.S. Congressional bar on funding of organizations that included communist members, but it also gave a sense of community to countries that had disparate histories and experiences with migration.

PICMME was a temporary measure until decisions could be made on a more lasting, although not necessarily permanent organization. Two acting directors were appointed to set up the new organization (Ducasse-Rogier 2001). At the fourth session of PICMME, October 13–21, 1952, the name was changed to the Intergovernmental Committee for European Migration (ICEM) and in November 1954, a constitution (which came in to force in February 1955) was adopted to provide greater stability to the organization. However, it was expected that ICEM would complete its work in three to five years (IO 1954).

ICEM was in some ways broader and in others narrower in its scope than the other principal migration organizations. The Brussels conference described the purpose of the organization:

> to make arrangements for the transport of migrants, for whom existing facilities are inadequate and who could not otherwise be moved, from certain European countries having surplus population to countries overseas which offer opportunities for orderly immigration, consistent with the policies of the countries concerned. (quoted in Perruchoud 1989)

Unlike UNHCR and the ILO, it would not focus on a specific category of migrants – refugees and labor migrants. Rather, its scope was broad enough to include all types of migrants, without regard to their purpose in moving to another country. However, the organization had a mandate to work only with European migrants.[1] The conferees in Brussels had agreed that the it would "engage itself solely in the overseas movement of people and that intra-European migration would be worked out by the countries concerned on a bilateral basis or some other agreed-upon method" (O'Connor 1952).

Perhaps the biggest difference between ICEM and the other organizations was that it was a state-led process apart from the UN and without the underpinnings of a convention or treaty. The governments that established the organization had no intent of adopting new rights frameworks, having debated and at least in the case of the United States decided against ratifying the 1951 Refugee Convention and the 1949 Migrant Worker Convention. ICEM was to serve state interests in carrying out migration-related activities that supported their national policies.

The ICEM constitution established a governance system that included a policy-making council of all members, an Executive Committee of nine member states, and a director-general and staff who would be headquartered in Geneva.

It is important to keep in mind that ICEM's activities were designed – at least at the beginning – to *expand* immigration opportunities. ICEM had a dual mission: to provide transport and logistical support for those migrants who had already been chosen for resettlement, and to help prepare the way for others to follow suit. As Perruchoud (1989) explains, "A further objective, explicitly stated, was to promote the increase of the volume of migration from Europe, by providing services which other international organizations were not in a position to supply."

---

[1] The Europeans could already be outside of Europe, as long as they could not return to Europe and could not readily remain where they were. For example, European refugees who had fled to China and later Hong Kong qualified for resettlement assistance.

Those services developed over time. During the meeting of the 1952 ICEM governing conference, members instructed "the committee to attempt to improve the selection and settlement services involved in the movement of migrants in the expectation that this would substantially speed up and increase movement" (IO 1953). The following year, the director-general of ICEM reported that provision had been made for training building laborers in Italy who would be migrating to Brazil. This was done in collaboration with the Brazilian and Italian governments and the ILO. In Greece, in collaboration with the UN Education, Social and Cultural Organization (UNESCO), a language training program for prospective migrants to Australia had been initiated. The director-general also reported that Brazil, Argentina, Chile, and Venezuela were making "definite progress" in the area of land resettlement (IO 1954).

Land resettlement was a new and controversial concept. ICEM was assisting countries, particularly in Latin America and Africa, to establish new settlements to receive immigrants. The idea was that these countries had "vast land tracts awaiting development" and "a continuing need for peripheral green belt" settlements to feed the rapidly growing cities (Marks 1957). In addition to the Latin American countries, ICEM experts had ascertained the interest of Costa Rica, Paraguay, and the Federation of Rhodesia and Nyasaland in developing such tracts. ICEM would assist in reviewing plans and surveys of areas proposed for settlement, assist governments in preparing the final project details, and provide advice on the selection of migrants (Marks 1957).

The main barrier, however, was finding the funds to establish the settlements. The ambivalence of the donors was clearly expressed by two U.S. delegates at the governing council in 1955. Francis E. Walter, who had been one of the cosponsors of the U.S. Immigration and Nationality Act of 1952, which had preserved national origins quotas, "reminded the meeting that ICEM was set up to find new areas of resettlement for European migrants. He expressed the hope that there would not be an increased dependence on the ability of the United States to absorb greater numbers of people" (IO 1955). On the other hand, George Warren, another U.S. delegate, "announced that the United States preferred a bilateral rather than a multilateral approach to the question of land settlement and that his government was not prepared to participate in an international financing fund for this purpose raised or disbursed by ICEM" (IO 1955). The United States might provide funding for technically sound projects on a bilateral basis, but not through ICEM.

Financing for its operations was a problem that went beyond the land resettlement projects. As early as 1953, the subcommittee on finance was reporting to the membership: "while contributions to administrative costs had been 'reasonably satisfactory,' those for operational costs had been less than hoped for, and that, combined with the delay in reimbursements for movements, this shortage had reached a point of endangering the cash position and the further operations of ICEM" (IO 1954). In early 1954, "a $2,600,000 budget deficit was reported to be threatening" (ibid.). The members set up a $3 million reserve fund of voluntary interest-free loans, but in 1955, the organization was still worried about a budget shortfall. In 1956, the director-general spoke of the ramifications of that year's shortfall: "It would be necessary for ICEM to reduce its grants for 1956 to voluntary agencies working in the field of migration; per capita grants would be diminished from $80 in 1955 to $35 for migrants to North America and $75 per migrant for other destinations" (IO 1956). Discussion also began about shifting at least some of the costs of transport from a grant to a loan that migrants would have to repay after settlement.

While struggling with finances, the new organization was already aware of the changing situation in Western Europe, where many of the region's economies had moved toward growth and high levels of employment. Whether the promotion of emigration to overseas locations continued to be a priority was the subject of debate at a conference in 1955 (IO 1956). Some attendees pointed out that there were still large numbers of Europeans without adequate employment, but others indicated that perhaps the three- to five-year timeframe for the organization had been appropriate. Then, in 1956, the need for large-scale resettlement of Hungarian refugees from Austria and Yugoslavia reminded the members that the situation in Europe remained unsettled. It also demonstrated the flexibility of ICEM to respond with UNHCR to refugee emergencies. Marks (1957) observed at the time: "As the influx of refugees swelled, ICEM virtually mortgaged its financial resources so that the flow out of Austria could continue without interruption. In the last six weeks of 1956 more than 80,000 Hungarian refugees were assisted in their westward trek. The figure reflects not only ICEM's effective marshalling of transport, but its equally effective enlistment of governments' cooperation in simplifying and otherwise speeding immigration formalities."

BROADENING THE MISSION AND MEMBERSHIP

Even with this capacity to respond to crises, European immigration to overseas locations would not be the principal focus of ICEM's activities for long. In the 1960s, many of the Italians, Greeks, and others who had been interested in permanently relocating abroad began participating instead in the temporary work programs implemented by their wealthier sister nations in Europe. In 1958, the ICEM council approved a pilot program for the vocational training center in Italy to train workers for both intra-European and overseas immigration (IO 1959). The following year, Belgium requested assistance in resettling Belgian citizens who had fled the fighting in the Congo. In 1961, U.S. delegate Francis Walker noted that "since the European refugee problem was considerably less critical and there was no longer a need for ICEM to 'siphon-off' western Europe's surplus population, the new task for the Committee should be to supply manpower to underdeveloped countries" (IO Summer 1961). Latin American countries emphasized their continuing need for immigrants.

A six-nation working group confirmed in a report to the council that ICEM should shift its focus to

> concentrate on providing needed assistance to Latin American countries in establishing the necessary infra-structure and facilities required for immigration, in planning and organizing group settlement and farm training projects, and by participating as an auxiliary agent in development projects administered by other agencies. (IO 1962)

At each of the council meetings, the issue of refugees continued to be on the agenda. The UNHCR made regular presentations that included the total number of refugees still remaining in Europe and a profile of their characteristics and needs. Over time, an increasing share of the refugees were disabled, until in 1962, the high commissioner reported that more than half of the 15,000 requesting resettlement "were handicapped refugees on whose behalf special efforts had to be made" (ibid.). At the same time, UNHCR reported its growing preoccupation with non-European refugees. The high commissioner reported to the ICEM council on the "urgent problem of new refugees elsewhere, particularly in North Africa, Togo, the Congo, and Tanganyika. He told the Council that he had just returned from Algeria where he had gone to help arrange the return of about 250,000 Algerian refugees" (ibid.).

Through the 1960s and 1970s, ICEM's role shifted from transporting immigrants from Europe to the traditional immigration countries to a broader mission to build capacity in both emigration and immigration countries. This work was enhanced by ICEM's participation, as a partner of UNHCR, in refugee crises around the globe. At the 1963 meeting of the council, ICEM's director-general proposed that the organization shift its focus to the following areas: (1) making the good offices and machinery of ICEM available in areas in which ICEM was not already operating; (2) establishing improved reception and placement services, especially in Latin America; (3) exploring the possibilities of making the fullest use of ICEM in carrying out governmental migration policies and programs; and (4) encouraging the settlement of European farmers in Latin America (IO 1964). A delegation of members of U.S. Congress, recognizing that a solution had been found for almost all displaced persons in Europe, nevertheless emphasized the need for ICEM to maintain a standby refugee resettlement capacity in case of a new emergency. This capacity helped ICEM resettle 40,000 Czechs displaced in 1968 after the Soviet invasion of their country.

By the end of the 1970s, it was clear that ICEM's mission was global, not European. In 1971, ICEM assisted UNHCR in the resettlement of 130,000 refugees from Bangladesh and Nepal to Pakistan; in 1972, it assisted in the evacuation and resettlement of Asians from Uganda; in 1973, a special resettlement program helped more than 31,000 Chileans resettle in fifty countries; and in 1975, ICEM launched its program to assist what would become the resettlement of more than 1 million Indochinese.

In 1979, the council gave formal recognition to this reality in a resolution "affirming 'that circumstances in the world today and for the foreseeable future will require ICEM to continue to provide its services on a global basis'" (quoted in Perruchoud 1989). In 1980, the council changed the name to the Intergovernmental Committee for Migration (ICM), dropping European although the resolution did not change the official name or the constitution. This shift was accompanied by a broadening of the membership so more countries that used or benefited from its services would join the organization. Also in the early 1980s, ICM launched new programs to assist countries in Africa and Asia to develop migration programs that would support their development. These programs were to attract highly skilled émigrés to return home temporarily or permanently to contribute what they had learned abroad to the building of their countries' economies, infrastructures, and governance.

In 1989, the metamorphosis to a global institution was completed when a new constitution went into force and the name was changed to its present formulation, the International Organization for Migration (IOM). The new constitution built on the resolutions of the Brussels conference and the constitution of 1953. Perruchoud (1989) describes five objectives of the new constitution:

> maintain the basic character, scope and organizational structure of ICM; recognize its global mandate and preserve its flexibility in carrying out its tasks; strengthen its basic humanitarian character and orientation; incorporate into the Constitution the substance of various resolutions approved by the Council in the course of the years; and reinforce the need for co-operation among international organizations on migration and refugee matters.

The constitution recognizes that "the provision of migration services at an international level is often required to ensure the orderly flow of migration movements throughout the world." The prologue further asserts "there is a need to promote the cooperation of States and international organizations with a view to facilitating the emigration of persons who desire to migrate to countries where they may achieve self-dependence through their employment and live with their families in dignity and self-respect." It recognizes the linkages between migration and the development of both receiving and origin states, and it acknowledges the need for cooperation and coordination among all parties (states, international organizations, and nongovernmental bodies) on migration and refugee matters. Particular attention is paid to research and consultation on the migration process and the specific situation and needs of migrants. The prologue ends by stating the need for the international financing of activities related to international migration.

Article 1 sets out the functions of the organization, specifying that IOM would make arrangement for the organized transfer of migrants and refugees, displaced persons, and other individuals when needed. IOM would also

> provide, at the request of and in agreement with the States concerned, migration services such as recruitment, selection, processing, language training, orientation

activities, medical examination, placement, activities facilitating reception and integration, advisory services on migration questions, and other assistance as in accord with the aims of the Organization.[2]

In a departure from the earlier focus on permanent settlement of immigrants, the new constitution included return migration; IOM would "provide similar services (as those listed above) as requested by States, or in cooperation with other interested international organizations, for voluntary return migration, including voluntary repatriation". The constitution also charged the organization with providing "a forum to States as well as international and other organizations for the exchange of views and experiences, and on the promotion of cooperation and coordination of efforts on international migration issues".

The principle of free movement of persons remains a condition of membership. After the Cold War and collapse of many communist regimes, recognition of the right of emigration was no longer a barrier in many countries. The basic governance system (council, Executive Committee, and director-general) remained in place, as did the headquarters in Geneva. The financing system also remained. The administrative part of the budget would be supported by cash contributions from member states in a proportional manner to be determined by the council and the member. The operational budget would be financed by voluntary contributions that could take the form of cash, in kind or in services from member states; other states; international organizations, governmental or non-governmental; other legal entities; or individuals. The donor may stipulate the terms and conditions for the use of the funds. Although its base of funding has broadened somewhat from earlier days, the budgetary situation remained very similar. The requirement that operational activities be funded through voluntary contributions had three major ramifications: (1) budget uncertainty, since it is not always clear if sufficient resources will be forthcoming to cover all of the activities that are needed; (2) a tendency to focus programs on areas or activities that are of interest to states, even if an objective analysis would question their priority; and (3) a high level of dependence on a few donors, especially the United States and EU countries, which often had their own interests and reasons to support certain types of programs. Louise Holborn's (1965) observation about UNRRA, IRO, and ICEM remained true for IOM in the years after the new constitution went into force: "the fact that certain countries seem to have preponderant influence in appointments and that the United States has provided the bulk of the money for the international administration and operations of these agencies does not make it easier to preserve a purely international atmosphere."

The financing mechanism and lack of an explicit protection mandate have also constrained IOM's ability to act independently of states or to criticize them

---

[2] All quotes from the IOM Constitution are from http://www.iom.int/cms/constitution.

if the protection needs of migrants called for such action. This puts IOM into sharp contrast with UNHCR, which is also dependent on states for financing but has a convention-based mandate to protect refugees. This gives UNHCR the authority to bring concerns about protection problems to the attention of states and, if the violations persist, even to the Security Council for corrective action. IOM does not have similar responsibility in the case of violations of migrant rights. It is primarily through its programs and field activities that IOM can contribute to the protection of migrants (IOM 2009).[3]

CURRENT ACTIVITIES OF IOM

In November 2007, IOM's council approved a new strategic focus for the organization. IOM's goal was summarized as follows: "to facilitate the orderly and humane management of international migration" (IOM 2007). Its member states encouraged the agency to maintain "its role as a leading global organization focusing on migration management" and "to address the migratory phenomenon from an integral and holistic perspective, including links to development, in order to maximize its benefits and minimize its negative effects" (ibid.).

To achieve that goal, IOM's member states set twelve strategic priorities, which would be carried out with the agreement of member states. These priorities are presented below, along with activities that IOM views as supportive of them (as reported in the 2010 Review of IOM's Strategy (IOM 2010b), presented to the council for consideration).[4]

1. **To provide secure, reliable, flexible and cost-effective services for persons who require international migration assistance.** This priority has been at the core of IOM's existence since its founding. "IOM's work under this Strategy point focuses on the provision of services to persons before, during and after the time of travel through its worldwide network of offices". The services are aimed at filling gaps in national programs and responses, and they include: application assistance, logistics and liaison duties, verification of documents, interviews and site visits, provision of country of origin information, the operation of visa application centers, DNA sampling and air transport, pre-migration information and

---

[3] This does not mean that serious violations of the rights of migrant workers do not get the attention of the Security Council. For example, Security Council Resolution 1973 (Available at http://daccess-dds-ny.un.org/doc/UNDOC/GEN/N11/268/39/PDF/N1126839.pdf?OpenElement) on Libya reiterated "its concern at the plight of refugees and foreign workers forced to flee the violence in the Libyan Arab Jamahiriya, welcoming the response of neighbouring States, in particular Tunisia and Egypt, to address the needs of those refugees and foreign workers, and calling on the international community to support those efforts."

[4] All quotes are taken from IOM 2010 found at https://www.iom.int/files/live/sites/iom/files/partnerships/docs/2010_IOM_Strategy_Review.pdf.

training about what is needed to succeed in the country of destination, health assessments, case processing, and arranging transport through agreements with a global network of air transport providers.

2. **To enhance the humane and orderly management of migration and the effective respect for the human rights of migrants in accordance with international law.** In addition to the services discussed above, IOM reports that it frequently responds to government requests for assistance in developing legislation and policies that are consistent with international norms and standards regarding the rights of migrants. It also provides training and capacity building regarding international migration law. The organization recognizes that it does not have a formal protection mandate but reports focusing on "practical, problem-solving approaches to ensure full respect for the human rights of migrants." In addition, the report describes the de facto protection offered by its operational activities in emergencies (providing life-saving interventions such as shelter, non-food items, health assistance), on behalf of trafficking victims, and in resettlement of vulnerable population. IOM also issues guidelines and standard operating procedures to address gender, age, and culture issues that may impede effective protection.

3. **To offer expert advice, research, technical cooperation and operational assistance** to states, intergovernmental, and non-governmental organizations and other stakeholders, in order to build national capacities and facilitate international, regional, and bilateral cooperation on migration matters. The report references advisory services, including the Capacity-Building in Migration Management Program, as an example of the type of technical assistance it provides to states. The project aims to improve border management, administrative, policy and legal frameworks. Often operating in coordination with other international organizations, IOM has helped establish regional centers such as the African Capacity-Building Center in Tanzania.

4. **To contribute to the economic and social development of States** through research, dialogue, design, and implementation of migration-related programs aimed at maximizing migration's benefits. The report emphasizes the need to focus on value-added programs since the interconnections between migration and development are areas of interest among numerous organizations. IOM's activities fall into two areas: supporting interstate dialogue and cooperation to enhance the positive potential of migration for development; and supporting and implementing practical steps to reduce migration pressures, enhance the development potential of migration, and help ensure that migration remains a choice for individuals and communities. More specifically, IOM points to the Migration for Development in Africa program and IOM's leadership in developing an inter-agency *Handbook on Mainstreaming Migration into Development Planning.*

5. **To support States, migrants and communities in addressing the challenges of irregular migration,** including research and analysis into root causes, sharing information and spreading best practices, as well as facilitating development-focused solutions. These activities overlap with its work to reduce human smuggling and trafficking (see 11). They include research on the causes and consequences of irregular migration; analysis of smuggling routes; and promotion of irregular migrants' access to basic health care, as a matter of good public health.

6. **To be a primary reference point for migration information, research, best practices, data collection, compatibility and sharing.** IOM conducts and commissions research to guide and inform migration policy and practice. It undertakes these activities in cooperation with academic research institutes (including the center that the author directs at Georgetown University) and think tanks. It supports publication of the peer-reviewed academic journal *International Migration* as a platform for policy relevant studies. IOM produces a biennial *World Migration Report* as well as a migration policy series of working papers. IOM is also greatly involved in the development of migration profiles for developing countries that need information and data on emigration and immigration patterns that affect their nation. In addition, it maintains a Global Human Trafficking Database.

7. **To promote, facilitate and support regional and global debate and dialogue on migration, including through the International Dialogue on Migration,** so as to advance understanding of the opportunities and challenges it presents, the identification and development of effective policies for addressing those challenges and to identify comprehensive approaches and measures for advancing international cooperation. IOM's convening power has expanded over the past sixty years, particularly through institution of the annual International Dialogue on Migration (IDM). IDM provides an opportunity for governments and observers to meet informally to discuss cutting-edge issues. The dialogue includes two workshops at which experts from government, international organizations, NGOs, the private sector, and academia exchange information and perspectives. There is also a concluding debate that coincides with the annual meeting of IOM's decision-making council. IOM provides secretariat services for a number of regional consultative processes, informal gatherings of governments within the same region or cross regions with interest in the same issues. IOM also assists the Global Forum on Migration and Development (GFMD) (discussed in greater detail in Chapter 8), by seconding staff to the governments preparing the sessions of the GFMD and hosting an independent support unit for the GFMD chair.

8. **To assist States to facilitate the integration of migrants in their new environment and to engage diasporas, including them as development partners.** This role is also a long-standing one for the organization,

consistent with its early promotion of permanent settlement but now applied to all migrants. The focus is to promote better understanding among host communities of the situation of migrants, enhance the capacity of migrants to adapt, and promote "harmonious coexistence between migrants and host communities." IOM has produced a compendium of migrant integration policies and practices. Operationally, it has recently implemented forty migrant integration projects, including language training and education programs. With regard to diaspora engagement, IOM promotes return of qualified nationals for permanent or temporary purposes within the context of such programs as Migration for Development in Africa. It gives special attention to medical personnel who wish to contribute to the development of the health sectors in their home countries. The agency also supports initiatives to build the capacity of diaspora organizations, including through workshops to develop the leadership of migrant women within the diaspora.

9. **To participate in coordinated humanitarian responses in the context of inter-agency arrangements in this field** and to provide migration services in other emergency or post-crisis situations as appropriate and relating to the needs of individuals, thereby contributing to their protection. IOM's activities in this area have grown substantially over the years, to the point that they now are among the largest and most well-funded programs within the organization. IOM has sought to fill gaps in the international system, particularly with regard to assistance to persons internally displaced by natural disasters. At the time of the report (2010), IOM had implemented 517 projects in this area, including 203 directly related to emergency responses and 314 to recovery, mitigation, and preparedness activities. IOM has played an important role in international responses to the May 2008 cyclone in Myanmar (Burma) and to the earthquake in Haiti and the floods in Pakistan in 2010. Within the context of the cluster approach described in Chapter 2, IOM has responsibility for camp coordination and camp management in cases of internal displacement from natural disasters. This responsibility can continue for many years, as witnessed by IOM's role in camp management in Haiti at the time of this writing (June 2012), two and a half years after the earthquake. IOM participates in other clusters, including shelter, health, protection, early recovery, and logistics.

10. **To undertake programs which facilitate the voluntary return and reintegration of refugees, displaced persons, migrants and other individuals** in need of international migration services, in cooperation with other relevant international organizations as appropriate, and taking into account the needs and concerns of local communities. Although not an original part of its mission, IOM has been involved in return programs for more than thirty years. This is also one of the most controversial parts of its operations since human rights groups often criticize the

agency for assisting governments in what they deem as involuntary return because the migrant's choice is between long-term detention or repatriation (Human Rights Watch 2007). As of 2010, IOM was implementing about eighty return programs, mainly from Europe, and since the implementation of the strategy in 2007, had helped return 80,000 migrants to 160 countries. The projects include individualized counseling, particularly for vulnerable groups such as unaccompanied minors, trafficking victims, and people with specific medical needs. The aim is sustainable return.

11. **To assist States in the development and delivery of programs, studies and technical expertise on combating migrant smuggling and trafficking in persons,** in particular women and children, in a manner consistent with international law. This is one of the most operational of IOM's activities, along with its role in camp management during disasters. The aim of some of the programs is to prevent trafficking through information campaigns and other educational processes and inform would-be migrants of safe migration alternatives. Other programs provide safe accommodation, medical, psychosocial, and legal support to trafficking survivors. Assisted return programs, which include training and assistance with establishment of small businesses, is a further area of activity. IOM also provides emergency humanitarian assistance to victims of trafficking in Africa, Asia, and Latin America. A final set of activities offer technical assistance to states to help them improve trafficking and smuggling legal frameworks and increase their administrative capacity to address these issues.

12. **To support the efforts of States in the area of labor migration, in particular short-term movements, and other types of circular migration.** The focus on temporary labor migration is a departure from the origins of IOM but consistent with state interest in circular migration, which both source and receiving countries see as beneficial. Source countries prefer that migrants bring skills and financial resources home to support new economic endeavors while destination countries want to fill labor demand without worrying about long-term integration of migrants. It is questionable whether the reality of temporary labor programs meets this desire, as the experience of the European guest worker programs attests. The old adage that there is nothing as permanent as a temporary worker is still familiar to many migration experts. Nevertheless, the aim of IOM's final strategic focus is to "provide project development and technical and strategic policy support to governments, civil society and private sector stakeholders ... to facilitate the formulation and implementation of labor migration policies and programs that optimize the developmental benefits of migration for both countries of origin and destination." Some of the IOM activities in this regard are undertaken with ILO, including development of a *Handbook on Establishing Effective Labour Migration Policies*.

The strategies outlined in the 2007 resolution and confirmed in the 2010 review show both consistency and change in IOM's mission. The main consistency has been in its focus on facilitation of orderly migration, which it has been doing for sixty years. Many of the specific actions, in terms of research, technical assistance, and training programs have been part of the IOM arsenal since its beginnings. So too have been the programs to facilitate the integration of migrants, an area in which the organization appears to have been more willing to innovate in earlier years. The commitment in the 1950s to supporting the establishment of new settlements for migrants in Latin America and elsewhere does not have equivalence today.

The organization's deference to the sovereign right of states to manage their migration policies remains a consistent focus though the broadening of its membership and the transformation of European states from supplicants seeking emigration opportunities to principal donors and receivers of migrants has caused the organization to redirect some of its attention. Certainly, the current focus on short-term movements and circular migration marks the growing dominance of countries without the history or tradition of permanent immigration that characterized the United States, Canada, Australia, and the principal immigration countries of South America.

IOM's work on capacity-building, research, and policy development in managing migration has taken new form in recent years. As discussed, early in its existence, the organization helped Latin American states develop their capacities to receive new immigrants. This work generally did not focus on broader issues of migration management – what types of policies states should consider as they set up their immigration or emigration policies. The activities were more operational in terms of helping states devise ways to best prepare migrants for emigration or adaptation to their new environments. In recent years, IOM's focus on migration policy has grown. The IDM was initiated at the fiftieth anniversary session of the IOM council in 2001. Until then, IOM organized such consultative events only on an ad hoc basis. IOM's support for regional consultative bodies and the GFMD has also grown, as has its research activities on behalf of greater policy coherence.

IOM has not, however, institutionalized its policy-related functions, in the way its migration management and emergency operations activities are organized as significant departments within the organization. Policy and research is subsumed within the Department of International Cooperation and Partnerships. By contrast, in UNHCR, the Policy Development Office reports directly to the high commissioner, with its evaluation component reporting to the deputy high commissioner. Although the organizational structure alone would not constrain the development of the policy function, the way in which IOM conceptualizes it is more telling. Much of what is described as policy work pertains to the organization's role in organizing the IDM and supporting state-owned consultations. There has been relatively little in-depth analysis of policy alternatives that states should consider adopting or policy approaches that IOM should adopt for its own initiatives.

More recently, however, as a result of structural changes adopted in 2009, steps are being taken to develop evidence-based policies for IOM's own use and that of its member states. The departments responsible for migration management services and operations and emergency have taken on new responsibilities in this area. An early example is the development of the Migration Crisis Operational Framework. The process began with compilation of lessons learned and research undertaken in situations in which migrants needed to be evacuated from countries experiencing conflicts and acute natural hazards. Under the leadership of the operations and emergency department, the operational framework was developed, discussed with key stakeholders (including during the 2012 IDM and the IOM-Civil Society consultations), then presented to the standing committee and finally endorsed by the council.

The evaluation component of IOM, although improving, has also been weak in relationship to the size of the organization's budget and the complexity of its programs. The evaluation unit is part of the inspector general's office, which is also responsible for audits. The office has been issuing approximately two internal evaluations per year. Another half-dozen or so external evaluations, often in combination with donors, are completed each year. These are generally programmatic evaluations, not policy or strategic ones. More recently, IOM has engaged external evaluators to address broader themes, such as the organization's response to the Libya crisis and its efforts to combat human trafficking. Evaluation results have not been posted on the internet but are available by request.

Another strategic function that is undergoing change pertains to migrant health services, although these are not listed separately in the strategy document. IOM has long taken leadership in the area of migrant and travel health. From its beginnings, the organization has conducted health examinations for millions of refugees and migrants seeking to move to other countries. The assessments aim to "reduce and better manage the public health impact of population mobility on the host communities of receiving countries, to facilitate the integration of migrants into host communities through the detection and management of health conditions in a cost-effective manner, and to provide information on the medical conditions of migrants" (IOM Health 2010a:47). In 2010 alone, IOM conducted more than 160,000 health assessments. Most were conducted on behalf of the U.S., UK, Canadian, Australian, and New Zealand governments. IOM spent about $43 million in 2010 on these activities. The examinations focus on communicable diseases such as tuberculosis but also identify migrants with HIV/AIDS and common diseases of migrants, including malaria and parasitic diseases, which could hamper their integration.

In recent years, IOM's focus has considerably broadened from these assessments. Its migrant health division notes "as new global migration health challenges emerged, IOM's work evolved accordingly. Currently, new IOM health programs aim to respond to a wide range of health challenges in different migration and displacement contexts" (ibid.). Its principal objectives are to ensure the migrants' right to health care; to avoid disparities in health status and morbidity among migrant populations; to reduce excess mortality and morbidity among migrant populations; and to minimize the health risks of migration (ibid.). The activities in support of these objectives fall into two main categories. First, IOM undertakes projects aimed at health promotion and assistance for migrants. These include technical assistance to governments in the establishment of migrant-friendly health systems; advocating for health policies and programs that take into account the needs of migrants; and strengthening partnerships in support of such policies and programs (ibid.). Particular focus is given to the development of policies for appropriate mental health and psychosocial support and HIV/AIDS prevention and treatment. Both of these require special attention to the vulnerability of migrants and refugees during all phases of their migration experience, including recognition of the risk of rape that many women face in transit or at their destination. Capacity-building for government health agencies is a major component of this work. Some of this work is supported by the IOM Development Fund (formerly the 1035 Facility) which allocates resources to helping developing countries and those with economies in transition (i.e., from centrally planned to market economies) to build their governance systems. Total funding for health promotion and assistance activities was $14.2 million in 2010.

A growing area of IOM's expanded health focus relates to its work in crisis situations. Until 2003, less than $500,000 of its funds was spent on health assistance for crisis-affected populations. The level of spending is still modest in a billion-dollar organization, but has averaged $6–9 million per year more recently. The services include primary health care provision and community health revitalization; medical evacuation and health rehabilitation; travel health assistance; and health referrals, facilitated hospital discharge, and assisted returns. These activities are linked with programs to provide clean water and sanitation during crises, as well as those aimed at rebuilding health-care infrastructure in post-crisis situations.

The health activities are just a small part of IOM's operational role in humanitarian emergencies. Perhaps the biggest point of departure for IOM is its operational activities in these situations. These go well beyond the organization's traditional role working with UNHCR in helping refugees return or repatriate (which it has always done). An increasingly large part of IOM's budget is now focused on providing humanitarian assistance, mainly but not solely to internally displaced victims of natural disasters. The chronology of events that IOM has posted on its website demonstrates this shift. During the 1990s, most of the emergency operations were within its early role of helping vulnerable migrants and refugees relocate from danger[5]:

---

[5] http://www.iom.int/jahia/Jahia/about-iom/history/1990s.

1990   Repatriated migrants stranded in the Middle East following the invasion of Kuwait by Iraq

1991   Assisted in the return of some 800,000 displaced Iraqi Kurds

1992   Provided logistical support and medical assistance to the displaced populations in former Yugoslavia

1993   Following the signing of the Mozambican peace agreement, organized the return of almost 500,000 displaced persons, demobilized soldiers, and vulnerable groups amongst the internally displaced and refugees.

1994   Assisted in the return of 1.2 million Rwandans from neighbouring countries and in the relocation of some 250,000 refugees inside former Zaire.

1995   Following the outbreak of war in Chechnya, IOM evacuated almost 50,000 vulnerable people to safety in Ingushetia and Daghestan

1996   Evacuates Kurdish populations from northern Iraq

1998   Provided shelter assistance to Hondurans left homeless by Hurricane Mitch.

1999   Organized the Humanitarian Evacuation Program airlifting some 80,000 Kosovar refugees

By the twenty-first century, however, the shift toward an operational role in internal displacement, especially from natural disasters escalates[6]:

2001   Road convoys delivered thousands of blankets and other non-food items from neighbouring countries to help internally displaced Afghans. In India, built shelters for the victims of the Gujarat earthquake

2002   Coordinated assistance to internally displaced Afghans in camps in the north and west of the country

2004   Set up operations in the Darfur region to assist IDPs

2005   Launched its largest ever emergency response following the December 26 Indian Ocean tsunami. Major logistics, emergency shelter and medical and other programs are launched in Indonesia's Aceh province, Sri Lanka and on Thailand's Andaman coast

      Asked by the Inter-Agency Standing Committee (IASC) to become the coordinating agency for emergency shelter in Pakistan-administered Kashmir and Pakistan's Northwest Frontier province [following the Pakistan earthquake]

2006   Extended logistical support and camp management expertise to relief efforts in the wake of the Yogyakarta earthquake in Indonesia, the conflict in Timor-Leste, and Typhoon Durian in the Philippines.

2007   Provided emergency aid to populations affected by Tropical Storm Noel in Haiti and the Dominican Republic, and to those displaced by other natural disasters in Angola, Ethiopia, Ghana, Mozambique, Sudan, Uganda, Mexico, Peru, Pakistan, Afghanistan and Indonesia.

---

[6] http://www.iom.int/jahia/Jahia/about-iom/history/21st-century.

2008 Responded to Cyclone Nargis in Myanmar, which affected 2.4 million people and left 140,000 dead or missing
2009 Provided shelter and non-food assistance to some 180,000 people displaced by fighting in Pakistan
2010 Rushed to Haiti's aid in response to the January earthquake which leaves over 200,000 dead and 1.9 million homeless
Responded to one of the worst floods in history to hit Pakistan, which damaged 1.7 million houses and left 11 million people homeless.

Emergency work dominates the chronology, but other activities are included. In some years, the number of refugees resettled, participation in key events, or the launching of new programs such as a new consumer campaign to raise public awareness of human trafficking merit inclusion. A running total of the millions of migrants directly assisted by IOM has not been updated since 2005, when it reached a total of 13 million. Previously approximately 1 million were added to the count every two to three years.

The shift toward emergency operations is reflected in the budget as well. In 2011, projects related to emergency and post-conflict situations accounted for $774 million of IOM's $ 1.27 billion expenditures. This contrasts with the $246 million spent on projects related to regulating migration, the next largest category of costs. These projects concentrated on return migration, border management, and human trafficking. Projects aimed at facilitating migration – labor migration and migrant processing and integration – received only $54 million, although many of the activities under migrant health ($73.3 million) and migration and development ($106.3 million) may well have supported that purpose.

IOM is dependent on voluntary contributions from governments; hence its budgets and expenditure reflect government priorities. The organization has reasons of its own to seek and accept funding for emergency operations. First, and most important, it is filling a gap in the international response system that other agencies have been much slower to close. IOM assumed responsibility for managing camps for IDPs in Afghanistan in 2001, prior to the post–September 11 intervention, only after UNHCR had determined that it had no mandate to respond to those displaced by drought as well as the ongoing instability in the country. UNHCR has since accepted responsibility for camp management and protection in cases of conflict. IOM continues as the lead for camp management in natural disasters but the gap in providing effective protection for those displaced by natural disasters remains, as will be discussed in Chapter 7.

Second, IOM has great flexibility to respond to new challenges. This is partly due to the nature of its constitution. At first glance, programs for IDPs should have been outside of the organization's mission. The constitution does not explicitly address the issue of internal migration, although most of the language in the preamble and the purposes and functions of the organization does refer to international migration. The term "displaced persons" is used in the context of its 1953 origins when it referred to those displaced across borders from the fighting and political instability during and after World War II. The term was used to describe a category similar to refugees, who by 1953 had a legal status based on a well-founded fear of persecution. On the other hand, the constitution does not restrict the organization's activities by defining in specific terms the categories of migrants of concern. IOM had the flexibility to assume new tasks without any restriction of its activities to international migrants, and no convention to define its mandate.

The emergency operations for IDPs are actually less of a mission stretch than some of the organization's other activities. In 2000, IOM assumed responsibility for administering several funds that had been allocated as reparations for abuses occurring as early as the Nazi era. One program settled claims with the victims of Germany's forced labor policies. IOM's "main responsibilities are to spread information and reach out to all potential claimants, to receive, process and review applications for compensation, to disburse compensation payments to successful applicants and to support the appeals processes for all categories of claims received under this program."[7] The IOM project Technical Assistance to the Administrative Reparation Program in Colombia aims to support the Colombian government in carrying out its Administrative Reparation Program, an initiative seeking to compensate victims of violence inflicted by illegal armed groups.[8] The program also focuses on land and property claims. With funding from the German government and the UN Peacebuilding Commission, IOM also supports the Sierra Leone Reparations Program.[9] Although all of these are laudable programs that benefit many victims of violence and abuse, the tie to IOM's migration mission is tenuous. IOM's explanation refers to the connection between reparations and establishing the conditions for return to post-conflict programs, but the German forced labor reparation program was implemented forty-five years after the end of World War II.

A third factor in moving IOM toward greater focus on emergency operations is its financing system. Almost all of IOM's funding is project driven. The organization has little of the unrestricted funding that UNHCR receives in support of its broad mission to assist and protect refugees. The dependence on project funding lessens IOM's ability to respond to many of the needs it identifies in the migration area. For example, the agency requested funding to help Congolese migrants who were deported from Angola in a series of sometimes brutal return programs. Donors did not step forward to finance the assistance to these migrants who were returning to some of the poorest areas of a country that has been locked in conflict and political insecurity for decades.

---

[7] http://www.iom.int/jahia/Jahia/activities/by-theme/claims-programmes/forced-labour-compensation-programme.

[8] http://www.iom.int/jahia/Jahia/activities/facilitating-access-to-reparation-for-victims-of-illegal-armed-groups-in-colombia.

[9] http://www.iom.int/jahia/Jahia/activities/support-for-the-sierra-leone-reparations-programme.

IOM has a standard overhead rate of 5 percent on project funds, which are used to support activities that are of more general interest. These include research, policy analysis, and the convening of conferences and workshops to discuss future trends in migration policy and programs. A portion of the overhead also goes to the IOM Development Fund. In practice, IOM's ability to help governments forge new consensus on migration policies has become highly dependent on its capacity to expand its operations into emergencies that receive more public attention and larger government resources.

IOM AND THE UNITED NATIONS

IOM was created as the state-owned alternative to existing multilateral organizations established to address refugee and labor migration issues. It was more explicitly an instrument of Western foreign policy than the other organizations. The United States dominated its budget and priorities far more than was the case with UNHCR and ILO. Nevertheless, the organization worked closely with UNHCR and, to a lesser degree, with ILO, from the start. As IOM's membership grew, and the Cold War origins diminished, the organization worked with the UN agencies even more closely. A fundamental question today is whether IOM should join the UN, and, if so, what form its affiliation should take.

Examining IOM's past and current interactions with the UN is a useful starting point for assessing the advantages and disadvantages of a closer relationship. The most important relationship since its founding has been with UNHCR. In his study of the cooperation between IOM and UNHCR, Elie (2010) points out that "on the whole, the mandates of the two institutions were designed to be complementary, creating potential grounds for cooperation." As discussed, IOM inherited the operational role of the IRO while UNHCR had the legal and protection role. IOM's mission was broader than UNHCR's but complemented the other institution's aim to find solutions for refugees with its capacity to facilitate their resettlement. Although there were initial tensions between the two organizations, as laid out by Elie (2010), both recognized the need to work together. For example, the two organizations had a joint office in Hong Kong to arrange the resettlement of European refugees. UNHCR issued travel documents and dealt with legal protection problems and provided for refugees' care and maintenance during their time in Hong Kong, while IOM (then ICEM) was responsible for their resettlement processing and arrangements for their transport. From the time of the Hungarian refugee crisis, when the Austrian government asked UNHCR to direct the emergency operation, IOM has been part of whichever coordination group has been established to address resettlement responsibilities. For its part, IOM has had the flexibility to assume responsibility for groups that did not come under the UNHCR mandate.

In more recent times, IOM and UNHCR have operated under a memorandum of understanding (MOU) signed in 1997. The aim of the MOU was "facilitating systematic, predictable, cooperative action between the two organizations. It seeks to build on the recognized expertise of each organization and to establish operational modalities of cooperation."[10] The MOU covers activities carried out on behalf of refugees, migrants, asylum seekers (including those whose cases were rejected), returnees, and IDPs. It also includes local populations affected by the presence of refugees, internally displaced persons, and returnees. It recognizes that UNHCR has primary responsibility for refugees, defined broadly to include "people outside of their own countries for reasons of feared persecution, armed conflict, generalized violence, foreign aggression or other circumstances which have seriously disturbed public order and, who, as a result, require international protection." IOM, in this context, was recognized to have a mandate to ensure orderly processing of migrants, including refugees. UNHCR's mandate extends to asylum-seekers whose claims have not yet been determined by relevant authorities, but the MOU expresses a joint willingness to assist governments with rejected asylum seekers provided the returns are carried out in a way that is consistent with humanitarian principles of both organizations. The MOU specifies that return should be seen as being primarily a bilateral matter between the countries of destination and origin. UNHCR's mandate also extends to returnees, predicated on substantive involvement to ensure that it takes place in conditions of safety and dignity. The duration and scope of UNHCR's activities will vary depending on the specifics of each situation. IOM has responsibility for providing migration services in support of repatriation.

The MOU recognizes that IOM has the principal responsibility for other migrants given its constitution's commitment to the principle that humane and orderly migration benefits migrants and society. UNHCR's interest arises from the recognition "that there can be links between involuntary displacement and many migratory movements." The MOU indicates that IOM has interest in a broad range of IDPs, including those uprooted by armed conflict, widespread violence, natural disasters, and human rights violations, largely "in view of the close interdependence between the problems of internal migration and those of international migration." By contrast, UNHCR's involvement is selective, generally applying only to those who would be classified as refugees had they crossed an international border. IOM and UNHCR will coordinate with each other to ensure complementarity of activities for local affected populations, focusing on groups living in areas directly affected by each organization's target populations of concern.

Two areas in which the organizations frequently collaborate concern mixed migration flows and the evacuation of migrant workers during humanitarian

---

[10] All quotes from the Memorandum of Understanding between UNHCR and IOM are found at http://www.refworld.org/docid/3ae6b31a70.html.

crises. Mixed migration occurs in two ways. First, bona fide refugees and migrants seeking work may be smuggled together. Determining who requires international protection and who might be an irregular migrant can be very difficult in such circumstances, particularly if they are all coming from unstable countries or regions. Second, the same individuals may have mixed motives in migrating – having left their countries to escape serious harm but choosing a destination based on economic opportunities and family ties. The UNHCR-IOM agreement implicitly recognizes the complexity of these situations. The agreement emphasizes the need to ensure that asylum seekers have the opportunity to present their claims for asylum and exhaust all avenues of appeal before being subject to removal. It also affirms that returns are "not only part of a viable migration policy but can contribute to maintaining the institution of asylum." Working together, the organizations can share the information needed to ensure that refugee principles are upheld and humane actions are taken to assist and protect those in need.

The need to evacuate migrant workers caught in crises has been a recurrent issue since it gained international attention after the Iraqi invasion of Kuwait and the resulting Gulf War. More recently, evacuations have taken place from Cote d'Ivoire as a result of civil conflict and from Libya during the airstrikes against the Qaddafi regime. In all of these cases, the evacuations took place in the context of large movements of refugees and IDPs. In the case of Libya, the political insecurity in North Africa more generally allowed an increase in irregular migration from sub-Saharan Africa, via Libya and Tunisia, toward Europe. The largest movements out of Libya were across the borders into Tunisia and Egypt, with nationals of those countries forming a large contingent of the migrant workers seeking safety. In their midst, however, were non-nationals from countries around the globe. There was also egress southward toward Niger and Chad. Among those at risk were refugees from third countries who had registered with UNHCR in Libya and asylum seekers who had been returned from Europe to Libya as part of a readmission agreement and detained in camps in Libya. Early in the crisis, UNHCR and IOM estimated that there were 8,000 Palestinian, Iraqi, Sudanese, Ethiopian, Somali, and Eritrean refugees registered with UNHCR in Libya. More than 3,000 more were seeking asylum. In addition, there were an estimated 1.5 million irregular migrant workers in Libya from Africa and Asia (UNHCR 2011). An estimated 500,000 people were internally displaced, often in areas beyond the reach of international agencies due to fighting and the government's intransigence.

By all accounts, the cooperation between UNHCR and IOM was exemplary. They formed the Humanitarian Evacuation Cell (HEC) early in the crisis. The HEC operated as a single unit, with a clear management structure. UNHCR raised funds for assisting Libyan refugees, third country refugees and asylum seekers, and IDPs while IOM sought funding for migrant workers who needed to be evacuated directly from Libya or one of the neighboring countries. By November, almost 800,000 migrants (not counting Libyans) had crossed the border or been evacuated directly from Libya, almost all going through Tunisia, Egypt, Algeria, Niger, and Chad. Of these, 216,021 third country nationals (that is, not nationals of the neighboring country itself) received transportation assistance by IOM and its partners via a combination of charter and commercial flights and land and sea vessels (IOM Middle East and North Africa Operations 2011). Some forty-five countries asked for IOM's help in evacuating, returning, and/or helping their citizens to reintegrate. The agencies also worked together to make sure the mixed migration flows to Europe – a small but highly visible portion of the total numbers – were treated in accordance with international standards, as defined in the MOU. These efforts were undertaken in the context of EU fears of a mass exodus and unwillingness to invoke special authorities to provide temporary protection to those fleeing North Africa.

While Libya was in turmoil, the two agencies were faced with a much less visible emergency in Cote d'Ivoire, where the civil war escalated and thousands were displaced. As in Libya, the displacement included a mixture of Ivoirian refugees and migrant workers from surrounding countries. IOM estimated that "Before the crisis in Ivory Coast, an estimated 40,000 Mauritanians were living and working in the country. The Malian ambassador to Abidjan also reported to IOM that about 20,000 Malian nationals required evacuation assistance. IOM estimates that at least 100,000 stranded migrants in Ivory Coast will need assistance".[11] Unlike the Libyan crisis, relatively little international attention was paid to the situation. IOM requested $41.6 million in March to carry out a range of operations including assisting IDPs, third country nationals, and stranded migrants in Cote d'Ivoire. As of September 2011, when conditions had stabilized in Cote d'Ivoire, it had received only 10 percent of the requested funding. UNHCR in turn had lead responsibility for protection of internally displaced and Ivoirian refugees in Liberia and other West African countries.[12] In contrast, IOM reported donations of $105 million during the same period for the migration crisis in Libya. Although the numbers of migrants needing assistance from the conflict in Libya were admittedly larger, the difference in scale was not of the same magnitude as the differential in support from international donors.

Responsibility for stranded migrants remains an area of international law and practice that is evolving but still highly dependent on foreign policy interests and media attention. Peter Sutherland, the Secretary General's Representative on Migration and Development, has called this issue to the attention of member states. Clearly, the country of origin has the principal responsibility to evacuate and protect its citizens in cases of conflict and natural disasters, but often the home country is unable or unwilling to fulfill its obligations. Many origin

---

[11] Quote found at http://www.iom.int/jahia/Jahia/media/press-briefing-notes/pbnAF/cache/offonce/lang/en?entryId=29543.

[12] Funding for UNHCR's work on behalf of refugees and IDPs was more generous. UNHCR's revised budget for its programs for 2011 was $47 million.

countries are poor and dependent on the remittances that migrants send home. Reintegrating them is a difficult challenge. Arguably, the Guiding Principles on Internal Displacement, referring not only to citizens but to those who leave their habitual residence, would apply to migrants, but countries in crises are often unable or unwilling to protect their citizens, let alone foreign nationals in their midst. It is questionable whether temporary workers would even be defined as habitual residents, especially in countries that see migrants as "guests" rather than permanent residents. Given these gaps, the issue of stranded migrants will remain a matter of concern for IOM and the broader international community.

The UNHCR-IOM MOU was developed following the signing of a broader UN-IOM agreement the previous year. The General Assembly granted IOM observer status in the UN in 1992. As a prelude to the UNHCR agreement, IOM had been accorded status as a "standing invitee" in the Inter-Agency Standing Committee (IASC), the principal mechanism for coordinating international organization responses in humanitarian crises. IOM's later assignment of lead responsibility for the cluster on camp management was a direct outgrowth of its participation in IASC deliberations.

The UN-IOM agreement indicated the terms of cooperation between the two institutions, which included collaboration and consultation, the expectation that each will attend meetings on migration-relevant topics at which intergovernmental organizations are invited to attend as observers; exchange of information and documentation; steps to ensure optimum use of statistical and legal information and efficient use of resources to compile, analyze, publish, and disseminate such information; administrative and technical cooperation to ensure complementary action at headquarters and field levels; and joint implementation of projects of common interest, where appropriate. The secretary-general of the UN and the director-general of IOM were to take appropriate measures to ensure effective coordination and liaison between their offices in carrying out the agreement. Organizations within the UN structure were not precluded from entering into supplementary arrangements, as witnessed by the UNHCR-IOM agreement.

IOM has signed twenty-six agreements with partner agencies, including with most UN agencies with migration-related interests, such as the World Health Organization (WHO), UN Women, UNICEF, and the UN Population Fund (UNFPA). IOM and the ILO have also had close working relationships. Both were founding members of the Geneva Migration Group, which is discussed in greater detail in Chapter 9. They have carried out joint research projects such as Intra-Regional Labour Migration Flows: Present Situation, Challenges and Opportunities, a regional study in Central America based on surveys and focus group sessions with more than 300 migrants and their relatives. They collaborate in developing handbooks and other resources, such as the OSCE-IOM-ILO *Handbook on Labour Migration for the Mediterranean*. In addition, they jointly operate technical assistance projects, such as Capacity-Building for Migration Management, which focuses on strengthening Europe-China cooperation on migration management through the targeted exchange of personnel, expertise, and information.

The broader IOM-UN relationship has been a continuing topic of debate during the past decade. In December 2002, the IOM council established a Working Group on Institutional Arrangements, which reported to the council in 2003. The Working Group focused on two main options: "keeping IOM outside the UN system or bringing it into the UN by transforming it into a specialized agency" (IOM 2003:5). Specialized agency status is negotiated with the Economic and Social Council and approved by the General Assembly under Articles 57 and 63 of the UN charter. The institutions must have mandates related to the areas of ECOSOC responsibility: economic, social, cultural, education, health, and related fields. They must also be intergovernmental bodies, established by an agreement among states that gives them their operating mandate. Their scope must be global, not regional or national. Specialized agencies keep their independence in terms of budget and programs but participate in the mechanisms used to coordinate UN efforts. They benefit from the immunities offered to the UN by member states and travel under UN *laissez-passer*. Because UNHCR was founded by the General Assembly, it is considered an arm of the UN itself, not a specialized agency. Because ILO predated the UN and had a great deal of independence in the League system, it joined the UN as a specialized agency. Other specialized agencies include the WHO, UNESCO, the World Bank, and the International Civil Aviation Organization.

In presenting its findings, the Working Group emphasized "the need for IOM to keep its qualities of flexibility, independence, efficiency, and responsiveness; they also stressed that IOM should remain the central body providing policy advice and services to the international community on migration" (IOM 2003: Annex III.2). In support of the status quo, the Working Group noted that a great deal of UN-IOM cooperation was already in place and could grow further in the future. The Working Group expressed concern, however, that the UN might decide to establish its own migration organization, or give responsibility for migration to one of its other agencies if IOM did not join as a specialized agency. The secretary general had already expressed concern that migration was the only major transnational issue that did not have a clear place within the UN apparatus but was rather scattered over a number of organizations.

There were constraints on IOM joining the UN stemming from some of this same interest in migration. The Working Group noted that "in the eyes of a number of close observers, the economic, social and political circumstances are not yet right or propitious. Indeed the enabling environment for such a change has unfortunately deteriorated considerably since 11 September 2001 on many fronts, including the now hugely important national security front" (IOM 2003: Annex I.21). Migration was not only a matter for ECOSOC but it also related to the work of the Security Council. The Working Group also raised issues of potential additional costs of becoming a specialized agency, not in the operating budget of IOM – which would remain under the direction of the council – but in the costs of participating in the UN coordination mechanisms. IOM could expect additional tasks if it became the UN agency for migration, as other UN agencies, NGOs, media, and others requested its assistance. These very issues were also benefits, though, in ensuring that IOM's perspectives on migration were fully represented within the UN and to the broader public.

The 2003 council opted for an "improved status quo" in the relationship between IOM and the UN. The aim was to renegotiate the agreement to strengthen the cooperation but to keep IOM out of the UN. Many member states believed that its flexibility would be hampered by joining the UN. The state-centered nature of the organization was its strength as far as they were concerned. Although the UN is also governed by its member states, the charter and body of international law that has developed under its umbrella meant that UN agencies appeared to be more independent of state will than IOM. The UN bureaucracy was generally seen as more cumbersome than IOM's though IOM used the UN personnel system and generally followed its auditing procedures.

An exchange of letters between the UN secretary general and the IOM director-general followed, in which IOM raised the possibility of participating in two of the UN governance structures without joining the UN. They were the Chief Executives Board (CEB) and the UN Development Group (UNDG). The CEB is the chief mechanism for coordinating decisions among the specialized agencies and the UN secretariat. The UNDG is the chief body through which UN work on all development issues is coordinated at the headquarters and field level. IOM already participated as an observer in its meetings and in UN country teams but the arrangements were ad hoc and varied between countries. The secretary general responded that specialized agency status was a prerequisite for membership in the CEB as well as any more formalized participation in the UNDG.

A 2007 IOM administration report included further analysis of the advantages and disadvantages of specialized agency status for IOM, pursuant to the council's request at its November 2006 meeting. Two new contexts were considered. First, the 2006 UN High Level Dialogue on Migration and Development was bringing new attention throughout the international community to issues long on IOM's agenda (see Chapter 8). Second were UN plans for a "One UN" approach to its field operations. As described in the report, "The ongoing 'One UN' reform process calls for a stronger integration of activities at the country level, and foresees new and strengthened common mechanisms for UN entities, under the title "one leader, one programme, one office, one budgetary framework" (IOM 2007:9). At that time, specialized agencies had discretion as to their participation in the process, but the status of non-UN agencies, such as IOM, was unclear. The report noted one potentially troubling development, the

possibility of creating, at the country level, a common Fund as a vehicle for receiving new resources pooled by donors to support unfunded portions of commonly planned activities. While modalities of such a Fund are still under discussion and may differ from one country to another, there are already indications that IOM in its current status might not be a direct beneficiary of the Fund – even in a context where it is integrated in the UN Country Team. (ibid.:9)

The concern was that implementation of the One UN strategy could make it more difficult for IOM to cooperate fully with the UN if it stayed out of the UN framework.

The increased activities in crisis situations also were discussed in the report as a further context for considering specialized agency status. The report concluded that

> Recognition for the Organization and its staff members of the legal status defined in the 1947 Convention on the Privileges and Immunities of Specialized Agencies, for example, is of increasing relevance for an organization with a growing global presence and activity base, often in insecure locations. Access to the UN *laissez-passer* would be a real advantage to IOM staff. These factors impact on cost-effectiveness and staff security. (ibid.:15)

No action was taken by the council, which turned its attention in 2008 to the election of a new director-general. For the first time in IOM's history, the election was not a foregone conclusion, with the U.S. nominee accepted by the other members. Instead, there were four candidates, including incumbent Director-General Brunson McKinley, a former State Department official the United States no longer supported; the U.S. candidate, Ambassador William Swing; Sergio Marchi, who had been Minister of Citizenship and Immigration Canada (CIC) and a member of the Global Commission on International Migration; and Luca Riccardi, Special Counselor for International Migration of the Italian Minister of Interior. Although Ambassador Swing had the most votes from the first ballot, it was not until the third that he received the requisite two-thirds of the votes. Ambassador Swing, as director-general-elect, pledged "open and transparent dialogue with the Member States on all matters (budget, personnel, delocalization, the IOM-United Nations relationship) and would consult them regularly and heed their concerns" (IOM 2008:5). He also articulated the need for IOM to develop new partnerships and increase the professionalism of its staff as it addressed the challenges of migration.

The issue of specialized agency status did not appear again on the council's agenda. Rather, attention turned to a review of the organization's structure, undertaken by the new director-general and designed to increase the quality and efficiency of the organization, particularly in light of the financial crisis. In its 2009 meeting, the council also heard from members of the Global Migration Group, which had been formed as a follow-up to the report of the Global Commission on International Migration as a way to improve coordination among UN-affiliated agencies and between the UN and IOM. Particularly in the context of IOM's emergency operations, attention focused primarily on developing practical working relationships with the UN within the cluster system for addressing humanitarian crises and at the field level. This has led to participation of IOM in most UN country teams. IOM also has greater access to the UN Multi-Partner Trust Funds for countries in which it operates and on issues of special concern to the organization. In addition, IOM has become part of the UN security system, which means it operates under UN protocols, including decisions on when it is safe to enter or remain in a specific country. IOM is assessed fees for its participation in the country teams and security system. This creates challenges when its project funding does not cover such costs. It also creates opportunities for even closer relationships with the UN in the future as IOM is already bearing some of the costs associated with being a part of the UN system.

CONCLUSION

IOM has grown significantly within the past decade in its staffing, funding, and near universality of its membership. It has also seen substantial evolution in its programs and priorities. Since the agency's founding as the logistics arm of the international community's response to migration pressures in Europe, it has become a global organization with new roles and relationships to other international bodies. It has proved to be highly flexible, responding in many cases more quickly to new developments than its peer agencies. Yet, it remains fundamentally a state-owned institution that is highly dependent on project funding to maintain its operations. That funding has led IOM to focus its activities increasingly on large-scale emergency operations. Although the council refers to its preeminence in migration management, helping states to develop balanced policies that protect the rights of migrants while serving the interest of states, only a fraction of the organization's funding goes to these types of programs. IOM continues to support global and regional dialogue on migration and makes important contributions to the knowledge available on the structure and impact of migration within the context of a budget that gives priority to operations. Questions still linger as to whether it has the capacity, resolve, and political support to take on a larger role in this area.

5

Trafficking in Persons

In recent years, trafficking of people for sexual exploitation and forced labor has become one of the fastest growing areas of international criminal activity and one that is of increasing concern to the international community. Great growth has also been seen in the smuggling of people across borders in defiance of immigration and criminal laws enacted by source, transit, and receiving countries. While international law treats the two issues separately, there are many interconnections between smuggling and trafficking, particularly when would-be migrants go into debt bondage in order to pay smuggling fees. Chapter 6 discusses smuggling in greater detail.

The attention to human trafficking is by no means new. In the nineteenth century, the term "white slavery" was used to describe trafficking in women for prostitution. This chapter begins with historical background information and then turns to the current conceptualization of trafficking in persons and its connection to human smuggling. Both human smuggling and human trafficking, as currently defined, involve illegal movements of people, but human smuggling does not require the coercion, deception, or exploitation that is part of the definition of trafficking. In human smuggling contexts, the migrant enters voluntarily into a monetary arrangement with the smuggler to be transported across an international border. In effect, the smuggled migrant is complicit in his or her own smuggling and the commission of the criminal offense, whereas the trafficked person is the victim of a criminal operation. In some cases, however, smuggling can turn into trafficking, particularly when a migrant is forced into bondage in order to pay off the smuggling fees. If the migrant was not told what would be required to repay the fees, and has no control over his or her labor after entry, then such debt bondage may meet the trafficking definition since the migrant was deceived into entering into an exploitative situation.

The chapter continues with descriptions of the policy frameworks for combating trafficking. It focuses particularly on Protocol to Prevent, Suppress and

Punish Trafficking in Persons, Especially Women and Children, part of the UN Convention against Transnational Organized Crime. The protocol was adopted in 2000 and went into force in 2003. The chapter discusses the provisions of the protocol. It also analyzes the reasons that the protocol entered into force so quickly and with ratifications from a wide range of governments. It contrasts these reasons with the situation described in Chapter 3 regarding the Migrant Workers Convention.

The next section discusses the range of international and regional agencies that are involved in anti-trafficking activities. Of particular interest is the United Nations Office on Drugs and Crime (UNODC), which serves as the secretariat of the Conference of the Parties to the UN Convention against Transnational Organized Crime and its protocols. UNODC's Global Program to Combat Trafficking in Persons comprises data collection, assessment, and technical cooperation. Also examined are the activities of the migration agencies already discussed in the book – IOM, ILO, UNHCR – as well as the UN Office of the High Commissioner for Human Rights and a range of other agencies with more specific focus (UNICEF on children, UN Women on women, etc.).

The chapter's conclusion is that the legal and institutional regime for protection of the victims of trafficking remains weak but the substantial proliferation of counter-trafficking activities in the past decade may well lead to more robust endeavors.

BACKGROUND

International agreements on trafficking in persons predated the establishment of the League of Nations. Although prostitution had a long history, the growth in empires in the nineteenth century led to an increase in the number of brothels to serve the military and civilian population in the colonies. Concerns about cross-racial sex precipitated the procurement of European women to fill those brothels. Limoncelli (2010:28–29) reports, "Imperial state-building and colonialism increased both the demand for prostitution and the supply of women for it, and the 'ethnosexual' politics of nation-states and empires facilitated trafficking as one component of the overall growth of prostitution." The primary supply countries were Italy, Poland, and Russia, and the primary destinations were the countries of the southern cone of South America and Southeast Asia and to a less extent the Middle East and North America (Limoncelli 2010). Cross-border trafficking within Europe also increased during this period of heightened mobility, as did the movement of non-European women within Asia (Limoncelli 2010).

Increased movement of women for prostitution provoked attention to the actual process of procurement for the brothels and the conditions of labor. Journalistic exposés raised concerns that many of the women were coerced or deceived into migrating without understanding the extent to which they were being procured to work in brothels.

The 1904 Treaty of Paris was known as the "international agreement for the suppression of the white slave traffic."[1] According to a contemporary account, "all the leading powers of Europe, from Spain to Russia, Turkey alone excepted, gave their adhesion. And with the approval of the Senate, the President of the United States, on June 15, 1908, proclaimed the adhesion of the United States to the treaty" (R.H.G. 1912:135). The treaty focused on "women of full age who have suffered abuse or compulsion, as also to women and girls under age." It aimed to provide "effective protection against the criminal traffic known as the 'White Slave Traffic.'" The focus was on trafficking across borders (Gallagher 2010). The agreement had four principal articles (emphasis added):

Article 1: Each of the Contracting Governments undertakes to *establish or name some authority charged with the coordination of all information relative to the procuring of women or girls for immoral purposes abroad.*

Article 2: Each of the Governments undertakes to have a *watch kept, especially in railway stations, ports of embarkation, and en route, for persons in charge of women and girls destined for an immoral life.* The arrival of persons who clearly appear to be the *principals, accomplices in, or victims of, such traffic shall be notified, when it occurs, either to the authorities of the place of destination, or to the diplomatic or consular agents interested,* or to any other competent authorities.

Article 3: The Governments undertake, *when the case arises, and within legal limits, to have the declarations taken of women or girls of foreign nationality who are prostitutes, in order to establish their identity and civil status, and to discover who has caused them to leave their country.* The information obtained shall be communicated to the authorities of the country of origin of the said women and girls, with a view to their eventual repatriation.

The Governments undertake, within legal limits, and as far as can be done, to *entrust temporarily, and with a view to their eventual repatriation, the victims of a criminal traffic when destitute to public or private charitable institutions,* or to private individuals offering the necessary security.

The Governments also undertake, within legal limits, and as far as possible, *to send back to their country of origin those women and girls who desire it,* or who may be claimed by persons exercising authority over them. Repatriation shall only take place after agreement as to identity and nationality, as well as place and date of arrival at the frontiers. Each of the Contracting Countries shall facilitate transit through its territory.

Article 4: Where the woman or girl to be repatriated *cannot herself repay the cost of transfer, and has neither husband, relations, nor guardian to pay for her, the cost of repatriation shall be borne by the country where she is in residence as far as the nearest frontier or port of embarkation in the direction of the country of origin, and by the country of origin as regards the rest.*

---

[1] All quotes from the 1904 treaty are taken from version found at http://www1.umn.edu/humanrts/instree/whiteslavetraffic1904.html.

The 1904 agreement focused on international exchange of information for purposes of interdicting trafficked women and girls at points of transit, relay of information about traffickers to the proper authorities (but no specifics on prosecution), social protection of trafficking victims through charitable organizations, return of trafficking victims, and, when needed, burden sharing in the cost of that return.

The 1910 International Convention for the Suppression of the White Slave Trade went further in defining trafficking and establishing the responsibilities of state parties. Traffickers were defined as being in two categories:

> Whoever, in order to gratify the passions of another person, has procured, enticed, or led away, even with her consent, a woman or girl under age, for immoral purposes, and Whoever, in order to gratify the passions of another person, has, by fraud, or by means of violence, threats, abuse of authority, or any other method of compulsion, procured, enticed, or led away a woman or girl over age, for immoral purposes.[2]

Hence, methods of compulsion are not required in the case of minors whose consent is not considered to be valid. Articles 1 and 2 specify that such persons "shall be punished, notwithstanding that the various acts constituting the offence may have been committed in different countries." For purposes of the first clause, "under age" was assumed to be those who had not yet completed their twentieth year. Parties to the convention were to pass legislation to ensure prosecution and punishment of the traffickers and to consider trafficking to be an extraditable offense.

By the time further action was taken on trafficking, the League of Nations had been established. The covenant of the League included a specific reference in Article 23 to trafficking, reflecting the seriousness with which this issue was seen at the time. In addition to the more general pledge that members would "endeavour to secure and maintain fair and humane conditions of labour for men, women, and children," they also committed to "entrust the League with the general supervision over the execution of agreements with regard to the traffic in women and children, and the traffic in opium and other dangerous drugs."[3]

In 1921, the League held a conference to consider further action regarding trafficking. The conference recommended dropping the conceptualization of trafficking as white slavery in that the offense involved all races. It also recommended expanding the protection for children to include boys as well as girls. The recommendations resulted in a new convention, International Convention for the Suppression of the Traffic in Women and Children, adopted the same year. This convention incorporated the definition of trafficking included in the 1910 convention, but it required parties to take "all measures to discover and

---

[2] All quotes from the 1910 treaty are taken from version found at http://www1.umn.edu/humanrts/instree/whiteslavetraffic1910.html.

[3] Quotes from the Covenant of the League of Nations are taken from the version found at http://avalon.law.yale.edu/20th_century/leagcov.asp.

prosecute persons who are engaged in the traffic in children of both sexes."[4]
It also increased the age of minors to those who had completed twenty-one
years. The convention included additional provisions to prevent trafficking.
First, the parties agreed to take "legislative or administrative measures regarding licensing and supervision of employment agencies and offices, to prescribe
such regulations as are required to ensure the protection of women and children seeking employment in another country." Second, they would "adopt
such administrative and legislative measures as are required to check the traffic
in women and children." These would take the form of "protection of women
and children travelling on emigrant ships, not only at the points of departure
and arrival, but also during the journey" In an early example of the type of
public information campaigns that have become ubiquitous in the trafficking
areas, parties would also "arrange for the exhibition, in railway stations and in
ports, of notices warning women and children of the danger of the traffic and
indicating the places where they can obtain accommodation and assistance."

The 1921 conference also recommended the establishment of a permanent committee to monitor progress in preventing trafficking of women and
children. Composed of experts from Britain, Denmark, France, Italy, Japan,
Poland, Rumania, Spain, and Uruguay, the committee invited representatives
from the United States to participate, although it was not a member of the
League. The chief of the U.S. Children's Bureau was appointed to the committee in an unofficial and consultative status. A number of NGOs also participated in the committee's discussions. The committee recommended that the
League collect information on applicable legislation, encourage governments to
prohibit employment of foreign women and children in licensed prostitution,
inform governments of the value of hiring women police to engage in counter-
trafficking activities, and support a major research study to provide additional
information about trafficking processes so that policies could be more targeted.

The League took further steps to curb the exploitation of labor with conventions in 1926 to suppress the slave trade and in 1930 to eliminate forced
and compulsory labor. In 1933, the organization returned to the issue of sex
trafficking and adopted the International Convention for the Suppression of
the Traffic in Women of Full Age. The offense was defined more broadly than
in the prior conventions. The first article states: "Whoever, in order to gratify
the passions of another person, has procured, enticed or led away even with
her consent, a woman or girl of full age for immoral purposes to be carried out
in another country, shall be punished."[5] Trafficking applies even if the woman

---

[4] All quotes from the 1921 convention are taken from version found at http://ec.europa.eu/anti-
trafficking/download.action;jsessionid=YX3mSQQDmQjJLzGJ1jQpJqZvFTFTTvBQoqFKtX
nlxPPw8rVSrqxh!-388123576?nodePath=/Legislation+and+Case+Law/International+
Legislation/United+Nations/1921+international+convention_en.pdf&fileName=1921+
international+convention_en.pdf&fileType=pdf.
[5] All quotes from the 1933 convention are taken from the version at http://www.oas.org/juridico/
mla/en/traites/en_traites-inter-women_1933.pdf.

is an adult and consented to being transported across borders to engage in "immoral purposes." Unlike the previous conventions, the 1933 one did not include provisions addressing prevention or protection of the trafficked women.

By 1937, the League of Nations was examining changes to the convention to strengthen the efforts to suppress not only trafficking but also prostitution. As with many of the issues discussed herein, the advent of fascism and the outbreak of World War II halted efforts to build international consensus on norms and standards. Following World War II, negotiations resumed and in 1949, the General Assembly of the new UN adopted the Convention for the Suppression of the Traffic in Persons and of the Exploitation of the Prostitution of Others. The preamble to the convention sets out the context, in determining that "prostitution and the accompanying evil of the traffic in persons for the purpose of prostitution are incompatible with the dignity and worth of the human person and endanger the welfare of the individual, the family and the community."[6]

Although the purposes are couched in human rights terms, the convention is primarily about law enforcement. The first two articles specify the offenders to be punished under the treaty:

Article 1: The Parties to the present Convention agree to punish any person who, to gratify the passions of another:

(1) Procures, entices or leads away, for purposes of prostitution, another person, even with the consent of that person;
(2) Exploits the prostitution of another person, even with the consent of that person.

Article 2: The Parties to the present Convention further agree to punish any person who:

(1) Keeps or manages, or knowingly finances or takes part in the financing of a brothel;
(2) Knowingly lets or rents a building or other place or any part thereof for the purpose of the prostitution of others.

Unlike its predecessor, the 1949 convention seeks punishment not only of the trafficker but also the brothel owner, manager, landlord, and financier. Like the previous conventions, there is no mention of punishment of the customers (the persons whose passions are gratified). Many of the provisions of the 1921 convention regarding the exchange of information, extradition, repatriation of the victims, and regulation of employment agencies to prevent recruitment for prostitution are found in the 1949 version as well, which superseded the earlier treaty once it went into force. Compared to the conventions on

---

[6] All quotes from the 1949 convention are taken from the version at http://www.ohchr.org/EN/ProfessionalInterest/Pages/TrafficInPersons.aspx.

migrant workers discussed in Chapter 3, the trafficking convention was well ratified, with eighty-two governments committing themselves to its terms. Many
of the principal destination countries did not become parties to the convention,
however. These included traditional immigration countries (the United States
and Canada) and larger receiving countries in Europe (e.g., United Kingdom,
Germany, and France).[7] Countries that legalized prostitution also found the
convention problematic since it treats voluntary engagement in prostitution as
trafficking. As Weissbrodt (2002) reports, "The requirement to treat all adult
participation in prostitution as trafficking has been cited as one reason why the
Suppression of Traffic Convention has been ratified by fewer States than the
other United Nations conventions against slavery."

In 1956, the UN addressed trafficking for forced labor in the Supplementary
Convention on the Abolition of Slavery, the Slave Trade, and Institutions and
Practices Similar to Slavery. Among the practices covered by the convention
were debt bondage, forced marriage, and "any institution or practice whereby
a child or young person under the age of 18 years, is delivered by either or
both of his natural parents or by his guardian to another person, whether for
reward or not, with a view to the exploitation of the child or young person
or of his labour" (United Nations 1956).[8] The convention required parties
to render the act of conveying persons in these categories across international
borders a criminal offense. The UN established a formal process for monitoring
implementation of the slavery convention in the form of a sub-commission
to the Economic and Social Council, which evolved into the United Nations
Working Group on Contemporary Forms of Slavery.[9] The Working Group
received information on slavery from governments and undertook its own
research on incidents of slavery (Bell n.d.).

CONTEMPORARY TRAFFICKING

A wide range of estimates exists on the number of trafficking victims around the
world. The U.S. State Department (2012) estimates "that as many as 27 million
men, women, and children around the world are victims of what is now often
described with the umbrella term 'human trafficking.'" The number includes
those who are trafficked domestically and internationally. This estimate
benefited from the work of ILO on forced labor. ILO estimates more than
20 million persons performing forced labor, a subset of those who are
trafficked.[10] The estimate is based on reported cases and has a margin of

---

[7] France signed the convention but did not ratify it.
[8] All quotes from the 1956 convention are taken from the version at http://www1.umn.edu/
humanrts/instree/f3scas.htm.
[9] When the Human Rights Council took over the work of the UN Commission on Human Rights,
the working group was eliminated and a special rapporteur on contemporary forms of slavery
was named.
[10] The ILO data do not include trafficking in organs or for marriages or adoptions.

error of 7 percent (i.e., the range is between 19.5 million and 22.3 million). In discussing the demographic composition of forced laborers, ILO concluded: "Women and girls represent the greater share of the total – 11.4 million (55%), as compared to 9.5 million (45%) men and boys. Adults are more affected than children – 74% (15.4 million) of victims fall in the age group of 18 years and above, whereas children aged 17 years and below represent 26% of the total (or 5.5 million child victims)" (ILO 2012). About 90 percent are believed to be working in the private sector. Almost one-quarter of these include victims of forced sexual exploitation, with the remainder engaged in other work, such as agriculture, construction, domestic work, or manufacturing. About 10 percent are engaged in public-sector forced labor, for example in prisons, or in work imposed by the state military or by rebel armed forces (ibid.). More than half of the forced laborers (11.7 million) are in the Asia-Pacific region, with the African region accounting for the second largest number (3.7 million). Proportionate to population, however, Central and Southeast Europe ranks highest, with 4.2 forced laborers per 1,000 inhabitants (ibid.). About 44 percent of the forced laborers have migrated internally or across international borders, predominately for sexual exploitation. The majority of the victims employed in their own communities are engaged in other types of labor.

Trafficking for labor and sexual exploitation takes a number of different forms. For example, child domestic servants, usually girls, are sold or given to families or distant relatives to serve as household help. They generally work extended hours and many experience sexual abuse by their employers. Often they are not paid for their services. In Africa, children, in principle, belong to the extended family so the placement of children in wealthier households of distant relatives is commonly a means for providing them with greater educational and employment opportunities (Fitzgibbon 2003). In fact, in West and Central Africa, training a girl to perform domestic duties from an early age is generally viewed as part of the natural education of girls, giving them skills to take care of their own families later in life. However, the practice often leads to exploitation and trafficking as recruiters lure them away from domestic work, or family members exploit their labor.

In Haiti, rural families send children to more affluent city dwellers to serve as *restaveks* in exchange for the child's room and board. The *restavek* tradition is widespread in Haiti, and although some children receive adequate care, it is typically fraught with abuse. Many employers force the children to work for long hours, without adequate provision of food or care. The government of Haiti estimates there are 90,000–120,000 children in coercive labor conditions as *restaveks*, but UNICEF estimates the number is much higher – between 250,000 and 300,000 (U.S. State Dept 2006).

Bonded labor is prevalent in many countries; whereby individuals are indebted to their employer and unable to stop working until the debts have been cleared. This practice occurs throughout the world, although concrete data is hard to acquire because it is often found in informal, unregulated, or illegal sectors of the economy. It is most common among the economically vulnerable and uneducated members of society, such as minority ethnic or religious groups, or the lowest classes or castes. In some cases, parents accept money in return for their children, who are forced to work for the money-lender until the debt is completely repaid. In other cases, entire families are enslaved as the debt passes from generation to generation. They live in extreme poverty, isolated from the rest of society, and have absolutely no control over their own lives. Many are illiterate and therefore unable to understand how much they owe and how long it should take to pay off their debt.

Commercial sexual exploitation has generally received a great deal of attention in the trafficking literature. The trafficking protocol considers "consent" irrelevant in the case of children; therefore, sexual exploitation of children in the sex industry is considered trafficking in persons. Children are sold, induced, tricked, or enticed into prostitution, and are often too young to fully comprehend or consent to the acts they are forced to perform. They are taken far from their homes or sold by their parents, and held in confinement where they are abused into submission and exposed to severe health risks including HIV infection and AIDS, other sexually-transmitted diseases, drug abuse, and physical and psychological abuse. As with most forms of trafficking, data on the number of people who are sexually exploited are not readily obtainable. The clandestine nature of the industry makes it impossible to move beyond general estimates.

Forced marriage, either through outright abduction, for purposes of receiving a bride price, or through arrangements for debt release is one of the most widespread, yet hidden forms of human trafficking. Girls as young as four are removed from their homes and families and taken to the living quarters of their new husbands who benefit from their sexual and domestic services. Around the world, an estimated 100 million girls will marry before their eighteenth birthday over the next decade; many of them forced into marriage by their parents or extended family members (Clark 2004). The countries with the highest rates of child marriages are (1) Niger (75 percent), (2) Chad (68 percent), (3) Central African Republic (68 percent), (4) Bangladesh (66 percent), and (5) Guinea (63 percent).[11] Endemic poverty results in young girls being regarded as an economic burden to the family and early marriage to an older man becomes a survival strategy.

Begging is another exploitative activity that generates trafficking. In Senegal, religious teachers (*marabouts*) sometimes bring students (*talibés*) from rural areas to urban centers and force them to roam the streets and beg for money from as early as six in the morning until well after dark. If they return to the school (*daaras*) without a sufficient amount of money, they are beaten and abused. A representative from Save the Children Sweden remarked

---

[11] Based on data from the International Center for Research on Women at http://www.icrw.org/child-marriage-facts-and-figures.

that there are *daaras* in Senegal that "resemble slave houses" (Moens et al. 2004).

Conflict also precipitates, and is inextricably linked to human trafficking. Conflict generates massive displacement of populations and results in extreme vulnerabilities, which often lead to abuse, exploitation, and trafficking. Displacement has profound effects on family and community networks, and social and cultural ties. It strips away economic opportunities, terminates dependable employment arrangements, disrupts educational opportunities, induces extreme forms of isolation and poverty, and destroys social structures. Many refugees and IDPs struggle to survive with inadequate shelter, little or no access to food or basic healthcare, and no protection. They are cramped together in makeshift dwellings, often in unhygienic conditions, leaving them disoriented and less able to resist exploitation as they desperately search for a means of survival. Whether the victims of conflict cluster in camps, flee into the countryside for refuge with friends or relatives, or become immersed into a community of the equally poor and dispossessed, they are among the most vulnerable populations in the world.

Displaced persons, especially women and girls, are particularly vulnerable to trafficking, which is likely to be related to gender-based violence in camp situations. Since women and children make up 75 percent of camp populations, they often become the sole source of income for their families. A lack of income-generating activities often forces them – either on their own accord or on that of their parents and/or husbands who barter their bodies – into prostitution and trafficking as a means of survival. Regardless of the reason for their displacement, they are forced into extreme poverty without the resources or assistance they need to provide for their children. Their vulnerability creates opportunities for male-dominated leadership structures within the camp, and traffickers outside the camp to carry out persistent violations of their rights and human freedoms.

Trafficking becomes more commonplace in areas where conflict strips away economic opportunities and breaks down law and order. Protracted, intrastate warfare is marked by violence that indiscriminately kills, violates, abducts, terrorizes, and explicitly targets civilian populations. Areas of conflict are easy targets for those interested in plundering a country's resources, including its people. The perpetrator, including governmental and nongovernmental military forces, thrive on and create war economies relying on violent and illegal activities such as trafficking and slavery. The following discussion focuses on the specific forms of trafficking that are inexorably linked to conflict itself.

Child soldiering is a unique and severe manifestation of human trafficking. Images of young boys carrying AK-47s and stories of forced conscription into the ranks of a country's military or rebel group pervade the popular press and have shed light on the unfortunate plight of millions of children around the world. As a result, a significant and growing body of international law and standards has emerged to prevent child recruitment and its potential links to displacement. The Convention on the Rights of the Child entitles all children under eighteen to the right of personal security. The Optimal Protocol on the Involvement of Children in Armed Conflict and ILO Convention 182 on the Worst Forms of Child Labor deal with trafficking of children into armed forces. Despite efforts by the international community, the recruitment of displaced children by national armed forces and/or militias has continued unimpeded in many countries (IDMC 2007). Worldwide, more than 500,000 children under the age of eighteen have been recruited into government or rebel armed forces in more than eighty-five countries. It is estimated that at any one time, more than 300,000 of these children are actively fighting.[12] The U.S. State Department (2012) reported the following governments as particularly egregious in their recruitment of child soldiers: Burma, Libya, Democratic Republic of the Congo, South Sudan, Somalia, Sudan, and Yemen.

Some children join voluntarily as a means of survival in a war-torn region whose economy has been destroyed. Children who are separated or displaced from their families and communities are at the greatest risk of recruitment and abduction by armed forces and rebel groups. At the same time, however, children who have been abducted or coerced into the ranks of government or rebel groups are displaced, usually internally, as a result of their abduction. They are physically relocated, often at great distances from their homes, and placed in harm's way. They also lack both the freedom and the means to return to their family or community, and are most at risk of subsequently becoming displaced if they return.

In conflict situations, sexual violence is often deliberately employed as a war strategy, making women extremely vulnerable to trafficking, particularly when the general level of violence against women is high (GTZ 2004). Women and girls may be abducted and used as combatants, laborers, spies, trainers, or sex slaves, yet no matter the purpose, sexual violence is almost always part of their exploitation.

Unfortunately, human trafficking does not stop when the conflict ends. In fact, post-conflict regions offer ideal conditions for traffickers, as they are frequently characterized by the absence of law, political instability, increased criminal activity, and dysfunctional law enforcement institutions. This highly volatile environment, coupled with social disintegration, destruction of livelihoods and a lack of economic activities following a war, provide numerous highly vulnerable people who are struggling to reconstruct their lives. A sudden increase in trafficking for sexual exploitation often occurs when foreign or international peacekeeping or civilian forces are deployed. Foreign soldiers bring money and time to post-conflict settings where both are regarded as priceless commodities. This increase in demand for sexual services is met with an increase in supply. The arrival of peace support missions often directly

---

[12] Amnesty International website, http://www.amnesty.org/.

coincides with growth in local sex markets around military and peacekeeping camps. Traffickers and local authorities in post-conflict regions are quick to enter and benefit from the emerging lucrative market, which represents an uncommon economic opportunity. International peacekeeping personnel have purchased trafficked women and children for sex or domestic labor, have permitted trafficking rings to flourish and have themselves engaged in trafficking persons (Picarelli 2002).

TOWARD A NEW NORMATIVE FRAMEWORK

Despite the adoption of the 1949 and 1956 conventions, ratification and implementation of the provisions related to trafficking did not receive significant attention by governments or international organizations until the 1970s. Two principal factors led to the reassessment of the phenomenon. First, trafficking of women and girls came on the agenda of the feminist movement and the attention of the series of World Conferences on Women held by the UN. Second, trafficking and smuggling of all types – weapons, drugs, and people – were increasingly seen as interconnected security issues given their links to organized crime.

The First World Conference on Women, held in Mexico City in 1975, sought to identify ways to promote ratification and implementation of the various conventions that addressed issues of concern to women. With regard to trafficking, the conference encouraged ratification of the 1949 convention. It also urged governments to adopt specific legislative and other measures "to combat prostitution and the illicit traffic in women, especially young girls. Special programmes, including pilot projects, should be developed in co-operation with international bodies and non-governmental organizations to prevent such practices and rehabilitate the victims."[13] The Second World Conference in 1980 recognized that there was limited action in this area and included a specific statement "deploring the scant interest shown by Governments and international organizations in this serious problem."[14] The final report urged governments to "recognize that women and children are not a commodity and that every woman and every child has the right to protection against abduction, rape and prostitution." It also brought issues related to trafficking to the attention of human rights and crime prevention and control authorities within the international system. Linking human rights and law enforcement would turn out to be an important step in gaining greater attention for trafficking as a transnational issue.

[13] All quotes from the report of the first world conference are taken from the report at http://www.un.org/womenwatch/daw/beijing/otherconferences/Mexico/Mexico%20conference%20report%20optimized.pdf.

[14] All quotes from the report on the second world conference are taken from the report at http://www.un.org/womenwatch/daw/beijing/otherconferences/Copenhagen/Copenhagen%20Full%20Optimized.pdf.

The Third and Fourth World Conferences, in Nairobi and Beijing respectively, also addressed trafficking issues. In Nairobi, the final report decried forced prostitution as a form of slavery resulting from economic degradation and women's dependence on men. The recommendations focused on prevention by giving women access to economic opportunities, including training and employment. The Beijing conference considered elimination of trafficking to be a strategic objective and had the most detailed recommendations. It also went well beyond sex trafficking to include forced labor. The Beijing Plan of Action urged governments to:

- Consider the ratification and enforcement of international conventions on trafficking in persons and on slavery;
- Take appropriate measures to address the root factors, including external factors, that encourage trafficking in women and girls for prostitution and other forms of commercialized sex, forced marriages and forced labour in order to eliminate trafficking in women, including by strengthening existing legislation with a view to providing better protection of the rights of women and girls and to punishing the perpetrators, through both criminal and civil measures;
- Step up cooperation and concerted action by all relevant law enforcement authorities and institutions with a view to dismantling national, regional and international networks in trafficking;
- Allocate resources to provide comprehensive programmes designed to heal and rehabilitate into society victims of trafficking, including through job training, legal assistance and confidential health care, and take measures to cooperate with non-governmental organizations to provide for the social, medical and psychological care of the victims of trafficking;
- Develop educational and training programmes and policies and consider enacting legislation aimed at preventing sex tourism and trafficking, giving special emphasis to the protection of young women and children.[15]

Trafficking in persons also emerged as an issue on the international law enforcement agenda. In the post–Cold War period, trafficking from the former Soviet Union and Eastern Europe had been linked to the emergence of Russian, Ukrainian, Georgian, Albanian, and other syndicates engaged in a wide variety of organized criminal activities. Asian groups, such as Chinese Triads and Japanese Yakuza, also appeared to engage in trafficking in addition to other criminal enterprises. There was some controversy, however, about the extent to which trafficking in persons met the definition of organized crime – in that the perpetrators often were loosely federated, engaged only in human trafficking, and not under a single hierarchical enterprise. Finckenauer (1998) made the distinction between crime that is organized (i.e., is efficient in its operations)

---

[15] All quotes from the fourth world conference are taken from the report att http://www.un.org/womenwatch/daw/beijing/pdf/Beijing%20full%20report%20E.pdf.

versus organized crime (i.e., involves criminal networks such as the Mafia who are already engaged in a wide array of criminal acts). Evidence of organized crime's involvement was scant in the late 1990s. An influential report issued by the U.S. State Department's Bureau of Intelligence and Research concluded, however, that this situation could well change:

> The international trafficking trade appears to be highly organized, involving sophisticated international networks of procurers, document forgers and providers, escorts, organizers, financiers, corrupt officials, and brothel operators.... The number of organized crime groups engaged in trafficking is likely to continue increasing, given the high profit potential and relatively low penalties. (Richard 1999:55)

Shelley (2010:3) explains the attraction of organized crime – whether in the traditional sense or the less hierarchical forms – to human trafficking: "Traffickers choose to trade in humans . . . because there are low start-up costs, minimal risks, high profit and large demand. For organized crime groups, human beings have one added advantage over drugs: they can be sold repeatedly." Governmental corruption aids and abets the process, as does the demand for exploitable labor in receiving countries.

In 2000, recognizing the growth in trafficking, as well as smuggling operations, the UN adopted two protocols that define the current phenomena of trafficking and smuggling. Both entered into force in 2003. The Protocol to Prevent, Suppress and Punish Trafficking in Persons, Especially Women and Children (hereafter called the Trafficking Protocol), which supplements the UN Convention against Transnational Organized Crime,[16] provides the first common normative definition on trafficking in human beings. It requires cooperation from states in combating trafficking and encourages them to pass preventative trafficking measures. The protocol defines trafficking (which includes trafficking within countries) as:

> The recruitment, transportation, transfer, harboring or receipt of persons, by means of the threat or use of force or other forms of coercion, of abduction, of fraud, of deception, of the abuse of power or of a position of vulnerability or of the giving or receiving of payments or benefits to achieve the consent of a person having control over another person, for the purpose of exploitation. Exploitation shall include, at a minimum, the exploitation of the prostitution of others or other forms of sexual exploitation, forced labour or services, slavery or practices similar to slavery, servitude or the removal of organs.[17]

Therefore, the defining elements of trafficking are the activity, the means, and the purpose, where: (1) The *activity* refers to some kind of movement either

---

[16] www.ohchr.org/english/law/protocoltraffic.htm.

[17] All quotes from the trafficking protocol are taken from the version at http://www.unodc.org/documents/treaties/UNTOC/Publications/TOC%20Convention/TOCebook-e.pdf.

within or across borders; (2) The *means* relates to some form of coercion or deception; and (3) the *purpose* is the ultimate exploitation of a person for profit or benefit of another (IOM 2004). Human smuggling holds some common elements with trafficking but it differs in a number of respects. A separate protocol to the Convention against Transnational Organized Crime, the Protocol Against Smuggling of Migrants by Land, Sea and Air (henceforth Smuggling Protocol), defines human smuggling as "the procurement, in order to obtain, directly or indirectly, a financial or other material benefit, of the illegal entry of a person into a State Party of which the person is not a national or a permanent resident." Illegal entry is defined as "crossing borders without complying with the necessary requirements for legal entry into the receiving State," including clandestine entry or entry through legal ports through the use of counterfeit or fraudulently obtained documents.[18]

Both human smuggling and human trafficking involve illegal movements of people, but human smuggling does not require the coercion, deception, or exploitation that is part of the definition of trafficking. In human smuggling contexts, the migrant enters voluntarily into a monetary arrangement with the smuggler to be transported across an international border. It is not surprising that as addenda to a convention on organized crime, the protocols focus particularly on the criminalization of smuggling and trafficking. For example, the Trafficking Protocol requires state parties to adopt "such legislative and other measures as may be necessary to establish as criminal offences the conduct set forth in article 3 of this Protocol [which provides the definition above], when committed intentionally." The protocol establishes the responsibility of state parties to cooperate in their law enforcement activities, with the aim of curbing smuggling and trafficking operations that cross international borders. The protocol spells out a number of areas of such cooperation, including the sharing of information, control of borders, technical assistance and training, security of documents, and other similar endeavors.

The protocols also set out guidelines for state parties regarding prevention and the protection of smuggling and trafficking victims. Generally, the language has fewer directives in these areas than in the law enforcement area. State parties, for example, "shall endeavour to provide for the physical safety of victims of trafficking in persons while they are within its territory." The protocol specifies that "in appropriate cases and to the extent possible under its domestic law, each State Party shall protect the privacy and identity of victims of trafficking in persons, including, inter alia, by making legal proceedings relating to such trafficking confidential." In this context,

---

[18] All quotes from the smuggling protocol are taken from the version at http://www.unodc.org/documents/treaties/UNTOC/Publications/TOC%20Convention/TOCebook-e.pdf.

Each State Party shall ensure that its domestic legal or administrative system contains measures that provide to victims of trafficking in persons, in appropriate cases:

(a) Information on relevant court and administrative proceedings;
(b) Assistance to enable their views and concerns to be presented and considered at appropriate stages of criminal proceedings against offenders, in a manner not prejudicial to the rights of the defence.

The protocol is more direct with regard to potential compensation, presumably from traffickers: "Each State Party shall ensure that its domestic legal system contains measures that offer victims of trafficking in persons the possibility of obtaining compensation for damage suffered."

State parties are encouraged, but not required, to adopt provisions to help trafficking victims to recover: "Each State Party shall consider implementing measures to provide for the physical, psychological and social recovery of victims of trafficking in persons." Among the areas to be considered are: appropriate housing; counseling and information; medical, psychological, and material assistance; and employment, educational, and training opportunities. For internationally trafficked persons, the protocol also encourages states to "consider adopting legislative or other appropriate measures that permit victims of trafficking in persons to remain in its territory, temporarily or permanently, in appropriate cases." And, in the case of international trafficking, the protocol includes specific provisions regarding return and reintegration of victims to their home countries. By contrast, it includes no provisions related to the return or reintegration of internal trafficking victims to their home communities.

In 2009, the UN issued its first global report on human trafficking, which gives some sense of progress in implementing the provisions of the protocol (UNODC 2009). In 2003, when the protocol went into force, only 5 percent of countries had action plans to combat trafficking. By 2008, 53 percent had adopted plans. Prior to 2003, 65 percent of the countries had no anti-trafficking legislation but that proportion was reduced to 20 percent by 2008 and additional governments were developing new laws. According to the report, many of the countries that did have counter-trafficking laws prior to adoption of the protocol had amended them to broaden the definition of trafficking to include forced labor and cover both adults and children. Prosecution and conviction of traffickers lagged behind these legislative actions but it is expected that they will increase as more countries begin to implement their new legislation.

INTERNATIONAL INSTITUTIONAL FRAMEWORKS

A wide array of international organizations have policies and programs aimed at combating trafficking through efforts to *prosecute* traffickers, *prevent* trafficking, *protect* the trafficked, and forge *partnerships* for more effective action. These are often referred to as the four Ps. The principal participants within and outside of the United Nations are[19]:

United Nations Office on Drugs and Crime (UNODC) serves as the secretariat of the Conference of the Parties to the UN Convention against Transnational Organized Crime and its protocols. It was established in 1997, with headquarters in Vienna and 54 field offices serving more than 150 countries (UNODC 2010). With regard to trafficking, in 2007 the General Assembly assigned UNODC the task of coordinating the Inter-Agency Coordination Group against Trafficking in Persons (ICAT) "to enhance cooperation and coordination and facilitate a holistic and comprehensive approach by the international community to the problem of trafficking in persons" (General Assembly 2006). Sixteen international organizations make up ICAT's membership. Also in 2007, UNODC was given responsibilities for management of the United Nations Global Initiative to Fight Human Trafficking (UN GIFT).

In 2010, the General Assembly, through the Global Plan of Action to Combat Trafficking in Persons, gave UNODC further responsibilities. These include the management of the UN Voluntary Trust Fund for Victims of Trafficking in Persons, Especially Women and Children. The fund is to provide humanitarian, legal, and financial aid to victims of trafficking in persons through governmental, intergovernmental, and non-governmental organizations. As of April 2012, only $1 million had been pledged, with less than half of that sum actually contributed. Awards of up to $25,000 had been given to NGOs.[20] The amount pales in comparison to the estimated $32 billion per year in profits to human traffickers.

UNODC was also tasked with servicing working groups of the Conference of the Parties on Trafficking in Persons and the research and publication of the biennial Global Report on Trafficking in Persons. Other activities include the drafting of model laws; dissemination of a toolkit to help countries combat trafficking; technical assistance to origin, transit, and destination countries; and maintenance of a database of case law related to trafficking. UNODC also runs the Blue Heart Campaign which aims to mobilize support and to inspire people to take action against human trafficking.

UNODC's funding is largely from voluntary contributions. Donors include "governments, consisting of major and emerging and national donors, UN Agencies, Multi-Donor Trust Funds, Inter-Governmental Organizations, International Financial Institutions (IFIs) and private donors, including private sector entities and foundations."[21] In 2010–2011, it received $242.9 million in

---

[19] There are also regional consultative processes that address trafficking issues, such as the Bali Process. These are discussed in Chapter 6.

[20] http://www.unodc.org/unodc/en/frontpage/2012/April/un-general-assembly-president-calls-for-re-doubled-efforts-to-end-human-trafficking.html.

[21] http://www.unodc.org/unodc/en/donors/index.html?ref=menuside.

voluntary contributions, representing an increase of 12.8 percent from the previous funding period but a decline from the record $246.9 million received in 2008. The funding for the unit responsible for trafficking and smuggling is entirely from voluntary contributions. UNODC's strategy on trafficking highlights the problems that this process creates: inconsistency in funding levels; lack of continuity in staffing, even for functions that should be seen as core ones such as servicing the working group responsible for monitoring implementation of the protocol; reliance on consultants to operate many programs; and donor driven programming that may give inadequate resources for important issues that contributors do not prioritize. UNODC's February 2012 Strategy on Human Trafficking and Migrant Smuggling signaled its intention to work toward resolving this problem.

International Organization for Migration has implemented 800 projects in over 100 countries, and has provided assistance to approximately 20,000 trafficked persons since 1994. "IOM operates from the outset that trafficking in persons needs to be approached within the overall context of managing migration."[22] This is both a strength and weakness of its trafficking program – a strength because it has allowed IOM to reach out to vulnerable persons who might be trafficked if denied other migration opportunities but a weakness because the organization's mandate to engage with such victims is highly dependent on the willingness of governments to support this policy framework. When legal alternatives are unavailable for would-be migrants, IOM can do little to address this cause of trafficking.

IOM's program has three main aims: "to provide protection and empower trafficked women, men, girls and boys; raise awareness and understanding of the issue; and bring justice to trafficked persons."[23] The strategy for tackling trafficking was set out in a concept paper in 1999. In 2000, IOM set up a specific office to coordinate its trafficking activities (Ducasse-Rogier 2001). Its program activities predated the strategy, implemented largely in the context of initiatives to reduce irregular migration from the Balkans and Southeast Asia (ibid.). Trafficking components were introduced as IOM staff realized that some irregular migration was characterized by high levels of coercion, deception, and exploitation.

IOM currently offers a range of assistance to trafficking victims, including accommodation in places of safety, medical and psychosocial support, skills development and vocational training, return and reintegration assistance, and resettlement to third countries in extreme cases. Many of its programs focus on children. For example, in Ghana, IOM has rescued, rehabilitated, and reintegrated more than 700 children into their communities of origin, most having been trafficked into the fishing industry. The aim is to sensitize the community to the dangers of trafficking, conduct home visits to see if the children can

---

[22] http://www.iom.int/jahia/page748.html.
[23] http://www.iom.int/jahia/page748.html.

be safely returned to their parents or need alternative placements, and follow up with assistance to enable the children to finish school or find a suitable apprenticeship.

The agency has also prepared a variety of handbooks and guidelines on assistance, including the *Handbook on Direct Assistance for Victims of Trafficking* and *Caring for Trafficked Persons: Guidance for Health Providers*. It also provides direct technical assistance to governments setting up counter-trafficking strategies. An evaluation of IOM's counter-trafficking operations found that one of IOM's major strengths was in capacity-building. IOM staff members were regarded as "highly skilled" and "very supportive" by partners inside and out of governments (Berman and Marshall 2010). Some stakeholders raised questions, however, about what they saw as a lack of systematic attention to the human rights dimension of trafficking, although the organization cites respect for the rights of trafficking victims as one of its core principles. The evaluation noted concerns related to

> how the organization responds to situations involving: closed shelters (those where victims are not allowed to leave); limited victim options for social integration; the extent to which voluntary return is actually voluntary; limited documentation as to how IOM supports victims in accessing their rights; and concerns expressed by respondents that IOM is not sufficiently outspoken about instances of human rights abuse within its area of mandate. (Berman and Marshall 2010)

The evaluators also noted, however, that IOM has devised a number of useful strategies that protect trafficking victims: "IOM's work to expand its victim support initiatives to other migrants in need; advocacy for the incorporation of human rights concerns in laws and policies; and expansion of options for vulnerable groups" (Berman and Marshall 2010).

One of IOM's principal areas of programming has been mass information campaigns to educate would-be migrants about the dangers and warning signs of trafficking. These campaigns are designed to prevent trafficking and to encourage would-be migrants to find legal means of working in other countries. The evaluation of IOM's counter-trafficking work found general appreciation for these activities but little evidence for their effectiveness in prevention:

> Respondents in three countries spoke highly of these campaigns, which use a wide range of techniques and have in some cases received international recognition. Yet there is limited documented evidence to demonstrate the relevance or effectiveness of IOM's information campaigns to preventing trafficking. In particular, no evidence was available as to the link between a person's lack of awareness and their likelihood of being trafficked. (Berman and Marshall 2010)

As with the other organizations involved in counter-trafficking, the vast majority of IOM's work is funded through voluntary contributions for specific short-term (generally one year) projects. The evaluation identified a number of weaknesses that emanate from this model of funding: "a reluctance to turn down any funding opportunity within the counter-trafficking area; an inability to offer job security to staff; a lack of resources for needs assessments; and difficulties in long-term planning and promoting sustainability" (ibid.). IOM tends to respond to donor requests rather than using more systematic criteria in determining what types of activities were needed (ibid.).

UN High Commissioner for Refugees has a responsibility to ensure that refugees, asylum seekers, IDPs, stateless persons, and other persons of concern do not fall victim to trafficking. The office has additional responsibility to ensure that those who have been trafficked and have well-founded fear of persecution upon a return to their country of origin are recognized as refugees and afforded the corresponding international protection.

In 2006, the UNHCR published guidelines on the application of the Refugee Convention to people who have been trafficked. The guidelines note that UNHCR's involvement in the issue of trafficking is essentially two-fold. First, UNHCR "has a responsibility to ensure that refugees, asylum-seekers, IDPs, stateless persons, and other persons of concern do not fall victim to trafficking" (UNHCR 2006b: 3). Secondly, UNHCR "has a responsibility to ensure that individuals who have been trafficked and who fear being subjected to perse-cution upon a return to their country of origin, or individuals who fear being trafficked, whose claim to international protection falls within the refugee def-inition contained in the 1951 Convention and/or its 1967 Protocol relating to the Status of Refugees are recognized as refugees and afforded the correspond-ing international protection" (3).

The guidelines in no way suggest that all victims of trafficking are entitled to refugee status, although they do demonstrate how some victims may have entitlements under the Refugee Convention. For example, they state that some acts – which are inherent to the trafficking experience – "constitute serious vio-lations of human rights which will generally amount to persecution" (ibid.:6). These include: abduction, incarceration, rape, sexual enslavement, enforced prostitution, forced labor, removal of organs, physical beatings, starvation, and the deprivation of medical treatment. The guidelines also state that

> the mere existence of a law prohibiting trafficking in persons will not of itself be sufficient to exclude the possibility of persecution. If a law exists but is not effectively implemented, or if administrative mechanisms are in place to provide protection and assistance to victims, but the individual concerned is unable to gain access to such mechanism, the State may be deemed unable to extend protection to the victims, or potential victim, of trafficking. (ibid.:9)

The guidelines include provisions related to the possible persecution upon the return of trafficking victims to the territory from which they have fled or were trafficked. For example, the guidelines state that reprisals and/or possible re-trafficking could amount to persecution depending on whether or not the acts feared involve serious human rights violations. In addition, the guidelines recognize that victims may fear ostracism, discrimination, or punishment by their family and/or the local community which could give rise to a well-founded fear of persecution, particularly if aggravated by the trauma suffered during or resulting from the trafficking process. Notably, the guidelines note that even if the ostracism does not rise to the level of persecution, "such rejection by, and isolation from, social support networks may in fact heighten the risk of being re-trafficked or of being exposed to retaliation, which could give rise to a well-founded fear of persecution" (ibid.:7).

Office of the High Commission for Human Rights (OHCHR) has been carrying out an anti-trafficking program entitled Eliminating Trafficking and Protecting the Rights of Trafficked Persons under the Agency's Voluntary Fund for Technical Cooperation in the Field of Human Rights. Through biannual resolutions on trafficking by the Commission on Human Rights, OHCHR is mandated to address human trafficking at the international, regional, and national levels.

OHCHR has gradually built up its migration and trafficking related work during the past decade. The work on trafficking is guided by the *Recommended Principles and Guidelines on Human Rights and Human Trafficking* issued in 2002. In keeping with the overall mission of UNHCHR, the human rights of "trafficked persons shall be at the centre of all efforts to prevent and combat trafficking and to protect, assist and provide redress to victims" (OHCHR 2002:3). The guidelines acknowledge that states have primary responsibility under international law "to act with due diligence to prevent trafficking, to investigate and prosecute traffickers and to assist and protect trafficked persons" (3). In carrying out their responsibilities, states should endeavor to ensure that "anti-trafficking measures shall not adversely affect the human rights and dignity of persons, in particular the rights of those who have been trafficked, and of migrants, internally displaced persons, refugees and asylum-seekers" (3). The guidelines also highlight that human rights abuses are both a cause and consequence of human trafficking.

Much of OHCHR's work is concerned with capacity-building. The focus of the activities is governments, international organizations, and nongovernmental agencies that work on trafficking issues. For example, OHCHR organized a consultation for members of the Arab League to help ensure that a newly developed Arab Strategy for Combating Human Trafficking included a human rights framework. OHCHR also administers the UN Voluntary Fund on Contemporary Forms of Slavery, which provides small grants to civil society organizations to combat slavery. Many of the funded projects are trafficking-related. In 2012, for example, projects included: a reintegration center for the victims of trafficking and people under risk of trafficking; protection of street children from trafficking; access to justice, education, and sensitization of traditional authorities as a means to combat trafficking in children; implementing progressive actions to address human trafficking; engaging communities in the fight against organ trafficking; and An Giang/Dong Thap Alliance for the Prevention of Trafficking (ADAPT) – Project Returnee Initial Support Essentials

(RISE).[24] At present, OHCHR has little field capacity to undertake programs on its own or to monitor conditions of trafficked persons. The 2011 annual report stated that

> A limited number of OHCHR field presences has begun to develop work on migration in their particular country or regional context. Yet more needs to be done to develop and strengthen their capacity to engage at the operational and field levels in order to monitor violations, advise on and address concrete migration issues through a human rights lens, including by supporting implementation of recommendations issued by human rights mechanisms. (OHCHR 2011)[25]

The special rapporteur on trafficking in persons, especially women and children is supported by OHCHR. The special rapporteur: (1) takes action on violations committed against trafficked persons and on situations in which there has been a failure to protect their human rights; (2) undertakes country visits in order to study the situation in situ and formulate recommendations to prevent and or combat trafficking and protect the human rights of its victims in specific countries and/or regions; and (3) submits annual reports on the activities of the mandate to the Human Rights Council.[26]

The special rapporteur's May 2012 mission to Gabon is indicative of the work of that arm of the human rights community. In her concluding statement, Joy Ngozi Ezeilo commended Gabon for ratifying the Trafficking Protocol and taking steps to enact legislation in support of the country's obligations as a party to the protocol. She also pointed to a range of deficiencies related to the trafficking of persons from other West African countries into Gabon: legislative provisions that applied only to children under the age of eighteen, leaving trafficked adults without protection; deplorable conditions in shelters for trafficked children; absence of any prosecution of traffickers; and weak coordination within the government ministries responsible for counter-trafficking activities. The report concluded with specific recommendations to address these issues.[27]

Often in coordination with colleagues with mandates on related issues, the special rapporteur takes specific complaints and communicates them to the relevant governments. For example,

> On 15 October 2010, the Special Rapporteur, jointly with the Special Rapporteur on the sale of children, child prostitution and child pornography, the Special Rapporteur on contemporary forms of slavery, and the Special Rapporteur on the human rights of migrants, sent a letter of allegation concerning an estimated 70,000 child bonded labourers who worked in the so-called 'rat mines' of Jaintia Hills, which is located in the North Eastern State of Meghalaya, India. (Ezeilo 2011)

[24] http://www.ohchr.org/Documents/Issues/Slavery/2012Projects.pdf.
[25] http://www2.ohchr.org/english/ohchrreport2011/web_version/ohchr_report2011_web/allegati/12_Migration.pdf.
[26] http://www.ohchr.org/EN/Issues/Trafficking/Pages/TraffickingIndex.aspx.
[27] http://www.ohchr.org/en/NewsEvents/Pages/DisplayNews.aspx?NewsID=12176&LangID=E.

The complaint went to the governments of India, Bangladesh, and Nepal – India being the receiving country and Bangladesh and Nepal the source countries of the trafficked children. Complaints regarding the treatment of individuals who claimed to be trafficked were also conveyed to proper authorities. In some cases, the governments explained their actions and/or took corrective measures; in other cases, the special rapporteur noted no government response to the communication.

The special rapporteur has also brought attention to the larger question of compensation for persons who have been trafficked. Her 2011 report to the Human Rights Council and General Assembly addressed trafficking victims' access to effective remedies. The report reviewed the international legal framework in place regarding compensation and proposed adoption of basic principles on the right to an effective remedy for victims. A number of countries have initiated processes by which trafficked persons can sue traffickers for compensation in civil courts or via employment tribunals. In other countries, mandatory restitution of lost wages to trafficked persons is part of the criminal sentencing of traffickers (OHCHR 2010).

The International Labor Organization conducts its trafficking work within the context of the Special Action Program to combat Forced Labor (SAP-FL). SAP-FL is part of broader efforts to promote the 1998 Declaration on Fundamental Principles and Rights at Work and its follow-up. Since its inception, SAP-FL has been concerned with raising global awareness of forced labor in its different forms. Several thematic and country-specific studies on human trafficking have since been undertaken.

Just as the other international organizations see trafficking from the perspective of their principal mandates (law enforcement, migration, refugees, human rights), ILO views the issues as they relate to employment. In explaining its work on trafficking, the organization states "Where the demand for cheap and flexible labour moves beyond the boundaries of legal migration, the trafficker provides a link between demand and supply" (ILO 2005:3). The organization also highlights that its "own experience shows that law enforcement alone cannot be an effective remedy for these problems. There is always a need for a dual approach, combining prosecution and law enforcement with employment-based and other social measures for prevention and the rehabilitation of victims" (ILO 2005:v).

In setting out the relationship between human trafficking and forced labor exploitation, ILO produced a guide for legislators that identified three principal areas of concern: criminalization of forced labor and eradication of the worst forms of child labor, prosecution of recruiters and other auxiliaries, and identification and protection of victims (ibid.). More fundamentally, ILO's strategy with regard to prevention focuses on finding decent work so that people are not vulnerable to the enticements of traffickers: "The ILO's approach to prevention is to promote productive work under conditions of freedom, equity, security and dignity, in which rights are protected and adequate remuneration and social coverage are provided" (ibid.:5). By incorporating trafficking into a broader labor rights framework, ILO hopes to address the root causes of trafficking, regardless of what form it takes. The organization highlights its own conventions on forced labor and migrant rights as appropriate complements to the trafficking protocol.

ILO has produced a training manual aimed at educating government officials, especially labor inspectors, employers' organizations, and trade unions on trafficking and its relationship to job placement systems. Recruitment agencies often place migrants into exploitative situations that can easily deteriorate into trafficking and forced labor. The manual emphasizes that deception of migrants in the recruitment process is often a prelude to trafficking. Deception can take the following forms:

> excess charging of fees for visas and other travel documents; processing and provision of fake travel documents without informing the migrant of their illegitimate status; recruitment for non-existent jobs; misrepresenting the job and work conditions (e.g. women going abroad who believe they will work as domestic help but end up in prostitution); providing the future migrant worker with a loan that is hard to pay back ..., leading to situations of debt bondage and forced labour. (ILO 2006b:21)

The manual recommends good labor practices that are consistent with the principles discussed in Chapter 3 and likely to curb the potential for trafficking. A follow-up handbook aimed at employers and businesses provides information about preventive and remedial action, reviews good practice in combating forced labor, and presents information relevant to senior business managers, human resource personnel, sourcing and social compliance staff, social auditors, and others (ILO 2008).

Other specialized UN agencies and funds have also addressed issues of human trafficking, largely in the context of their own mandates. For example, UNICEF focuses particularly on protection of children from trafficking and through its Innocenti Research Centre hosts a Child Trafficking Research Hub; UN Development Program (UNDP) aims to identify the factors that increase women's and girls' vulnerability to trafficking and to develop responses for the facilitation of safe mobility; UN Women addresses the trafficking of women within the context of violence against women and focuses on improving data and information systems related to trafficking in women; UNESCO has undertaken policy-oriented research on specific factors leading to the trafficking of women and children in pilot countries in Africa and Asia; UNAIDS aims to address the root causes of human trafficking, including poverty, limited access to education and jobs, and social and cultural attitudes and practices that devalue women, girls and, children; and UNFPA sees trafficking as being directly related to gender inequality, lack of women's empowerment, violence against women, and reproductive health issues.

Rounding out these activities is the International Criminal Police Organization (INTERPOL), the world's largest intergovernmental police organization, with 186 member countries. Created in 1923, it facilitates cross-border police cooperation and supports and assists all organizations, authorities, and services whose mission is to prevent or combat international crime. With regard to trafficking, INTERPOL describes four areas of activity: "(1) Operations and projects – concrete action in the field to dismantle human trafficking networks; (2) INTERPOL tools – technical tools and systems for sharing information globally; (3) Partnerships – strengthening our approach by working across sectors; and (4) Events and conferences – bringing together experts from across the world."[28] INTERPOL has an Expert Working Group on Trafficking in Human Beings, which raises awareness of emerging issues, promotes prevention programs and initiates specialized training. The Working Group has promulgated a manual of best practices for law enforcement investigators with information on how to investigate trafficking for sexual exploitation, trafficking for forced labor, trafficking for domestic servitude, and trafficking for organ removal. INTERPOL also provides a standardized format for reporting cases of trafficking and smuggling.

Recognizing the complexity of the international system, UN GIFT was launched in 2007 to provide a more coherent framework for many of these efforts. It is managed by UNODC in cooperation with ILO, IOM, UNICEF, UNHCR, and a regional body, the Organization for Security and Cooperation in Europe (OSCE). UN GIFT's mission statement describes the aim as:

> The United Nations Global Initiative to Fight Human Trafficking (UN.GIFT) aims to mobilize state and non-state actors to eradicate human trafficking by (i) reducing both the vulnerability of potential victims and the demand for exploitation in all its forms; (ii) ensuring adequate protection and support to those who do fall victim, and (iii) supporting the efficient prosecution of the criminals involved, while respecting the fundamental human rights of all persons. In carrying out its mission UN.GIFT will increase the knowledge and awareness on human trafficking; promote effective rights-based responses; build capacity of state and non-state actors; and foster partnerships for joint action against human trafficking.[29]

UN GIFT's strategy focuses on three elements. The first involves building awareness of human trafficking, particularly through support for innovative public-private partnerships. The second strategy is to increase the knowledge base about trafficking. "The research component of UN.GIFT aims to deepen understanding of human trafficking by better data collection, analysis and sharing, as well as joint research initiatives."[30] The third element is technical assistance, helping states develop more effective policies and programs,

---

[28] http://www.interpol.int/Crime-areas/Trafficking-in-human-beings/Trafficking-in-human-beings.

[29] http://www.ungift.org/knowledgehub/en/about/.

[30] http://www.ungift.org/knowledgehub/en/about/goals.html.

including the development of a standardized methodology to collect and analyze national data on human trafficking. UN GIFT was launched with a grant from the United Arab Emirates and subsequently received additional financial support from the governments of Australia, Austria, Belgium, Canada, and Switzerland as well as a number of international organizations. It can also receive contributions from members of the public.

Heightening awareness of trafficking is a principal focus of UN GIFT's activities. In summer 2012, for example, it collaborated with the NGO Stop the Traffik (sic) to install public art during the Olympic Games in London aimed at raising awareness about trafficking victims' experiences. UN GIFT also supports research projects to collect data and statistics on trafficking trends and helps forge new alliances that bring together state and non-state actors bodies endeavoring to stop human trafficking.

Ensuring cooperation among the broader set of agencies rests with the Inter-Agency Coordination Group against Trafficking in Persons, for which UNODC serves as secretariat as discussed. A first meeting of the agencies participating in ICAT set out its overall aim "to improve coordination and cooperation between UN agencies and other international organizations to facilitate a holistic approach to preventing and combating trafficking in persons including protection of and support for victims of trafficking" (ICAT 2006:7). Its functions include providing a platform for exchange of information, experiences, and good practices and encouraging, supporting, and reviewing the activities of the members of ICAT to ensure "a full and comprehensive implementation of all international instruments and standards of relevance for the prevention and combating of trafficking in persons and protection of and support for victims of trafficking" (ibid.:7). The agencies would meet annually.

A questionnaire to the member agencies revealed barriers to cooperation, including failure to share meaningful project data between counterparts, particularly because other agencies are often perceived not only as collaborators, but also as competitors for scarce resources (UNODC 2010). The failure to cooperate led to duplication of activities and waste of funds due to a lack of knowledge about activities undertaken by other organizations; fragmented information and technical assistance activities, lack of information sharing resulting in loss of time and resources for collecting already available knowledge, and scattered research and data (ibid.). A 2010 report described more fully the activities of each of the member organizations, identified gaps, and provided recommendations. Most of the gap analysis dealt only with issues related to individual organization mandates rather than a coherent strategy to outline areas in which collaboration would be useful.

A theme throughout the analysis was the gap in protection of trafficked persons. Although each agency highlighted the need to protect those who had been trafficked, the gap analysis revealed the limited mandate and operational capacity of the international organizations in this regard. Several agencies have protection responsibilities for specific populations – for example, UNHCR for

refugees and asylum seekers and UNICEF for children. IOM sees protection as
a key priority but it does not have a formal protection mandate. OHCHR has
a protection mandate but does not have the physical presence or operational
capacity in many countries that would be needed to address protection issues.
Issues of sovereignty remain major constraints on developing an effective protection capacity. All international organizations recognize the ultimate authority and responsibility of governments to protect trafficked persons through all
stages from prevention to reintegration or resettlement. Yet, as is the case with
other vulnerable populations, relying totally on state protection is inadequate.
This is especially true when organized criminal elements corrupt government
officials in order to profit from trafficking.

In 2012, ICAT launched a public consultation to determine how best to
fill gaps. The overview paper prepared for the online consultation set out five
areas in which greater progress is needed: (1) the international legal framework
relating to trafficking in persons; (2) evaluating anti-trafficking responses; (3)
preventing trafficking in persons by addressing demand; (4) preventing trafficking in persons by addressing vulnerabilities; and (5) providing effective
remedies for trafficked persons. In each case, ICAT outlined the nature of the
problem, options for consideration and questions to be addressed.

CONCLUSION

Despite more than 100 years of interest in trafficking, the international regime
(that is, the legal norms and international institutional frameworks) to address
human trafficking is in its infancy. The principal legal framework for combating modern-day trafficking went into force in 2003, and the institutional
structures to help states implement the Palermo Protocols are only now being
fully developed. It appears that states recognize the need for multilateral cooperation in combating trafficking, which explains the relatively rapid ratification
of the protocols. This is in sharp contrast to the UN Convention on the Rights
of Migrant Workers and Members of their Families. Yet, the Palermo Protocol is weak in laying out the rights of trafficked persons and it is cautious in
assigning responsibilities to governments to prevent trafficking or protect those
who have been trafficked. As a normative framework, it stands between the
well-ratified instruments that define the rights of refugees and the much less
agreed upon frameworks for migrant workers.

This chapter has demonstrated that a large number of international organizations have developed programs during the past decade to address trafficking
but no single organization is responsible for combating the phenomenon in
a holistic manner, focusing on all elements of an effective counter-trafficking
strategy. While millions are spent each year on efforts to prevent trafficking,
prosecute those who engage in this activities, and protect the victims, little
is known at present about the efficacy of any of these endeavors or on how
activities in one sphere (for example, prosecution) affect activities in the others

(prevention and protection). The various coordination mechanisms established to reduce duplication and address gaps in responses have not been evaluated to determine their effectiveness. Without such specific information, the jury is still out on the impact of the norms and institutions established to address human trafficking.

6

Migration and International Security

This chapter examines one means through which an emerging international migration regime should be understood: cooperation in addressing international security challenges arising from increased global mobility. The focus of this chapter is the establishment of mechanisms to share information and coordinate actions to reduce the risk of migration for source, transit and destination countries. Two distinct issues are addressed from a security perspective: unauthorized/irregular migration and movements of terrorists and criminals. The issues covered include regulation of short-term cross-border movements for business and tourism – what Rey Koslowski (2011) has described as the international travel regime. The engagement of international organizations that are not usually considered a part of the migration system (e.g., the International Civil Aviation Administration) will be examined. Of particular interest is the evolving normative framework for addressing issues of human smuggling. The security dimension of refugee and asylum movements will be referenced as they pertain to these issues, with the broader connections having been discussed in Chapter 2.

The interconnection between migration and security concerns raises challenges for governments in three areas: (1) how best to cooperate in ensuring that those who pose security threats are not able to carry out their activities cross borders; (2) how to accomplish this task without overly impeding legitimate, beneficial international mobility; and (3) how to ensure that individual rights and privacy are protected in the process. In an age of globalization, in which eradicating barriers to business travel and tourism is a core objective, finding the appropriate balance between facilitation and control is difficult. Similarly, respect for privacy and rights calls for protection of the individual against intrusions by the state but security often necessitates some exceptions in the interest of the public good. A key issue discussed in this chapter is the role of international bodies in setting priorities and principles that will reach the correct balance among these interests.

The chapter will examine initiatives in the post–September 11 era to exchange information to deter the mobility of terrorists. In 2006, the UN adopted a resolution on counter-terrorism intended

> to encourage the United Nations Counter Terrorism Committee and its Executive Directorate to continue to work with States, at their request, to facilitate the adoption of legislation and administrative measures to implement the terrorist travel-related obligations, and to identify best practices in this area, drawing whenever possible on those developed by technical international organizations such as the International Civil Aviation Organization, the World Customs Organization and the International Criminal Police Organization.[1]

One area of such cooperation has been efforts to improve the exchange of airline passenger information and its verification before passengers are permitted to fly.

In discussing consultative processes that primarily address the control of unauthorized migration, the chapter sets out the relative merits of regional versus global arrangements. It focuses particularly on the Bali Process in Asia and the Budapest Process in Europe, whose agendas are heavily concerned with migration and security issues.

BACKGROUND

The interconnections between migration and security are complex. Migration is often a result of economic, political, and social insecurity but it can also itself be a destabilizing factor. Traditionally, security has been viewed in terms of relationships among states. Rudolph (2003:604) suggests a broader conceptualization that is more relevant to understanding the interconnections between migration and security: "the 'national interest' of states can be defined largely along three dimensions: (1) geopolitical security, (2) the production and accumulation of material wealth, and (3) social stability and cohesion." All three factors are important in understanding the formulation of migration policies. According to Rudolph (2003:616), "the empirical evidence suggests that military security interests do not wholly dominate migration policy as one might predict. Societal security remains salient, and economic interests continue to serve as a powerful counterweight." This may occur because governments are "caught between economic forces that propel them toward greater openness (to maximize material wealth and economic security) and political forces that seek a higher degree of closure (to protect the demos, maintain the integrity of the community, and preserve the social contract" (Hollifield 2004).

---

[1] All quotes from the 2006 Resolution (A/RES/60/288) are from the version found at https://www.un.org/en/terrorism/strategy-counter-terrorism.shtml.

In one of the earliest examinations of the interconnections between migration and security, Myron Weiner (1992–93:103) noted, "migration can be perceived as threatening by governments of either population-sending or population-receiving communities." Weiner argued that a security lens was as important as a political economy one in understanding the causes and impacts of migration. He described the need for a

> security/stability framework for the study of international migration which focuses on state policies toward emigration and immigration as shaped by concerns over internal stability and international security. Such a framework would consider political changes within states as a major determinant of international population flows, and migration – including refugee flows – both as a cause and a consequence of international conflict. (ibid.:94)

Weiner identified five ways in which migration might be seen as a security concern: (1) "when refugees and migrants are regarded as a threat – or at least a thorn – in relations between sending and receiving countries; (2) when migrants or refugees are perceived as a political threat or security risk to the regime of the host country; (3) when immigrants are seen as a cultural threat, (4) as a social and economic problem for the host society; and (5) when the host society uses immigrants as an instrument of threat against the country of origin" (Weiner 1990:405). To this list may be added situations in which the source country uses emigration as an instrument of threat against the destination country. The Cuban government, for example, used its control over exit as an instrument of its foreign policy against the United States, opening ports of exit at strategic points and, as in the case of the Mariel boatlift, releasing criminals from prisons and forcing them onto boats ferrying passengers to Florida.

All of these security threats can be real or perceived. To some extent, it does not matter since perception is often as relevant to the policy-making process as the actuality of threat. As Weiner (1992–93:104) notes, "It is necessary to find an analytical stance that, on the one hand, does not dismiss fears, and, on the other, does not regard all anxieties over immigration and refugees as a justification for exclusion."

Adamson (2006:191) considers the migration and security linkages in discussing the ways in which migration affects the nature of violent conflict in the international system. She argues "Migration flows can interact with other factors in three ways to exacerbate conditions that foment violent conflict in the international system: by providing resources that help to fuel internal conflicts; by providing opportunities for networks of organized crime; and by providing conduits for international terrorism." As examples, she notes the role of diaspora groups in arming insurgencies, the recalcitrance of refugees and displaced persons to join peace processes, and the spill-over effects when militants use refugee camps to launch attacks on their home countries. By contrast, Fagen and Bump (2006) outline a number of ways in which diaspora groups have contributed to peace by rebuilding essential infrastructure, including health and educational facilities, participating in a constructive way in peace negotiations, and using remittances to provide an alternative source of income to demobilized soldiers and civilian returnees.

The security implications may be quite different for three principal groups of migrants. The first category includes refugees – that is, those who cross international borders as a result of persecution, conflict, or political instability. Their flight is often the direct consequence of insecurity but, too often, the conflict that led to their predicament crosses borders with them. The second category is composed of irregular migrants – that is, those who move without authorization to enter destination countries. A large proportion of those who enter another country illegally do so with the assistance of human smugglers. The third category may be better characterized as mobile populations, rather than migrants, in that they do not intend to settle in the destination country for even short periods. They are business travelers, students, and tourists who present security concerns because terrorists and criminals can utilize the pathways available to legitimate travelers.

The security implications may also vary substantially depending on the way in which migration occurs. For example, rapid movements of people, often because of natural disasters or other emergencies, generally appear to pose greater security risks than more gradual labor migration. This is especially likely when authorities in destination countries are unprepared to handle the inflow of people. Highly visible migrants, such as those arriving by boat, often appear more threatening than larger numbers of migrants crossing land borders or arriving by air. Migrants entering without inspection will generally be seen as more threatening to a destination country than those who enter through legal channels after verification of their identity and reasons for travel. A caveat here is misuse of visa systems by those who receive permission to enter using fraudulent means – either through counterfeit documentation or by lying about the purpose of the trip. The extent to which organized criminal networks are involved in the migration flows or migrants are involved in organized criminal activity, including gangs, is another variable affecting the perception and reality of threat.

Destination countries are not alone in experiencing the security implications of migration. Countries of origin and transit may also be affected. Expulsions and evacuation of migrant workers during crises may disrupt remittances from overseas workers to countries that are highly dependent on these funds. Many of these same countries are ill-prepared to reintegrate migrants into their poor economies. Smuggling generally requires the complicity of government officials in origin, transit, and destination countries; such corruption may undermine the rule of law not only in this area but in others as well. Countries of origin may also experience significant loss of its tertiary educated population, making it all the more difficult to provide for the economic, health, and educational security of those who remain behind. Although remittances may help compensate for some of the loss, the origin country may end up in a cycle requiring ever more emigration to provide for its population.

It is important to keep in mind that the security implications are not one-sided. International migration can provide security benefits to source and destination countries. As Adamson (2006:185) notes, "if states have the capacity to design and implement effective policies that 'harness the power of migration,' international migration flows can enhance, rather than detract from or compromise, state power." Immigrants bring new ideas, technical skills and expertise that can help the destination country's security. An extreme case certainly was the flight of scientists from persecution in Europe, which gave the Allied powers an edge in the development of the atomic bomb, decryption of codes, and other war-related technological advances. Source countries have benefited from the emigration of citizens who, on return home, used skills and financial resources developed abroad to help establish strategic industries, improve health and education, or even serve in government ministries responsible for enhancing security.

The many positive aspects of migration have led many scholars and some policy makers to be cautious in using security language in discussing migration. They fear that the security discourse feeds into xenophobia. Huysmans (2000: 752) for example, writes:

> the political process of connecting migration to criminal and terrorist abuses of the internal market does not take place in isolation. It is related to a wider politicization in which immigrants and asylum-seekers are portrayed as a challenge to the protection of national identity and welfare provisions. Moreover, supporting the political construction of migration as a security issue impinges on and is embedded in the politics of belonging in western Europe.

Ibrahim (2005:163) equates linking migration and security to racism, stating:

> freedom of human mobility has nearly disappeared. Instead, powerful words are travelling the globe unhindered: risk and security. They are being strung together with the present "migration phenomena," leaving migrants bound by the chain of the new security discourse: the securitization of migration. This discourse is racism's most modern form.

Collyer (2006:268) takes a more balanced view in concluding from his study of the French government's response to Algerian migrants: "Migration policy has become one of the most significant influences on migration and security is the dominant force behind migration policy. Any understanding of human movement must therefore incorporate notions of security at both an empirical and theoretical level."

NORMATIVE FRAMEWORK

There exists no comprehensive instrument or set of rules specifically devoted to migration and security. Nevertheless, security is a feature in all international law, including the conventions that define the rights of migrants and refugees and the obligations of states toward them. The extent to which concerns about national security permit parties to derogate from their obligations varies. For example, the 1951 Refugee Convention provides that the right to *non-refoulement* (that is, the obligation of states not to return refugees to where they would face persecution) does not apply to any refugee "whom there are reasonable grounds for regarding as a danger to the security of the country in which he is, or who, having been convicted of a final judgment of a particularly serious crime, constitutes a danger to the community of that country." In contrast, the UN Convention against Torture and Other Cruel, Inhuman or Degrading Treatment forbids member countries to "expel, return ('refouler') or extradite a person to another State where there are substantial grounds for believing that he would be in danger of being subjected to torture."[2] No exception is provided for national security.

International law may also give parties to certain conventions the right to enforce national immigration laws in areas that are adjacent to their borders as a matter of national security.

> Under the United Nations Convention on the Law of the Sea ("UNCLOS") and customary maritime law, states are entitled to enforce domestic laws including immigration laws in their territorial seas and on ships bearing their flags. UNCLOS extends the right to enforce certain types of domestic law, including immigration controls, to "contiguous zones" (which extend an additional twelve miles from the end of the territorial sea). (Fisher et al. 2003:94)

On the high seas, by contrast, states may not interfere with foreign flag vessels for purposes of enforcing immigration law unless the flag state consents (ibid.). The right to leave a country is guaranteed in a number of international conventions, but this right can be subject to restrictions that are necessary for the maintenance of public order, public safety, or national security. Restrictions on the right to leave have been justified on "national security grounds for military personnel, persons subject to a mandatory national service requirement, and persons subject to criminal proceedings or sentences" (ibid.:111). Countries also impose restrictions on where their citizens can travel. Even where an outright ban is not imposed, countries may restrict the right to spend their currency in designated countries.

---

[2] See Convention Against Torture and Other Cruel, Inhuman or Degrading Treatment or Punishment, Art. 3(1), December 10, 1984, G.A. Res. 39/46, 39 UN GAOR Supp. (No. 51), UN Doc. A/39/51, at 197 (1984).

Part 4 of the Migrant Workers Convention provides for freedom of movement for those legally working in the country: "1. Migrant workers and members of their families shall have the right to liberty of movement in the territory of the State of employment and freedom to choose their residence there." It includes the national security escape clause in paragraph two:

> The rights mentioned in paragraph 1 of the present article shall not be subject to any restrictions except those that are provided by law, are necessary to protect national security, public order (ordre public), public health or morals, or the rights and freedoms of others and are consistent with the other rights recognized in the present Convention.

Similar language granting freedom of movement does not appear in Part 3, which sets out the rights of all migrants regardless of their legal status. This provides states more leeway in detaining or restricting the movements of those without authorization. States are to abide, however, by prohibitions against arbitrary detention and requirements that detainees be provided prompt access to a court (Fisher et al. 2003). No exception is made for national security except in cases of a declared state national emergency (ibid.).

The authority of countries to expel is constrained in a number of ways, subject to national security. For example,

> States may not engage in collective expulsions of aliens. In other words, expulsions must be based on individualized determinations of need for each alien. Moreover ... aliens are entitled to several specific procedural protections prior to being expelled, including review by a competent authority and the opportunity to submit reasons against the expulsion. These procedural rights, however, may be denied if "national security" so requires. (ibid.:117)

Article 32 of the Refugee Convention permits parties to expel refugees for reasons of national security and public order, and "such expulsions may be ordered without a hearing for the refugee if 'compelling reasons of national security' so require" (ibid.:119).

MIGRATION AND SECURITY CHALLENGES IN PRACTICE

This section focuses on two areas in which migration has been viewed through a national security lens: the mobility of terrorists and the role of organized crime in human smuggling. Each is treated separately since the topics raise somewhat different – although in some cases related – issues in forging international cooperation.

Immigration and Terrorism

The security implications of migration have taken on new meaning as terrorism has become a global problem. Even before the events of September 11, 2011, governments had worried that terrorists would take advantage of weaknesses in border security to enter other countries. The wakeup call for the United States came in 1993 when putative asylum seekers were implicated in the bombing of the World Trade Center in New York and shooting deaths outside the Central Intelligence Agency building in northern Virginia. The 1995 domestic terrorist attacks in Oklahoma City, initially blamed on foreign terrorists, paved the way for new legislation. In 1996, Congress passed the Effective Death Penalty and Anti-Terrorism Act, which in combination with later legislation, put in place special policies and procedures for the removal of persons suspected of terrorist activities.

September 11 raised further questions not only in the United States but globally about the capacities of governments to prevent the movement of terrorists across borders. Given the transnational nature of the terrorist problem, international cooperation appeared to be essential to controlling these movements. Nevertheless, the bases for such cooperation were not obvious. One of the principal barriers was lack of consensus about what constituted terrorism. Efforts to forge an international consensus on the meaning of terrorism had begun in the 1930s with negotiation of the League of Nations Convention for the Prevention and Punishment of Terrorism, which was adopted in 1937 but never went into force. Terrorism was defined in highly state-centric terms. Article 1 defined acts of terrorism as "criminal acts directed against a State and intended or calculated to create a state of terror in the minds of particular persons, or a group of persons or the general public" (Saul 2006). More specifically, the convention referred to any willful act causing death or grievous bodily harm or loss of liberty to heads of state, their spouses, and other public officials when the act is directed against them in their public capacity. Also included was willful destruction of, or damage to, public property; willful acts calculated to endanger the lives of members of the public; and manufacturing, obtaining, possessing, or supplying of arms, ammunition, explosives, or harmful substances with a view to committing any of the previously cited actions. Conspiracy, incitement, willful participation, and assistance knowingly given toward the commission of a terrorist act were also to be punishable as acts of terrorism. Pertinent to migration issues, the convention also specified that the fraudulent manufacture and use of passports and equivalent documents were to be punished.

As with other League of Nations conventions, World War II intervened and the convention never went into force. Afterwards, little further action was taken in addressing the overall issue of terrorism but a number of conventions tackled specific elements. Among the most pertinent[3]:

- The 1973 Convention on the Prevention and Punishment of Crimes against Internationally Protected Persons. The convention included diplomatic

---

[3] Quotes from UN Conventions related to terrorism are taken from the versión found at https://www.un.org/en/terrorism/instruments.shtml.

agents, protected heads of state, members of their families, and other public officials, including representatives of international organizations. It focused on the intentional murder, kidnapping, or violent attack against persons or premises, private accommodation, or means of transport.

- The 1979 International Convention against the Taking of Hostages, which addressed the seizure, detention, and threats designed to compel a third party – a state, international organization, natural or juridical person, or a group of persons – "to take or abstain from doing any act as an explicit or implicit condition for the release of the hostage."

- The 1997 International Convention for the Suppression of Terrorist Bombings, which defined the offense as unlawful and intentional delivery, placement, discharge, or detonation of an explosive in, into, or against a place of public use, a state or government facility, a public transportation system, or an infrastructure facility "with the intent to cause death or serious bodily injury or with the intent to cause extensive destruction of such a place, facility or system, where such destruction results in or is likely to result in major economic loss."

- The 1999 Convention for the Suppression of the Financing of Terrorism proscribed funding of the actions described in the other conventions and added: "Any other act intended to cause death or serious bodily injury to a civilian, or to any other person not taking part in the hostilities in a situation of armed conflict, when the purpose of such act, by its nature or context, is to intimidate a population, or to compel a government or an international organization to do or to abstain from doing any act."

- The 2005 International Convention for the Suppression of Acts of Nuclear Terrorism defines the offence as unlawful and intentional possession of or use of radioactive material or device with the intent to cause death or serious bodily injury or to cause substantial damage to property or to the environment. It also applies to damaging a nuclear facility in a manner that releases or risks the release of radioactive material, including when it is done to compel a government, international organization, or natural or legal person to do or refrain from doing an act.

In addition, the 2010 Convention on the Suppression of Unlawful Acts Relating to International Civil Aviation and its Protocol criminalize the acts of using civil aircraft as a weapon and using dangerous materials to attack aircraft or other targets on the ground.

Efforts to enact a comprehensive convention with a universal definition of terrorism have failed to reach agreement. According to the UN, such a convention

> would complement the existing framework of international anti-terrorism instruments and would build on key guiding principles already present in recent anti-terrorist conventions: the importance of criminalization of terrorist offences, making them punishable by law and calling for prosecution or extradition of

the perpetrators; the need to eliminate legislation which establishes exceptions to such criminalization on political, philosophical, ideological, racial, ethnic, religious or similar grounds; a strong call for Member States to take action to prevent terrorist acts; and emphasis on the need for Member States to cooperate, exchange information and provide each other with the greatest measure of assistance in connection with the prevention, investigation and prosecution of terrorist acts.[4]

One of the impediments to agreement on a universal definition pertains to state-sponsored terrorism – determining when a military or police action by a government is an act of terrorism and when it is a legitimate exercise of state sovereignty (Walter et al. 2004). Another disagreement is on the issue often referred to as "one person's freedom fighter is another's terrorist." Some of the earlier conventions made clear that the end does not justify the means – specifying, as does the convention on financing terrorist acts, that "criminal acts within the scope of this Convention are under no circumstances justifiable by considerations of a political, philosophical, ideological, racial, ethnic, religious or other similar nature." Agreement on language capturing this sentiment for all aspects of terrorism has been more elusive.

In lieu of a comprehensive convention, the Security Council has passed a series of resolutions and the General Assembly adopted a Global Counter-Terrorism Strategy that together provides the basis for broad international cooperation. Security Council Resolution 1373, adopted in September 2001, makes several specific references to migration issues. First, it calls on governments to "prevent the movement of terrorists or terrorist groups by effective border controls and controls on issuance of identity papers and travel documents, and through measures for preventing counterfeiting, forgery or fraudulent use of identity papers and travel documents."[5] It also instructs states to "take appropriate measures in conformity with the relevant provisions of national and international law, including international standards of human rights, before granting refugee status, for the purpose of ensuring that the asylum seeker has not planned, facilitated or participated in the commission of terrorist acts" and "to ensure, in conformity with international law, that refugee status is not abused by the perpetrators, organizers or facilitators of terrorist acts, and that claims of political motivation are not recognized as grounds for refusing requests for the extradition of alleged terrorists." Security Council Resolution 1390 "imposed travel bans on individuals or entities who are terrorists or support terrorist activities, namely Osama bin Laden and members and associates of the Taliban and Al-Qaeda" (Ginsburg and Tanaka 2011: 163).

---

[4] http://www.un.org/terrorism/instruments.shtml.
[5] Quotes from Security Council Resolution 1373 are found at http://www.un.org/en/sc/ctc/specialmeetings/2012/docs/United%20Nations%20Security%20Council%20Resolution%201373%20(2001).pdf.

The 2006 General Assembly Counter-Terrorism Strategy laid out a four-point strategy based on the Security Council resolutions. In adopting the strategy, the UN condemned terrorism "in all its forms and manifestations, committed by whomever, wherever and for whatever purposes, as it constitutes one of the most serious threats to international peace and security."[6] The terms "whomever, wherever and for whatever purposes" accomplished the aims of those who wanted the definition to encompass state-sponsored terrorism and to bar a defense based on political, religious, ideological, and other bases without requiring agreement on the specifics.

The plan of action's four pillars included: (1) measures to address the conditions conducive to the spread of terrorism; (2) measures to prevent and combat terrorism; (3) measures to build states' capacity to prevent and combat terrorism and to strengthen the role of the UN system in this regard; and (4) measures to ensure respect for human rights for all and the rule of law as the fundamental basis of the fight against terrorism. A number of migration and refugee related provisions are included as sub-points.

Conditions Conclusive to the Spread of Terrorism

The plan of action refers to the need to counter "marginalization and the subsequent sense of victimization that propels extremism and the recruitment of terrorists." Although it does not specify marginalization of migrants, the strategy was adopted in the context of terrorist acts committed by immigrant and second generation youth in Europe. The first report of the working group that has been gathering an inventory of practices to combat radicalization includes a number of programs aimed at minorities, many of whom are of immigrant background.

The plan echoes the EU's 2005 strategy to address radicalization. One of its three components focuses on promoting security, justice, democracy, and opportunity for all.

> These conditions may include . . . lack of political and economic prospects, unresolved international and domestic strife; and inadequate and inappropriate education or cultural opportunities for young people. Within the Union, most of these factors are not present, but within individual segments of the population they may apply and there may also be issues of identity in immigrant communities. (European Union 2005:4)

Significantly, the EU issued principles of immigrant integration in 2004. Although not directly tied to the issues of radicalization, the integration strategy makes the case that "uncertainty and unequal treatment breed disrespect for the rules and can marginalise immigrants and their families, socially and economically" (EU 2004:22).

---

[6] All quotes from the General Assembly resolution, which sets forth the strategy and plan of action, are found at https://www.un.org/en/terrorism/strategy-counter-terrorism.shtml.

Prevent and Combat Terrorism

The measures to prevent and combat terrorism encourage countries to ratify the Convention against Transnational Crime and its protocols, including those on human trafficking and smuggling. The UN plan of action takes specific aim at measures related to asylum-seekers. States are encouraged "to take appropriate measures, before granting asylum, for the purpose of ensuring that the asylum seeker has not engaged in terrorist activities." After granting asylum, steps should be taken to ensure that refugee status is not used for organizing, instigating, facilitating, participating in, financing, encouraging, or tolerating terrorist activities.

Although there is little evidence of bona fide asylum-seekers or refugees being engaged in terrorist activities, the experience in the United States with terrorists misusing the asylum system to enter the country no doubt contributed to this section of the plan as it had the Security Council resolution. Complicating the situation, refugees come in disproportionate numbers from countries that are considered state supporters of terrorism; Somalia, Sudan, Afghanistan, Iran, and Iraq have produced refugees at the same time as they permitted or even encouraged terrorism. Determining who has been persecuted by these governments and who has been supported can be a difficult challenge.

Immediately after September 11, and despite the fact that none of the hijackers had been asylum applicants, UNHCR issued a statement of principles regarding terrorism and asylum. The agency began by citing concerns that preoccupation with terrorism would erode support for protection of refugees. Expressing the view that "Current anxieties about international terrorism risk fuelling a growing trend towards the criminalisation of asylum-seekers and refugees," UNHCR sought to reassure governments that existing legal frameworks and procedures could effectively distinguish between bona fide refugees and terrorists seeking to abuse the system (UNHCR 2001: para 2). The report concluded that "the international refugee instruments do not provide a safe haven to terrorists and do not protect them from criminal prosecution. On the contrary, they render the identification of persons engaged in terrorist activities possible and necessary, foresee their exclusion from refugee status and do not shield them against either criminal prosecution or expulsion" (UNHCR 2001: para 3). The Refugee Convention bars the granting of refugee status to those who have committed crimes against humanity, war crimes, particularly serious non-political acts, and actions that are in violation of the Charter of the United Nations. Most acts of terrorism can be defined as being within one or more of these categories.[7]

---

[7] The application of these standards varies from country to country, often depending on how terrorism and support for terrorism are defined. In the United States, for example, the U.S. Patriot Act bars admission of foreign nationals who have provided material support to terrorist organizations, defined broadly to include "groups of two or more individuals, whether organized or not," (Public Law 107–56—OCT. 26, 2001 115 STAT. 347) which engage in proscribed

Capacity Building and Border Controls

Measures to enhance capacity-building in addressing terrorism focus largely on regulation of entry and exit across international borders. In the UN plan of action, governments are encouraged "to continue to work within the United Nations system to support the reform and modernization of border management systems, facilities and institutions, at the national, regional and international level." The focus on border security is understandable in light of the report of the National Commission on Terrorist Attacks upon the United States (9/11 Commission). The 9/11 Commission concluded that "had the immigration system set a higher bar for determining whether individuals are who or what they claim to be . . . it could have potentially excluded, removed, or come into further contact with several hijackers who did not appear to meet the terms for admitting short-term visitors" (National Commission 2004: 384). Interestingly, a number of plotters failed to obtain visas, largely because as Yemeni citizens coming from a poor country they were considered at high risk of overstaying their visas. By contrast, the Saudi applicants were considered good prospects for admission because they came from a wealthier country with many economic and foreign policy ties to the United States. The 9/11 Commission found that a number of the hijackers had requested new passports to avoid showing that they had been previously in Pakistan, with access to Afghanistan. Others had altered passports. Some had been observed participating in terrorist gatherings but the intelligence information had not been matched to the immigration alert systems.

The concerns of the 9/11 Commission have been echoed in other countries. Consular officers and immigration inspectors usually have only a limited time to review passports and visas. The consular officers and inspectors would probably have been unable to identify the suspected terrorists even with additional time, however, because they did not have access to needed information in the law enforcement and intelligence databases. At the time of the terrorist attacks, most consular and immigration officers used name-based systems that were effective only if applicants used names that had been entered into the database. False names, supported by fraudulent documentation, could help an individual to evade identification. Moreover, intelligence services were generally reluctant to enter data from classified sources into immigration control

activities. There is no exception for providing material support under duress, which is particularly problematic for refugees. Even minimal support is prohibited. Applications for asylum have been put on hold because the applicant paid a ransom for the release of relatives kidnapped by insurgents or had been forced to cook, clean, and provide sexual services to the insurgents that had captured them (Sridharan 2008). In effect, what gives refugees a well-founded fear of persecution becomes the basis for denial of admission and, if they are already in the country, the potential for deportation. The legislation permits admission only if the Secretary of State and Secretary of Homeland Security specifically waive the application of the material support bar.

systems, fearing exposure of informants. In all too many cases, there was no actionable intelligence about visa applicants whose terrorist activities had not come to the attention of government authorities. Without this sensitive information, detection systems could never function effectively in preventing known terrorists from entering the country.

Governments have subsequently taken steps to help ensure that visa look-out systems receive more timely law enforcement and intelligence information to uncover fraud and abuse. Among the innovations are the use of machine readable passports and visas that are more difficult to counterfeit; greater use of biometrics, including fingerprints and digitized photos taken at time of application and matched to the person using the visas at ports of entry; and guidelines regulating the exchange of intelligence, law enforcement, and immigration information. Measures taken within individual countries have been complemented by initiatives to further information exchange among governments. For example, the United States and the EU negotiated an agreement on exchange of airline passenger information, which provides access to data that go well beyond what is included in passports – dates of travel and travel itinerary, ticket information, address and phone numbers, means of payment used, credit card number, travel agent, seat number, and baggage information (European Union 2012).

At the global level, the International Civil Aviation Organization (ICAO), which became a UN specialized agency in 1946, became responsible for developing passport standards in 1968 (Koslowski 2011, Salter 2003). As air hijacking increased in the 1970s, ICAO also focused on developing standards to increase aviation security, including by setting standards travel documents. In undertaking its standard setting role, ICAO notes: "It is a fundamental precept that if public authorities are to facilitate inspection formalities for the vast majority of air travelers, those authorities must have a satisfactory level of confidence in the reliability of travel documents and in the effectiveness of inspection procedures" (ICAO 2006:1.2). In effect, facilitation and control are mirror images of the same phenomenon, not principles in conflict with each other.

In 1980, ICAO member states agreed to standards for the issuance of machine readable travel documents (Koslowski 2011). It established a technical advisory group that has investigated new biometric technologies to increase the security of the documents still further. This work began prior to September 11 but accelerated in the aftermath of the terrorist attacks.

A basic concept underlying ICAO's work is global interoperability. The term is defined as "the capability of inspection systems (either manual or automated) in different States throughout the world to exchange data, to process data received from systems in other States, and to utilize that data in inspection operations in their respective States" (ICAO 2006:iii). In 2003, the Air Transport Committee of the ICAO governing council endorsed a recommendation that the universal biometric identifier on passports be a photo of the face, although governments could use fingerprints or iris scans for additional security. They also urged governments to move toward storing the passport data, including the biometric, in an electronic chip, such as Radio Frequency Identification (RFID) systems.

Adoption of RFID would allow faster transfer of data as passengers go through passport controls than is the case with machine readable technology that requires an inspector to physically swipe the document through a reader (Koslowski 2011). Such technology is seen as a way to facilitate travel while increasing security by enabling inspectors to quickly determine if the holder of a passport or visa is in fact the person to whom it was issued (ICAO 2006). The debate over the technology has focused largely on privacy concerns. Critics have been dubious that countries would produce and embed computer chips in a way that could not be read by those without a legitimate need for the information. Passport covers with aluminum fiber or other materials that shield the chip and encryption of data are aimed at averting this problem (Juels et al. 2005). ICAO also gave increased prominence to ways of preventing fraud, alteration, and counterfeiting of passports and chips.

Capacity Building and Money Laundering

A second relevant area of capacity-building discussed in the UN plan of action relates to money laundering. The plan encourages "the International Monetary Fund, the World Bank, the United Nations Office on Drugs and Crime and the International Criminal Police Organization to enhance cooperation with States to help them to comply fully with international norms and obligations to combat money-laundering and financing of terrorism." One target of such cooperation has been the informal system of financial transfers called Hawala. Hawala has been used extensively by immigrants to transfer money to their families in the Middle East, Africa, and South Asia because it is usually less expensive than more formal banking services. Law enforcement agencies are concerned that the same informality makes Hawala attractive to terrorists and organized crime as a means of laundering money. After September 11, a number of Hawala outlets, particularly those serving Somalia, were closed down. Since these were the main mechanisms through which Somalis abroad could send funds to their families, the shutdowns had serious repercussions for many innocent persons.

Terrorism, Migration, and Human Rights

With regard to human rights and the rule of law, the UN plan encourages countries to ensure that "any measures taken to combat terrorism comply with their obligations under international law, in particular human rights law, refugee law and international humanitarian law." Protecting the rights of persons suspected of terrorist activities while still addressing the serious security problems posed by terrorism continues to be a challenge for governments. In the days immediately following September 11, a rash of attacks against people believed to be of Arab or Muslim descent raised serious fears of a broad backlash against immigrants and immigration. An Amnesty International report[8] issued the first week in October 2001 cited more than 540 attacks on Arab-Americans and at least 200 on Sikhs in the week following the attacks on the World Trade Center and Pentagon. According to Amnesty, these attacks occurred in countries as diverse as Poland, India, the United Kingdom, and Denmark as well as the United States.

In the United States, at least, these attacks were relatively short-lived. A number of factors appear to have dampened the most egregious overreactions to Arab-Americans and Muslim immigrants. Elected public officials at the federal, state, and local levels played an important role in deflecting anger that may have otherwise been directed at immigrants. President Bush, Mayor Guiliani, and other officials quickly distinguished between the vast majority of law-abiding immigrants and the very few terrorists who had attacked the country. Visits to mosques and cultural centers, as well as highly visible meetings with Muslim and Arab community leaders, demonstrated that Islam and terrorism are not one and the same thing. At the same time, some early and vehement denunciations of terrorism by Muslim and Arab immigrants helped to alleviate public concerns. Public leaders demonstrated that they have great capacity to affect public perceptions, and, fortunately, this leadership was used to help protect minorities from abuses.

The terrorist attacks nevertheless raised concerns about the status of ethnic and religious minorities in developed countries. Several of the hijackers had spent considerable time studying or working in Europe and/or North America. At least two accused terrorists were naturalized citizens of European countries. This raised serious questions about the process of integration of religious and ethnic minorities in the West. If immigrants who are exposed to democratic values and institutions nevertheless turn to terrorism, one must question whether their experiences in the West have marginalized and radicalized them. This issue, of course, returns us to the first pillar of the UN strategy – addressing marginalization of minorities as a component of the plan to address conditions conducive to radicalization.

Irregular Migration and Human Smuggling

The second principal issue on the migration-security agenda has been irregular migration, with particular attention to the role of human smuggling operations. Irregular migration is a global phenomenon that is already large and has grown significantly over the past decades. Generally, irregular migration for employment purposes is driven by the same forces that propel people to move through legal channels: a ready supply of people, particularly from

---

[8] "Caught in the Backlash: Human Rights under Threat Worldwide in Aftermath of September 11 Attacks," *Amnesty International*, October 3, 2001.

developing countries, seeking greater economic opportunities; a demand for cheap labor in destination countries; and networks that are able to match workers to employers.

In contrast to legal immigration, however, irregular migration is the resort of those who are unable to enter under the often strict requirements imposed by governments on their temporary or permanent foreign worker programs. These requirements may be numerical – rigid limits on the number of visas issued each year, or they may be qualitative educational, occupational, or skill requirements. They may be imposed on employers, rather than workers – requirements regarding wages, working conditions, or benefits in addition to what are often costly administrative procedures to obtain permission to hire legal foreign workers.

Employers may prefer irregular workers if the costs of participating in legal foreign worker programs exceed the risks posed by the hiring of irregular migrants. Moreover, networks (family, relatives, labor recruiters and sometimes smugglers and traffickers) are often very efficient in arranging the employment of irregular migrants, reducing costs still further since the networks take care of recruitment, vet the new workers, and may even train them until the newcomers are proficient. For their part, migrants may trust these informal networks more than government programs that may be unreliable and costlier even when considering the heavy risks that irregular migration entails, particularly to the safety and security of the migrants.

The term "irregular migration" encompasses two principal sets of migrants: those who move from their country of destination, often through transit countries, and enter a country of final destination without authorization; and those who enter the destination country with legal documents, having been inspected at a port of entry, but then violate the terms of their admission by overstaying their visa and/or working illegally. Unauthorized entry occurs in a number of different ways. Irregular migrants cross land borders between official ports of entry, and they arrive by sea, often in makeshift boats or rafts. They also use fraudulent documents in order to gain entry through official ports of entry. Counterfeit passports, visas, and other identity documents may be used. The migrants may use the documents to board flights and then destroy them before landing in the destination country. They may also enter via impostor documents, using legitimate papers obtained through illegitimate means. They often use documents belonging to people who bear a superficial likeness to their own appearance. Such documents may be possessed by family or friends, or they may be purchased for the specific purpose of gaining admission. This type of unauthorized migration is often arranged by smuggling operations, as will be discussed in greater detail later in this chapter.

A much safer form of irregular migration is visa abuse. For example, migrants obtain legal permission to enter a destination country, often as a tourist, and then overstay the period that the visa covers. Another method is to obtain a longer-term visa that does not permit employment, such as a foreign student visa, and then work in contravention of the terms of their admission. In still other cases, the migrants enter as temporary workers but fail to leave when their period of work authorization ends. In some cases, migrants seek the visa knowing that they plan to violate its terms. As with those who come clandestinely, they may seek the visa on their own or obtain it through the assistance of smugglers. In other cases, the migrants have no intention of overstaying or working illegally, but circumstances change and they enter into irregular status.

Efforts to Curb Irregular Migration

The potential to stop irregular migration in its entirety is remote, particularly in liberal democracies that shun authoritarian mechanisms to control the movements of their populace. It is also difficult to address because irregular migration serves many economic interests – of migrants who earn higher incomes than they could at home; employers who have a willing source of cheap labor; and consumers who pay less for goods and services than might otherwise be the case.

It is seen as a security threat, however, because irregular migration can undermine the rule of law. Generally, smuggling operations cannot function effectively without the aid of corrupt officials in source, transit, and destination countries. It also thrives when there is access to counterfeit and fraudulently obtained documents, which in turn creates opportunities for identity theft. Many irregular migrants work in the underground economy, allowing unscrupulous employers to violate labor laws with little impunity since the irregular workers are unlikely to complain to authorities.

Added to these concerns is the human security cost to the migrants who enter through unauthorized channels or who remain illegally in the country. Clandestine migration is dangerous, as is evident in the statistics on deaths along the U.S.-Mexico border or in the Mediterranean Sea. When migrants cross deserts, are packed in containers, or take to the seas in rickety boats, they put themselves at risk of serious harm. When they use the "services" of professional smugglers who are only interested in profit, their lives are at further risk. Irregular migrants who do arrive safely to their destination find themselves in very vulnerable situations as they attempt to elude authorities and work illegally. They have few rights and face the risk of apprehension and removal.

Efforts to reduce irregular migration generally are three-fold: (1) prevention of future irregular migration through a combination of law enforcement mechanisms, legal alternatives for migration, and measures to address the underlying causes of the movements; (2) regularization of those who have gained equities in the host countries and whose continued presence is considered beneficial to all parties; and (3) removal of those who pose a threat to the host country. Many of these measures are addressed through domestic policies but some require substantial international cooperation. This is particularly the case in terms of border enforcement and removal policies, although even decisions on issues such as regularization can have ramifications for other countries. For the purposes of this chapter, however, issues requiring international standards will be given specific attention.

Countries tend to fall into two camps with regard to enforcement: those that follow the "island" model, focusing their activities on the border; and those that follow an interior model, focusing their enforcement on activities inside their countries. Although no country is exclusively in one or the other category, these paradigms help explain the preponderance of policy approaches. The island model is generally characteristic of the Anglophone countries (whether they are islands or have contiguous neighbors) that tend to eschew national identity documents and sweeps of immigrant neighborhoods or businesses that employ immigrants. The emphasis is on keeping irregular migrants out, not on finding them after they have entered. By contrast, many other countries tend to focus more heavily on interior enforcement, with greater willingness to ask residents with foreign appearances for identity documents and stronger systems for enforcing sanctions against employers who hire irregular workers.

States are increasingly seeking to enforce their domestic immigration laws beyond their own borders, which inevitably leads to greater need for international cooperation. For governments, the best opportunity to manage risk is to do so as far away from the border as possible. The further away, the more time government officials have to examine the individual and his travel documents. Once travelers reach the border, inspection officers are pressed to make quick decisions to not unduly inconvenience bona fide travelers. Visa issuance is generally considered to be the first line of defense against irregular migration, particularly of those deemed likely to overstay their permission to remain in the host country. Pre-clearance and pre-inspections by destination-country immigration personnel are additional ways to prevent the arrival of irregular migrants. Many countries deploy immigration officials to work with foreign governments and airline personnel to identify persons traveling with fraudulent documents and to combat smuggling and trafficking operations.

Pre-enrollment of frequent travelers clears certain foreign nationals for admission, allowing greater time and attention to be paid to visitors about whom the authorities have less information. The Secure Electronic Network for Travelers Rapid Inspection (SENTRI) pre-clears crossers at the U.S.-Mexico border to determine: (1) if they have a secure residence in one of the border towns, and (2) if they pose any security risk. Frequent commuters apply and pay a fee for this special privilege. Applicants submit to biographical background checks against criminal, law enforcement, customs, immigration, and terrorist indices; a ten-fingerprint law enforcement check; and a personal interview with an officer of the U.S. Customs and Border Protection agency. Technically, the system combines security pre-screening with biometrics and fast crossing/inspection. Those who are not pre-screened are required to comply with more extensive checks at the port of entry to determine if they are admissible.

Sanctions against carriers who transport migrants ineligible to enter a destination country are a further means of preventing irregular migration. Domestic law in a number of states requires common carriers (including, in various combinations, sea, air, and land carriers) servicing their territories internationally to verify travel documents of all boarding passengers. Financial fines are imposed upon carriers that fail to comply.

The strategies just described refer to the front doors through which migrants try to enter destination countries. Irregular migrants also enter through back doors, bypassing official ports of entry. They cross land borders and arrive by sea. Measures to curb clandestine entries include personnel to patrol borders and seaways; fences to make it more difficult for migrants to cross land borders; sensors, cameras, and other technology to help identify those seeking entry; and lighting to make it more difficult to cross without recognition. Interdiction on the high seas, preferably close to the embarkation point, is used to deter boat departures. Policing of borders is often done with some level of cooperation among affected countries. For example, Frontex, the EU border agency, plans, coordinates, implements, and evaluates joint operations using staff from member states at the external sea, land, and air borders.[9]

A further area needing international cooperation concerns removal of irregular migrants from the destination country. Obtaining cooperation can be problematic. Return of migrants who have been sending remittances to their families can create economic difficulties for the source country. Deportation of migrants who have committed criminal acts is often the most controversial, particularly when the migrants learned their craft in the host country. It can pose the most significant security problem for both countries. For example, members of criminal gangs that had their origins in Los Angeles have been deported to El Salvador and subsequently established flourishing branches in their home country.

Generally, removal takes place on the basis of bilateral or regional agreements that set out the roles and responsibilities of all parties. The readmission agreements usually pertain to nationals of one country to be repatriated to another country, but a new trend is to negotiate terms under which countries agree to accept third country nationals who transited their territory to reach the ultimate destination country. Spelled out in the agreements are such issues as: the evidence to be used in determining the nationality of the returnee, transit arrangements, protection of personal data, and rules on costs. In the case of third country nationals, there is often a provision in which the transit country agrees to respect international law, particularly in determining whether to repatriate migrants to their home countries.

Despite the supposed adherence of parties to international human rights standards, a 2010 report of the Council of Europe raised concerns that

---

[9] http://www.frontex.europa.eu/about/mission-and-tasks.

irregular migrants who are returned to a country which is not their country of origin might risk ending up in an unsustainable situation, notably in terms of social rights. There is also a risk that third country returnees are shuttled back to their country of origin without having had the possibility to submit an asylum application in any of the countries through which they pass. (Council of Europe 2010:8)

A readmission agreement between Italy and the Qaddafi regime in Libya raised particular concerns; not only was the government repressive toward its own citizens, it was also not a party to the Refugee Convention and had no domestic asylum system (Council of Europe 2010).

Addressing Human Smuggling

The growth in human smuggling (as well as trafficking, as described in Chapter 5) as a major part of irregular migration has been a significant factor in encouraging ever more international cooperation. These criminal operations have proven to have a global reach, able to move migrants from China to the United States, Afghanistan to Australia, and Africa to Europe – to give just three examples. Statistics on human smuggling are even more difficult to obtain than those on human trafficking, however.

A search of the websites of major national, regional, and international offices that focus on smuggling yield no definitive statistic comparable to the widely quoted numbers generated by the U.S. Trafficking in Persons report or the ILO report on forced labor. The Human Smuggling and Trafficking Center in the U.S. State Department notes: "Each year, hundreds of thousands of illegal migrants are moved by international smuggling organizations, often in harsh or even inhuman transit conditions, from their countries of origin to the United States. UN estimates indicate that human smuggling has grown to a $10 billion per year global criminal industry."[10]

The numbers of smuggled appear to approach the estimated numbers of those who illegally migrate, as per INTERPOL's statement: "Criminal networks which smuggle human beings for financial gain increasingly control the flow of migrants across borders. Due to more restrictive immigration policies in destination countries and improved technology to monitor border crossings, willing illegal migrants rely increasingly on the help of organized people smugglers."[11] However, estimates of those who migrate illegally are themselves very contentious.

Smuggling takes many forms, and can lead to any of the types of trafficking discussed in Chapter 5. In some cases, people cross international borders through clandestine means. Such smuggling occurs across land borders (for example, from Mexico into the United States) or across sea routes (Africa into

[10] http://www.state.gov/p/inl/41444.htm.
[11] http://www.interpol.int/public/THB/PeopleSmuggling/Default.asp.

Europe). The trip can be very direct, going across a contiguous border, or very indirect, going via any number of transit countries. Smugglers arrange for the transport, safe houses en route, and in some cases, documentation to be used after the migrant gains entry. In the United States, this process is referred to as "Entry without Inspection" (EWI), meaning that the smuggled migrant enters the country without coming into contact with government officials who usually determine if someone has the legal right to enter.

In other cases, the smugglers arrange for migrants to cross borders through legal ports of entry. The smugglers provide a range of services, such as arranging for legitimate visas (fraudulently obtained) or counterfeit documents that allow the migrant to reach the ports of entry. Since many developed countries sanction airline and other carriers who transport persons who do not have the right to enter, the smugglers help the migrants bypass the requirements imposed by the carriers. They may instruct migrants to destroy counterfeit documents before they arrive at the port of entry, or attempt entry with the passports and visas that are provided as part of the smuggling package. The smugglers may provide instructions to the migrant to claim asylum or other relief from deportation if apprehended at the port of entry. At the Mexican border with the United States, smugglers rent valid border crossing cards to migrants attempting to enter the United States. The smugglers match the migrant to an often-stolen card with a photo that is similar in appearance. The successful migrant returns the card after crossing the border so it can be rented to other would-be migrants with similar physical characteristics.

Smuggling groups vary from "mom and pop" outfits to highly organized transnational criminal operations. The individual who is smuggled may have little idea of the extent of organization involved in his or her smuggling. He or she may be recruited by an acquaintance in the home village who offers to arrange transport. Sometimes, the acquaintance is seeking to cover the costs of his or her travel to the destination. Yet, if the distances are great, it is likely that much of the smuggling is actually in the hands of professionals with the capacity and contacts to transport people through a number of transit countries to the final destination or to produce the types of documents that will pass muster with carriers and officials. Although the migrants' exposure may be only to his or her acquaintance, behind the local face of the smuggling operation may be a much more organized criminal syndicate.

Smuggling can be as exploitative as trafficking, and as dangerous to the person being transported. As Koser (2008) recounts, "The means of transport used by migrant smugglers are often unsafe, and migrants who are travelling in this way may find themselves abandoned by their smuggler and unable to complete the journey they have paid for. Using the services of smugglers, many migrants have drowned at sea, suffocated in sealed containers or have been raped and abused while in transit."

The normative framework for addressing human smuggling is delineated in the Smuggling Protocol. The aim of the protocol is "to prevent and combat the smuggling of migrants, as well as to promote cooperation among States Parties to that end, while protecting the rights of smuggled migrants" (Article 2).[12] As discussed earlier, smuggling is defined as "the procurement, in order to obtain, directly or indirectly, a financial or other material benefit, of the illegal entry of a person into a State Party of which the person is not a national or a permanent resident" (Article 3). In contrast to trafficking, the protocol applies only to cross-border activities. It assumes the migrant who is smuggled has made the arrangements on a voluntary basis and, therefore, is complicit in the crime. Nevertheless, it recognizes that migrants may be victimized by the smugglers. It establishes that prosecution for the offenses covered in the protocol applies only to the smuggler, not to the smuggled migrant (Article 5).

This protocol requires state parties to establish: (1) smuggling; (2) producing, providing, or possessing fraudulent travel or identity documents; and (3) enabling through illegal mechanisms a person to remain illegally in the country to be criminal offences, "when committed intentionally and in order to obtain, directly or indirectly, a financial or other material benefit" (Article 6). The Smuggling Protocol establishes the responsibility of state parties to cooperate in their law enforcement activities, with the aim of curbing smuggling operations that cross international borders. The protocol specifies several areas of such cooperation, including the sharing of information, control of borders, technical assistance and training, and other similar endeavors.

As with responses to the mobility of terrorists, the Smuggling Protocol gives special attention to the security of documents. State parties are

> (a) To ensure that travel or identity documents issued by it are of such quality that they cannot easily be misused and cannot readily be falsified or unlawfully altered, replicated or issued; and (b) To ensure the integrity and security of travel or identity documents issued by or on behalf of the State Party and to prevent their unlawful creation, issuance and use. (Article 12)

With regard to prevention, the Smuggling Protocol requires state parties to provide or strengthen information programs to increase public awareness of the fact that smuggling is "a criminal activity frequently perpetrated by organized criminal groups for profit and that it poses serious risks to the migrants concerned." Regarding the underlying reasons that migrants might fall prey to smugglers, the protocol leaves more discretion, saying

> each State Party shall promote or strengthen, as appropriate, development programs and cooperation at the national, regional and international levels, taking into account the socio-economic realities of migration and paying special attention to economically and socially depressed areas, in order to combat the root socio-economic causes of the smuggling of migrants, such as poverty and underdevelopment.

---

[12] All quotes from the Smuggling Protocol are found at http://www.unodc.org/unodc/treaties/CTOC/.

The Smuggling Protocol requires state parties to follow applicable international laws in affording protection to the victims of smuggling operations, particularly the right to life and the right not to be subjected to torture or other cruel, inhuman, or degrading treatment or punishment. Also, "each State Party shall take appropriate measures to afford migrants appropriate protection against violence that may be inflicted upon them, whether by individuals or groups," and specifies that "States Parties shall take into account the special needs of women and children" (Article 16).

Return of smuggled persons is a further area covered in the protocol: Countries have an absolute obligation in the case of nationals "to facilitate and accept, without undue or unreasonable delay, the return of a person who has been [smuggled]" (Article 18). In the case of immigrants with permanent residence who are being smuggled into a third country, the country of permanent residence is encouraged to consider accepting the return. The protocol underscores that states continue to have obligations under international law to ensure that refugees are not forcibly returned:

> Nothing in this Protocol shall affect the other rights, obligations and responsibilities of States and individuals under international law, including international humanitarian law and international human rights law and, in particular, where applicable, the 1951 Convention and the 1967 Protocol relating to the Status of Refugees and the principle of non-refoulement as contained therein. (Article 19)

Institutional Mandates Regarding Irregular Migration and Human Smuggling

In contrast to the wide array of international organizations with mandates regarding trafficking, there are relatively few institutions with explicit mandates on irregular migration and human smuggling. Unlike the international coordination mechanisms on human trafficking (i.e., ICAT), there is no single coordination mechanism for human smuggling.

UNODC, in its capacity as the secretariat of the Conference of the Parties to the UN Convention against Transnational Organized Crime and its protocols, has responsibility for monitoring human smuggling activities. Until recently, its counter-smuggling activities were eclipsed by its counter-trafficking ones. For example, in UNODC's 2010 annual report, there is a full section on human trafficking but only three mentions of smuggling – and those were generally descriptions of the protocols to the organized crime convention.

In its strategy on human trafficking and smuggling, however, UNODC affirmed that it would be seeking resources to increase its programs related to human smuggling. It explains the shift to changes in the international community's interests:

> While the international community has placed a greater emphasis on the implementation of the Protocol on Trafficking in Persons over the last ten years, this

is starting to change as the significance and consequences of the crime of migrant smuggling have come to the world's attention. UNODC intends to continue to expand its work relating to migrant smuggling to respond to the increasing requests of Member States. (UNODC 2012)

The intent is to increase staffing expertise on human smuggling to meet expected new demands.

This is not to say that UNODC has completely ignored human smuggling. In January 2012, the organization published an International Framework of Action to Implement the Smuggling of Migrants protocol. The framework outlines the principal provisions of the protocol and provides recommendations for its implementations. UNODC also undertakes more operational programs with respect to human smuggling. These include:

> Capacity-building for states – The publication of the Model Law against the Smuggling of Migrants, which was developed in response to a request by the General Assembly to promote and assist the efforts of States to become party to and implement the Protocol; development with Interpol and Europol of basic training modules on preventing and combating migrant smuggling; and preparation of a Toolkit to Combat Smuggling of Migrants to provide guidance, showcase promising practices and recommend resources in thematic areas addressed in the separate tools.

> Technical Assistance – UNODC is assisting governments in West and North Africa in implementing the Protocol and strengthening their criminal justice systems and holding training workshops for prosecutors on investigating and prosecuting migrant smuggling.

> Research and intelligence gathering – UNODC supports projects to assess and counter the various threats posed by human smuggling; published the Global Review and Annotated Bibliography of Recent Publications on Smuggling of Migrants;" and prepared analyses of specific smuggling issues, such as the publication "Smuggling of migrants into, through and from North Africa" and a 2011 report on the involvement of organized criminal groups in the smuggling of migrants from West Africa towards the European Union.[13]

UNODC's regional program for West Africa is representative. It assists Benin, Burkina Faso, Cape Verde, Côte d'Ivoire, the Gambia, Ghana, Guinea, Guinea Bissau, Liberia, Mali, Mauritania, Niger, Nigeria, Senegal, Sierra Leone, and Togo "in building capacities and strengthening cooperation mechanisms among law enforcement and prosecution authorities to effectively prevent, investigate and prosecute smuggling of migrants, and to develop effective cooperation mechanisms with third countries."[14] The project focuses

---

[13] For more information on UNODC's activities, see https://www.unodc.org/unodc/en/human-trafficking/smuggling-of-migrants.html#Response.

[14] http://www.unodc.org/nigeria/en/law-enforcement-capacity-building-in-west-africa-to-prevent-and-combat-smuggling-of-migrants.html.

on evidence-based research, elaboration of national counter-smuggling of migrants' policies that enhance intra-agency cooperation, capacity-building for law enforcement officers, establishment of trained national counter-smuggling of migrant units, and the facilitation of regional cooperation and information exchange.

IOM, in contrast to its explicit anti-trafficking program, does not have a similarly focused anti-smuggling program. Much of its work on human smuggling appears to be within the context of its activities related to irregular migration more generally. In particular, IOM operates a range of return and reintegration programs that assist those illegally residing in a destination country to repatriate. Corresponding programs for stranded migrants focus on assistance to migrants in transit countries. Many of them are in the situation because the smuggling operation has failed to gain their entry into a country of final destination. IOM's technical assistance to governments includes help in formulating and implementing anti-smuggling provisions. The agency also publishes research reports on human smuggling, focusing on such corridors as West Africa, Central Asia, and East Asia.

Within this general area, IOM is perhaps best known for its voluntary return and reintegration programs for irregular migrants. During the past decade, IOM has assisted approximately 330,000 migrants through these return programs (IOM 2010). In recent years, the largest numbers of returns have been from the United Kingdom, Germany, and Austria. The countries of origin with the largest numbers of returnees in 2009 and 2010 were Brazil (mostly from Portugal), Iraq, Russian Federation, and Kosovo (ibid.). Participants include those whose asylum applications have been rejected as well as those who never applied for asylum or withdrew an application before a decision was made. A small proportion has legal status in the host country but do not have resources to return home. Unaccompanied and separated children are beneficiaries in a number of countries. The host countries include ones of long-term residence and those serving as a transit site for migrants seeking to reach final destinations. Some countries participate in the programs as both hosts of transit migrants and origins of others.

IOM's own assessment of the return programs shows the need for more systematic long-term evaluation of their effectiveness. Compared to forced returns, there are many benefits to migrants, source, and destination countries from a voluntary, assisted model of repatriation. These include the opportunity for planning of both the timing and means of departure and the reintegration after arrival in the home country. Destination country governments cite the lower cost of assisted return relative to forced return (European Migration Network 2011) but there are few studies that have analyzed return mechanisms from a cost-effectiveness perspective. Critics of the return programs often raise questions about whether they are truly voluntary, particularly when they occur in the context of failed asylum applications or other decisions to deny a legal status to irregular migrants. Webber (2011:103) explains the problem:

"Voluntary return is . . . offered as a less painful alternative to continued destitution followed by (inevitable) compulsory return, and it is generally impossible for the returnee to make an informed choice about the country to which they are returning." Many of the returnees are going back to countries newly emerging from ethnic or religious conflict. Most of the Russian returnees, for example, are from Chechnya. Others are returning to Iraq and Afghanistan. Compounding the problem is the poor economic situations in those countries, which makes reintegration even more difficult.

UNHCR is particularly concerned with protection of smuggled migrants who may be seeking asylum. The agency often points out that because of restrictive admission policies, asylum-seekers may have few options other than smuggling to reach places of guaranteed safety. As with trafficking, UNHCR field offices seek to combat smuggling by strengthening the legal framework and access to justice; awareness raising among refugee communities; awareness raising among UNHCR staff and counterparts; support to survivors and groups at risk; and inter-agency coordination.[15]

UNHCR's work on human smuggling is often performed in the context of its activities on mixed migration. In 2007, UNHCR issued a ten-point plan of action on refugee protection and mixed migration. In explaining the need, UNHCR writes:

> While refugees and asylum seekers account for a relatively small portion of the global movement of people, they increasingly move from one country or continent to another alongside other people whose reasons for moving are different and not protection-related. More often than not such movements are irregular, in the sense that they take place without the requisite documentation and frequently involve human smugglers and traffickers. (UNHCR 2007:1)

Special focus is given to irregular maritime migration – that is, the use of boats to smuggle migrants across borders. The challenges include differentiating asylum-seekers (and others in need of protection) from labor migrants, but also safeguarding lives at sea, maintaining the integrity of the search and rescue regime, and ensuring the smooth flow of maritime traffic (UNHCR 2007).

These concerns have led to the engagement of the International Maritime Organization (IMO) in counter-smuggling efforts. IMO first entered this field in 1993 when the *Golden Venture* came aground in New York with a shipload of Chinese migrants. Concerned about unsafe conditions that put passengers at risk, IMO first considered a separate convention but determined that it did not have the competence to promulgate one. Instead, the agency continues to press for state ratification and implementation of the Smuggling Protocol. The International Civil Aviation Organization is also concerned with smuggling operations when they lead governments to restrict mobility and impose new

---

[15] http://www.unitarny.org/mm/File/3%20Traffic%20Report%20SG%20G0310460.pdf.

requirements on carriers. IMO and ICAO operate jointly in search and rescue operations when smuggling ships are lost at sea.

As in trafficking operations, INTERPOL focuses on the law enforcement side of smuggling. It provides assistance to "frontline law enforcement agencies dealing with people smuggling, such as border police or immigration authorities, to receive instant responses for queries on stolen or lost travel documents, stolen motor vehicles and wanted criminals." INTERPOL also provides technical assistance and training, changing its geographic priorities as the smuggling operations shift their locus of operations.

There are also a number of regionally focused organizations and consultative processes that work toward greater intergovernmental collaboration in reducing irregular migration and curbing human smuggling. The International Centre for Migration Policy Development (ICMPD), established in 1993, has fifteen member states (Austria, Bosnia and Herzegovina, Bulgaria, Croatia, Czech Republic, Hungary, the Former Yugoslav Republic of Macedonia, Poland, Portugal, Romania, Serbia, Slovakia, Slovenia, Sweden, and Switzerland) and works internationally. It has what is referred to as a competence center on illegal migration and return (in addition to a separate center on trafficking), which seeks to "cooperate with and implement capacity building projects with countries of origin, transit and destination and facilitates dialogue between the stakeholders."[16]

Perhaps the most active intergovernmental focus on irregular migration is in the form of consultative mechanisms, not institutions. The Global Forum on Migration and Development, which will be discussed in greater detail in Chapter 8, has held roundtables on irregular migration. These focus largely on the rights of irregular migrants and efforts to prevent irregular migration through more targeted development aid. More relevant to the migration-security nexus are regional consultative processes, in which governments meet informally to exchange information and develop strategies to address issues of mutual concern. Two of these are emblematic of the type of intergovernmental activities in which these consultative processes engage. Both are significant in the attention given to irregular migration and to the fact that their memberships include source, transit, and destination countries.

First is the Bali Process on People Smuggling, Trafficking in Persons and Related Transnational Crime, with forty-six members, largely drawn from Asia and the Pacific region and including IOM and UNHCR as full members. There are also about twenty non-Asian participating countries and international and regional organizations that are observers to the process. It is co-chaired by Australia and Indonesia. With an agenda heavily influenced by security issues, working groups and meetings focus on issues of documentation, including identity management, visa integrity, and lost and stolen passports; return of irregular migrants; and immigration intelligence gathering. The discussions

---

[16] http://www.icmpd.org/Capacity-Building.1555.0.html.

tend to be very practical. An assessment of regional consultations concluded: "The Bali Process mentions the importance, which is generally recognized, of migration's root causes, but moves forth in practice by tackling topics of immediate importance in a regional context: legal frameworks, interdiction, customs and intelligence cooperation, victim protection, and borders" (Hansen 2010:23).

At the 2011 ministerial meeting, member states agreed to a regional cooperation framework underpinned by the following core principles:

1. Irregular movement facilitated by people smuggling syndicates should be eliminated and States should promote and support opportunities for orderly migration.
2. Where appropriate and possible, asylum seekers should have access to consistent assessment processes, whether through a set of harmonised arrangements or through the possible establishment of regional assessment arrangements, which might include a centre or centres, taking into account any existing sub-regional arrangements.
3. Persons found to be refugees under those assessment processes should be provided with a durable solution, including voluntary repatriation, resettlement within and outside the region and, where appropriate, possible "in country" solutions.
4. Persons found not to be in need of protection should be returned, preferably on a voluntary basis, to their countries of origin, in safety and dignity. Returns should be sustainable and States should look to maximise opportunities for greater cooperation.
5. People smuggling enterprises should be targeted through border security arrangements, law enforcement activities and disincentives for human trafficking and smuggling.[17]

An observer of the Bali Process concluded that "a key aim of the Bali Process is to enhance operational cooperation on law enforcement" (Kohler 2011: 80). Therefore, a core focus is on "strengthening the technological and human capacity to process and share intelligence, and on developing cooperative approaches to law enforcement" (ibid.). The 2012 report of activities of the annual meeting of senior officials gives a glimpse of how the Bali Process functions in support of these aims. Much of the work is accomplished through workshops and ad hoc groups that tackle a specific issue.

• A Workshop on Biometrics for Identity and Integrity in Immigration was held. Participants agreed "to consider developing a framework of voluntary minimum standards to facilitate sharing biometrics to strengthen immigration integrity within the legal framework of member countries."

---

[17] Bali Process activities are described in greater detail at http://www.baliprocess.net/.

- A Voluntary Reporting System on Migrant Smuggling and Related Conduct in support of the Bali Process was reported by UNODC as being close to completion; members were asked to indicate interest in participating in a pilot phase to test the system.
- An information resource on policies, procedures and approaches to "Protection, Repatriation and Resettlement" was underway, with country papers having been prepared.
- IOM reported on plans for a Secure Portal on Effective Exchange of Data (SPEED) website which was being designed to provide a secure and centralized portal to facilitate timely information collection and dissemination among members of the Bali Process.
- The Technical Experts Group on Irregular Movement by Air had been expanded to address irregular movement by land and sea.
- The Regional Immigration Liaison Officer Network (RILON) was serving as a forum for sharing information on irregular movements by air in major hub locations. (Bali Process 2012)

The Budapest Process, a consultative forum of more than fifty governments and ten international organizations, is also noteworthy for its focus on the security ramifications of migration. It involves states from the wider European region (EU member states, the Balkans, members of the Commonwealth of Independent States, and others) and is supported by the ICMPD. The aim is to exchange information and experiences in dealing with topics such as irregular migration, visas, border management, trafficking in human beings, smuggling of migrants, readmission, and return. As with the Bali Process, the Budapest Process works through ad hoc groups, workshops, and joint training operations and information exchange. For example, a recent meeting of the Working Group on the Silk Routes Region (hosted by Turkey and including the Central Asian republics of the former Soviet Union) emphasized the need for consistent training of border and immigration officials. The working group decided to hold an annual training program targeting the officials of all interested states on such as issues as combating smuggling of migrants and trafficking in persons as well as document security (Budapest Process 2011). Other working groups have focused on cooperation among border guards in the Black Sea region, migration flows from specific areas (such as the Horn of Africa), irregular migration and asylum, determining penalties for smuggling and trafficking offenses, and other similar issues.

CONCLUSION

Security concerns place new challenges on migration policy. Yet, migration has not received the same level of attention as what are seen by academics and policy makers as more traditional problems of national security. During the Cold War, as Collyer (2006:257) explains, "security was viewed in big picture, militaristic terms by classic international relations theorists who viewed states as the only significant actors; its end brought about a growing awareness of a range of security issues not associated with inter-state relations, including migration." Despite the increased attention to irregular migration and, especially, the mobility of terrorists, migration does not rank high on the international security agenda. This stems, at least in part, from the fact that migration in general does not pose serious security risks and is more likely seen as an economic benefit. Irregular migrants, the group most likely to be addressed in a security framework, are probably seeking entry to work rather than to undermine national safety. Irregular migration may be a hot political issue but it seldom reaches the highest levels of public policy concern. Terrorism is another matter but even there, the principal focus has been "the war on terrorism" and not the movement of terrorists. As this chapter demonstrates, however, there has been increased international cooperation around border security and documentation issues.

The result is that there has been little political will to take serious action at either the national or international level to organize an effective response to irregular migration. Instead governments have done enough to satisfy public opinion but not invested significant political or financial capital in curbing irregular migration. Koser (2005) summarized the issue very well in a report prepared for the Global Commission on International Migration:

> Irregular migration poses very real dilemmas for states, as well as exposing migrants themselves to insecurity and vulnerability. Most states have, nevertheless, failed to manage or control irregular migration effectively or efficiently. What is therefore required are new, more effective and coherent approaches to address the issue of irregular migration, that recognise both the concerns of states in this respect and the need to protect the rights of irregular migrants.

The relative inattention in the international arena to human smuggling – certainly in comparison to human trafficking – is nevertheless surprising, as are the piecemeal efforts to reduce the potential that terrorists could use these networks for their own purposes. Human smugglers are as ruthless in their activities as are traffickers, even if the relationship with the migrant is not as long-term. Some smugglers are of the mom and pop variety and may, indeed, be the migrant's relative or neighbor, whereas others are engaged in a broad variety of organized criminal activities that demonstrate little regard for human life. Migrants have been left to die in shipping containers, vans and trucks, and on rafts and small vessels. Coastal police patrolling the waters between Italy and Albania reported to this author finding flotillas of speedboats carrying smuggled arms, drugs, and people. When encountered, the smugglers threw the people overboard in order to escape with the contraband, knowing that the police would have little recourse other than to halt pursuit to rescue the migrants.

Even without the human cost, the lack of serious attention to combating human smuggling makes little sense from a law enforcement perspective. Governments spend billions on border controls, but as Jandl (2007) reports, "More important than upgrading controls at the borders, however, are measures directed at 'deep' investigations against smugglers, ranging from the harmonization and sharpening of penal law against smugglers to cross-border investigations and the tackling of corruption." The very fact that UNODC has only recently committed to enhancing its role in the development and implementation of counter-smuggling activities is emblematic of the problem. Neither governments nor the international organizations that they fund have seen the development of mechanisms for international cooperation on human smuggling as a priority despite the promulgation of the Smuggling Protocol. Yet, they recognize that smuggling operations are themselves transnational in nature and will not be addressed effectively through unilateral action.

Hence, despite the growing security discourse about migration since the end of the Cold War, there has been relatively little follow-through in establishing the type of mechanisms for international cooperation that are characteristic of higher order security issues. Where cooperation has taken place, it has been within the framework in place since global passport standards were set after World War I. The focus has been on ensuring more effective documentation and sharing of information about short-term international travelers, rather than ensuring the legality of longer-term international migration.

7

Migration, the Environment, and Climate Change[*]

In 1990, the Intergovernmental Panel on Climate Change (IPCC) warned that significant levels of migration could occur as a result of changing climatic conditions. This was not the first time, however, that the nexus between migration and the environment was a topic of international attention. The concept of environmental migration proved to be controversial, largely because of the difficulty in measuring the extent to which environmental factors compel people to move. Since the 1980s, when the term "environmental refugees" was coined (El-Hinnawi 1985), experts within the environmental and migration fields have differed in their characterization of the phenomenon.

Dun and Gemmene (2008) places those concerned with the interconnections in two groups – alarmists and skeptics. The *alarmists* see the environment as a principal cause of population movements, emphasize the forced nature of the migration (hence, the term "refugee"), and often project that hundreds of millions of persons will be affected, frequently without differentiating between those who will move short distances to safer ground versus those who will move thousands of miles to new countries. The *skeptics*, by contrast, raise questions about the models used to generate estimates of those who will be forced to migrate and emphasize that pull factors in destination locations are often more important than push factors at home in determining whether, where, and in what volume people will migrate. Perhaps it is not surprising that some environmentalists have been particularly alarmist, often using the threat of mass migration as a reason that immediate action should be taken to address climate change and other environmental problems. Migration experts, concerned about a potential backlash against migrants, and misuse of terms like refugee

---

[*] Sections of this chapter first appeared in Susan Martin, "Climate Change and Governance," *Global Governance: A Review of Multilateralism and International Organizations* 16.3. Copyright 2010 by Lynne Rienner Publishers, Inc. Used with permission by the publisher.

(carefully defined in international law) have tended to join the camp of the skeptics.

Recognizing the complexity in determining causality, and the broader context in which the environment affects population movements, the IOM has offered the following broad definition of environmental migrants: "Environmental migrants are persons or groups of persons who, for compelling reasons of sudden or progressive change in the environment that adversely affects their lives or living conditions, are obliged to leave their habitual homes, or choose to do so, either temporarily or permanently, and who move either within their country or abroad" (IOM 2007a).

Policy makers have been slow to develop national, regional, or international laws, policies, or organizational responsibilities – that is, a system of governance – to manage environmentally induced migration. This situation derives in part from uncertainties about the actual impacts of the environment on migration, particularly as exacerbated by climate change. Despite recognition that some form of migration related to environmental change is likely to occur, addressing these anticipated movements is hampered by the paucity of policy or appropriate institutional responses.

This chapter opens with a brief discussion of the potential impact of climate change on migration patterns. It discusses the principal pathways by which environmental change may affect migration, either directly or, more likely, in combination with other factors. The chapter continues with an examination of existing capacities to address these forms of movement and discusses gaps in governance. It concludes with recent discussions within the context of the UN Framework for a Climate Change Convention and the GFMD.

CLIMATE CHANGE AND MIGRATION

While new research is emerging on the relationship between climate change and migration (Renaud et al. 2007, Brown 2007, Raleigh et al. n.d., Hugo 2008, Kniveton et al. 2008, Kolmannskog 2009, Lazco and Aghazarm 2009, White 2011, UK Foresight 2011), there is no consensus regarding the current or likely future scale of migration resulting from climate change. Estimates vary substantially and often conflate those who move one mile inland with those who may need to move thousands of miles away to other countries. Without such basic information as to the numbers likely to move, locations, and expected duration, developing an appropriate policy framework is exceedingly difficult.

There are four paths, in particular, by which environmental change may affect migration either directly or, more likely, in combination with other factors:

1) Changes in weather patterns that contribute to longer-term drying trends that affect access to essential resources such as water and negatively

affect the sustainability of a variety of environment-related livelihoods including agriculture, forestry, fishing, and so forth;

2) Rising sea levels that render coastal and low-lying areas uninhabitable in the longer-term;

3) Increased frequency and magnitude of weather-related natural disasters, such as hurricanes and cyclones that destroy infrastructure and livelihoods, requiring people to relocate for short or long periods;

4) Competition over natural resources that may exacerbate pressures leading to conflict, which in turn precipitates movements of people.

The first two scenarios are likely to create conditions that cause large-scale displacement, often in emergency situations. The third and fourth scenarios are likely to cause slow onset migration, in which people seek new homes and livelihoods over a lengthy period of time as conditions in their home communities gradually worsen.

Vulnerability or resilience to these situations – that is, the capability to cope or adapt to them – will determine the degree to which people are forced to migrate. The availability of alternative livelihoods or other coping capacities in the affected area generally determines the scale and form of migration that may take place. The urgency to migrate may be less pressing in slow-onset processes, such as intense drought and rising sea levels, as compared to such natural disasters as hurricanes, cyclones, and typhoons, or human disasters, such as conflict. But if alternative livelihoods are not available within a reasonable timeframe, then migration may be the best or only option available, even in slow-onset situations.

Developing countries with a large proportion of people directly involved in agriculture, herding and fishing are particularly sensitive to environmental changes and to natural disasters. As Collinson (2010:4) suggests, "many of the world's poorest and most crisis-prone countries will be disproportionately affected by climate change owing to higher exposure to climate-related hazards such as droughts and floods, pre-existing human vulnerabilities and weak capacities for risk reduction measures."

However, even highly destructive natural hazards will not necessarily result in humanitarian crises that cause massive displacement. Generally, the efficacy of national and international policies, institutions and humanitarian responses influence whether people are able to cope in a manner that allows them to recover their homes and livelihoods. In Bangladesh, for example, severe events such as cyclones are only one part of the broader migration picture. As Collinson (2010:2) further observes, "national governance structures and the state's capacity to provide services and maintain institutions are of key importance in influencing the humanitarian impacts of climate change and associated displacement and migration in different contexts."

Conflict may further undermine the capacity of people to cope with climate change, leading to greater displacement than might have been the case in a more peaceful environment. Economic and social development is often delayed or even reversed in the context of prolonged conflict, leading to greater vulnerability and decreased capacity to cope with the effects of climate change.

The type of migration that occurs as a result of either slow or rapid-onset situations will depend, at least in part, on prior institutional experience and capacity to address the needs of affected people as well as previous migration patterns. In Jalisco and Zacatecas, Mexico, for example, weather cycles, in combination with other push and pull factors (particularly U.S. labor demand), have contributed to a century of migration to the United States and to urban centers in Mexico. These Mexican states lie at a crossroads between arid and arable land, and have experienced drought cycles that prompted population movements. Understanding the history of this migration is essential to realizing the ways in which further desertification due to climate change may affect future movements.

Philip Martin (2010) argues that even without climate change, the coming years are likely to witness continuing large-scale migration out of the agricultural sector, particularly in developing countries where farm incomes are significantly lower than non-farm incomes. Climate change, specifically global warming, is likely to accelerate this pace of migration. Several economic models project that global warming will have more effects on where farm production takes place than on global farm output, with new areas becoming viable for farming as a result of higher temperatures. However, far more people in developing regions are likely to be displaced by global warming than those likely to find jobs in these new farming areas. Many of the agricultural regions that will benefit are located in developed countries where mechanization of new farm operations is probable.

Past and current unsustainable development practices compound problems and pose more immediate challenges than global climate change. In St. Louis, Senegal, for example, a combination of a large dam system on the Senegal River and a poorly planned flood protection canal for St. Louis have contributed to significant coastal erosion that threatens to inundate and displace several small communities. The canal – originally just four meters wide – has grown to more than a kilometer in width, with the ocean threatening not only coastal communities, but also barrier beaches in a national park. Local fishing and farming communities are losing their livelihoods as salt water intrudes, thereby contributing to internal migration pressures. In Jalisco, Mexico, many farmers switched from traditional crops to agave as demand for tequila rose, only to experience falling prices as soil was eroded by new pesticides. Similarly, pollution from urban areas and livestock is affecting both the quantity and quality of water in the Lake Chapala-Lerma-Santiago river basin.

Climate change increases preexisting vulnerability by allowing more extreme weather-related shocks to affect highly fragile livelihood systems and vulnerable populations. Sea-level rise, for example, worsens already extreme pressures on land due to high population density and growth.

Living in a mid-income country with relatively low fertility rates, Mexicans may be less vulnerable to some kinds of environmental changes, in part because many people have the assets and networks needed for migration. On the other hand, many residents of Bangladesh and Senegal display high levels of vulnerability in terms of poverty, rapid population growth, landlessness, and loss of livelihoods, but those very factors limit the availability of assets that can be used to migrate. Such very high levels of vulnerability may mean that migration, particularly that resulting from acute natural disasters, will occur with little forewarning and under emergency conditions that bode ill for the security and well-being of the displaced.

Many movements from both slow and rapid-onset situations are likely to be immediately across borders, from one poor, developing country into another. Such migration may be particularly challenging as the receiving countries will probably have few resources and legal structures, or little institutional capacity to respond to the needs of the migrants. Geographical proximity may also mean that destination areas face similar environmental challenges as areas of migration origin (e.g., drought, desertification) and may offer little respite.

It is important to keep in mind that migration can have positive as well as negative consequences for the affected populations and the communities to which they migrate. The negative impacts stem particularly from emergency mass movements, generally those related to the rapid-onset natural disasters and to competition for resources that may result in conflict. These movements most closely resemble refugee movements and often require large-scale humanitarian assistance. The negative effects may also be more extreme if receiving communities, particularly urban areas, are unprepared to absorb large numbers of spontaneous migrants. The more positive consequences occur when migration is a voluntary coping strategy that allows people time to weigh alternatives and use migration as a way to reduce household risk (Morton 2008).

Climate change-induced migration is not a single event. Different issues arise at each stage of environmental migration. The first stage is pre-migration, when actions to prevent, mitigate, and help individuals adapt to environmental hazards are initiated. Mitigation of the causes of climate change is the most critical need but it will require considerable political will, time, and resources to take the steps that are needed to protect the environment.

In the meantime, increasing attention is being turned to adaptation and disaster risk reduction and their relationship to migration. *Adaptation* refers to "initiatives and measures to reduce the vulnerability of natural and human systems against actual or expected climate change effects" (IPCC 2007). *Disaster risk reduction* involves "systematic efforts to analyse and manage the causal factors of disasters, including through reduced exposure to hazards, lessened vulnerability of people and property, wise management of land and the environment, and improved preparedness for adverse events" (UNISDR 2009). Identifying vulnerabilities is essential in each case since the "characteristics and circumstances of a community, system or asset ... make it susceptible to the damaging effects of a hazard" (ibid.). Adaptation and disaster risk reduction can involve steps to reduce the need for individuals to migrate to avoid harm. Alternatively, it can involve migration as an adaptation or risk reduction strategy enabling a community or household to cope with changes and, perhaps, reduce risk for others.

Movement is the second stage of environmental migration. Migration can be planned or spontaneous, involving individuals and households or entire communities. It can be internal, with people moving shorter or longer distances to find new homes and livelihoods within their own countries, or it can be international when people relocate to other countries. It can proceed as an orderly movement of people from one location to another, or it can occur under emergency circumstances. It can be temporary, with most migrants expecting to return home when conditions permit, or it can be permanent, with most migrants unable or unwilling to return. Each of these forms of migration requires significantly different approaches and policy frameworks. Depending on the specific situation, the environmental migrants may resemble labor migrants, seeking better livelihood opportunities in a new location, or they may resemble refugees and IDPs who have fled situations beyond their individual control.

Most migration occurring from climate change is likely to be internal, although a portion will undoubtedly be international. In the most extreme cases, particularly in the context of rising sea levels, the entire population of an island nation may need to be relocated. The third stage of the cycle involves return or settlement in another location and the integration of migrants. The decision as to whether return is possible involves a range of variables, including the extent to which the environmental causes – either direct or indirect – are likely to persist. Policies in the receiving communities and countries, depending on whether the migration is internal or international, will also affect the likelihood for return or settlement in the new location. In addition to immigration policies, other policies affecting return and settlement include land use and property rights, social welfare, housing, and employment. Additional factors include the extent to which migrants are able to find decent living conditions and pursue adequate livelihoods. Integration is also affected by plans and programs to mitigate future dislocations from environmental hazards, coming full circle to a focus on prevention, adaptation, and risk reduction.

INTERNATIONAL NORMS AND CLIMATE INDUCED MIGRATION

There are no international instruments that specifically address migration stemming from climate change or other environmental factors. Persons migrating because of environmental factors have the same rights and responsibilities of others who cross international borders. As with other migrants, they enjoy all of the human rights applicable in international law. The UDHR, the ICCPR, and the International Covenant on Economic, Social and Cultural Rights (ICESCR) define the basic rights of all persons. If they migrate as workers, the UN Migrant Workers Convention and the conventions sponsored by the ILO would apply (see Chapter 3). Environmental migrants who use irregular means of entry may be covered under the Trafficking and Smuggling Protocols (see Chapters 5 and 6, respectively).

Some environmental migrants may be covered under the 1951 UN Convention Relating to the Status of Refugees and its 1967 protocol. While few persons who migrate purely for environmental reasons are likely to meet the definition of a refugee (see Chapter 2), those fleeing because of competition for resources arising from climate change may qualify if they are unable to access resources because of a "protected" characteristic (i.e., race, religion, nationality, membership of a particular social group, or political opinion). In Africa, the scope of coverage might be greater because the 1969 OAU Convention Governing the Specific Aspects of Refugee Problems in Africa includes those who, "owing to external aggression, occupation, foreign domination or *events seriously disturbing public order in either part or the whole of his country of origin or nationality*, is compelled to leave his place of habitual residence in order to seek refuge in another place outside his country of origin or nationality" (emphasis added). To the extent that climate change seriously disturbs public order, persons forced to leave their homes may be covered.

For the internally displaced, the Guiding Principles on Internal Displacement would apply since it encompasses people who are forced to leave their homes because of natural or human-made disasters. The African Union Convention on Internal Displacement explicitly recognizes that there will likely be displacement from climate change, stating in Article 4: "States Parties shall take measures to protect and assist persons who have been internally displaced due to natural or human made disasters, including climate change."[1]

The relative absence of applicable international law mirrors the situation at the national level. Immigration laws of most destination countries are not conducive to reception of large numbers of environmental migrants, unless they enter through already existing admission categories. Typically, destination countries admit persons to fill job openings or to reunify with family members. Employment-based admissions are usually based on the labor market needs of the receiving country, not the situation of the home country. Family admissions are usually restricted to persons with immediate relatives (spouses, children, parents, and, sometimes, siblings) in the destination country.

Humanitarian admissions are generally limited to refugees and asylum-seekers (i.e., those who fit the definition in the UN Refugee Convention). Some countries have established special policies that permit individuals whose countries have experienced natural disasters or other severe upheavals to remain at least temporarily without fear of deportation. The United States, for example, enacted legislation in 1990 to provide temporary protected status (TPS) to

---

[1] Quote taken from version of Convention at http://www.unhcr.org/4ae9bede9.html.

persons "in the United States who are temporarily unable to safely return to their home country because of ongoing armed conflict, an environmental disaster, or other extraordinary and temporary conditions."[2] Environmental disaster may include "an earthquake, flood, drought, epidemic, or other environmental disaster in the state resulting in a substantial, but temporary, disruption of living conditions in the area affected." In the case of environmental disasters, as compared to conflict, the country of origin must request designation of TPS for its nationals.

Importantly, TPS only applies to persons already in the United States at the time of the designation. It is not meant to be a mechanism to respond to an unfolding crisis in which people seek admission from outside the country. It also only pertains to situations that are temporary in nature. If the environmental disaster has permanent consequences, a designation of TPS is not available or it may be lifted, even for those presently in the United States, When the volcano erupted in Montserrat in 1997, TPS was granted and then extended six times. In 2005, however, the grant was ended because "it is likely that the eruptions will continue for decades, [and] the situation that led to Montserrat's designation can no longer be considered 'temporary' as required by Congress when it enacted the TPS statute."[3]

At the EU level, the "Temporary Protection Directive establishes temporary protection during 'mass influxes' of certain displaced persons. The term 'mass-influx' refers to situations where large numbers of people are suddenly displaced and where it is not feasible to treat applicants on an individual basis. It was decided that 'mass-influx' was to be defined on a case-by-case basis by a qualified majority of the Council" (Kolmannskog 2009). Sweden and Finland have included environmental migrants within their immigration policies. Sweden includes within its asylum system persons who do not qualify for refugee status, but have a need for protection. Such a person in need of protection "has left his native country and does not wish to return there because he or she – has a fear of the death penalty or torture – is in need of protection as a result of war or other serious conflicts in the country – is unable to return to the native country because of an environmental disaster."[4] The decision is made on an individual, not group basis. Although many recipients of this status are presumed to be in temporary need of protection, the Swedish rules foresee that some persons may be in need of permanent solutions. Similarly, in the Finnish Aliens Act, "aliens residing in the country are issued with a residence permit on the basis of a need for protection if . . . they cannot

---

[2] Public Law 101–649 (Immigration Act of November 29, 1990), Section 302.
[3] "Termination of the Designation of Montserrat Under the Temporary Protected Status Program; Extension of Employment Authorization Documentation," *Federal Register* 69.128 (Tuesday, July 6, 2004). Available at http://www.uscis.gov/sites/default/files/ilink/docView/FR/HTML/FR/0-0-0-1/0-0-0-94157/0-0-0-94177/0-0-0-96204.html.
[4] Quote is found in the Swedish Aliens Act available at http://www.government.se/content/1/c6/06/61/22/94531dbc.pdf.

return because of an armed conflict or environmental disaster" (Kolmannskog 2009).

A number of countries provide exceptions to removal on an ad hoc basis for persons whose countries of origin have experienced significant disruption because of natural disasters. After the 2004 tsunami, for example, Switzerland, the UK, and Canada suspended deportations of those from such countries as Sri Lanka, India, Somalia, Maldives, Seychelles, Indonesia, and Thailand. A number of governments announced similar plans after the 2010 earthquake in Haiti. It should be emphasized, however, that there is no international law that would compel or even encourage other governments to follow similar policies.

To date, there are no examples of legislation or policies that address migration of persons from slow-onset climate changes that may destroy habitats or livelihoods in the future. For the most part, movements from slow-onset climate change and other environmental hazards that limit economic opportunities are treated in the same manner as other economically motivated migration. Persons moving outside of existing labor and family migration categories are considered to be irregular migrants. In the absence of a strong humanitarian basis for exempting them from removal proceedings (which is unlikely in the slow-onset situation), these migrants would be subject to the regular systems in place for mandatory return to their home countries. Because their immediate reasons for migrating would be similar to that of other irregular migrants – that is, lack of economic opportunities at home and better economic opportunities abroad – there would be little reason for destination countries to manage these movements outside of their existing immigration rules.

INSTITUTIONAL ROLES AND RESPONSIBILITIES

Just as the international legal frameworks for addressing climate-induced cross-border migration are weak, so are the institutional roles and responsibilities at both the international and the national levels. This is not to say that there is a total absence of governance. Among the plethora of international organizations that have some responsibilities related to international migration there is significant interest in addressing issues related to climate change. Perhaps the most important active international organization in this area has been IOM. It has been a focal point for discussion of environmental migration since 1992 when IOM co-hosted a series of consultations on the interconnections between the environment and migration, in the context of the UN Conference on Environment and Development (UNCED) in Rio de Janeiro. Since then, IOM has published working papers and books on climate change and migration, and worked with UN agencies and experts to define more precisely the category of environmental migration.

IOM describes its aims in addressing climate change, environment and migration in the following terms:

First, to prevent forced migration resulting from environmental factors to the extent possible

Second, where forced migration does occur, to provide assistance and protection to affected populations, and seek durable solutions to their situation

Third, to facilitate migration as an adaptation strategy to climate change.[5]

The agency has assumed the lead role of the international system in managing camps set up for people displaced by natural disasters. A compendium of its activities related to environmental migration includes: research to assess the evidence about climate change and potential displacement to guide program development (e.g., a study of climate change and migration in smallholder farming areas in Zimbabwe); population tracking systems to inform action (e.g., village assessments in the Sudan); helping governments develop adaptation strategies that build on the potential of migration to reduce risk (e.g., development of an innovative model of temporary and circular migration in Colombia that is tied to environmental factors); addressing sustainability of livelihoods to reduce emigration pressures in areas facing longer-term environmental problems (e.g., a project in Azerbaijan to develop an efficient and sustainable water supply system in drought-prone areas and one in Indonesia to promote sustainable agriculture); helping governments build capacity to respond to climate induced displacement (e.g., a five year program in the North Pacific for disaster mitigation, relief and reconstruction and one in Trinidad and Tobago to develop standard operating procedures for mass migration emergency response); reducing the impact of forced migration (e.g., setting up community information centers in Bangladesh to reduce forced migrants' vulnerability); helping migrants find durable solutions (e.g., a program to educate displaced Pakistanis on earthquake-resistant construction to assist return) (Quesada 2009). The compendium shows a robust array of projects but as with other IOM activities (as discussed in Chapter 4), the capacity to engage in these activities is dependent on targeted donor support.

UNHCR has addressed issues related to climate change and displacement, raising both the humanitarian and security ramifications of environmental factors. As early as 2007, High Commissioner Antonio Guterres gave voice to his concerns:

> When we consider the different models for the impact of climate change, the picture is very worrying. The need for people to move will keep on growing. One need only look at East Africa and the Sahel region. All predictions are that desertification will expand steadily. For the population, this means decreasing livelihood prospects and increased migration. All of this is happening in the absence of international capacity and political will to respond. (Guterres 2007)

---

[5] http://www.iom.int/jahia/Jahia/migration-climate-change-and-environment.

The following year Assistant High Commissioner for Protection Erika Feller summarized the dilemma before the Executive Committee: "New terminology is entering the displacement lexicon with some speed. The talk is now of 'ecological refugees,' 'climate change refugees,' the 'natural disaster displaced.' This is all a serious context for UNHCR's efforts to fulfill its mandate for its core beneficiaries.... The mix of global challenges is explosive, and one with which we and our partners, government and non-government, must together strike the right balance" (Feller 2008). In an address before the Security Council in November 2011 – with famine and displacement in Somalia heavily on his mind – High Commissioner Guterres returned to the theme: "we should be addressing the more complex issue of the way in which global warming, rising sea levels, changing weather patterns and other manifestations of climate change are interacting with and reinforcing other global imbalances, so as to produce some very powerful drivers of instability, conflict and displacement" (Guterres 2011:3).

In the lead up to the Ministerial Conference in December 2011 that marked the sixtieth anniversary of UNHCR, the organization commissioned new research on climate change and displacement. Preparatory meetings were held in Bellagio and Oslo to discuss gaps in the international response to the evolving phenomena. The initial hope was that governments would back reforms in the institutional arrangements, particularly for responding to natural disasters. This would have helped clarify under which situations UNHCR should take leadership in assisting and protecting victims. There was no inclination, however, on the part of the governments for UNHCR to become more systematically involved with migrants who cross borders because of natural disasters or climate change. The Ministerial Conference instead gave very indirect acknowledgement of the problem but did little to resolve it:

> We note that today's challenges in providing protection and achieving solutions continue to be serious, interconnected and complex.... We will reinforce cooperation with each other and work with UNHCR and other relevant stakeholders, as appropriate, to deepen our understanding of evolving patterns of displacement and to agree upon ways to respond to the challenges we face in a changing global context. (UNHCR 2011)

In June 2012, Guterres returned to the issue of climate change and environmental disasters in launching a new report on the impact of environmental factors on displacement in East Africa. At the Rio +20 conference that marked progress in implementing the recommendations in the 1992 UNCED, he noted: "This report confirms what we have been hearing for years from refugees. They did everything they could to stay at home, but when their last crops failed, their livestock died, they had no option but to move; movement which often led them into greater harm's way."[6] Despite Guterres's efforts, the document

---

[6] Press Release at http://www.unhcr.org/cgi-bin/texis/vtx/search?page=search&docid=4fe3129d6 &query=guterres%20environment%20(rio,r%C3%ADo).

describing the outcomes of the Rio +20 conference had no mention of refugees or displaced persons. The section on migration included rather vague entreaties to governments "to promote and protect effectively the human rights and fundamental freedom of all migrants regardless of migration status" (UN 2012: 29). The report encouraged bilateral, regional, and international cooperation in support of this aim.

Other international organizations have shown more targeted responses. For example, the ILO has focused on climate change mitigation and adaptation in the context of its commitment to decent work standards, observing "The world can ill afford to invest the massive resources required to address the climate crisis in ways that do nothing to tackle the global job crisis and poverty" (ILO 2007). UNESCO published a volume entitled *Migration and Climate Change*. During its chairmanship of the GMC, UNESCO also negotiated a statement on climate change and migration that was adopted by the member organizations (see below). UNICEF plans to issue a volume of essays on the impact of climate-induced migration on youth.

CLIMATE CHANGE AND MIGRATION IN INTERNATIONAL FORUMS

Although there has been little progress in establishing legal or institutional responsibilities for people displaced by climate change, the issue has come to the attention of numerous intergovernmental forums. Four in particular bear further examination in providing some guidance on the direction being taken by the international community on this emergent problem.

Climate Change and Migration in the UN Framework Convention on Climate Change

From 2008 onward, migration and displacement have been on the agenda of the climate change negotiations undertaken in the context of the Conference of the Parties of the UN Framework Convention on Climate Change, known by the acronym COP.[7] The discussions have been largely within the context of negotiation of text regarding adaptation policies and programs. The Copenhagen Accord, adopted at the fifteenth COP session in December 2009, highlighted the importance of adaptation strategies:

> Adaptation to the adverse effects of climate change and the potential impacts of response measures is a challenge faced by all countries. Enhanced action and international cooperation on adaptation is urgently required to ensure the implementation of the Convention by enabling and supporting the implementation of adaptation actions aimed at reducing vulnerability and building resilience in developing countries, especially in those that are particularly vulnerable, especially least developed countries, small island developing States and Africa. We agree that

[7] My thanks to Koko Warner, my co-author in several reports of international discussions on climate change and migration, for helping me understand the COP process and outcomes.

developed countries shall provide adequate, predictable and sustainable financial resources, technology and capacity-building to support the implementation of adaptation action in developing countries. (Copenhagen Accord 2009)

National adaptation programs of action (NAPAs) are the principal mechanisms through which low-income developing countries identify their needs and programs. The governing legal accord is the UN Framework Convention on Climate Change (UNFCCC), which states that NAPAs "provide a process for Least Developed Countries (LDCs) to identify priority activities that respond to their urgent and immediate needs to adapt to climate change–those for which further delay would increase vulnerability and/or costs at a later stage."[8] As of October 2008, thirty-eight countries had submitted plans.[9] NAPAs have serious limitations as a mechanism for identifying the full range of adaptation needs and plans. The UNDP assessed NAPAs in its 2007/2008 *Human Development Report*:

> First, they provide a very limited response to the adaptation challenge, focussing primarily on "climate-proofing" through small-scale projects.... Second, the NAPAs have, in most countries, been developed outside the institutional framework for national planning on poverty reduction. The upshot is a project-based response that fails to integrate adaptation planning into the development of wider policies for overcoming vulnerability and marginalization. (UNDP 2007:188)

NAPAs nevertheless remain one of the few planning instruments for LDCs that are facing the prospect of large-scale dislocations due to climate change. The Copenhagen conference made some progress in identifying funding mechanisms to support adaptation initiatives. Paragraph 8 of the Copenhagen Accord specifies:

> Scaled up, new and additional, predictable and adequate funding as well as improved access shall be provided to developing countries, in accordance with the relevant provisions of the Convention, to enable and support enhanced action on mitigation, including substantial finance to reduce emissions from deforestation and forest degradation (REDD-plus), adaptation, technology development and transfer and capacity-building, for enhanced implementation of the Convention. (Copenhagen Accord 2009)

The parties to the accord pledged to provide $30 billion (U.S. billion) for the period from 2010 to 2012, with funding allocated between adaptation and mitigation. The most vulnerable developing countries, such as the LDCs, small-island developing states, and African countries, will be given priority for adaptation programs. Developed countries also committed to a goal of mobilizing jointly $100 billion (U.S. Billion) dollars a year by 2020 to address

---

[8] https://unfccc.int/national_reports/napa/items/2719.php.
[9] All NAPAs referenced herein can be accessed at http://unfccc.int/national_reports/napa/items/2719.php.

the needs of developing countries. The extent to which projects related to migration will be funded is unknown.

Despite some progress on defining the importance of adaptation, the COP15 negotiations in Copenhagen were largely seen as a failure. This called into question the efficacy of climate negotiations in a UN forum. As a result, there was pressure to create a package of balanced outcomes for the next year's negotiations, which would take place in Cancun, Mexico. The intent was to deliver results concrete enough to restore faith in the UNFCCC process. Accordingly, delegates concentrated on finding elements suitable for inclusion in a possible Cancun Adaptation Framework.

The language on migration and displacement was placed in the context of a broader range of adaptation issues found in Article 14. Article 14 begins with a general statement that "Invites all Parties to enhance action on adaptation under the Cancun Adaptation Framework, taking into account their common but differentiated responsibilities and respective capabilities, and specific national and regional development priorities, objectives and circumstances."[10] The measures to be undertaken regarding migration are in subsection (f):

> Measures to enhance understanding, coordination and cooperation with regard to climate change induced displacement, migration and planned relocation, where appropriate, at national, regional and international levels.

The negotiating language focused on enhancing understanding of the phenomenon and increasing coordination and cooperation, rather than offering concrete solutions. The final document reinforced the importance of the issue but was not controversial in terms of what was being asked (i.e., voluntary measures to enhance understanding, coordination and cooperation). While the topic of migration and displacement itself has the potential to be divisive, the way that it had been couched and presented to UNFCCC delegates (voluntary, not embedded in normative language, not linked to contentious issues) prepared the grounds for its inclusion. An advantage of Article 14f is that those items mentioned in the Cancun Adaptation Framework are viewed in practical terms by many ministries as types of activities that may qualify for adaptation funding.

With adoption of specific language on displacement, migration, and planned relocation, attention in 2011 turned to implementation. The negotiations in Durban (COP17) in December 2011 achieved a roadmap for a legally binding international agreement on climate change. They also led to a series of key decisions to implement the Cancun Agreements, including financing for adaptation, arrangements for the Adaptation Committee, and others. It is too soon to know whether governments will follow up with concrete proposals and a

---

[10] All quotes from the Cancun adaptation framework are found at https://unfccc.int/files/adaptation/cancun_adaptation_framework/adaptation_committee/application/pdf/1_cp.16.pdf.

firm commitment to funding projects that focus on displacement, migration, and planned relocation.

Global Forum on Migration and Development

The issue of climate change and migration was raised at the third round of the GFMD discussions (for more information on the GFMD, see Chapter 8). There were two brief references to climate change in the report of the civil society meeting of the GFMD in Athens. Roundtable 1, in discussing the root causes of migration, recommended "Send[ing] a clear message from the GFMD to the Copenhagen Conference on climate change that the threats to and interests of migrants and potential migrants should be high on the policy agenda of the conference."[11] Roundtable 3, in discussing data, research and policy coherence, noted "Climate change must increasingly be taken into consideration in the context of both migration and development." The government meetings of the GFMD struck a similar tone, recommending that policy makers "Give serious consideration to the impact of climate change on migration and to joint efforts to face this challenge" and referred to the need for "mainstreaming and integrating migration into development planning processes, including . . . National Adaptation Plans of Action concerning climate change (NAPAs)."

When the government of Mexico assumed leadership of the GFMD discussions for 2010, it proposed putting the issue of climate change, migration, and development more firmly on the agenda in a roundtable of its own. Responsibility for the government roundtable was assumed by the UK and Bangladesh, with support from Chile, Ecuador, France, Germany, Ghana, Mauritius, Mexico, Switzerland, and IOM. The background paper was written by Ronald Skeldon of the UK Department for International Development (DFID) with input from Susan Martin at Georgetown University. Martin, with Koko Warner, also wrote the background paper for the parallel discussions that took place during the Civil Society Days.

After presenting a review of the literature on climate change and its impact on migration, the government background paper laid out a set of questions for discussion:

   i. How can the quality of data and research on climate change, migration and development be improved and what should future priorities be?

  ii. What can countries learn from National Adaptation Programmes of Action (NAPAs) and Disaster Risk Reduction Strategies (DRRs) and their integration into national development planning? How can migration be included in such frameworks?

 iii. What can be done to manage risks in vulnerable zones and communicate information to populations who may be at risk, as well as contingency

---

[11] All references to the Athens GFMD are found at http://www.gfmd.org/en/docs/athens-2009.

planning for the possibility of relocation or resettlement? What are the implications for development policy?
iv. What are the key challenges for migration and development policy in destination countries? Are there ways in which adaptation support could be provided to countries where climate change is gradual and people have time to plan how to respond, for example, through temporary migration programmes?
v. How best can the international community assist the most vulnerable countries, especially the poorest among them, to address climate-induced displacement of populations?
vi. How could governments and other stakeholders strengthen consultations on policy challenges and solutions related to climate-induced migration?[12]

Unlike the UNFCCC discussions, the GFMD results in a rapporteur's summary and not negotiated text of an agreement. Nevertheless, the rapporteur generally seeks to present areas in which there was a great deal of consensus. The report on the climate change, migration and development discussions touched on the following four major points:

Data and Analysis
The discussions acknowledged conceptual difficulties and lack of empirical data but recognized that "this is an area deemed too important to ignore" The roundtable emphasized the need to collect data and bring them together on a continuous and systematic basis.

Geographical Scale
The UK paper had made the now common assertion that most displacement from climate change is likely to be internal (that is, within the borders of the affected countries) indicating that discussions of climate change and migration might be of relatively less importance for a forum that focuses primarily on international migration. Representatives of small island states immediately countered this assertion, pointing out that there is no interior in many of their countries to which affected populations could resort in the face of rising sea levels.

The rapporteur acknowledged that geography and size *do* matter in developing responses to climate change displacement. "Small island countries are different: for them internal migration is not an option." Thus a need to develop this topic at the local, regional, and global level was acknowledged. As one representative very eloquently put it, "climate change does not stop at borders."

[12] All references to the Athens GFMD are found at http://www.gfmd.org/en/docs/mexico-2010.

Multi-Sectoral Issues

The discussions recognized that these issues cut across different areas, "not the least of which food and water security, the basic factors of life." The roundtable emphasized the need to discuss migration and displacement from climate change in multiple forums, including the UNFCCC, and to integrate these issues into NAPAs, Disaster Risk Reduction Strategies (DRRs), and Poverty Reduction Strategy Papers.

Legal and Institutional Arrangements

The roundtable consensus was that new instruments and institutional arrangements were needed to tackle the complex issues arising from climate change induced migration and displacement, but it was recognized that binding agreements are the result of complex negotiations. The rapporteur indicated: "One must deal with complex issues, such as development, migration, humanitarian issues, and climate change which are interconnected, while at the same time trying to achieve as well policy coherence in all of them".

In keeping with the nonbinding nature of the discussions, the roundtable recommended the following ways to follow up on the discussions:

1. In order to expedite data and analysis exchange and sharing, first experiences and best practices are of the utmost importance. A virtual library may be a useful way of sharing this information.
2. A need exists to strengthen the dialogue at local, regional and global level on the interconnections on climate change and migration. RT participants welcomed and encouraged future discussions on this issue in the context of the Global Forum.
3. The need to begin discussions as to the appropriate legal and institutional arrangements to address these important issues was recognized.

Climate change and migration was not on the agenda of the 2011 GFMD concluding debate in Geneva. Nevertheless there were side meetings on the topic at both the government meeting and Civil Society Days that kept the issue alive. Most notably, the UK government presented its report on *Migration and Global Environmental Change*, prepared under the supervision of the office of the chief scientific adviser. This most authoritative study done to date on the impact of environmental drivers on migration concluded:

> Environmental change will affect migration now and in the future, specifically through its influence on a range of economic, social and political drivers which themselves affect migration. However, the range and complexity of the interactions between these drivers means that it will rarely be possible to distinguish individuals for whom environmental factors are the sole driver ('environmental migrants'). Nonetheless there are potentially grave implications of future environmental change for migration, for individuals and policy makers alike, requiring a strategic approach to policy which acknowledges the opportunities provided by migration in certain situations. (Foresight 2011:6)

A new statement by the GMG was also unveiled at the GFMD. The GMG recommended:

- To adopt gender-sensitive, human rights- and human development-oriented measures to improve the livelihoods of those exposed to the effects of climate change and increase their resilience, in order to counter the need for involuntary movements.
- To pay particular attention to the human rights situation of all people affected by the consequences of climate change, regardless of their legal status: international human rights law, including the fundamental principle of non-discrimination, as well as specific instruments such as the Guiding Principles on Internal Displacement, should guide States' action towards people who are displaced as a result of environmental factors.
- To explore the complex interrelations between climate change and human mobility in order to collect data, develop expertise and build capacity to address this challenge, and to achieve close cooperation between the climate and social sciences communities to this end.
- To address the migration impacts of both sudden and slow-onset effects of climate change.
- To recognize migration as an adaptation strategy to environmental risks and to make migration an option available to the most vulnerable. Immigration policies could take into account environmental factors in the likelihood of cross-border movement and consider opening new opportunities for legal migration.
- To assist the least-developed countries in responding to climate change by mainstreaming migration and mobility in national adaptation plans.
- To incorporate the relationship between climate change and migration in Poverty Reduction Strategies and national development strategies. (GMG 2011:2)

The statement concluded that "In the long term, States may wish to review existing legal instruments and policy framework to identify possible new solutions to the situation of those who move in relation to climate change" (ibid.:3).

UNHCR and the Nansen Initiative

As discussed earlier, in 2011, UNHCR launched a series of consultations to mark its sixtieth anniversary that focused on these looming gaps in international responses to displacement. An expert meeting in Bellagio concluded:

> There is a need to develop a global guiding framework or instrument to apply to situations of external displacement other than those covered by the 1951 Convention, especially displacement resulting from sudden-onset disasters. States, together with UNHCR and other international organizations, are encouraged to explore this further. Consideration would need to be given to whether any

such framework or instrument ought also to cover other contemporary forms of external displacement. (UNHCR 2011b)

A consultation in Oslo that included government representatives began with a focus on climate change but soon determined: "From a protection perspective, it makes little sense to distinguish between displacement caused by a non-climate related natural hazard (e.g. volcanic eruption, earthquake) and by a climate-related natural hazard (e.g. storm or flood)" (Nansen Conference 2014). The Nansen Principles adopted by the Oslo conference also concluded that "A more coherent and consistent approach at the international level is needed to meet the protection needs of people displaced externally owing to sudden-onset disasters. States, working in conjunction with UNHCR and other relevant stakeholders, could develop a guiding framework or instrument in this regard" (ibid.:5).

In October 2012, the governments of Norway and Switzerland, at the urging of UNHCR, launched the Nansen Initiative, to address the legal and protection gap for people displaced across borders owing to environmental change and extreme weather events. As described by Walter Kälin (2012: 49), the envoy to the chairmanship of the initiative, it will address issues of "international cooperation and solidarity; standards for the treatment of affected people regarding admission, stay and their access to basic rights; and operational responses including funding mechanisms and responsibilities of international humanitarian and development actors." The intent is not to develop a soft law framework similar to the Guiding Principles on Internal Displacement. Rather, the aim is to foster dialogue and consultation that will identify problems in current arrangements and potential new avenues of cooperation to address them.

IOM and the International Migration Dialogue

In 2012, IOM devoted its annual International Migration Dialogue (IMD) to the issue of Managing Migration in Crisis Situations. IOM describes the IMD as an "opportunity for governments, inter-governmental and non- governmental organizations and other stakeholders to discuss migration policy issues, in order to explore and study policy issues of common interest and cooperate in addressing them."[13] The 2012 theme was broader than climate change in encompassing "large-scale, complex migration flows due to a crisis which typically involve significant vulnerabilities for individuals and communities affected. A migration crisis may be sudden or slow in onset, can have natural or manmade causes, and can take place internally or across borders" (IOM 2012: 1). Nevertheless, climate change was a backdrop to much of the discussion at the opening workshop that focused on the migration consequences of crises. The participants concluded: "The effects of climate change already give rise

[13] http://www.iom.int/jahia/Jahia/international-dialogue-migration.

to forced migration, and to potentially large migration crises in the future. Temporary displacement due to natural disasters and the need for permanent migration solutions, especially where countries are affected by sea level rise, were underlined as some of the most acute challenges" (IOM 2012:1–2).

Placing climate change in the broader context of humanitarian crises addressed one perceived shortcoming in previous efforts to address the issues arising from environmental change. A narrow focus on climate change assumed that the international frameworks for addressing displacement in other similar situations were adequate. In essence, the question asked is: "why hurricanes and not earthquakes?" Or, in other words, should those displaced by disasters that are more numerous or intense because of climate change deserve greater international attention than those stemming from other forces? Even in slower onset situations, such as loss of livelihood from intensified drought or rising sea levels, is the connection to climate change relevant to the formulation of solutions? Should those who are forced to move from these situations be treated any differently or more generously than who lose their livelihoods, for example, by global economic policies? These are not easy questions to answer. Addressing the full complement of crises may be one approach to the problem.

CONCLUSION

Discussion of policies to manage environmental migration is in its infancy. As understanding of the various ways that environmental change affects migration patterns increases, governments are beginning to consider how to manage the implications of these interconnections. Much of the attention to date focuses on internal migration, largely in the context of adaptation strategies and, to a lesser degree, movements that may arise as a result of natural disasters and climate change-induced conflict. Few potential destination countries have explicit policies to manage migration in slower onset situations, unless affected populations migrate through the normal immigration policies that give preference to family reunification and employment-based admissions. While potential destination countries have asylum or resettlement systems to manage admission of persons who cannot return home because of a well-founded fear of persecution, none have systems in place to manage admission of migrants who cannot remain or return home because of environmental threats. At best, destination countries have policies to defer deportation of people coming from countries with natural disasters, but these are generally post-disaster measures and ad hoc in their implementation. In sum, no major destination country has a proactive policy designed to resettle victims of environmental hazards.

Given the current gaps, more attention needs to be placed on identifying and testing new frameworks for managing potential movements. Attention needs to be given to both sides of the environment and migration nexus: identifying adaptation strategies that allow people to remain where they currently live and work, and identifying resettlement strategies that protect lives and livelihoods when migration becomes necessary. Since internal migration is the most likely outcome for those affected by climate change and other environmental hazards, highest priority should be given to policies and programs aimed at managing these issues within the most affected countries.

Some international migration may nevertheless be needed, particularly for the citizens of low-lying island nations, necessitating identification of appropriate admissions policies in potential destination countries. Particular attention should be placed on determining who cannot be relocated within their home countries, either because of widespread habitat destruction (again, as in the case of certain island states) or because relocation would pose security risks that could provoke violence or even conflict. Some attention should also be addressed to the slow-onset situations in which loss of livelihoods generates emigration pressures. In the absence of legal opportunities to immigrate, at least some who lose livelihoods as a result of climate change and other environmental hazards will become irregular migrants. The challenge in these cases is determining, as discussed, whether these individuals should be given priority over others who migrate solely in search of better opportunities. There is reason to doubt that many destination countries will answer this question in the affirmative. With the exception of their refugee and asylum policies, countries tend to base their admissions policies on their own national interests, prioritizing admission of persons who will contribute to economic growth, meet labor shortages, or have close family ties in the destination county. While exceptions may be made for environmentally induced migrants whose situation most resembles that of refugees, there is less likelihood that governments will make an exception for those who resemble economic migrants. Yet at least in the case of island states that are affected by rising sea levels, the absence of an appropriate international response could render large numbers of people stateless because they are unable to remain at home, but have no legal recourse for entry elsewhere.

8

Migration and Development

The issue of migration and development is now firmly on the international agenda. As the previous chapters have indicated, the concept is not new. During the past century, however, the concept of development has changed. Initially, development was viewed in primarily economic terms – what would augment economic growth in poor countries. More recently, development has been conceived in broader terms. The UNDP argues, for example, that development "is about much more than the rise or fall of national incomes. It is about creating an environment in which people can develop their full potential and lead productive, creative lives in accord with their needs and interests."[1] The Millennium Development Goals adopted at the Millennium Summit of world leaders in 2000 are based on this understanding of development. Governments committed to make progress in eight areas: ending poverty and hunger, achieving universal education, reducing gender inequality, improving child and maternal health, combating HIV/AIDS, ensuring environmental sustainability, and developing a global partnership for development.[2]

In the periods after both World Wars, the interconnection between reconstruction and resettlement of displaced persons received considerable attention. With the end of the Cold War, it is not surprising that attention turned once more to role that migration plays in development and vice versa. Almost fifteen years ago, the International Conference on Population and Development (ICPD) in Cairo produced a twenty-year plan of action that included ways in

---

[1] http://hdr.undp.org/en/humandev/. UNDP was influenced by the Nobel Prize-winning economist, Amartya Sen's *Development as Freedom* Sen views the aim of development as the expansion of the real freedoms of persons (i.e., political freedom, economic security, access to knowledge, etc.). Expanding freedom enhances the capabilities of people to not only choose among a number of options but also to pursue a particular choice. In this sense, the expansion of freedoms is the primary end and the principal means of development.

[2] http://www.un.org/millenniumgoals/global.shtml.

which developing countries could accelerate development to make emigration unnecessary. The cooperation of industrial countries was required via "financial assistance, reassessment of commercial and tariff relations, increased access to world markets and stepped-up efforts . . . to create a domestic framework for sustainable economic growth with an emphasis on job creation" (UN 1995: 68).

What is often called the migration-development nexus incorporates two elements: ways in which migrants can be a resource for the development of their home communities and ways in which development aid and processes can reduce pressures for migration, particularly irregular movements of people. After a brief discussion of the relationship between migration and development, this chapter discusses the ways in which the international community has addressed these issues, with particular focus on the establishment of the Global Forum on Migration and Development. It will also discuss the emergence of new actors in the migration debate, including the World Bank and the UN specialized agencies focusing on development.

MIGRATION AND DEVELOPMENT

Ideally, migration should be voluntary on the part of the migrant and the receiving community, not forced by economic or political conditions in the home community. Similarly, migrants should be able to return voluntarily to home communities that are economically stable and safe. Academicians exploring the relationship between economic development and emigration tend to agree that improving the economic opportunities for people in source countries is the best long-term solution to "distress migration" – i.e., when migrants have little choice but to move in search of better opportunities. Almost uniformly, however, they caution that emigration pressures are likely to remain and possibly increase before the long-term benefits accrue: "The transformations intrinsic to the development process are at first destabilizing. They initially promote rather than impede migration. Better communications and transportation and other improvements in the quality of life of people working hard to make a living raise expectations and enhance their ability to migrate" (U.S. Commission 1990:34).

Several researchers agree with what economist Philip Martin refers to as a "migration hump." As levels of income rise, emigration would at first increase, then peak and decline. The experience of such countries as Italy and South Korea in transitioning from emigration to immigration countries gives credence to this theory.

In the interim, migrants can contribute to economic development through their financial resources as well as their skills, entrepreneurial activities, and support for democratization and human rights. They do so individually and collectively. For example, while individuals remit to their families, associations of migrants often band together to raise and remit funds for infrastructure development and income generation activities in their home communities.

Remittances

Individual remittance transfers continue to be an important source of income for many families in developing countries. The World Bank (2006:88) noted that "remittance growth has outpaced private capital flows and official development assistance (ODA) over the last decade." Remittances represented more than 15 percent of GDP in ten countries. While most flows are from more developed to less developed countries, the World Bank (2006) estimated that nearly 30 percent of remittances flow from one developing country to another.

The World Bank (2011) estimated that worldwide remittance flows in 2010 exceeded $440 billion (U.S. billion). The report noted:

> From that amount, developing countries received $325 billion, which represents an increase of 6 percent from the 2009 level. The true size, including unrecorded flows through formal and informal channels, is believed to be significantly larger. Recorded remittances in 2009 were nearly three times the amount of official aid and almost as large as foreign direct investment (FDI) flows to developing countries. (World Bank 2011:x)

Patterns of remitting appear to vary depending on the form of migration (temporary vs. permanent), gender of the sender and receiver of the remittance, geographic region, educational level of the remitter, family and household linkages of the remitter to the home country, and other similar factors. Unfortunately, the research base for fully understanding these variations and their impact is not adequate. For example, studies have only recently been examining gender differences in remitting behavior, in terms of either the sending of remittances or their use upon receipt.

Until the past decade, researchers, economists, and development agencies tended to dismiss the importance of remittances or emphasize only their negative aspects. They often argued that money sent back by foreign workers was spent largely on consumer items and seldom was invested in productive activities that would grow the economies of the developing countries. They also feared that recipients of remittances would become dependent on them, reducing incentives to invest in their own income-generating activities. Adverse impacts on exchange rate appreciation from large monetary inflows could also undermine the profitability of cost-sensitive trade items, such as crops and manufactured items.

Moreover, excessive consumerism, they argued, would lead to inequities, with remittance-dependent households exceeding the standard of living available to those without family members working abroad. Government attempts to encourage or require investment of remittances were often heavy-handed and led to few economic improvements. Critics pointed out that remittances would diminish over time as the foreign workers settled in their new communities and lost contact with their home communities. Sometimes, wives and children would be left behind, with the all-important remittances no longer contributing to their livelihood.

Many of these problems still exist, but recent work on remittances shows a far more complex picture. The scale of remittances has grown so substantially in recent years that experts now recognize that remittances have a far greater positive impact on communities in developing countries than previously acknowledged. Perhaps most important, remittance flows are a more stable source of revenue for many countries than foreign trade, foreign direct investment, and foreign aid (Ratha 2003). Remittances also tend to be counter-cyclical, flowing to countries experiencing financial crises, natural disasters, or conflict – when other forms of aid and investment may be reduced. Remittances to post-conflict and post-disaster countries have been used for reconstruction after years of civil war, hurricanes, and earthquakes. At the macro-economic level, remittances may be used to secure financing and improve a country's creditworthiness. Such experts as Edward Taylor at the University of California at Davis argue that even consumer use of remittances stimulates economic development, particularly when spent locally. The multiplier effects of remittances can be substantial, with each dollar producing additional dollars in economic growth for the businesses that produce and supply the products bought with these resources.

Nevertheless, there continues to be skepticism as to the long-range impact of remittances on growth. The World Bank (2006:86) concludes from the existing literature, "The evidence on the effect of remittances on long-term growth is inconclusive." In part, the difficulty lies in the factors that may have induced migration in the first place. Countries with large emigration have often not made economic reforms that would facilitate more productive uses of remittances. Investment of remittances is largely determined by such factors as relaxation of exchange and capital controls, banking practices, taxation policies, level of corruption, and general business climate. These policies affect the willingness of migrants to send remittances through formal channels, save money, or invest in job-producing enterprises.

The role of remittances in regards to poverty reduction appears more straightforward. As private resources, most remittances go to families that make rational choices as to their use. For these families, remittances often represent an important difference in their standard of living. Further, remittances appear to have a positive impact on investment in education and health services. As one summary of the literature concludes, "Since the increased investments in education and health contribute to human capital formation, it is likely that remittances may benefit developing countries' long-term growth prospects" (Agunias 2006:25). In fact, according to research conducted for the World Bank, "international remittances – defined as the share of remittances in country GDP – has a strong, statistical impact on reducing poverty. On average, a 10 percent increase in the share of international remittances in a country's GDP will lead to a 1.6 percent decline in the share of people living in poverty" (Adams and Page 2003:1). The beneficial impact on rural households is particularly strong.

Although remittances hold promise for development and poverty reduction, they are not a panacea. Moreover, they are by no means a substitute for Official Development Assistance (ODA). Remittances may help alleviate poverty in families with migrants but they do not reach everyone in need and may thus increase inequality. Many donor countries tend to channel their ODA to the poorest of the poor; these individuals generally have too little financial or human capital to benefit from opportunities for migration. In the absence of ODA, it is unlikely that any improvements would be made in their health, education, or income.

The cost of remitting money to home communities has also been an area of concern. The costs can be exceedingly high. The market appears to be responding to this situation, with greater competition leading to lower transfer costs, but more needs to be done in this area. To date, the business is dominated by wire transfer companies rather than financial institutions that offer a wider range of services to customers. Immigrants often mention that they use a few well-established companies because of their greater reliability. The greater entry of banks and credit unions could help reduce costs and abuses even further. To the extent that credit unions, for example, reinvest transfer fees in the remittance-receiving communities, the development potential could be further increased. There are new initiatives in this area. The InterAmerican Development Bank's Multilateral Investment Fund supports programs to enable the transmission of remittances through financial institutions that work with low-income clients, such as credit unions and micro-finance institutions.

Remittances are often used to help families address emergency needs that could, perhaps, be better addressed through other means – or prevented altogether. For example, many households use some portion of their remittances to deal with emergency health care needs because they lack access to routine health care and do not have insurance coverage. The Mexican Migration Project asks respondents how their family members use remittances. According to one research study, "the largest single reported use of remitted or saved funds was health care expenses for family members. Among those who remitted (approximately 60 percent of respondents) fully three-quarters reported that some share of the funds were used for health care expenses" (DeSipio 2000). At the same time, many migrants have not taken advantage of an initiative by the Mexican government that enables them to purchase health insurance for families in Mexico for a very low rate per month. Such cross-border health coverage, purchased in the United States for relatives at home, could be a more effective use of remittances than the funding of emergency care. Since many migrants return periodically to their home communities, such cross-border programs could also provide the largely uninsured U.S. residents with a source of health care.

Greater financial literacy among remitters, as well as clearer information about the actual costs of transferring funds, would also reduce abuses in this area. Financial literacy programs have many benefits for both immigrants and financial institutions. A particularly useful initiative was pioneered in Rogers, Arkansas (Schoenholtz 2005). The curriculum covers such issues as basic banking services, how to write checks, how to establish a credit history, how to buy a house, and retirement planning. The training program is offered by a local bank, in cooperation with corporations in the area. With greater financial literacy, the largely immigrant workforce has become better educated consumers, who are less likely to be victims of abusive and predatory financial practices. The bank that offered the courses significantly increased its customer base for a number of bank products – a win-win situation for both (Schoenholtz 2005).

It is well to remember that it is often the poorest residents of wealthy countries that are sending remittances abroad. Many migrants have low incomes, often living in poverty, yet they remit billions of dollars to their home countries. While beneficial to the families and societies at home, it is well to ask if the remittances come at a cost to those settling abroad. What trade-offs are they making to save sufficient resources to remit? Are they unable to make investments in education and skills upgrading, for example, in order to send the billions home?

Brain Drain

Brain drain, or the migration of highly skilled individuals, remains a problem as well as an opportunity for many countries. As a study for the ILO found, "The percentage loss of tertiary skilled persons is far greater than that of secondary schooled persons, while the loss of primary schooled persons is very small. . . . Emigration selects those who can afford it, whose skills are in demand abroad, and who stand to benefit most (the tertiary educated)" (Lowell and Findlay 2001). When the emigration of highly skilled professionals reaches a critical mass – for example, 30 percent of those with graduate degrees – the negative impacts on particular sectors (such as health care and education) can be massive. Overall, the loss of highly educated migrants can also represent a loss in economic growth potential if not offset by other factors.

The effects are not all negative, however. The prospect of employment in other countries can also stimulate interest in higher education. Because only a portion of the graduates leave, a country may benefit from an increase in educated persons even if emigration of skilled persons continues (Lowell and Findlay 2001). In addition, if the investment climate is poor or there are no jobs for highly educated professionals, their departure may not negatively affect the country of origin, which would not have benefited from their skills if they had remained.

The impact of high-skilled migration varies depending on the sector in which the migrants work. One result can be a virtuous cycle of information technology workers who migrate and then form networks that bring contracts and expertise back to their home countries. In contrast to this model is the vicious cycle of health professionals whose migration reduces the likelihood that poor countries will be able to meet their Millennium Development Goals related to child mortality, maternal health, and HIV/AIDS. Some countries have policies designed to retain health professionals and other key skilled workers by improving salaries, working conditions, and research facilities, and offering other inducements to remain or return.

Circulation and Return

Migrants returning temporarily or permanently bring needed skills to their home countries. Programs that identify migrants with specific skills needed by their home countries and facilitate return with reintegration contribute to economic development, as does support for migrants who plan to open small businesses upon their return. The skills may be needed for economic development, but they may also be required to help move the source country toward greater democratization and respect for human rights. For example, migrants who have legal training may be helpful in developing new judicial systems and establishing the rule of law. There is a caveat, however. Migrants who return may be negatively selected – that is, those who have not succeeded in the destination country may be the most likely returnees. Whether they have acquired skills useful for development is the key question.

Many countries hope to build on the human capital of their émigrés by inducing them to return. Multilateral and bilateral programs to support return are notably small. Operated by the UN Development Program, the TOKTEN project (Transfer of Knowledge through Expatriate Nationals) aims to persuade migrants established abroad to return at least temporarily and contribute to their homeland's development. Similar opportunities for migrants to bring their skills home are offered by the IOM. For example, the Return for Qualified Afghans Program offers comprehensive assistance packages to qualified Afghans who would like to return to their home country to work in the public and private sectors. The Migration for Development in Africa (MIDA) program provides a wider range of activities through which migrants can contribute to the development of their home countries, including virtual return (using information technology to transfer skills), investment, short or sequenced visits, and permanent relocation. The numbers of migrants who use these programs are small and their long-term impact on development is largely unstudied. France, for example, funds an assisted return program as part of its development strategy (Martin et al. 2006). The potential for expansion of the program appears to be limited. Many of the small businesses begun by returnees are not sustainable because the owners did not have previous experience in the Malian economy.

Diaspora Communities

Diasporas often seek to promote economic development through investments in businesses, infrastructure, education, and health. Some governments actively seek such investment. The likelihood that members of the diaspora will invest is enhanced by reforms in the economy and banking institutions that would also attract foreign direct investment from other sources. Home Town Associations (HTAs) raise funds for their communities of origin, sometimes with matching funds – as in the case of Mexico's 3-for-1 program, under which the federal, state, and local governments match the HTA contributions.

These programs tend to be small, and there is insufficient evidence to judge their effectiveness. Some research indicates, however, that HTA support has the potential to grow to significant size. According to one study: "Consider the Salvadoran 'United Community of Chinameca': their first largesse was $5,000 to build a school, and then they built a septic tank worth $10,000. Later they constructed a Red Cross clinic at a cost of $43,000, and bought an ambulance worth $32,000."[3] There has been a recent trend towards encouraging the HTAs to invest in small businesses and manufacturing activities, in order to produce new jobs for villagers. These are truly grassroots initiatives that involve community-to-community development.

Diaspora communities can also help stimulate political reforms that improve conditions in home countries. Mexican migrants in the United States have been consistent forces for democratization and better governance in their home country, and Mexican political candidates have responded by campaigning extensively in U.S. communities. The new political leadership in a number of post-conflict countries urged their citizens abroad to provide not only financial resources for rebuilding the country, but also technical expertise as they established new democratic institutions.

The experience of the diaspora is not always positive in stimulating respect for democratic values. Some returning migrants appear particularly reluctant to expose women and girls to Western values if it means undermining cultural traditions, maintaining that they would never allow their wives or daughters to migrate with them to Europe or North America. In some cases, returning migrants appear to have become more socially and religiously conservative as a result of their own migration experience.

HTAs and their home communities may not have the technical expertise to determine the best ways to invest in community development. The strength of a grassroots initiative can become its weakness if HTAs and local villages disagree about the best use of the remittances or if they invest the funds unwisely. There are some initiatives underway to provide technical assistance and training in this regard. For example, the InterAmerican Foundation funds such assistance through the Fundacion para la Productividad del Campo, also known as APOYO, in several Mexican states. The InterAmerican Development Bank has held several conferences and regional workshops to stimulate discussion of mechanisms to increase the development payoff of remittances.

---

[3] B. Lindsay Lowell and Rodolfo O. de la Garza, *The Developmental Role of Remittances in U.S. Latino Communities and in Latin American Countries*, Washington, DC: InterAmerican Dialogue, June 2000.

Gender, Migration, and Development

International migration profoundly affects gender relations, particularly the role of women in households and communities. The impacts are complex. In many respects, migration enhances the autonomy and power of women. When women from traditional societies migrate to advanced industrial societies, they become familiar with new norms regarding women's rights and opportunities. Outside employment may provide financial resources that had never before compensated their labor. Even if their pay is pooled with that of other family members, this new wage-earning capacity often gives women greater ability to direct household priorities.

Women who are left at home when their husbands migrate also experience changes in their role. The stay-at-home spouses may now have greater household and economic responsibilities. Although they may still be financially dependent on remittances from their overseas relatives, the women may have substantial autonomy over decisions about how the funds will be used. Should their husbands fail to return home, or stop sending remittances, the women may have to assume even greater responsibility for themselves and their children.

In other respects, migration can serve to reinforce traditional gender roles. This is particularly the case when women are expected to preserve cultural and religious norms that appear to be threatened. This process could be seen, for example, in Afghan refugee camps in Pakistan, where *purdah*, the separation of men and women, was practiced more rigidly than in Afghanistan itself. Upon return to Afghanistan, the Taliban leaders retained the intensified practice, imposing it on the whole country. International migration can also lead to generational tensions, particularly when children adapt more quickly than their parents to a new language and social system. Seeing their children adopt unfamiliar practices may prompt some immigrant women to recommit themselves and their families to more traditional and often patriarchal mores. Male migrants may return home also intending to buttress traditional norms. For example, interviews conducted in Mali by this author indicated that some men who had lived in France had sought to bring their daughters home to undergo female circumcision (also known as female genital mutilation) because it was illegal in France. Some of them had succeeded but others reported that their wives and daughters remained abroad because they did not want to undergo the procedure.

Immigration rules can also reinforce traditional roles. Many migrant women obtain legal residency status through family reunification or formation so their ability to exercise rights may be limited by their spouse's willingness to support their immigration claims. Migrant women who are victims of spousal abuse, for example, may be unwilling to leave the abuser if he controls access to their legal status. In recognition that immigration laws can make women and their children vulnerable, the United States passed legislation permitting abused women to petition on their own for permanent residence.

It is not only the role of women that may change dramatically through international migration. Men must often adjust to their wives' and daughters' new participation in the labor market and their greater economic autonomy as wage-earners. Men who migrate on their own for work often find themselves responsible for household activities that they had previously seen as solely the purview of women. Similarly, men left behind by migrating spouses may be required to assume parenting roles previously unfamiliar to them.

INTERNATIONAL COOPERATION ON MIGRATION AND DEVELOPMENT

As discussed, the interconnections between migration and development have long been on the international agenda. IOM, in particular, identified migration for development as a major theme of its work as early as 1960, largely in the context of its work in Latin America. The IOM council passed Resolution 223 (XIII) authorizing an expansion of its activities to include assistance to countries in Latin America to help them absorb highly skilled workers from Europe with the aim of facilitating economic development (Ducasse-Rogier 2001). The programs included assessment of labor needs, recruitment of workers, vocational training, and placement services. A special fund was established in 1965 to provide financial incentives for would-be migrants who possessed needed skills. The agency also engaged in settlement programs to stimulate commercial agriculture (ibid.). By the 1980s, programs for what was often dubbed "Return of Talent" – meaning the repatriation of highly qualified migrants whose skills were needed at home – were proliferating as concerns about brain drain mounted. Initially, these programs targeted the needs of African countries but soon came to include developing countries throughout the world (ibid.). IOM was joined in these endeavors by the UNDP, which launched the TOKTEN program to assist university professors and other professionals to return temporarily to help build the knowledge base and institutions of developing countries.

A second manifestation of interest in migration and development focused on people displaced by conflict. As discussed in earlier chapters, a number of international organizations have been charged with responsibility to find solutions for refugees and displaced persons. Generally, three options might be available: repatriation once conditions in the home country permit such return, long-term settlement with possibility of citizenship in the country in which asylum was first found, or resettlement to a third country. Problems of underdevelopment have often constrained the potential for both local settlement and repatriation. In the 1980s, UNHCR began to address these barriers in Africa. Convening the International Conference on Refugees in Africa (ICARA), UNHCR hoped to convince both the African countries and donors that it would be more humane and financially advantageous for everyone if refugees in camps were permitted to integrate into the host country economies. The discussions broke down, however, when donors proposed that the African countries pay for integration of refugees with their existing development aid, whereas the African governments – not surprisingly – argued that additional funding was needed to cover the costs of settling the refugees. Even if donors had agreed to additional funds, the African countries were skeptical about the long-term costs of settlement. From their perspective, as long as refugees remained in camps, the international community would pay for their care and maintenance. They feared, probably correctly, that once the refugees were integrated, the donors would lose interest and funding would dissipate and then disappear.

It was not until the end of Cold War conflicts, which allowed millions of refugees to return home that the relationship between refugee aid and development was resurrected. This time the focus was on how refugee repatriation would fit into the reconstruction of countries that had been destroyed by war. UNHCR funded "Quick Impact Projects" that were aimed at helping home communities receive refugees back into their midst. These projects usually involved the employment of both locals and returnees on projects, such as rebuilding infrastructure, thus benefitting all. Many of the projects proved useful in the short term but unsustainable once the refugee funding ended. To bridge the transition between refugee relief and development, UNHCR tried to form partnerships with development agencies, such as the World Bank. The hope was that these agencies would assume longer-term responsibility for the projects and make repatriation effective for both the refugees and the communities. Too often, however, the gap between refugee aid and development remained wide and unbridgeable.

International Conference on Population and Development

Beyond these efforts to address brain drain and solutions for refugees, attention to the interconnections between migration and development remained sporadic. Nor was there much attention to addressing the development-related causes of migration. The situation began to change in 1994, however, with the incorporation of migration into the agenda of the ICPD that convened in Cairo. The principal focus of the conference was on fertility and reproductive health, but a section of the Plan of Action (PoA) that resulted from the discussions addressed movements of people. The inclusion of migration on the agenda was recognition that there are three major ways in which population size and distribution are influenced: births, deaths, and relocation of people.

The ICPD PoA devoted a full chapter to international migration, stressing the need for a "comprehensive approach to migration management and policy development by States and other concerned actors."[4] The PoA focused on the duality referenced previously – that development affects migration and

---

[4] All quotes from the ICPD PoA are taken from the version available at http://www.unfpa.org/
public/home/publications/pid/1973.

vice versa. It noted that economic, political, and cultural interrelations play an important role in the flow of people between countries, whether they are developing, developed, or with economies in transition. In its diverse types, international migration is linked to such interrelations and both affects and is affected by the development process. International economic imbalances, poverty, and environmental degradation, combined with human rights violations, absence of peace and security, and the varying degrees of development of judicial and democratic institutions all influenced international migration. The PoA also recognized that migration could have multi-faceted ramifications:

> Orderly international migration can have positive impacts on both the communities of origin and the communities of destination, providing the former with remittances and the latter with needed human resources. International migration also has the potential of facilitating the transfer of skills and contributing to cultural enrichment. However, international migration entails the loss of human resources for many countries of origin and may give rise to political, economic, or social tensions in countries of destination.

The migration-related objectives of the PoA were three-fold:

(1) To address the root causes of migration, especially those related to poverty;
(2) To encourage more cooperation and dialogue between countries of origin and countries of destination to maximize the benefits of migration to those concerned and increase the likelihood that migration has positive consequences for the development of both sending and receiving countries;
(3) To facilitate the reintegration process of returning migrants.

The PoA focused separately on documented migrants, those without documentation, and refugees and displaced persons. While emphasizing the sovereign responsibility of governments to determine who would be admitted to their territory, emphasis was placed on ensuring the protection of basic rights and safety of migrants in all of these categories. The root causes of all of these types of migration were also addressed.

With regard to documented migration, the PoA placed special attention on actions that would decrease discrimination against migrants. It encouraged governments to provide for "equality of opportunity and treatment in respect of religious practice, working conditions, social security, participation in trade unions, access to health, education, cultural and other social services and to the judicial system and equal treatment before the law." Governments were also "urged to promote, through family reunion, the normalization of the family life of legal migrants who have the right to long-term residence."

The PoA sections regarding undocumented migration aimed to reduce such movements, to protect irregular migrants from exploitation and other abuses, and to ensure that those in need of international protection received it. The plan urged governments to cooperate in addressing the problems of undocumented migration and to establish "effective sanctions against those who organize undocumented migration, exploit undocumented migrants or engage in trafficking in undocumented migrants, especially those who engage in any form of international traffic in women, youth and children."

The provisions regarding refugees, asylum-seekers, and displaced persons emphasized ensuring adequate protection and assistance while finding durable solutions. Recognizing the large number of women and children who are displaced, the PoA gave special attention to these populations:

> Refugees, particularly refugee women, should be involved in the planning of refugee assistance activities and in their implementation. In planning and implementing refugee assistance activities, special attention should be given to the specific needs of refugee women and refugee children. Refugees should be provided with access to adequate accommodation, education, health services, including family planning, and other necessary social services.

ICPD succeeded in raising awareness of the migration-development nexus among organizations concerned with development but it led to relatively little change in the ways governments approached these issues. The PoA included few migration-related provisions that were not already on the agenda of IOM and UNHCR. Nor did it determine the best way to move forward in the area of migration and development.

2006 High Level Dialogue on Migration and Development[5]

Following the ICPD, there was disagreement among states regarding the benefits or value of convening a conference specifically on international migration and development. Many were reluctant to support global discussions of migration. In 1997, after consulting with member governments about the desirability of an international conference on migration, United Nations Secretary General Kofi Annan found insufficient consensus to plan such a meeting. He concluded:

> The disparate experiences of countries or subregions with regard to international migration suggest that, if practical solutions are to be found, they are likely to arise from the consideration of the particular situation of groups of countries sharing similar positions or concerns with the global international migration system. In the light of this, it may be expedient to pursue regional or subregional approaches whenever possible. (Annan 1997: para. 55)

In fact, proliferation of regional and cross-regional consultative processes was already underway. Some of these included like-minded countries experiencing similar challenges as source or destination countries. Examples included the Colombo Process that focused "on the management of overseas employment

---

[5] My thanks to Philip Martin and Sarah Cross, who co-authored with me, "High Level Dialogue on Migration and Development," published in *International Migration*. This section draws on that article with the permission of the co-authors.

and contractual labour for countries of origins in Asia"[6] and the Intergovernmental Consultations on Migration, Refugees, and Asylum that brought together destination countries in Europe, the Americas, and Oceania. Others were composed of both source and destination countries, such as the Regional Migration Conference (RCM), otherwise known as the Puebla Process, that includes Canada, the United States, Mexico, the Central American countries, and the Dominican Republic, and the Abu Dhabi Dialogue between the countries in the GCC and the members of the Colombo Process. Subregional consultative processes have been established in the southern cone and Andean regions of South America, the Migration Dialogue for Southern Africa, and the Migration Dialogue for Western Africa.

Despite this growth in regional mechanisms to stimulate cooperation, discussion continued on ways in which the UN itself could be a forum for dialogue on migration and development. The High Level Dialogue on Migration and Development (HLD) formally arose from General Assembly Resolution 58/208 in December 2003, which agreed to devote a high-level dialogue to international migration and development in 2006.[7] In 2005, the secretary-general reported on the organizational details of the HLD to the General Assembly. It adopted Resolution 60/227 to convene the HLD on September 14–15, 2006, in New York. The resolution directed the HLD to explore the "overall theme of the multidimensional aspects of international migration and development in order to identify appropriate ways and means to maximize its development benefits and minimize its negative impacts" (UN Resolution 2005).

The tone for the HLD shifted subtly but markedly from that of the ICPD. Whereas the migration section of the Cairo PoA began with the assertion that all governments "should seek to make the option of remaining in one's country viable for all people," the HLD preparations recognized the reality of international migration and sought to explore ways it might speed up development.

The General Assembly determined that the HLD would include four plenary meetings for statements by leaders of participating states, and four interactive roundtables. To assist in the preparation of the HLD, Peter Sutherland was appointed in January 2006 as Special Representative of the Secretary-General of the United Nations on International Migration and Development. He emphasized the need for "a non-adversarial, non-finger-pointing dialogue where you [source and destination countries] can exchange best practices, learn how best to deal with the issues" ("Global" Migration News 2007).

In anticipation of the HLD, there were several preparatory events around the world during 2006, including the July Informal Interactive Hearings with NGOs, Civil Society and the Private Sector, in New York; the June and July

---

[6] http://www.colomboprocess.org/.

[7] For a contemporary analysis of the HLD, see Philip Martin, Susan Martin, and Sarah Cross, "High-level Dialogue on Migration and Development," *International Migration* 45.1 (March 2007).

Panel Discussions on International Migration and Development, in New York and Geneva, respectively; the June International Symposium on International Migration and Development in Turin; the Thirty-Ninth Session of the Commission on Population and Development in New York in April; and the May Expert Group Meeting on International Migration and Development in the Arab Region: Challenges and Opportunities in Beirut, Lebanon.

At the HLD, four roundtables were organized around the following themes: (1) the effects of international migration on economic and social development; (2) measures to ensure respect for and protection of the human rights of all migrants and to prevent and combat smuggling of migrants and trafficking in persons; (3) multidimensional aspects of international migration and development, including remittances; and (4) promoting partnerships and capacity-building and the sharing of best practices at all levels. Participants included high-level state representatives, officials from UN agencies and programs, the executive secretaries of two regional commissions, the director-general of the IOM, and representatives of various NGOs, civil society groups, and the private sector.

While the issues covered in the round-table discussions were at the heart of the HLD, the statements delivered during the plenary sessions often went well beyond the designated round-table topics. The statements of each delegate reflected the particular concerns of individual states and often provided useful insights into national policies. Thus, during the plenary meetings, perspectives of states became discernible through the topics they chose to address (or not address), the weight they placed on the various issues, and the ways in which they framed their concerns. There was considerably more agreement than disagreement among states on substantive issues, but they differed significantly in deciding on the process of promoting cooperation.

In two roundtables, participants explored the migration-development nexus, highlighting the "substantial positive impacts of international migration on social and economic development, while noting certain negative impacts as well."[8] In this regard, participants "called on countries of origin to take a more proactive approach to enhancing the development impact of migrants' contributions and savings. Collaboration among governments, civil society, and the private sector in this endeavor was encouraged.

In plenary statements, states generally agreed that well-managed migration could be a positive force for development. In particular, they stressed the potential of co-development, that is, the cooperation between receiving and source states to improve the economic and social conditions in both places, especially by enlisting migrant communities in development efforts. With proper national policies and active engagement of the diaspora, migration could be an engine

---

[8] All quotes from the High Level Dialogue are taken from the reports available at http://daccess-dds-ny.un.org/doc/UNDOC/GEN/N06/571/02/PDF/N0657102.pdf?OpenElement.

for development. Participants discussed the numerous ways in which this might be achieved.

Remittances, estimated at $232 billion (U.S. billion) in 2005,[9] were a major focus of discussions in this area. Rapidly increasing remittances inspired many states to suggest that remittances create a win-win-win situation for migrants and countries of origin and destination. States recognized the importance of finding ways to maximize the developmental impact of remittances. Many countries, both source and destination, called for efforts to make the transfer of remittances cheaper, faster, and more reliable. Many noted their own progress, such as through working with banking or other financial institutions to improve the access of migrants and their families to banking services and to reduce the cost of wire transfers. To maximize the developmental impact of remittances, many countries of origin also recognized, as the Albanian delegate declared, that because "sound policies will stimulate remittances and channel them into productive investments," it is necessary to "provid[e] facilities for investment . . . and shorten the procedures for establishment of private enterprises."[10]

Since remittances are sent to migrants' families and are used primarily for consumption, rather than investment, many states stressed that such funds are private and therefore should not be seen as a substitute for ODA. Some countries, primarily in the north, added that remittances are "not substitutes for national development efforts." In the words of the U.S. representative, they "will have a greater overall impact on development in countries of origin when those countries undertake economic and social reforms that create an environment conducive for asset building, entrepreneurship, and investment." At the same time, many developing countries called for continued "investment, trade, foreign aid and debt relief" to bolster the development impact of remittances.

Many source countries pointed out that remittances would not offset losses from brain drain. As the Caribbean Community (CARICOM) representative observed, "the *total losses* due to skilled emigration outweigh the recorded remittances for the Caribbean Region on average, and for almost all the individual Caribbean countries." This reference to the problem of brain drain was echoed by many states, particularly with regard to the loss of professionals in the health and education sectors. A number of destination countries acknowledged the brain-drain problem and highlighted the importance of trying to minimize its negative impacts through the "more ethical and disciplined

[9] The ground work for the discussion of remittances was laid by the World Bank's Global Economic Prospects 2006 report (www.worldbank.org/prospects/gep2006), which urged more guest worker programs to benefit migrants and developing countries: "Managed migration programs, including temporary work visas for low-skilled migrants in industrial countries, could help alleviate problems associated with a large stock of irregular migrants, and allow increased movement of temporary workers."

[10] Quotes from delegates to the HLD are found at http://www.un.org/migration/statements.html.

recruitment policies," as the EU representative urged. Some states pointed to their efforts to help countries retain needed professionals: "A priority of the Irish Government aid programme is to support our partner countries to improve management and working conditions of health workers so that they are encouraged to continue working in their own countries."

While many countries dwelled on the negative impacts of brain drain, several also highlighted initiatives underway to promote "brain gain." Source and destination countries agreed that this could be achieved by engaging migrants in development through improved diaspora relations, policies to encourage return, or circular migration and the transfer of skills and knowledge back to countries of origin.

Source countries highlighted the importance of their diasporas and many, like the Albanian representative, pointed to progress in "efforts in creating the necessary conditions and incentive structure for the engagement of Diaspora in the country's development." Many agreed that because the temporary return of migrants to their countries of origin can provide brain gain and stimulate development, it is important, as the Mexican representative urged, to "develop new schemes that allow for the mobility and circularity of people."

To maximize further the developmental benefits of migration, some countries called for increased portability of pensions. In a similar vein, there was a call for destination countries to encourage the return and reintegration of migrants, as the representative of the Philippines urged, "by helping the sending country who absorbs all the burden of providing for its elderly and previously productive nationals."

To ensure that migration and development are addressed jointly, numerous countries called for the further integration of migration policies into national poverty-reduction strategies. The British delegate noted that "donors are more likely to get behind countries' efforts to manage migration effectively if it appears in national strategies." Governments urged increased coordination of such policies and pointed to successful examples.

The HLD also tackled the issue of human rights of migrants, beginning with recognition that migrants were first and foremost human beings possessing fundamental rights. "Human rights should be considered part of the necessary under-girding linking international migration to development since, as delegates stressed, only when the human rights of migrants were recognized and safeguarded could the positive contributions of migrants to countries of origin and destination be fully realized." Participants agreed all states had the obligation to protect the rights of all migrants, regardless of status. In addition, there should be particular concern for migrants more vulnerable to exploitation, such as women and children. States addressed the crucial role of social, economic, and cultural rights in the successful integration of migrants in receiving countries, pointing out that governments had the obligation to oppose discrimination and xenophobia and to promote tolerance. Toward that end, roundtable participants urged governments to ratify and implement relevant ILO and UN conventions that provide protection for human rights, including the Migrant Workers Convention.

Plenary statements acknowledged that migrants are human beings endowed with inviolable rights that all governments are obligated to protect. While most countries expressed at least passing concern for migrant rights, a division emerged between source and destination countries in emphasis, with source countries asserting the sanctity of migrant rights more frequently and more forcefully than their receiving counterparts. A number of source countries listed human rights as a top priority of migration policy, and some argued that concern for human rights should trump state sovereignty. A sizeable number of states, source and destination, made little or no mention of rights at all. Some countries with questionable human rights records themselves made quite forceful claims that countries hosting their migrants should respect human rights.

The destination countries that addressed migrant rights generally did so by affirming their long-standing commitments to human rights. "The respect for human and labour rights of migrants is essential. The EU instruments are in this regard clear and unequivocal," said the EU delegate. Many pointed to their ratification of the major international human rights instruments.

A few source countries urged increased ratification of the Migrant Rights Convention. One such appeal came from the Turkish representative, who reported, "We are not happy to see that except few countries, many migration receiving states have not yet ratified 'The UN Convention on the Protection of the Rights of all Migrant Workers and Members of their Families.'"

Several countries expressed concern about potential discrimination against migrants and called for equal protection of migrant rights by destination countries. Azerbaijan echoed the sentiments of other countries in raising the "urgent issue [of] the provision of the rights of migrants. We . . . are deeply concerned at recently increased facts of racism and xenophobia towards migrants." Moreover, several took the opportunity to highlight, often in quite critical terms, the existing discrimination and denial of rights facing migrants in destination countries. In the words of the representative from Turkey, "In many parts of the world immigrant populations are experiencing irksome difficulties in accessing education, housing and job opportunities. Unbearable discriminations, racism and cultural discrimination are becoming a major problem." The Nigerian delegate offered a similar perspective, noting that his country was "concerned with the degrading treatment of migrants, in particular, the vulnerable groups, and calls on states to fulfill their human rights and labour obligations to migrants."

Some destination countries echoed the importance of preventing discrimination, xenophobia, and exploitation in host societies. Expressed by destination countries, however, this sentiment was usually framed in the affirmative, confirming commitment to equality. For example, the EU statement declares, "Labour migration policies need to be supported by measures of integration including equal treatment and the prohibition of discrimination of any kind including social and economic rights, in order to prevent abusive practices and to promote decent and productive work for all migrants."

A wide range of countries agreed on the importance of incorporating coherent policies, capacity-building, and interstate cooperation (bilateral, regional, or global) into the effort to address international migration. The importance of the three areas of governance was summed up well by the representative of Cyprus:

> Through international cooperation and coordination of our policies we can maximize the beneficial effects of international migration to development and minimize the negative ones. We need, however, to build capacity in both countries of origin and destination in order to formulate coherent migration policies, in an integrated and a holistic way. Cooperation in this area is essential, not only between governments, but also with non-government actors, such as the civil society, the private sector and international organizations.

A number of states echoed the need for greater coherence both within and between states regarding migration policies, and linking migration policies with related policies (such as economic/developmental, social, employment/labor, health, and security). They further highlighted the importance of capacity-building in countries of origin to help those governments formulate and implement migration policies. Some developing countries pointed to progress in their national capacity-building efforts, often assisted by IOM, while others appealed to the international community for more support in this endeavor.

Many statements acknowledged that the transnational nature of migration required transnational coordination. Although almost all states agreed that countries need to work together to achieve positive outcomes in migration, they differed somewhat in the value they ascribed to bilateral, regional, and international cooperation. A number of countries, particularly the United States and Australia, attached more significance to regional cooperation; many, including Iran, Mozambique, and the Dominican Republic, highlighted their successful participation in regional cooperative schemes. Some countries, such as Albania and Greece, highlighted the benefits of particular bilateral agreements, but the general tone of source countries was to encourage more international cooperation, especially in fighting trafficking, facilitating remittances, and combating brain drain. They urged more international cooperation, for, as the Mexican representative asserted, "No country can address migration alone."

While the discussions regarding coherence, capacity-building, and cooperation generally yielded consensus, there was an occasional accusatory note. The representative of the Russian Federation, for example, declared:

> Experience shows that the countries of origin of migrants often resort to a passive stand, shifting the responsibility for their citizens on to the receiving host-countries and benefiting from their activities. We call on all the participants of this process to approach this cooperation in a more responsible manner in the spirit of equal burden sharing and partnership.

From source countries periodically came corresponding charges about the "lack of will in the cooperation for development" of destination countries, with the Cuban representative, for example, arguing that "today's facts put into question the existence of that will by the industrialized world."

Most differences were on more procedural issues – that is, on how to move the debate forward. The disagreement manifested itself in what might be considered the organizational details, such as whether the forum would be conducted within or outside of the UN, who should be involved, how much to build on existing (primarily regional) efforts, and whether and how to link the forum to other migration-related entities and programs. These differences did not appear to fall along any major extant fault lines, including any North-South divide.

Most states supported continuing dialogue at the international level, but they differed in their views of the appropriate venue and nature of the dialogue. One group emphasized the need for, in the words of the Irish representative: "the establishment of . . . a forum which would be nonbureaucratic, open-ended, state owned, consultative and non-decision making and would provide a framework for continued dialogue on challenges which face all our societies in the areas of migration and development." Another group favored continuing the dialogue at the global level, but preferred that it be conducted more formally, within the UN. Countries represented by the Group of 77 and China took this position, noting that the dialogue "is too important not to have it within the United Nations."

There was some opposition to any forum, whether independent or within the UN system. Such opposition came from a distinct minority, but nevertheless a very important one that included the United States and Australia. Their statements warned of duplication of efforts and expressed a preference for follow-up at the regional level. According to the American delegate, "We are not interested in grand and elaborate global dialogues simply because we have seen the inherent weakness that results from their size and scope. They lumber under the great weight of rounds and rounds of conversation, far removed from immediate problems and realistic solutions."

The rejection by countries that explicitly opposed the forum, often destination countries, did not constitute a source-destination divide. Most of the EU countries favored establishing a global forum. Likewise, source countries were divided over the issue of whether the dialogue should take place within or outside of the UN.

A large number of states were noncommittal, expressing general support for continued international dialogue and cooperation, but making no specific mention of the proposed forum. New Zealand, for example, urged caution, voicing concern over the potential duplication of efforts and insisted that any new forum must add value to existing efforts. In outlining their preferred follow-up, several states underscored the potentially vital role of IOM and the Global Migration Group (GMG) in future coordination of efforts. A number of statements included an appeal similar to that of the African, Caribbean, and Pacific

Group of States (ACP), which encouraged an "inclusive approach to migration, including the involvement of non-state actors (NGOs, business, trade unions and civil society)." The secretary-general concluded, "Clearly, there is no consensus on making international migration the subject of formal, norm-setting negotiations. There is little appetite for any norm-setting intergovernmental commission on migration" (Annan 2006).

Global Forum on Migration and Development

With no agreement on continuing the discussions within the UN, the default outcome of the HLD was a more informal process that would be state-owned. With the encouragement of Peter Sutherland, the Belgian government announced at the HLD that it would be hosting a Global Forum on Migration and Development (GFMD) in 2007 and invited interested governments to participate. More than 160 governments accepted the invitation.

The GFMD subsequently proceeded as a state-led process. It has two principal components. The core of the GFMD is a meeting of government officials, which relies primarily on the governments themselves to plan and execute. The second part is a gathering of nongovernmental representatives, called the Civil Society Days (CSD). The CSD precedes the government meeting with the aim of contributing recommendations on the issues to be discussed by the officials. A common space provides the opportunity for the two groups to meet jointly, usually on the last afternoon of the CSD and first morning of the government meetings. Representatives of international organizations participate in both parts of the forum as observers. For brevity, the government meeting will be described as the GFMD, the nongovernmental as CSD, and the overall process as GFMD/CSDs.

The past, present, and future countries that host the GFMD form a troika in preparing for the annual government meeting. The host country assumes responsibility for the implementation of each forum, chairing all preparatory meetings and the forum itself. The co-chairs from the country that organized the previous forum and, once a decision is made, from the country that has agreed to host the next one jointly provide guidance to the current chair and work toward achieving some continuity in the discussions.

The government process relies on a Steering Group, composed of governments that are actively engaged in the preparations. It is balanced between developed and developing countries and includes representatives from all regions. It meets at regular intervals to provide "sustained political and conceptual support to the Forum and . . . to ensure continuity of the process."[11] The Steering Group provides substantive input into the agenda of the GFMD, the various roundtables, and the materials disseminated to participants. The Special Representative of the UN Secretary General on International Migration

[11] http://www.gfmd.org/en/process/supporting-framework/steering-group.

and Development is invited to participate in Steering Committee meetings but is not a member of the group.

The Friends of the Forum is open to all state members. Specialized agencies of the UN and other international organizations participate as observers as do representatives of the CSD. The Friends of the Forum provide an opportunity to keep potential participants in the forum up to date on preparations and to receive input on the substance of the deliberations.

Initially, the CSDs were organized by private foundations chosen by the host country, with the idea that these organizations would bring financial resources to the process. Their support was supplemented by generous contributions from the MacArthur Foundation and, in most cases, the host government. The gain in financing was often lost, however, in lack of continuity from one CSD and the host foundations' lack of previous expertise in migration issues. In preparation for the fifth CSD in Geneva, the Swiss government asked the International Catholic Migration Commission to organize the meeting; this was the first time that an organization dedicated to migration issues took on this role. Mauritius continued the practice. The MacArthur Foundation and several European governments provide financial resources to help underwrite the costs. The CSD has an international advisory committee that helps guide the preparations. The participants are generally drawn from five sectors: development organizations, migrant rights groups, trade unions, private-sector employers, and academia. Priority is given to organizations that are migrant or diaspora-led. The CSD meetings generally discuss the same issues that will be on the GFMD agenda but the organizers have added or substituted topics that they believe should garner more attention from governments.

The GFMD/CSDs also provide space for representatives of the People's Global Action on Migration, Development, and Human Rights – a parallel process that permits larger numbers to gather in workshops to discuss a range of migration issues – to present their findings to the delegates.

Much of the work of the GFMD/CSD is organized around roundtables. Roundtables focus on a wide range of issues that link migration and development. Some issues come up for repeat discussion while others tend to be raised because of the host country's particular interests or because of such pressing events as the global financial crisis that could not be ignored. Issues addressed across roundtables in different venues included:

- Human capital development and labor mobility: maximizing opportunities and minimizing risks, with sessions on highly skilled migration, particularly between developing and developed countries; temporary labor migration and its contribution to development, the role of the private sector and other non-state agencies in temporary labor migration, and how circular migration and sustainable return can serve as development tools.
- Remittances and other diaspora resources: increasing their net volume and development impact, with sessions on increasing the beneficial effects of

these migrant resources (reducing the costs of, and formalizing, remittance transfers); increasing the micro impacts of remittances; leveraging the macro impacts of remittances; and strengthening diaspora contributions to development.

- Rights of migrants: Rights have been discussed from both a normative (that is, the international conventions that apply to migrant rights) and practical (that is, what can be done on the ground to reduce abuse) framework. The underlying assumption is that enhancing the rights of migrants contributes to human development.
- Increasing legal admission options and reducing irregular migration. In Manila, this roundtable began with a normative statement: Secure, legal migration can achieve stronger development impacts. The sub-sessions focused on fostering more opportunities for legal migration and managing migration to reduce the negative impacts of irregular migration. Similar themes were pursued in Athens, where particular focus was given to reducing the costs of international migration to increase the development payoffs. Circular migration also received attention as a model for managing labor flows. These themes were also on the Mexico agenda, with focus on reducing irregular migration and enhancing prospects for legal admissions.
- Integration and reintegration of migrants. In Athens, roundtables examined the extent to which offering options for integration of labor migrants in destination countries improved their working and living conditions while also positioning them to contribute to their home country, either through financial or social remittances, or eventual return.[12]

In addition, roundtables focused on emerging issues, such as the impact of the financial crisis on migration patterns, migrant well-being and the flow of remittances. The GFMD roundtables have also provided the opportunity to raise issues at the migration-development nexus that had not yet received sufficient attention in other venues. In 2010, as discussed in Chapter 7, the Mexican government put climate change, migration, and development on the agenda in anticipation of the Cancun climate summit.

A recurring area of discussion at all GFMDs has been enhancing policy and institutional coherence and promoting partnerships for migration and development, with sessions on latest initiatives and progress for measuring migration and development-related impacts, coherent policy planning and methodology to link migration and development, and regional consultative processes on migration and development. After discussing policy coherence and data and research in separate roundtables in Brussels, they were brought together in Manila. The participants recommended establishing a working group that

---

[12] This discussion is drawn from reviewing the final reports, background papers and other materials prepared for the Global Forums. These are available on the GFMD website: www.gfmd.org (last accessed on June 6, 2013). The author has also drawn on her participation at the GFMDs that have been held to date (with the exception of the 2012 one held in Mauritius).

would help governments to identify the evidence base for developing more coherent migration and development policies. The working group hosted a preparatory workshop to the discussions in Mexico that examined models for evaluating and assessing the impact of migration and development policies and programs on migrants, countries of origin, and countries of destination. Subsequent meetings have focused on evaluation methodology, mainstreaming of migration into development planning, and the preparation of migration profiles to help countries better understand the nature, characteristics, and impact of migration.

Working papers are prepared for each roundtable session, and a number of specialized surveys of government policies and practices have been undertaken to support the discussions. Some of the papers are prepared by government officials and others are commissioned by experts. Generally, a developed and developing country co-chair each of the roundtable sessions, overseeing preparations for the discussions that would take place when all of the governments are present at the GFMD. The roundtable preparation process, by this author's observation, serves a confidence-building role in its own right as governments bring different perspectives into the discussions about the papers while weighing which ones are sufficiently based on evidence to merit inclusion in the final paper.

At the first meeting, the forum also included a side event, the "Marketplace," in which countries could request services, including technical assistance from other governments or international organizations. A password-protected website allowed countries to present their requests prior to the Brussels meeting. Some thirty-two such requests were discussed in the Marketplace. They included requests for assistance in "developing information systems for immigration control, formulating national migration policies, training of immigration officers, combating human trafficking, mobilizing expatriate communities for development, and facilitating the reintegration of nationals."[13] The GFMD process had no resources, however, to ensure that these requests were met, demonstrating a gap in the process of moving from consultation to action.

One of the most ambitious new initiatives promoted in Brussels was a proposal by Mauritius on circular migration. As co-chair of Roundtable 1, Financial Secretary Ali Mansoor, Ministry of Finance in Mauritius,[14] presented a model program showing how circular migration could be used to build skills in its workers to help the country deal with the restructuring of its economy. The restructuring was expected to lead to widespread unemployment in certain sectors. Mauritius proposed to conclude bilateral agreements that would identify ways to ensure greater circularity by linking short-term migration to small and

---

[13] Report of Proceedings, Global Forum on Migration and Development, Brussels, 2007, p. 153. Available at http://gfmd.org/en/gfmd-documents-library/brussels-gfmd-2007/cat_view/934-brussels-gfmd-2007/983-report-of-the-proceedings.html.

[14] Mauritius hosted the GFMD in 2012 and Mansoor led the preparations.

medium enterprise development in Mauritius. In the aftermath of the GFMD, Mauritius entered into negotiations with several EU countries and Canada. The first group of circular migrants left for Canada in March 2008 under a special agreement to work in the food processing companies in Alberta and Manitoba provinces. Reflecting the high visibility of such schemes in Mauritius, the Minister of Finance spoke to the migrants as they left for Canada, explaining that the circular migration program "will improve the living conditions of the workers and give them an opportunity to start a small business once they come back home after their stay in Canada."[15] The Marketplace has given way to a Platform for Partnerships that highlights effective collaborations.

It is too soon to make any conclusions regarding the effectiveness of the GFMD in promoting international cooperation. The continued enthusiasm of the participating governments,[16] as witnessed by the successful completion of GFMD sessions in six countries, the establishment of a small support structure, and working groups that allow for discussions between formal annual meetings, indicates that many countries find it a useful way to exchange information, form partnerships, and tackle difficult issues. Yet, the GFMD is by no means at a point where it serves the regime functions that Krasner outlined: despite the discussions of migrant rights, it has not attempted to set out norms, nor would the member states accept that as a role of the GFMD. The GFMD is not a mechanism to build agreement on decision rules to guide state to state negotiations over migration policy. While some progress in this direction is occurring at the bilateral and regional level, with successful promulgation of migration agreements, little has been done toward establishing rules to help states formulate a global agreement on movements of people. Many of the more concrete cooperative projects raised during the Brussels Forum were small-scale pilot programs, such as the Mauritius proposal. Whether these initiatives can be scaled up to address the broad challenges posed by international mobility of labor is still to be tested. Finally, the GFMD is not set up to address institutional gaps or duplications within international organizations.

One encouraging development is the decision by the United States to be an active participant in the GFMD. In Brussels, the United States was represented by a member of its mission to the EU, who had instructions to observe but not participate in the discussions. There was no senior official in Manila and only a very small delegation in Athens. U.S. skepticism of multilateral processes is well known and, in the case of migration, long-standing. It is worth noting that the Clinton administration was as negative toward a UN Conference on

---

[15] Net News Publisher, *Mauritius Workers Leave for Canada under special migration program*, March 9, 2008. Available at http://www.netnewspublisher.com/mauritius-workers-leave-for-canada-under-special-migration-program, last accessed on October 10, 2010.

[16] It should be noted here that governments are less enthusiastic about hosting the GFMD, as compared to participating in it. Argentina and Spain backed out of their offers to host, citing financial concerns.

International Migration as the Bush administration had been. Both administrations were more enthusiastic supporters of regional consultative mechanisms, believing they would be more productive venues for discussion and debate. In effect, concerns about the effectiveness and efficiency of UN conferences and opposition to the introduction of any new UN organizations have tended to be bipartisan ones in the United States.

Many of the U.S. concerns about inflating the role of the UN in an area in which it had relatively little expertise were heeded, however, when the HLD rejected the idea of a UN-embedded consultation mechanism and established a state-owned process. And in 2008, when the General Assembly was faced with a resolution proposed by Mexico to integrate the GFMD more closely into the UN, a majority of governments reinforced their opposition to converting the GFMD into a UN process.

These actions may have helped reverse some of the U.S. reluctance to become actively engaged in the GFMD although the Obama administration's support for multilateralism is also important and was warmly welcomed by other governments. An international migration process without the United States makes little sense. Not only is the United States the largest destination country of migrants, it is also the single largest source of remittances. In absolute terms it is the largest donor of ODA. Whether a new international system for international cooperation on migration and development could overcome opposition from the clear hegemonic power in this area is debatable. Fortunately, under the Obama administration, the United States has been much more engaged with other governments and civil society on the GFMD. The delegation in Mexico was headed by the assistant secretary for Population, Refugees, and Migration – the most senior official in the U.S. foreign policy apparatus with responsibilities for migration – and included representatives from several other agencies. Although still not convinced that migration issues are better negotiated at the global instead of bilateral or regional levels (a fair question), the United States has shown itself open to debating these issues with other governments.

In determining future success, another factor to consider is the route that the GFMD is following in promoting international cooperation on migration and development. The GFMD has no decision-making authority, and it has shied away from discussion of new normative frameworks. At present, the GFMD is clearly a vehicle for discussion, not action. Only the Marketplace provided an opportunity for the implementation of new initiatives, and its role was short-lived. This is not to say that there is no follow-up to the recommendations of the GFMD, but their implementation depends solely on the interest of individual countries.

2013 High Level Dialogue on Migration and Development

The successful series of GFMDs paved the way for a second HLD in October 2013. Following much the same pattern as the 2006 HLD, the 2013 meeting included plenary sessions and roundtables. It also provided the opportunity for countries to make statements about their perspectives on migration and development. Unlike the earlier meeting, however, the 2013 HLD had a negotiated document that was adopted at the start of the discussions. Led by the Mexican government, the declaration reinforced the need and benefits of international cooperation in addressing the complex issues raised by international migration. It also called on states to "promote and protect effectively the human rights and fundamental freedoms of all migrants, regardless of their migration status, especially those of women and children."[17] Further, the declaration took a strong stance against xenophobia, violence against migrants, and human trafficking, calling on states to take action against these phenomena. While there is little that is controversial in the declaration, the very fact that there was a declaration was significant. Previously, governments had great difficulty in coming to agreement on the value of a negotiated outcome on migration in the context of the UN deliberations. The previous years of consultation appeared to have introduced some new willingness to engage in setting out an agenda for cooperation.

INSTITUTIONAL RESPONSES OF DEVELOPMENT AGENCIES

The past two decades haves seen a new set of international development organizations becoming increasingly involved in migration-related activities. The interest has been galvanized, in part, by the various conferences, dialogues, and forums on migration and development discussed in this chapter. The growing magnitude of migration and, especially, remittances has been important in its own right in raising the visibility of the interconnections between these phenomena and development. As remittances exceeded ODA and equaled or surpassed trade and investment in developing countries, the importance of migration could no longer be ignored by those concerned with development. A review of the principal development actors highlights this new awareness as well as the gap between interest and actual implementation.

A number of organizations have derived their migration-related activities from a relationship to the major international gatherings that have put the concept of migration and development on the global agenda. For example, the UN Department of Economic and Social Affairs (UN-DESA) has played a crucial role, especially in the context of the HLD on International Migration and Development. It is the primary source of information on matters related to international migration and development for the General Assembly, ECOSOC, and its functional commissions. "UNDESA's activities in this area are part of its overall responsibilities for the analysis of development prospects

---

[17] Quotes from the Declaration of the 2013 High Level Dialogue are found at http://www.ilo.org/wcmsp5/groups/public/-ed_protect/-protrav/-migrant/documents/meetingdocument/wcms_226556.pdf.

globally, and aim at providing the foundation for the policy debate on maximizing the benefits of international migration for development."[18] The principal focal point for its international migration activities is the UNPD, which
collects data on the number of international migrants in each country. The
UNPD also surveys countries on their attitudes about international migration
and the nature of their policies. It served as the de facto secretariat for the
HLD in 2006 and was involved in preparations for the HLD that took place
in 2013.

UNFPA work on migration is guided by the ICPD PoA. More specifically,
UNFPA focuses on four principal areas: the role of migration in social-economic
development, the relationship between migration and women and migration
and young people, and the impact of migration on human rights. Within this
thematic focus, UNFPA seeks to improve data, research, and institutional
capacity for formulating, implementing, monitoring, and evaluating migration policies and programs; promote policy dialogue on migration issues; and
advocacy on migration issues.

UNFPA carries out relevant activities at both the headquarters and field level.
At headquarters, UNFPA supports a range of research and publications, crossing the disciplines and drawing on a wide set of perspectives from academia as
well as the policy world. Some of the publications result from UNFPA's own
activities, whereas others are by experts supported by UNFPA. A particular
contribution was the focus on migration in the flagship publication, *State of
the World's Population*, in bringing attention to issues specifically related to
women and migration. Since these annual reports reach a broad audience concerned with population and development, the focus on migration helped raise
awareness of the importance of migration in understanding both population
and development issues.

UNFPA works closely with IOM on its migration activities. Under an MOU,
the two organizations agreed to collaborate on a number of areas intersecting
their areas of competence:

1. Strengthening the knowledge base and promoting capacity development
   in the area of migration as part of existing regional and country programmes;
2. Incorporating sexual and reproductive health into health responses for
   migrants, mobile populations and populations of humanitarian concern;
3. Preventing and responding to Smuggling and Trafficking in Women and
   Girls and all forms of violence, including Sexual and Gender Based Violence; and
4. Monitoring the Migration of Health-Care Workers. (UNFPA-IOM
   2006)

---

[18] http://www.globalmigrationgroup.org/en/gmg-members.

Joint initiatives include advocating for better data and research, actions to raise awareness of the issues covered in the MOU, training, and facilitating policy dialogue. In some cases, the MOU outlines more operational collaborations, such as ensuring the availability of translation at sexual and reproductive health services.

Although international migration is a key issue in all of the UNFPA's five regions, some are more engaged than others on migration matters. All are aware of the importance of international migration and work with regional partners and other UN agencies. All regions seek to inform national governments and regional actors about migration and development and try to facilitate discussions among them. Most pursue collaborative work with other UN agencies, IOM, and other organizations, as well as intergovernmental regional organizations and national governments. One of the most notable regional projects is one in Latin America financed by the Spanish Development Ministry, which focuses on the sexual and reproductive health of migrant women and children in five specific border regions: Argentina-Bolivia, Ecuador-Colombia, Costa Rica-Nicaragua, Haiti-Dominican Republic, and Mexico-Guatemala. This project includes promotion and protection of sexual and reproductive health, HIV/AIDS prevention, and protection against gender-based violence in the particularly vulnerable and exploitative context of border regions. In this respect, it combines UNFPA expertise in both reproductive health and migration. Few other regional or country offices have implemented programs that build so systematically on UNFPA's mission.

In contrast to these institutions, the World Bank has developed an interest in migration because of the substantive importance of remittances and mobility to its broader mission – worldwide poverty alleviation. In 2006, the World Bank devoted its flagship publication, *Global Economic Prospects*, to international migration. The choice of migration as a topic showed the new importance that the institution was paying to the phenomenon. Coming out at the time of the HLD, the publication argued that "Greater emigration of low-skilled emigrants from developing to industrial countries could make a significant contribution to poverty reduction" (World Bank 2006:xv). The report also asserted that international migration "can generate significant economic gains for migrants, origin countries, and destination countries" (World Bank 2006: 26). It acknowledged that migration also can have important political and social consequences (World Bank 2006) but these issues were not discussed at length, given the publication's focus on economic prospects.

The Migration and Remittances Unit and Migration Research Group within the World Bank have been integral to efforts to improve data on migration and remittance flows and to conducting research on the impacts of migration on development. The Migration and Remittances Unit is based within the Development Prospects Group, which reports to the Development Economics Senior Vice President of the World Bank. Overall, the Prospects Group provides "information and analysis on global trends in the world economy, especially on trade, financial flows, commodity prices, remittances flows, and the impact of these trends on developing countries. The Group's global projections underpin country and regional projection exercises and are central to the Bank's short-term monitoring activities."[19]

The Migration and Remittances Unit produces a fact book that provides up to date information about immigration and emigration patterns as well as the inflow and outflow of remittances. The efforts of the World Bank, in coordination with regional banks such as the InterAmerican Development Bank and the Asian Development Bank, have led to significant improvements in the capacity of central banks in many countries to determine how much money is sent by migrants to their home countries. The unit was also pivotal in collecting bilateral migration data that shows emigration and immigration between countries of origin and destination. Previously, the only data available on international migration were the numbers of migrants resident in destination countries; there were no reliable data on the number of migrants exiting their home countries. The bilateral data have been important in contributing to the understanding of the extent to which migration is a so-called South to South phenomenon – meaning that many migrants move from one developing country to another, not just from developing countries in the south to developed countries in north.

The Migration Research Group is part of the Development Economics Research Department, which also reports to the Senior Vice President for Development Economics. The Development Research Group is the "World Bank's in-house research department, which aims to conduct research to guide development policy for the Bank and external clients alike. With eight programs, it produces the majority of the Bank's research."[20] The Migration Research Group is located within the trade and international integration area. Its aim is to expand knowledge about the impacts of migration on source and destination countries and to identify the migration policies, regulations, and institutional reforms that will improve development outcomes. The migration work has led to publication of several books, including those on the determinants of migration, international migration of women, and brain drain.

Several other offices within the World Bank have programs or focal points related to migration and development. The Poverty Reduction and Economic Management (PREM) Network and the Human Development Network undertake migration-related activities. Their aim is to integrate understanding of migration dynamics into the technical assistance provided to governments

---

[19] http://econ.worldbank.org/WBSITE/EXTERNAL/EXTDEC/EXTDECPROSPECTS/0,,content
MDK:20267500~menuPK:476908~pagePK:64165401~piPK:64165026~theSitePK:476883,
00.html.
[20] http://econ.worldbank.org/external/default/main?menuPK=469435&pagePK=64165236&pi
PK=64165141&theSitePK=469382.

in areas of concern to their unit. PREM has published a variety of reports, including one disseminated in 2012 on the impact of the financial crisis on migration patterns and remittance flows. The Social Protection Unit of the Human Development Network helps governments to assist individuals, households, and communities to better manage the income and welfare risks that affect vulnerable groups, including migrant workers.

The World Bank and UNFPA are not alone in devoting one of their principal publications to migration and development. In 2009, the UNDP's Human Development Report focused on human mobility and development. It covered both internal and international migration, a departure in that most agencies have dealt with the two issues separately. A common element, according to the report, is that "migration can expand...choices – in terms of incomes, accessing services and participation, for example – but the opportunities open to people vary from those who are best endowed to those with limited skills and assets."[21] The publication is generally positive about the contribution of migration to human development (through such avenues as increased household incomes and improved access to education and health services, as well as empowerment of traditionally disadvantaged groups) but it also addressed "risks to human development...where migration is a reaction to threats and denial of choice, and where regular opportunities for movement are constrained."[22]

A still further set of organizations link their involvement in migration to the conventions and core missions that otherwise guide their work. For example, UNICEF focuses specifically on migration-affected children and youth, examining the situation of those who migrate and those left behind by migrating parents. The agency "is particularly concerned with reducing the often severe social costs of migration and remittances for children in developing countries, and engages in local capacity-building efforts and policy dialogues aimed at generating social protection measures and legislative reforms that in UNICEF's view are fundamental to the realisation of the rights of affected children and women as well as to effective development."[23] Much of its activities are undertaken by its country offices. Only one full time staff member works on migration at the headquarters level. In contrast to some of the other development agencies that view migration as a mostly positive phenomenon for migrants and their families, often ignoring the costs, UNICEF frequently raises serious questions about the impacts of migration on children who are deprived of parental contact:

> While remittances may help reduce poverty and spur economic development, the effects of brain drain and parental absence can take their toll. Children and women

[21] http://hdr.undp.org/en/reports/global/hdr2009/.
[22] Ibid.
[23] http://www.unicef.org/socialpolicy/index_migration.html.

left behind must frequently take on full household responsibilities and endure social stigmatization. "UNICEF country studies also suggest that children and adolescents left behind may be at greater risk for drug abuse, teenage pregnancy, psycho-social dysfunction and criminal behaviour."[24]

UNICEF highlights the applicability of a broad set of international standards in discussing the rights of migrants – norms that go beyond the migrant worker conventions. Its work is especially guided by the UN Convention on the Rights of the Child (CRC), which having been ratified by every country except the United States, South Sudan and Somalia, is the most widely accepted set of norms. Article 2 of the CRC makes clear that "States Parties shall respect and ensure the rights set forth in the present Convention to each child within their jurisdiction without discrimination of any kind, irrespective of the child's or his or her parent's or legal guardian's race, colour, sex, language, religion, political or other opinion, national, ethnic or social origin, property, disability, birth or other status."[25] Accordingly, parties to the CRC pledge they will not discriminate against migrant children in access to primary education, healthcare, safety, and so forth on the basis of their or their parents' migration status.

UN Entity for Gender Equality and the Empowerment of Women (UN Women) brings a "gender-equality and women's empowerment approach to international migration and human development via its work on Empowering Women Migrant Workers to Claim their Rights and Celebrate their Contribution" (UNWomen 2011:1). UN Women's work reflects its priorities in implementing the Convention to Eliminate all Forms of Discrimination Against Women. At global, regional, and country levels, UN Women focuses on "gender-responsive migration governance in line with the CEDAW General Recommendation No. 26 on Women Migrant Workers, and other international human rights standards on migration" (ibid.:2). Activities include:

> knowledge generation and management; providing technical and financial assistance to creating, implementing and monitoring gender-responsive policies, plans, programs and budgets on migration; facilitating gender-sensitive service delivery environments; capacity-strengthening for women migrant workers and their associations to claim their rights; engaging with mainstream accountability mechanisms to uphold women migrant workers' rights; linking with practitioners on gender equality, women's economic empowerment and climate change to identify convergence areas for policy advocacy; supporting intergovernmental processes like the GFMD to prioritize the gender dimensions of migration; and playing a lead role on women's migration in UN interagency mechanisms and processes. (ibid.:2–3)

---

[24] http://www.unicef.org/socialpolicy/index_migration.html.
[25] Quotes from the Convention on the Rights of the Child are from http://www.ohchr.org/en/professionalinterest/pages/crc.aspx.

The United National Education, Social and Cultural Organization's (UNESCO) migration activities are part of the attention to social development and transformation. In its own words, the agency "places emphasis on the human face of migration. It addresses the implications of the movement of people within its fields of competence, firmly embedding its interventions in a human rights framework."[26] Its budget request for 2010–2011 notes that

> through the creation of ad hoc research networks and of innovative spaces enabling exchanges between researchers and policy-makers, UNESCO will in particular engage in the study of the integration of migrants and the protection of their rights in the societies where they settle, and the introduction of free movement agreements within regional integration zones, as well as the impact of climate change and environmental trends on migration. (UNESCO 2010)

UNESCO would also be giving special emphasis to the major urban challenges linked to migration in a joint UNESCO/UN-HABITAT project. Further activities would focus on urban policies and citizenship to prevent and mitigate urban conflicts (UNESCO 2010).

A range of other international organizations also sees a connection between migration and their principal activities as described in their membership in the GMG.[27] The UN Conference on Trade and Development (UNCTAD) addresses migration under its three pillars (research and analysis, technical assistance, and intergovernmental consensus-building). UNCTAD actively promotes coherence and global understanding by offering strategic policy analysis and practical solutions on the nexus between migration, trade, and development as well as the impact of remittances on poverty in developing countries.

The UN Institute for Training and Research's (UNITAR) "mandate is to strengthen the effectiveness of the United Nations system through capacity development activities for member states." UNITAR promotes inter-agency collaboration and inclusive dialogue among all relevant stakeholders in the migration field. "The Institute offers a neutral platform for networking, trust building, and the exchange of information and advanced policy thinking amongst government representatives and the broader international community." UNITAR collaborates with IOM in hosting policy forums at UN headquarters in New York. It also contributes to the GFMD and relevant UN General Assembly discussions. A specific area of emphasis is on international migration law. UNITAR offers certified training on this subject.

The WHO's work on migration "is guided by the Resolution on the Health of Migrants which was endorsed by the 61st World Health Assembly in 2008." The resolution asks states to "take action on migrant sensitive health

---

[26] http://www.unesco.org/new/en/social-and-human-sciences/themes/international-migration/.
[27] The descriptions of the remaining GMG members are adapted from http://www.global migrationgroup.org/en/gmg-members. Quotes come from this source.

policies and practices and directs WHO to promote migrant health on the international agenda, in partnership with other organizations and interregional cooperation." In 2010, WHO held a global consultation on migrant health. The meeting reached consensus on priority areas including: "monitoring migrant health, migrant sensitive health systems; policy and legal frameworks; and networks and multi country frameworks." An important contribution is the WHO Global Code of Practice on the International Recruitment of Health Personnel, which addresses the migration of health personnel and its impact on health systems in especially developing countries. The code was accepted during the Sixty-Third World Health Assembly. It promotes the ethical international recruitment of health personnel as part of strengthening health systems.

And, of course, the ILO, whose work was described in greater detail in Chapters 1 and 3, focuses on migration as part of its decent work agenda.

One of the benefits of this interest in migration on the part of development organizations has been fruitful collaboration between these agencies and IOM in preparation of a *Handbook on Mainstreaming Migration into Development Planning*. The handbook was the outgrowth of deliberations at the GFMD. The roundtables on policy coherence questioned the extent to which national development agencies had the tools to take migration into account in preparing Poverty Reduction Strategy Papers, national development plans, activities related to the achievement of the Millennium Development Goals (MDGs), and other development plans. After setting out the benefits to considering migration in a holistic way in development planning, the handbook proposes possible institutional arrangements to ensure appropriate consideration of migration and its implications. It also presents effective practices adopted by countries that do integrate migration into their plans. The handbook, although principally written and funded by IOM, received input from all of the development agencies that are members of the GMG. Their participation lends credibility to the proposed options for mainstreaming migration. Chapter 9 will discuss in greater detail the role of the GMG in coordinating migration activities across international organizations.

CONCLUSION

Migration and development has become the principal rubric through which governments and many international organizations are cooperating in the migration arena. As an issue, migration and development lends itself to a collaborative approach – particularly in contrast to some of the other issues discussed in this book. Migration and development is often described as a way to create a win-win-win situation out of the movements of people – a win for migrants, for source countries, and for destination countries. The conclusions of the World Bank's *World Economic Prospects* report highlighted this approach in discussing the economic gains for migrants as well as origin and destination countries. Given this context, the relative success of the HLD and the GFMD in bringing countries together to discuss migration and development is not surprising. Whether these are a harbinger of more systematic cooperation on other issues is the subject of Chapter 9.

9

Towards the Future

This final chapter discusses recent and potential future efforts to improve international cooperation in managing migration.[1] It focuses on the extent to which the international community is prepared to move in the direction of greater collaboration, identifying barriers to further action in developing a "migration regime." It will also discuss the potential frameworks for addressing both forced and voluntary migration as well as the linkages and interconnections between the two dominant modes of migration. Of particular concern will be the identification of laws, policies, and institutional arrangements to address the complex, mixed migration that an issue such as climate change raises. Although the chapter sets out the many reasons that an international regime would be beneficial, it is also realistic about the obstacles to implementation. It concludes that the rather hesitant steps already taken toward developing new frameworks for interstate cooperation and international organization coordination have been helpful in building confidence but, at some point, these steps must result in actions that demonstrate the benefits of global cooperation. The chapter sets out a number of discrete areas in which cooperation may be forthcoming.

RECENT INITIATIVES

Many national governments remain reluctant to consider the establishment of a single international migration regime that meets the criteria discussed in the introductory chapter – that is, to quote Krasner (1983) again, a "set

[1] This chapter draws from an earlier publication, Martin, "International Cooperation on Migration and the UN System." The full published version of this publication is available from http://www.palgrave.com/products/title.aspx?pid=523980. The author has covered similar issues in "International Migration and International Cooperation: An Overview."

of norms, decision rules and procedures which facilitate the convergence of expectations." Yet, the twenty-first century has seen some very tentative steps in that direction. This section discusses two such efforts. The first, launched by the Swiss government, focused on intergovernmental cooperation, while the second, begun by Secretary-General Kofi Annan and taking form in the establishment of the GMG, dealt with many of the international organizations discussed in this book.

Berne Initiative

In 2001, the Swiss government launched the Berne Initiative as a:

> States-owned consultative process with the goal of obtaining better management of migration at the regional and global level through co-operation between States. As a process, the Berne Initiative enabled governments from all world regions to share their different policy priorities and identify their longer-term interests in migration, and offers the opportunity of developing a common orientation to migration management, based on notions of co-operation, partnership, comprehensiveness, balance and predictability.[2]

The initiative was the brain-child of Jean-Daniel Gerber, director of the Federal Office for Refugees (which was later renamed Federal Office for Migration) in the Swiss Department of Justice and Police. Formerly, he held several trade-related positions in the Swiss Ministry of Foreign Affairs and served as executive director and then dean of the board of the World Bank Group. When he took on responsibility for migration issues, he was struck by the absence of international governance principles or structures, particularly in contrast to the regimes in place for international trade and capital flows (personal communication 2001). After discussions with officials within the Swiss and other governments and a range of migration experts, Gerber recognized that the migration field was far from adopting similar systems to those of the WTO or World Bank. He determined that a more informal, state-led process might help identify areas of common interest while addressing the concerns of many governments about their sovereign right to formulate and implement immigration policies.

To launch the initiative, the Swiss government invited governments from both developed and developing countries to participate in a consultation in Berne in which modalities for promoting cooperation were discussed. The governments of Sweden (through the participation of Jan O Karlsson, minister for Development Co-operation, Migration, and Asylum) and the Philippines (through Patricia A. Sto. Tomas, secretary of the Department of Labor) played an active role in ensuring that the perspectives of destination and source countries alike would be represented in the outcomes of the process. The IOM

---

[2] The Goal of the Berne Initiative, April 2003. Available at http://www.iom.int//DOCUMENTS/OFFICIALTXT/EN/Goal_E.pdf.

served as secretariat for the initiative and a number of experts (the author included) were asked to prepare resource materials and moderate panels. The initiative also hosted workshops and regional consultations before organizing a final global meeting to bring the findings together into a set of recommendations. The Swiss government funded a parallel process that resulted in the first comprehensive analysis of the source and scope of international law on migration. It explored international norms on state authority to regulate migration, freedom of movement, forced migration, human rights, family unification, trafficking and smuggling of migrants, national security, rescue at sea, health, development, integration, and nationality (Aleinikoff and Chetail 2003).

The Berne Initiative differed from later processes such as the GFMD in taking a more holistic approach to international migration and its connections to other issues. As Solomon and Bartsch (2003:1) described the discussions:

> It was emphasized that the root causes of migration are related to broader economic, social, and development issues. Regulated migration could contribute, among other things, to fostering economic growth, good neighborly relations, security, the rule of law, and cultural diversity. On the other hand, the participants noted that there is growing dissatisfaction with the way in which irregular migration is occurring at present, in particular regarding the increasing involvement of international criminal organizations in smuggling and trafficking. The undermining of state sovereignty and security by uncontrolled and irregular migration was identified as a major concern for many countries, both in developing and industrialized regions, with important financial, economic, social, and legal implications.

The participants in the first meeting of the Berne Initiative set out certain principles that should apply in any effort to promote international cooperation. These included:

- Equal possibilities for interested countries to participate in the establishment of a common framework;
- Partnership, trust, and transparency in inter-State co-operation on migration issues;
- Recognition of the importance of conducting economic, social, and cultural policies in a manner that would not trigger mass migration;
- Recognition of the principle of orderly, safe, and dignified legal migration versus disorderly and illegal migration, and consideration of the rights of migrants;
- Examination of various categories of migratory flows (labor, family reunion etc.), and the extent to which relevant laws and procedures meet the interests of States and migrants;
- Joint fighting of trafficking and smuggling of human beings, with particular attention devoted to children and women;
- Respect for basic readmission principles in the context of coherent return policies, and respect for the principle of non-refoulement;

• Recognition that migration questions must be addressed in a balanced way as they are interrelated with broader development issues like, inter alia, the creation of employment opportunities, the access to education and health services, the preservation of a safe environment. Migration should not be a substitute for transfer of capital and technology. (Summary and Conclusions of the Chair 2001:5)

Through the regional and international consultations, the Berne Initiative developed an International Agenda for Migration Management, which includes "common understandings for the management of international migration" and "Effective Practices for a Planned, Balanced, and Comprehensive Approach to Management of Migration" (Berne Initiative 2003).

The common understandings briefly restated international law, but they went well beyond conventions to achieve consensus on principles and norms to undergird international cooperation. This framework recognized the benefits of legal avenues of migration and the integration of immigrants, but also emphasized the need to reduce irregular migration and curb such abuses as smuggling and trafficking as well as racism and xenophobia. Twenty common understandings were listed (see Table 9.1).

The effective practices focused on mechanisms to promote international cooperation. Specific policies to regulate entry and stay for work purposes, family union, study, and humanitarian resettlement were recommended. Measures were also outlined to prevent irregular migration and manage return. Due attention was further given to mechanisms to protect the rights of migrants and ensure that refugees would not be subject to *refoulement*. Programs to more effectively integrate immigrants and regulate naturalization and citizenship were presented. The effective practices also addressed the nexus between migration and such issues as development, trade, security, health, and the environment.

The strength of the Berne Initiative was the state-led consultative process that brought source, transit, and destination countries together to build consensus on common understandings and effective practices. The governments that participated were serious in tackling the issues and little rancor was expressed about the differences in policies or views. That is not to say that differences did not exist, but the participating governments took pains to explain their positions and avoid criticizing other governments for holding different perspectives.[3] The governmental participants generally worked in ministries that were directly responsible for migration matters, bringing expertise on the

---

[3] This commentary is based on the author's participation in the two international meetings and one regional consultation, as well as discussions with other participants in all of these processes. Although the government participants tended to be polite in their remarks, some of the nongovernmental participants in the regional consultation attended in Santiago, Chile, did use more incendiary language in attacking destination countries (especially the United States) for what they considered to be policies that were hostile to migrants.

TABLE 9.1. *Common Understandings: Berne Initiative*

---

1. The continuing movement of people across borders is an integral feature of a rapidly globalizing world.
2. Humane and orderly management of migration benefits both States and migrants.
3. The prime responsibility for the management of migration lies with States: each State has the right and duty to develop its own legal framework on migration and to protect the security and well-being of its population, consistent with existing international principles and norms.
4. According to customary international law, States are required to protect and respect the fundamental human rights and dignity of migrants, irrespective of their status; the special needs of women and children, the elderly and the disabled require particular attention. Similarly, migrants are required to comply with the laws of the host State.
5. All States share a common interest in strengthening cooperation on international migration in order to maximize benefits.
6. The implementation of comprehensive and coherent national migration policies is key to effective international migration policies and cooperation in this field. Support for capacity building in those States lacking adequate resources, structures or expertise can make a useful contribution in this regard.
7. Relevant bilateral, regional and global instruments provide a solid foundation for the development of cooperative approaches to migration management.
8. Compliance with applicable principles of international human rights, refugee, humanitarian, migrant workers and transnational organized crime laws is an integral component of any migration management system, at the national, regional and international levels.
9. Cooperation and dialogue among all interested stakeholders, in particular Governments, international organizations, non-governmental organizations, civil society, including migrant associations, employer and worker organizations, and the media, are important elements for effective migration management partnerships and the development of comprehensive and balanced migration management policies.
10. Bilateral, regional and inter-regional consultative processes are key to the development of cooperative migration management and contribute to cooperation at the global level.
11. Effective migration management is achieved through balanced consideration of economic, social, political, humanitarian, developmental, health and environmental factors, taking into account the root causes of migration.
12. There is a close and complex relationship between migration and development; properly managed, that relationship can contribute to the development of States and their populations.
13. Providing adequate and regular channels for migration is an essential element of a comprehensive approach to migration management.
14. Prevention and reduction of irregular migration is a shared responsibility among all States with the support of other stakeholders.
15. Enhanced efforts are needed to combat human trafficking, migrant smuggling and other forms of international criminality affecting migrants and to provide support to victims.

16. Integration of migrants fosters social cohesion and political stability, maximizes the contributions migrants can make, and reduces instances of racism and xenophobia.
17. The family is the basic unit of society and deserves special attention. In the context of migration, family separation impedes integration, whereas facilitation of family reunion can contribute to maximising the positive effects of social and cultural integration of migrants in the host community.
18. The dissemination of accurate, objective and adequate information on migration policies and procedures enables migrants to make informed decisions. It is also needed to inform public opinion and ensure support for migration and migrants in host societies.
19. The systematic collection, analysis and exchange of timely, accurate and comparable data on all aspects of migration, while respecting the right to privacy, are important for migration management at national, regional and global levels.
20. Further research on all aspects of migration is needed to better understand the causes and consequences of international migration.

Source: Berne Initiative. (2003). *An International Agenda for Migration Management.*

substance of the issues to the table. At the same time, the weakness of the Berne Initiative was its relative exclusion of non-state representatives. Although staff of international organizations, NGOs, and academic experts participated in the international and regional meetings, the process was dominated – purposefully – by governments. There was little opportunity for external actors to voice their concerns or recommendations. This diminished some of the credibility that the initiative might have gained through a more inclusive process.

Doyle Report

While the Berne Initiative was considering modes of interstate cooperation, the UN was considering its own role in migration management. The secretary-general asked his Special Adviser Michael Doyle, Howard Brown Professor of International Relations at Columbia University, to convene a working group to present recommendations for future UN involvement in migration issues. Doyle's starting point was similar to Gerber's. He noted at a UN meeting in 2002 that "international migration was an integral part of globalization, yet it had not received the concerted international attention that other aspects of globalization, such as the trade of commodities, had received" (UNDESA 2003). In analyzing the international system, Doyle identified numerous agencies within and outside of the UN that worked consistently on migration issues. He concluded, however that "International migration is lightly institutionalized within the United Nations system. . . . No organization has the broad mandate that would allow the international community better to meet the challenges of internationalization by coordinating action, developing preventive strategies, and fostering constructive solutions" (Doyle 2004:4).

There were significant differences, however, in views as to which organization was best situated to take on such a mandate. Moreover, discussions were still continuing within the IOM governing board about the feasibility and desirability of that organization joining the UN system. As a result, the Doyle Report recommended that the secretary-general establish a commission to make more specific recommendations about the assignment of long-term responsibilities for migration.

Global Commission on International Migration

Following the recommendation of the Doyle Report, UN Secretary-General Annan asked Switzerland and Sweden – key participants in the Berne Initiative – to provide financial and technical support for what became the Global Commission for International Migration (GCIM).[4] The GCIM was mandated to "provide the framework of a coherent, comprehensive and global response to the issue of international migration" (GCIM 2005:vii). Co-Chaired by Jan Karlsson, former Swedish minister for Development Co-operation, Migration, and Asylum, and Mamphela Ramphele, former managing director, World Bank and vice-chancellor of the University of Cape Town in South Africa, the commission brought together nineteen members from source, transit, and destination countries. All experienced leaders in their own countries and internationally, the commissioners engaged in a consensus-building initiative, holding regional consultations, engaging the expertise of researchers, consulting with the governments that formed a core group of supporters, and wrestling with many difficult issues that had no easy or ready solutions.

The GCIM tried to tackle the institutional framework in which migration should be managed. It began where the principal responsibility rests – with the state. After a discussion of state sovereignty, the GCIM urged states to establish coherent national migration policies based on agreed objectives and consistent with international law. National policies should also take into account related policy issues, such as the role of international migration in relation to economic growth and development and security. Governance should follow suit, with mechanisms for coordination among ministries responsible for these various aspects of policy. This meant coordination among agencies responsible for different aspects of migration policy and n between the migration agencies and other parts of government.

Capacity is a further area in which the commission saw the need for improvement in national responses. Here, the report called upon the international community to support the efforts of states to formulate and implement national migration policies. Because of the paucity of well-run immigration systems,

---

[4] For a contemporary analysis of the Global Commission, see Philip Martin and Susan Martin, "Global Commission on International Migration: A New Global Migration Facility," *International Migration* 44/1: 5–12, 2006.

this might lead to a "blind leading the blind" scenario. Nevertheless, the commission recognized that there had been some progress in identifying effective practices (or at least more effective than the norm). The report noted that the Berne Initiative had vetted many of these initiatives and its recommended practices could be a model for building state capacity.

The commission extolled the benefits of bilateral and regional cooperation before embarking on the thornier issues of international cooperation. It laid out a two-phase reform process. In the long term, the commission concluded, a fundamental overhaul would be required to bring the disparate migration-related functions of the UN into a single organization. The commission set out various options for this entity, but did not make recommendations on its mandate, size, or shape, a shortcoming that may have reflected an inability of the commissioners to reach consensus on the issue. One option would create a new agency for all migration issues, possibly by merging the IOM and the UNHCR. A second would designate a lead agency from among the existing UN agencies (such as UNHCR or the ILO). A third was to bring IOM into the UN system to take a lead on issues of voluntary migration, leaving UNHCR as the key institution on forced movements.

The commission gave equal weight to the first and third options, mentioning little about how the second would work. In explaining the benefits of merging IOM and UNHCR, the commission contended that the historical mandates of the two organizations do not reflect contemporary realities, in that the distinctions between voluntary and forced migrants have become blurred. There is overlap in their migration routes and a large number are in a grey zone between the two categories (for example, they may have left because of violence or persecution but chose a destination with better economic opportunities). The commission was cognizant, however, that there would be serious barriers to a merger of UNHCR and IOM, including the possible dilution in UNHCR's mandate for refugee protection, the difficulties in combining organizations with very different cultures and approaches (a rights-based protection approach for UNHCR and a service approach for IOM), and the considerable negotiation that would be needed for a merger.

Incorporation of IOM into the UN system as the global agency for economic migration had certain advantages from the commission's perspective, but it also posed several barriers. The commission noted that IOM already assumes a number of the required functions of such an agency, but its mandate for protection of migrants is weak and member states and donor governments prefer its independence and flexibility.

The commission avoided making a solid recommendation as to which option the UN should pursue. Rather, it recommended that they be "taken forward at an appropriate moment in the context of the ongoing process of reforming the UN" (GCIM 2005:76). For the short-term, GCIM recommended enhanced coordination among the existing UN international organizations with migration responsibilities, via an Inter-Agency Global Migration Facility that would coordinate policy planning and analysis in areas that cross the mandates of several institutions. This new facility would also engage in capacity building efforts, consultations, data collection, and similar activities. There is little detail in the commission's report about how such a facility would operate, what benefits would accrue from its establishment, and what impact it would have on more fundamental reform of the UN system.

Global Migration Group

The GMG appears to have taken on some of the commission's recommended coordination activities. It is an outgrowth of the Geneva Migration Group, which was in turn the outgrowth of a UNHCR/IOM consultative process. The Geneva Migration Group included IOM, ILO, OHCHR, UNCTAD, UNHCR, and UNODC. According to participants,[5] the Geneva Migration Group was relatively successful in providing a forum for the member agencies to share issues and concerns. Agency heads generally participated in its meetings. As one respondent noted, the heads of agencies knew each other reasonably well and, being Geneva-based, they were able to have face-to-face discussions. The Geneva group was not meant to be a decision-making body; rather, it provided an opportunity for discussion of issues that crossed the mandates of the major agencies with policy and operational responsibilities in the migration area.

Following the GCIM report, the membership was expanded to include UN-DESA, UNDP, UNFPA, the World Bank, UNESCO, UNICEF, the United Nations Regional Commissions, and UNITAR. The terms of reference were updated and the coordination body was renamed the Global Migration Group as its membership was now worldwide. In 2010, WHO and UN Women were admitted, bringing the total GMG membership to sixteen agencies.

According to its terms of reference, the aim of the GMG is to "promote the wider application of all relevant international and regional instruments and norms relating to migration, and the provision of more coherent and stronger leadership to improve the overall effectiveness of the United Nations and the international community's policy and operational response to the opportunities and challenges presented by international migration."[6] The GMG, whose chairmanship rotates among member agencies, is primarily consultative in nature, with regular sharing of information its primary function. The heads of agencies are supposed to meet quarterly to guide the work of the GMG.

---

[5] The author has gleaned the following assessments of the GMG and its predecessor from conversations with staff who have participated in the GMG meetings. These discussions were under conditions of anonymity in order to gain an honest appraisal of the working relationships at the GMG.

[6] http://www.globalmigrationgroup.org/pdf/Final%20GMG%20Terms%20of%20Reference_prioritized.pdf.

The terms of reference detail a number of areas in which the GMG should focus:

- Establishing a comprehensive and coherent approach in the overall institutional response to international migration;
- Providing direction and leadership in a system-wide context and promoting interest, dialogue and debate on migration-related issues, including trade and development aspects, with governments, employers' and workers' organizations and civil society;
- Contributing to greater consistency in policy formulation and program implementation;
- Exchanging information and expertise to improve understanding, inter-agency cooperation and collaboration, to promote synergies and avoid duplication;
- Identifying critical issues, opportunities, challenges, weaknesses, gaps and best practices along the migration "life cycle";
- Pooling efforts in and exchanging results of research, data collection and analysis;
- Agreeing on common positions, responses and actions in addressing specific situations or themes;
- Agreeing on common activities to develop and exchange thematic expertise among staff such as training programs, especially in the field of capacity building, and inter-agency transfers;
- Reinforcing the human rights, labor rights, human security and criminal justice dimensions of migration governance and management, with a focus on the protection and well-being of migrants, including victims of trafficking;
- Contributing to major initiatives of GMG members and the international community such as the 2006 General Assembly High Level Dialogue on Migration and Development and the follow-up to the recommendations of the Global Commission on International Migration;
- Enhancing the efforts of individual states, regional bodies, regional and global consultative processes; and
- Finding appropriate mechanisms to interact with states.

There has been no formal evaluation of the functioning or impact of the GMG. The public records of the GMG are scant. For example, the most recent work plan on its website is from 2011. Its main record is in its published reports and other documents. Of particular note is a report on migrant rights produced in commemoration of the sixtieth anniversary of the UDHR. GMG also initiated a survey of capacity-building activities undertaken by the member agencies and serves as a conduit for input to and follow-up from the GFMD. The handbook on mainstreaming migration into development planning (see Chapter 8) began as an initiative of several members of the GMG and was endorsed by the group as a whole. The GMG also adopted a statement on the impact of climate change on migration, which was circulated widely at the GFMD meeting in Geneva and reprinted on its website in multiple languages.

Discussion by the author with staff of member agencies reflects some dissatisfaction with the GMG. Representatives of organizations with major migration-related activities found a declining interest on the part of senior officials, particularly heads of agencies, to use the GMG as their principal means of consultation or coordination with the heads of other agencies. Having grown to sixteen agencies, the GMG includes too diverse a range of organizations, with some whose principal focus is migration and others for whom migration is a peripheral issue. Some agencies have a primarily migrant-rights focus while others are more concerned about economic development or migration management. Whereas there is reason for the agencies with a principal migration focus to meet regularly at the most senior level, there appears to be less reason for those with a marginal interest to give the GMG serious attention unless they are taking their turn as chair. Although participants praised a number of agencies for their leadership in convening the GMG, the six-month rotating chair and the absence of a secretariat make it difficult to achieve consistency and sustainability in its activities. At a high-level meeting of GMG agencies at the end of 2012, a working group was established to consider a number of structural changes, including a one-year rotation of the chair, establishment of a secretariat, and elaboration of a more systematic financing mechanism.

As a mechanism for coordination and consultation, the GMG does not have the authority to identify gaps or duplications of effort and assign responsibilities to its member agencies. The GMG, like its predecessor is consultative and not decision-making in its activities. Some participants complain that far too much time is spent on procedural issues, including the criteria for GMG membership, rather than on substantive issues. The relevant discussions often focus on the GFMD and the UN HLD, events of interest to all of the members, rather than the much thornier issues covered in the terms of reference – particularly identifying what is needed to establish a comprehensive and coherent approach to international migration. To some extent these failures relate to the nature of a consultative process that includes organizations with varying interest in migration. It also reflects ambivalence on the part of states and of the UN secretariat as to the role that the GMG should play in building a more coherent set of policies and institutional responses to migration.

Forced Displacement

At the same time that the international community has been considering new approaches to labor and other forms of voluntary migration, an equal focus has been placed on the need for improved cooperation in protecting and responding to the needs of forced migrants. The international regime for addressing refugee movements is well-established, as discussed in Chapter 2, but UNHCR's principal mandate covers those defined in the Refugee Convention – persons who are unable to return to their home countries because of a well-founded fear of persecution on the basis of their race, religion, nationality, political opinion, or a membership in a particular social group. As new categories of forced migrants have emerged, such as those displaced from natural disasters and climate change, international responses have been slow to emerge. There are no conventions comparable to the Refugee Convention to provide norms for government responses if environmental migrants cross their borders, as discussed in Chapter 7. The UNHCR does not consider such migrants to be under its mandate, even though the agency has been called upon to offer assistance when there is large-scale displacement from natural disasters such as the South Asian tsunami or Pakistan earthquake.

IOM was one of the first international organizations to recognize the potential large-scale movements from environmental harm, but to date its role has primarily been to stimulate research and discussion of the topic. Until recently, neither agency had undertaken any systematic examination of the adequacy of international responses to displacement generated by other humanitarian crises, such as nuclear accidents. Clearly, the recent earthquake, tsunami, and nuclear disaster in Japan raised serious questions about what might happen if such a sequence of events occurred in a less developed country with fewer resources of its own. As discussed in greater detail in Chapter 7, concerns about climate change have generated considerable debate about the need for a normative and institutional framework to address these forms of displacement. So far, however, there has been relatively little progress in either norm- or institution-setting. Whether UNHCR's Nansen Initiative or IOM's IDM leads to new approaches is still to be seen.

In the meantime, Peter Sutherland, the secretary-general's representative on International Migration and Development took leadership, along with the United States and the Philippines, in putting the needs of migrant workers trapped during emergencies onto the agenda of the 2013 HLD on Migration and Development. A roundtable on migrant rights focused specific attention on this issue, as did the opening comments by the UN secretary-general and closing comments by the deputy secretary-general.

TOWARDS A MORE EFFECTIVE NORMATIVE FRAMEWORK

Arguably, there is ample international law setting out the rights of migrants even though the principal migrant-centric instruments are not widely ratified. Failures in protecting migrant rights arise from the lack of implementation of these standards at the national level. Nevertheless, some gaps remain, especially in determining who other than refugees deserve international protection because their own governments are unable or unwilling to fulfill their obligations. Addressing these gaps or, for that matter, increasing adherence to already adopted international norms is unlikely to be accomplished through the promulgation of still more conventions.

In the absence of greater willingness of countries to ratify international conventions setting out the rights of migrants, an alternative approach is to build greater state acceptance of a set of basic norms that address issues at the core of migrant vulnerability to abuses – what Thomas Alexander Aleinikoff, (former dean of the Georgetown University Law Center and current deputy UN high commissioner for refugees) has called an International Bill of Rights for Migrants (Georgetown University 2010). Justin Gest (2010:646) suggests that states are more likely to accept limitations on their sovereignty when the focus is on fundamental rights ("minimum rights that afford migrants equal opportunity to subsist, succeed, and participate in their new society") than in respect to "those entitlements which benefit individuals and families beyond this baseline minimum – these are *supplemental*. A migrants' rights regime suggests that fundamental rights should be extended to all people, regardless of citizenship, by virtue of their situated coexistence, codependency, and co-humanity." To gain further adherence to this concept, Gest (2010:647) recommends positing these rights "as a selection of fundamental entitlements that are excerpted from the regimes to which states are already subject."

This approach is similar to the one taken in development of the Guiding Principles on Internal Displacement. The value of these guidelines is they do not constitute a binding instrument such as a treaty or convention but they reflect and are consistent with existing international law and have become a standard for developing national practice. There are thirty clearly articulated principles that fall into five areas: general principles that set the basic framework; principles related to protection from displacement, which set out the rights that people have to remain within their own home communities; principles related to protection during displacement, which set out the basic rights of those who must relocate; principles related to humanitarian assistance, which set out the obligations of states and the broader international community; and principles related to return, resettlement, and reintegration.

Although they are not binding international law, the Guiding Principles on Internal Displacement have stimulated the development of national law in many countries with large numbers of IDPs and a regional convention in Africa. Some of the countries that have adopted laws based on the Guiding Principles have not implemented the provisions in the intended spirit but they have become important in galvanizing the means by which the internally displaced and human rights groups have pressed in courts and elsewhere for improvements in treatment. In Colombia, for example, the internally displaced sued the government and the Supreme Court required the government to take action to implement the provisions adopted based on the Guiding Principles. In Georgia, the displaced used the Guiding Principles to advocate for greater flexibility to vote in the places in which they were currently residing, rather than in their communities of origin.

A similar process is already underway with regard to an International Migrants Bill of Rights (IMBR), drafted by a coalition of students at American

University in Cairo, Georgetown University Law Center, Hebrew University in Jerusalem, and London School of Economics, with the assistance and input of legal experts. The draft was presented at a symposium at Georgetown University and the IMBR and commentaries by invited experts were published in the *Georgetown Immigration Law Journal* in 2010. The IMBR contains nineteen articles that set out core human rights which apply to all international migrants. Article 1 defines a migrant very broadly to include "a person who has left a State of which he or she is a citizen, national, or habitual resident."[7] The definition applies regardless of the causes of migration (forced or voluntary), duration of stay (temporary or permanent), legal authority to be in the destination country, or connections to the labor force. It is therefore more comprehensive in its scope than any existing international instrument. This very comprehensiveness is its strength but also its weakness, in that states may be more reluctant to endorse some of its provisions in relationship to those with irregular status.

Many of the articles focus on the legal rights of migrants, including equal protection under the law. The equal protection clause is expansive in its treatment:

(1) All persons, including migrants, are equal before the law. Migrants are entitled to the equal protection of the law on the same basis as nationals of the State in which they reside. In this respect, the law shall prohibit any discrimination and guarantee to migrants equal and effective protection against discrimination on any ground such as race, color, sex, language, religion, political or other opinion, national or social origin, property, birth, or other status.

(2) Distinctions in the treatment of migrants are permissible, including in the regulation of admission and exclusion, only where the distinction is made pursuant to a legitimate aim, the distinction has an objective justification, and reasonable proportionality exists between the means employed and the aims sought to be realized.

The way the non-discrimination provisions are applied (that is, what is a legitimate aim in establishing distinctions in the treatment of migrants) is central to the issue of "numbers versus rights" discussed in relationship to the ILO and Migrant Workers Conventions. As Broude (2010:562) points out in his commentary on the IMBR, "Strict requirements of equality can impact the willingness of states and constituencies to allow immigration, which in turn can reduce global inequities. Equal protection . . . should not be drafted too sweepingly, lest they throw the baby of migration liberalization out with the bathwater of protecting vulnerable migrants from abusive discrimination."

---

[7] All quotes from the IMBR are found at http://www.law.yale.edu/documents/pdf/Clinics/ITC_InternationalMigrantsBillofRights.pdf (pp. 399–407).

Some articles in the IMBR focus on due process in relationship to removal, detention, and other immigration-related proceedings. Others set out core civil and political rights, identifying those that should apply to all migrants: for example, freedom of thought, conscience, and religion; freedom of expression, including the freedom to seek, receive, and impart information and ideas of all kinds; the rights of peaceful assembly and of association; the right to the security of person and protection by the state against violence, bodily harm, or expression inciting violence; liberty of movement within the territory of the host state (except for those in removal proceedings); and right to identity documents. A further set of provisions describe economic, social, and cultural rights, including access to emergency medical care and disaster relief; special protection for women and children during a reasonable period before and after childbirth; benefits of any social welfare or insurance program to which they have contributed; and the right to enjoy their own cultures and to use their own languages. With regard to labor rights, there is a firm prohibition against servitude, slavery, or forced labor. The IMBR also specifies that migrants should be protected by laws regarding "minimum wages, minimum working age, maximum hours, safety and health standards, protection against dismissal, and the rights to join trade unions, to organize, or to take part in collective bargaining." A number of articles apply specifically to children, including the right to education.

Despite its principal focus on existing international law, the IMBR attempts to fill some gaps in existing conventions. Most notably, it establishes a right to family unity, at least for those in lawful status, which is not addressed in most migration-related international conventions. Article 18 specifies that "Dependent family members of migrants have a right to derivative immigration status and timely admission to the country in which a migrant is lawfully settled." This right is founded in broad "principles that underlie the right to respect for family life, especially as it relates to children: (1) that family is the natural and fundamental unit of society and (2) that maintaining the family unit is in the best interests of the child" (Mrazik and Schoenholtz 2010:651).

The IMBR has a broader non-*refoulement* provision than is found in the Refugee Convention: "No migrant shall be returned to a country where there are substantial grounds for believing he or she would be in danger of being subjected to a serious deprivation of human rights that would threaten the migrant's life or freedom." In this case, the criterion is serious deprivation of human rights, not fear of persecution. Interestingly, the prescription against forcible return does not apply to persons at serious risk of loss of life, property, or livelihood due to natural or human-made disasters. As formulated, they do not address the normative gap outlined in Chapter 7.

The IMBR is a good starting point for serious discussions among states on what should be the fundamental rights guaranteed to all migrants. Not all of its provisions are likely to remain intact, and some states and NGOs will argue that the focus of limited time and resources should be on ratification of the

Migrant Workers Convention, rather than on what might be called a "soft law" approach. Nevertheless, given the reluctance of destination countries to ratify the Migrant Workers Convention, and continuing abuses that many migrants experience, gaining greater clarity as to what governments recognize as fundamental rights would be a step in the right direction.

Setting of norms is important but abuses by the very governments that have drafted and ratified the conventions that guarantee rights is all too common. Putting an International Migrants Bill of Rights into practice is the next step. Acer and Goodman (2010:531) describe the challenge:

> While the discussions surrounding the proposed IMBR may help to focus greater attention on the human rights of migrants, much greater attention–and commitment–is needed to ensure that the human rights of migrants are actually protected by States. The laws, policies, and practices of many States fail to provide essential protections to migrants, and existing protections continue to be eroded as States escalate migration enforcement and detention.

Cholewinski (2007:270) agrees that: "A 'protection gap' ... exists between the fine rhetoric of international human rights and labour standards and their enjoyment and implementation in practice."

To return to Krasner's definition of a regime, beyond norms are the decision-rules and procedures which facilitate a convergence of expectations among states as to appropriate policy and practice. While there is much to criticize in governmental actions related to migrant rights, there are ample examples of national programs taken by source, transit, and destination countries that appropriately balance interests in immigration control with respect for the rights of migrants. These activities fall into several categories, including strategies to prevent abuses, in particular by better informing migrants of their rights and ways to assert them; education, monitoring, and where necessary, prosecuting abusive recruiters and employers of migrants; establishing standard contracts to regulate the relationship between employers and foreign workers; initiatives (including hotlines and safe houses) to help migrants whose rights have been violated; reintegration programs for returned migrants and survivors of human trafficking; and provisions for temporary or permanent legal status for those who are unable to return home.[8]

One important role for an international migration regime is to advise governments on their responsibilities to protect migrant rights, inform them of effective practices to fulfil their obligations, assess compliance, and take action where there are violations. As discussed in the preceding chapters, a number of international organizations and individual actors, such as the special rapporteurs on migrant workers and trafficking, play important roles in this regard. None, however, has a comprehensive mandate. And, no process is in place

---

[8] For a more detailed exposition of effective practices adopted by governments, see Martin and Abimourched 2009.

comparable to the procedures in the World Trade Organization for holding governments accountable for violations. Nor does any international body now have a responsibility to balance migrant rights issues against other important considerations in the setting of migration policies – for example, economic or security interests. The next section turns to recommendations for the institutional arrangements that might address these gaps.

TOWARDS A MORE COHERENT INSTITUTIONAL MIGRATION REGIME

Governments do not yet appear willing to endorse institutional arrangements that would go beyond the GMG to the setting of standards or negotiation of common migration policies. They do see the need for continuing dialogue. They also recognize the need for technical assistance and capacity building if states are to manage migration more effectively. The GFMD is the beginning of a process that may lead to new forms of interstate cooperation, but there is a long path from these first steps to a fully integrated international migration regime with well-articulated norms and well-functioning institutions.

Recognizing the limitations that states have put on it, the UN has tended to focus on coordination and consultation, rather than the assignment of responsibility for migration to one clearly mandated agency within (or outside) of the UN. The GCIM suggested that merger of UNHCR and IOM might be one way to approach the issue. In my view, such a merger would not serve the needs of either the voluntary or forced migration systems. The causes of movements are indeed crucial in determining what type of regime makes most sense. Because refugees and displaced persons have been forced to leave their homes because of conflict, repression, and, in the case of environment and disasters, the inability of governments to offer protection (and in some cases, assistance), the international community's first priority is to restore that protection or find a substitute for the state that is unwilling or unable to fulfill its responsibilities. The second priority is to find solutions to the displacement so those affected can return home or resettle elsewhere. These are addressed in the context of decisions on international security often left to the Security Council.

In contrast to forced migrants, voluntary ones have chosen to relocate. They are drawn by family networks, study, work, and a range of other opportunities in the destination country. While they have a right to leave and reenter their home country, they do not have the right to be admitted to or remain elsewhere – however compelling are the reasons for seeking entry.[9] States retain substantial discretion in determining whether to admit migrants and what criteria and mechanisms to use in defining eligibility for admission. To the extent

---

[9] A possible exception to this statement is the case of spouses and minor children of those who reside in another country. The right to family unity is an evolving area of international, regional and national law.

that they find it more practical and beneficial to cooperate with other states in making these decisions, it is their decision. The priority for the international voluntary migration regime is therefore how to best manage this process, which includes ensuring respect for the rights of the migrants. In determining best policies, issues of voluntary migration intersect with a different range of concerns than forced migration – for example, movement of goods, services, and capital on the one hand, and movement of those who pose security risks on the other.

The separate causes and contexts of voluntary and forced migration argue for separate institutional arrangements with a link to accommodate issues that fall in the nexus of the two regimes. In previous work (Martin 2006), I have recommended the establishment of a UN High Commissioner for Forced Migrants. Superseding UNHCR, its mandate would include refugees covered under the 1951 UN Convention Relating to the Status of Refugees as well as individuals internally and externally displaced because of repression, conflict, natural disasters, environmental degradation, and other humanitarian crises. There are many benefits to be achieved by consolidation. A single agency would ensure more comprehensive and consistent approaches. The High Commissioner for Forced Migrants would be tasked with ensuring that all persons displaced by the same events are afforded comparable treatment, regardless of their location, and that the resolution of the situations causing displacement would take into account all parties that have been displaced. The office would have the mandate to negotiate access and protection of forced migrants with governments and insurgent groups in both home and host countries of forced migrants. It would be responsible for developing a consolidated appeal for funding that would show donors the full range of financial needs in all countries affected by the displacement. Antonio Guterres, the UN High Commissioner for Refugees, has stated that his agency should become the UN Agency for Forced Displacement, indicating potential progress in this regard. In November 2006, the secretary-general's High-Level Panel on UN System-Wide Coherence stated: "A clear allocation of responsibility within the UN system is needed. The Office of the UN High Commissioner for Refugees must reposition itself to provide protection and assistance for displaced people in need, regardless of whether they have crossed an international border" (Secretary General's High Level Panel 2006:15).

The most immediate issue regarding forced migrants is setting the institutional responsibility for those who are displaced by humanitarian crises that do not fall within the context of the refugee definition. In this regard, UNHCR's recent note, "Climate change, natural disasters and human displacement: a UNHCR perspective," states that: "it is legitimate to ask whether new legal protection instruments might be needed for cross-border movements that are induced by climate-related reasons. UNHCR is not seeking an extension of its mandate, but it is our duty to alert the international community to the protection gaps that are emerging" (UNHCR 2008:9).

Regardless of its own concerns about mandate, UNHCR will no doubt be called upon to extend its good offices to these populations. The question is: By what criteria should UNHCR engage with those displaced by climate change, natural disasters, and other crises? To answer this question, it is necessary to identify UNHCR's mandate and capabilities relative to the rest of the international community. I argue that UNHCR has evolved to protect persons whose own governments cannot or will not provide such protection. Other UN and international agencies, such as the IOM, have a demonstrated capacity to provide assistance to persons displaced by natural disasters and environmental hazards, but only UNHCR has a history of providing protection to displaced populations.

Following this line of reason, one can divide forced migrants into three categories based on the extent to which their own governments fulfill their obligations to protect them. In the first group are individuals whose governments are *willing and able* to provide protection. Those displaced by natural disasters and climate change in wealthy, democratic countries generally, though not always, fall into this category. There are examples of poorer and more authoritarian governments that also have good track records of demonstrating they are willing and able to protect their citizens affected by natural disasters and environmental hazards. Generally, displacements in these contexts are internal, not international since the forced migrants are able to find assistance from their own governments and have few reasons to cross an international border. There is a limited role for the international community, although other governments and international organizations may offer assistance – for example, in the form of search and rescue teams, financial aid for rebuilding homes, health professionals and other experts in disaster relief. There would be no role for UNHCR to involve itself since there is no need for protection from the international community.

The second group includes forced migrants in situations in which governments are *willing but unable* to protect persons displaced by disaster or environmental hazards. Certainly, poor countries that do not have the financial capacity to provide assistance may fall into this category. They would like to protect their citizens from harm but do not have the capacity or resources to do so. If the affected population moves within the country of origin to find safety, a government may well attempt to fulfill its protection responsibilities by calling on the international community to assist. There would be little reason for UNHCR to involve itself because protection is not at stake, but the broader international community has an important role to play in ensuring that it buttresses the willing state's ability to provide protection by offering financial and other aid. Of course, UNHCR might be called upon for material goods and expertise, as has been the case in some of the massive displacements occurring from natural disasters, but this population would not otherwise fall within its mandate.

The third group includes displaced persons whose governments are *unwilling* to provide protection to their citizens, regardless of their ability to do so. This would include situations in which the government has the capacity to provide protection, but is unwilling to offer it to some or all of its citizens. For example, the government may not spend its resources on political opponents or ethnic or religious minority groups. Failed states would also fit into this category because they have neither the willingness nor the ability to protect their citizens.

These are the situations in which UNHCR can play a constructive role in promoting protection for persons whose rights have been violated by states that are unwilling and/or unable to ensure their safety. In cases of internal displacement, UNHCR would need to use the same criteria the agency uses in determining whether to intervene in conflict displacement situations. The form of intervention would differ depending on the circumstances. If the agency were able to reach the affected populations, UNHCR would have an obligation to offer both assistance and protection. If state sovereignty or security conditions precluded direct access, UNHCR could still play an important role as an advocate for unprotected persons, up to and including encouraging the Security Council to intervene.

More complicated are cases in which large numbers move across borders because of the unwillingness of their own government to provide protection. In such situations, the need for international protection will be determined by the destination country's policies and the extent to which the displaced would be harmed if returned home. If the destination country is willing and able to provide assistance and protect the cross-border population, there would be little reason for the international community to become involved. On the other hand, if the destination country is unwilling or unable to assist and protect the forced migrants, or it attempts to return the forced migrants to the home country without adequate guarantees of their protection, UNHCR would have cause to offer its assistance and protection. The complication, of course, is the absence of international law defining the rights of persons with a well-founded fear of harm from natural disasters or environmental hazards and the responsibilities of states towards them. One can nevertheless posit that if the country of origin's ability to provide protection and assistance is buttressed by the international community and the cross-border migrant could return safely, the destination country would be well within its right to return the migrants without international intervention. On the other hand, if protection is unavailable in the home country, and returnees would be seriously harmed, then the destination country as well as the international community has a greater responsibility to offer its protection. As in conflict-induced displacement, UNHCR could offer its assistance as a way to encourage the country of destination to permit the cross-border migrants to remain until it was safe to return or other solutions are found for them.

This would still leave the institutional arrangements for voluntary migration. Here, I am persuaded that the IOM has the strongest capacities to take on the range of activities needed. Only IOM among international organizations has the expertise and staffing to help governments to develop and implement rational, effective policies in cooperation with other states. The agency has a robust membership of more than 150 states and field presence in more than 100 countries. IOM already hosts the IMD, which could encompass a larger number of states, particularly if IOM were to become a part of or more closely affiliated with the UN, probably as an independent specialized agency.

IOM's work in four broad areas of migration management corresponds to the agenda of many states: (1) migration and development; (2) facilitating migration; (3) regulating migration; and (4) forced migration. IOM activities that cut across these areas include the promotion of international migration law, policy debate and guidance, protection of migrants' rights, migration health, and the gender dimension of migration.[10] IOM provides a range of services related to capacity-building, migration management, migrant health, migration and development, return assistance, and counter-trafficking. My proposal would reduce its activities related to forced migration, transferring them to UNHCR.

IOM also serves as secretariat to many of the regional consultation mechanisms and houses the light support structure for the GFMD. Establishing a more formalized secretariat within IOM might help provide continuity and the expertise needed to ensure that the best available information is brought into the forum. The GFMD would not lose its state-owned character but preparations would be embedded in an organization that could provide technical assistance, programs, and other resources needed to carry out agreed-on plans of action, at least on a pilot basis. With success, such implementation could also lead to standard-setting and negotiated agreements, which governments now shy away from but may in the future see as mutually beneficial. It might also allow a broadening of GFMD's mandate to cover important issues beyond migration and development (such as the security implications of international migration).

There are three major challenges that IOM would have to overcome if it were to become the focal point for a new global regime on voluntary migration. The first is its lack of a clear set of norms and decision rules. IOM's mission statement appears to provide such a framework ("IOM is committed to the principle that humane and orderly migration benefits migrants and society"[11]) but it also acknowledges that IOM has no legal protection mandate for migrants, as compared to UNHCR for refugees. IOM's constitution references a specific list of purposes and functions of the organization, but none of the items relates to a responsibility toward migrants, stating rather a range of

---

[10] http://iom.int/jahia/Jahia/pid/2.
[11] http://www.iom.int/jahia/Jahia/about-iom/mission/lang/en.

services that IOM would provide to states. While I would argue that tying IOM to a specific convention is not needed to establish a mandate for protection of migrant rights, IOM's constitution would need to be amended to establish a legal obligation for protection that would be as clear as its current mandate to assist states in their management of migration. Such a statement would not be in contradiction with a principle already established in the constitution that IOM "shall recognize the fact that control of standards of admission and the number of immigrants to be admitted are matters within the domestic jurisdiction of States."[12] Rather, it would recognize that once having entered a state, migrants have certain rights that must be protected.

A second barrier pertains to the way in which IOM receives its financial resources from states. While state members provide for administrative costs on the basis of agreed-on assessments, the operational budget comes mostly from voluntary, earmarked allocations for specific programs and activities. Only a small portion of the operational funding is available for discretionary activities, mostly derived from the indirect costs associated with earmarked resources. Two problems arise from this funding process. First, many of the "regime-building" functions of IOM – for example, its policy, research, and legal analysis units – are largely funded as a discretionary activity, as compared to its service functions, which are generally funded through earmarks. This creates a vicious cycle: as long as states are reluctant to see an international migration regime develop, they are unlikely to earmark funds for this purpose, restricting IOM's activities in this area. This in turn limits the ability of the organization to demonstrate the value of having a more robust international migration regime, which reinforces state reluctance. The second problem arises from the type of earmarked funding it receives. About half of the organization operational budget is for activities referenced as movement, emergency, and post-crisis migration management. The next largest category is for regulating migration with facilitating migration covering a smaller share.[13] Because of the heavy dependence on the indirect costs derived from earmarked programs, IOM's ability to undertake activities related to building an international migration regime would be heavily compromised if its forced migration activities were to shift to UNHCR unless states were willing to earmark funds specifically for these purposes.

The third and principal barrier to this proposal is the reluctance of key states to see IOM more closely tied to the UN or to an evolving international migration regime. IOM is often described by government representatives as a lean, efficient organization that has the capacity to respond quickly to the needs of states. In effect, its current constitution and focus is what states see

---

[12] International Organization for Migration, Constitution, p. 12. Available at http://www.iom.int/jahia/webdav/site/myjahiasite/shared/shared/mainsite/about_iom/iom_constitution_eng_booklet.pdf.

[13] http://iom.int/jahia/webdav/shared/shared/mainsite/about_iom/en/council/96/MC2258.pdf.

as its strength. It is also the reason many civil society organizations criticize IOM as undertaking the bidding of states with too little regard for the rights of migrants. For IOM to become the principal focus of international institutional responsibility on migration management, it would need to better balance its dual responsibilities – toward states and toward migrants. Whether states will permit this to happen will depend largely on the discussions taking place in regional and global forums to determine what forms of interstate cooperation are mutually beneficial to source and destination countries, as well as to the migrants themselves. If these forums lead to the conclusion that a more robust international regime would be mutually beneficial, the reforms to IOM's mission and mandate would help achieve that goal.

Increasing IOM capacity to help states manage voluntary migration should not be seen as a signal to other international organizations to lessen their activities in this area. With its century of experience and tripartite governance structure, the ILO especially should continue to play an important role in bringing governments, employers, and trade unions together in forging new approaches to labor migration and protecting the rights of migrant workers. To engage in such activities, ILO's migration-related funding and staffing would need to be enhanced. The same observation can be made about the other members of the GMG, many of which have very few staff members whose primary responsibility relates to the relationship between migration and the mission of their agency.

One final point to be made about these institutional arrangements is that assigning greater responsibility to UNHCR and IOM for forced and voluntary migration, respectively, would not obviate the need for coordination. What is now referred to as mixed migration, or more broadly, the intersection between voluntary and forced movements requires mechanisms to address the complexities inherent in large-scale mobility. Moreover, the nexus between migration and such areas as development, labor, peacemaking/peace-building, security, trade, and capital flows will require coordination between the two institutions outlined herein and those responsible for these other policy issues. Thus, the GMG would continue to play a role in ensuring that migration issues remain on the agenda of the development and security agencies already involved. A more coherent regime for managing migration and protecting the rights of migrants would, however, allow such coordination to take place among policy equals.

Bibliography

"About Human Development." *Human Development Reports*. UN. Available at http://hdr.undp.org/en/humandev/.

"About Us." *The World Bank-Prospects*. Available at http://econ.worldbank.org/WBSITE/EXTERNAL/EXTDEC/EXTDECPROSPECTS/0,,contentMDK:20267500~menuPK:476908~pagePK:64165401~piPK:64165026~theSitePK:476883,00.html.

Acer, Eleanor, and Jake Goodman. (2010). "Reaffirming Rights: Human Rights Protections of Migrants, Asylum Seekers, and Refugees in Immigration Detention." *Georgetown Immigration Law Journal* 24: 507–31.

Acharya, Arun Kumar. (2004). "Agrarian Conflict, Internal Displacement, and Trafficking of Mexican Women: The Case of Chiapas State." UNAM, Mexico for the 2004 Annual Meeting of Population Association of America, Boston.

Adams, Richard H. Jr. and John Page. (2003). International Migration, Remittances, and Poverty in Developing Countries. World Bank Policy Research Working Paper 3179, December. Available at http://elibrary.worldbank.org/doi/pdf/10.1596/1813-9450-3179.

Adamson, Fiona B. (2006). "Crossing Borders: International Migration and National Security." *International Security* 31.1: 165–99.

Adelman, Howard and Susan McGrath. (2007). "To Date or to Marry: That Is the Question." *Journal of Refugee Studies* 20: 376–80.

Agunias, Dovelyn Rannveig. (2006). *Remittances and Development Trends, Impacts, and Policy Options: A Review of the Literature.* Washington, DC: Migration Policy Institute.

Alcock, Antony Evelyn. (1971). *History of the International Labor Organization.* New York: Octagon.

Aleinikoff, Thomas Alexander, and Vincent Chetail. (2003). *Migration and International Legal Norms.* The Hague: T.M.C. Asser Press.

"The Alexandria Protocol; October 7, 1944." *The Avalon Project: Documents in Law, History and Diplomacy*. Lillian Goldman Law Library, Yale University. Available at http://avalon.law.yale.edu/20th_century/alex.asp.

Alfredson, Lisa. (2002). "Child Soldiers, Displacement, and Human Security." Coalition to Stop the Use of Child Soldiers.

Al Husseini, Jalal. (2010). "UNRWA and the Refugees: A Difficult but Lasting Marriage."*Journal of Palestine Studies* 40.1: 6–26.

Aliens Act. (2005). Sweden. Published 22 June 2006. Available at http://www.government.se/content/1/c6/06/61/22/bfb61014.pdf.

"Amnesty International | Working to Protect Human Rights." Available at http://www.amnesty.org.

An Analytical Review 10 Years on from the Adoption of the UN Trafficking in Persons Protocol. Rep. ICAT, 2010.

Annan, Kofi. (1997). "International Migration and Development, including the Convenng of a United Nations Conference on International Migration and Development: Report of the Secretary-general," UN Doc. No. A/52/314, September 18.

———. (2006). The Secretary-General Address to the High-Level Dialogue of the General Assembly on International Migration and Development, New York, 14 September 2006. Available at http://www.un.org/migration/sg-speech.html.

Arnold-Forster, W. (1946). "U.N.R.R.A.'s Work for Displaced Persons in Germany." *International Affairs (Royal Institute of International Affairs 1944–)* 22.1: 1–13.

Bain, J. Arthur. (1897). *Life of Fridtjof Nansen: Scientist and Explorer: Including an Account of the 1893–1896 Expedition.* London: Simpkin, Marshall, Hamilton, & Kent.

Bali Process. (2012). *Co Chairs' Statement.* Sixth Meeting of Bali Process Ad Hoc Group Senior Officials. Bali, Indonesia, 1 June 2012. Available at http://www.baliprocess.net/ministerial-conferences-and-senior-officials-meetings.

Bashford, Alison, and Sarah Howard. (2004). "Immigration and Health: Law and Regulation in Australia, 1901–1958." *Health and History* 6.1: 97–112.

Basri, Carole. (2003). Jewish Refugees from Arab Countries: An Examination of Legal Rights – A Case Study of the Human Rights Violations of Iraqi Jews 26 Fordham *Int'l L.J.* 711 (2002–2003).

Bauer, Stephan. (1919). *International Labor Legislation and the Society of Nations.* Trans. Annie M. Hannay and Alfred Maylander. Washington, DC: Government Printing Office.

Bell, Jessica. n.d. *Contemporary Slavery and International Law.* University of Denver.

Belser, Patrick, Michelle de Cock, and Farhad Mehran. (2006). *ILO Minimum Estimates of Forced Labor in the World.* Geneva: International Labor Organization.

Bellamy, Alex J., and Sara E. Davies, eds. (2010). Special Issue: Protecting IDPs and Refugees, Global Responsibility to Protect, vol. 2. No 1–2.

Berman, Jacqueline, and Phil Marshall. (2010). *Evaluation of the International Organization for Migration and Its Efforts to Combat Human Trafficking.* Oslo: Norwegian Agency for Development Cooperation.

Berne Initiative. (2003). *An International Agenda for Migration Management.* Rep. Berne: Berne Initiative.

Betts, Alexander. (2011). *Global Migration Governance.* Oxford: Oxford University Press.

Bhagwati, Jagdish. (2003). "Borders Beyond Control." *Foreign Affairs.* January/February. Available at http://www.foreignaffairs.com/articles/58622/jagdish-n-bhagwati/borders-beyond-control.

Black, Magge. (1995). *In the Twilight Zone: Child Workers in the Hotel, Tourism and Catering Industry*. Geneva: International Labor Organization.

Blackburn, Melissa. (1994). "A Tradition of Slavery," in *Anti-Slavery Reporter*. London: Anti-Slavery International.

Bohning, Roger. (1991). "The ILO and the New UN Convention on Migrant Workers: The Past and Future." *International Migration Review* 25.4: 698–709.

Bohning, W. R. n.d. *The Integration of Migrant Workers in the Labour Market: Policies and Their Impact*. Geneva: International Labour Office, International Migration Papers.

Bosniak, Linda S., and Aristide Zolberg. (1992). "State Sovereignty, Human Rights and the New UN Migrant Workers Convention." *Proceedings of the Annual Meeting (American Society of International Law)* 86: 634–41.

Breuil, Brenda C., Dina Siegel, Piet Van Reenen, Annemarieke Beijer, and Linda Roos. (2011). "Human Trafficking Revisited: Legal, Enforcement and Ethnographic Narratives on Sex Trafficking to Western Europe." *Trends in Organized Crime* 14: 30–46.

"British White Paper of 1939." (2008). *The Avalon Project: Documents in Law, History and Diplomacy*. Lillian Goldman Law Library, Yale Law School. Available at http://avalon.law.yale.edu/20th_century/brwh1939.asp.

Brookings Bern Project on Internal Displacement. (2007). When Displacement Ends: A Framework for Durable Solutions. *UNHCR Refworld*. Available at http://www.unhcr.org/refworld/docid/469f6bed2.html.

Broude, Tomer. (2010). "The Most-Favoured nation Principle, Equal Protection, and Migration Policy." *Georgetown Immigration Law Journal* 24: 553–63.

Brown, Eleanor. (2007). The Ties that Bind: Migration and Trafficking of Women and Girls for Sexual Exploitation in Cambodia. Geneva: International Organization for Migration.

"The Brussels Migration Conference." *Social Service Review* 26.1 (1952): 86–87.

Budapest Process, 2nd Meeting of the Working Group on the Silk Routes Region. Nevsehir, June 7–8, 2011.

Calavita, Kitty. (1984). *U.S. Immigration Law and the Control of Labor: 1820–1924*. London: Academic Press.

Carson, J. (1993). "Young's Town: 'Prison Camp' and Slave Dungeon for Child Workers," *Child Workers Philippines*, Vol. 1, No.1. Manila: Kamalayan Development Center.

Cartagena Declaration on Refugees Adopted by the Colloquium on the International Protection of Refugees in Central America, Mexico and Panama, Cartagena de Indias, Colombia, November 22, 1984.

Cassel, Doug. (2005). "Equal Labor Rights for Undocumented Migrant Workers." *Human Rights and Refugees, Internally Displaced Persons and Migrant Workers*. Leiden: Martinus Nijhoff.

Chamie, Joseph, and Mary G. Powers. (2006). *International Migration and the Global Community*. New York: Center for Migration Studies.

Cholewinski, Ryszard. (1994). "The Protection of the Right of Economic Migrants to Family Reunion in Europe." *The International and Comparative Law Quarterly* 43.3: 568–98.

⸻. (1997). *Migrant Workers in International Human Rights Law: Their Protection in Countries of Employment*. Oxford: Oxford University Press.

CIA World Factbook. (2012). Langley: Central Intelligence Agency. Available at https://www.cia.gov/library/publications/the-world-factbook/rankorder/2004rank.html.

Clark, Bruce. (2004). "The Implications of Early Marriage for HIV/AIDS Policy." Brief based on background paper prepared for the WHO/UNFPA/Population Council Technical Consultation on Married Adolescents. New York: Population Council.

Clark, Michelle A. (2003). "Trafficking in Persons: An Issue of Human Security." *Journal of Human Development* 4.2: 247–64.

Cobban, A. (1945). *National Self-Determination*. London: Oxford University Press.

Coghlan, Deirdre, and Gillian Wylie. (2011). "Defining Trafficking/Denying Justice? Forced Labour in Ireland and the Consequences of Trafficking Discourse." *Journal of Ethnic and Migration Studies* 37.9: 1513–26.

Cohen, Roberta. (2007). "Response to Hathaway." *Journal of Refugee Studies* 20: 370–76.

Collinson, Sarah. (2010). *Developing Adequate Humanitarian Responses*. Washington, DC: German Marshall Fund of the United States.

Collyer, Michael. (2006). "Migrants, Migration and the Security Paradigm: Constraints and Opportunities." *Mediterranean Politics* 11.2: 255–70.

"Colombo Process." (2014). *Colombo Process*. Available at http://www.colomboprocess.org/.

Committee on Migrant Workers. (2010). November 22–December 3. Available at http://www2.ohchr.org/english/bodies/cmw/cmws13.htm.

Compendium of IOM's Activities in Migration, Climate Change and the Environment. (2009). Rep. Geneva: International Organization for Migration.

Copenhagen Accord, following the United Nations Climate Change Conference, December 2009. Available at http://unfccc.int/resource/docs/2009/cop15/eng/l07.pdf.

Corbett, David. (1951). "Immigration and Canadian Politics." *International Journal* 6.3: 207–16.

"Council of Europe." (1953). *International Organization* 7.1: 153–63.

Council of Europe. (2010). *Readmission Agreements: A Mechanism for Returning Irregular Migrants*. Council of Europe Parliamentary Assembly, pp. 1–21.

Cushman, Bernard. (1946). "Labor Laws: A Reconsideration." *The Antioch Review* 6.3: 410–25.

De Guchteneire, Paul, Antoine Pecoud, and Ryszard Cholewinski. (2009). *Migration and Human Rights: The United Nations Convention on Migrant Workers' Rights*. Cambridge: Cambridge University Press.

Dennett, Raymond. (1945). "UNRAA Report." *Far Eastern Survey* 14.1: 7–8.

DeSipio, Louis. (2000). Sending Money Home . . . For Now: Remittances and Immigrant Adaptation in the United States. Washington, DC: InterAmerican Dialogue.

Discussion Note: Migration and the Environment at the Ninety-Fourth Session of the IOM. November 1, 2007. MC/INF/288. Available at http://www.iom.int/jahia/webdav/shared/shared/mainsite/about_iom/en/council/94/MC_INF_288.pdf.

"The Displacement of Population in Europe." (1943). *Population Index* 9.4:233–236.

"Document – Caught in the Backlash: Human Rights under Threat Worldwide in Aftermath of September 11 Attacks." *Amnesty International*. Amnesty International, October 3, 2001.

Doyle, Michael W. (2004). "The Challenge of Worldwide Migration." *Journal of International Affairs* 57.2: 1–5.

Ducasse-Rogier. (2001). *International Organization for Migration, 1951–2001.* Geneva: International Organization for Migration.

Dun, Olivia, and François Gemmene. (2008). *Protection of Environment, Forced Migration and Social Vulnerability International Conference.* Bonn, Germany.

D.W. (1946). "Success of a Mission: U.N.R.R.A. in Yugoslavia." *The World Today* 2.8: 376–83.

Edelenbos, Carla. (2009). "Committee on Migrant Workers and Implementation of the ICRMW" in Paul de Guchteneire, Antoine Pecoud and Ryszard Cholewinski, eds. *Migration and Human Rights: the United Nations Convention on Migrant Workers.* Cambridge: Cambridge University Press and Paris: UNESCO:100-120.

Elie, Jerome. (2010). *IOM from 1951–53: The Creation of PICMME/ICEM.* Report. Geneva.

El-Hinnawi, E. (1985). *Enviro1.mental Refugees.* New York, United Nations Development Program.

Emerson, Herbert. (1943). "Postwar Problems of Refugees." *Foreign Affairs* 21.2: 211–20.

"End-of-Mission Statement by the Special Rapporteur on Trafficking in Persons, Especially in Women and Children." *United Nations Human Rights Office of the High Commissioner for Human Rights.* UN. Available at http://www.ohchr.org/en/NewsEvents/Pages/DisplayNews.aspx?NewsID=12176.

"The Evian Conference on Refugees." *Bulletin of International News* 15.14 (1938): 16–18.

EU. (2004). Council of European Union. *Justice and Home Affairs, 2618th Council Meeting.* Brussels: EU.

————. (2005). Council of European Union. *The European Union Strategy for Combating Radicalisation and Recruitment to Terrorism.* Brussels: EU.

————. (2012). Council of European Union. *Council Adopts New EU-US Agreement on Passenger Name Records (PNR).* Luxembourg: EU.

European Migration Network. (2011). *Programmes and Strategies in the EU Member States fostering Assisted Return to and Reintegration in Third Countries.* Brussels: European Union.

Ezeilo, Joy N. (2011). *Report Submitted by the Special Rapporteur on Trafficking in Persons, Especially Women and Children.* UN. Available at http://daccess-dds-ny.un.org/doc/UNDOC/GEN/N10/483/11/PDF/N1048311.pdf?OpenElement.

"Facilitating Access to Reparation for Victims of Illegal Armed Groups in Colombia." *International Organization for Migration.* IOM. Available at http://www.iom.int/cms/en/sites/iom/home/what-we-do/reparation-programmes/facilitating-access-to-reparation-for-vi.html.

Fagen, Patricia W., and Micah N. Bump. (2004). *REMITTANCES IN CONFLICT AND CRISES: How Remittances Sustain Livelihoods in War, Crises, and Transitions to Peace.* Rep. Washington, DC: International Peace Academy.

Feingold, David. (2005). "Human Trafficking" September/October Issue of Foreign Policy.

Feller, Erika. (2008). Statement by UNHCR Assistant High Commissioner for Protection at the 42nd Meeting of the Standing Committee, Agenda Item 3, June 24.

Finckenauer, James O. (1998). *Russian Mafia in America: Immigration, Culture, and Crime.* Boston: Northeastern University Press.

Finkelstein, Monte S. (1988). "The Johnson Act, Mussolini and Fascist Emigration Policy: 1921–1930." *Journal of American Ethnic History* 8.1: 38–55.

Fischbach, Michael R. (2002). "The United Nations and Palestinian Refugee Property Compensation." *Journal of Palestine Studies* 31.2: 34–50.

Fisher, David, Susan Martin and Andrew Schoenholtz. (2003). "Migration and Security in International Law." In T. Alexander Aleinikoff and Vincent Chetail. *Migration and International Legal Norms.* The Hague: TMC Asser Press.

Fitzgibbon, Kathleen. (2003). "Modern-Day Slavery: The scope of trafficking in persons in Africa." *African Security Review* 12(1).

Forsythe, David P. (1983). "The Palestine Question: Dealing with a Long-Term Refugee Situation." *Annals of the American Academy of Political and Social Science* 467: 89–101.

Fourth Bali Regional Ministerial Conference on People Smuggling, Trafficking in Persons and Related Trasnational Crime. Bali, Indonesia, March 29–30, 2011.

"Frequently Asked Questions." *UNRWA.* United Nations Relief and Work Agency for Palestine Refugees in the Near East. Available at http://unrwa.org/etemplate.php?id=87.

Friedmann, W. (1952). "Migration and World Politics." *International Journal* 7.3: 196–203.

"Funds and Partners: UNODCBudget." *United Nations Office on Drugs and Crime.* UN. Available at http://www.unodc.org/unodc/en/donors/index.html?ref=menuside.

Fyfe, Alec. (1989). *Child Labor.* Oxford: Polity Press.

Gagnon, Jason, and David Khoudour-Casteras. (2011). Tackling the Policy Challenges of Migration: Regulation, Integration, Development. Paris: OECD.

Gallagher, Anne. (2010). "Trafficking, Smuggling and Human Rights: Tricks and Treaties." *Human Rights Quarterly* 23.4.

Gargan, Edward. (1992). "Bound to Looms by Poverty and Fear, Boys in India Makes a Few Men Rich," *New York Times,* July 9.

Gatrell, Peter. (1997). "Refugees in the Russian Empire, 1914–1917: Population Displacement and Social Identity," in *Critical Companion to the Russian Revolution, 1914–1921.* Bloomington: Indiana University Press.

Geddes, Andrew. (2011). *International Migration.* Thousand Oaks, CA: Sage.

"General Assembly President Calls for Redoubling of Efforts to End Human Trafficking." *United Nations Office on Drugs and Crime.* UN. Available at http://www.unodc.org/unodc/en/frontpage/2012/April/un-general-assembly-president-calls-for-re-doubled-efforts-to-end-human-trafficking.html.

General Assembly. (2006). Improving the coordination of efforts against trafficking in persons, Resolution 61/180 adopted by the General Assembly on 20 December 2006. Available at http://www.un.org/en/ga/search/view_doc.asp?symbol=A/RES/61/180&Lang=E.

Georgetown University Law Center International Migrants Bill of Rights Initiative. (2010). "International Migrants Bill of Rights" Georgetown Law Student Series. Paper 7 available at http://scholarship.law.georgetown.edu/spps_papers/7.

Gest, Justin. (2010). "Avoiding Evasion: Implementing International Migration Policy." *Georgetown Immigration Law Journal* 24: 639–49.

GCIM. (2005). *Migration in an Interconnected World: New Directions for Action.* Geneva: Global Commission on International Migration.

G. J. v. H. G. (1952). "Refugees: An Unsolved Problem." *The World Today* 8.8:324–332.

"Global Economic Prospects 2006: Economic Implications of Remittances and Migration." *Data & Research*. The World Bank. Available at http://econ.worldbank.org/external/default/main?pagePK=64165259.

"Global: Population, Remittances, HLD." (2007). *Migration News* 14.2:1.

"GMG Members." *Global Migration Group (GMG)*. Available at http://www.globalmigrationgroup.org/en/gmg-members.

GMG. (2011). Statement on the Impact of Climate Change on Migration. Geneva: GMG. Available at http://www.globalmigrationgroup.org/uploads/english.pdf.

Goodrich, Carter. (1947). "Possibilities and Limits of International Control of Migration." *The Millbank Memorial Fund Quarterly* 25.2: 153–60.

Gordenker, Leon. (1987). *Refugees in International Politics*. New York: Columbia University Press.

Government of the Netherlands. (2005). "The UN International Convention on the Protection of All Migrant Workers and Members of their Families of 1991," prepared for the Global Commission on International Migration, January.

Ghosh, Bimal. (2003). *Elusive Protection, Uncertain Lands: Migrants' Access to Human Rights*. Geneva: International Organization for Migration.

Gregory, Charles N. (1921). "The International Labor Organization of the League of Nations." *The American Journal of International Law* 15.1: 42–50.

GTZ. (2004). "Armed Conflict and Trafficking in Women: Desk Study" Sector Project against Trafficking in Women: Eschborn.

Guerrero, Eileen. (1994). "Bonded Labor of Children on Rise in Philippines." *Associated Press*, June 7.

Guterres, António. (2007). Keynote Speech by UN High Commissioner for Refugees, Third Symposium on Corporate Social Responsibility and Humanitarian Assistance. Tokyo, November 26. Available at http://www.unhcr.org/admin/ADMIN/476132d911.html.

———. (2011). Statement by UNHCR High Commissioner for Refugees at the United Nations Security Council Briefing, "Maintenance of International Peace and Security: New Challenges to International Peace and Security and Conflict Prevention." New York, November 23.

Hambro, Edvard. (1957). "Chinese Refugees in Hong Kong." *The Phylon Quarterly* 18.1: 69–81.

Hansen, Randall. (2010). *An Assessment of Principal Regional Consultative Process on Migration*. Rep. Geneva: International Organization for Migration.

Hansen, Randall, Jobst Koehler, and Jeannette Money. (2011). *Migration, Nation States, and International Cooperation*. New York: Routledge.

Hasenau, Michael. (1991). "ILO Standards on Migrant Workers: The Fundamentals of the UN Convention and Their Genesis." *International Migration Review* 25.4: 687–97.

Hasenclever, Andreas, Peter Mayer and Volker Rittberger. (1997). *Theories of International Regimes*. Cambridge: Cambridge University Press.

Hathaway, James C. (2007). "Forced Migration Studies: Could We Agree Just to 'Date'?" *Journal of Refugee Studies* 20: 349–69.

Hatton, T. J., and Jeffrey G. Williamson. (1998). *The Age of Mass Migration: Causes and Economic Impact*. New York: Oxford University Press.

Heim, Susanne. (2010). "International Refugee Policy and Jewish Immigration under the Shadow of National Socialism." In *Refugees from Nazi Germany and the Liberal European States*. Oxford: Berghahn Books.

Hernandez-Pulido, Ricardo, and Tania Caron. (2003). "Protection of Children and Young Persons." *Fundamental Rights at Work and International Labour Standards*. International Labour Organization.

"History–1990's." *International Organization for Migration*. IOM. Available at http://www.iom.int/cms/en/sites/iom/home/about-iom-1/history/1990s.html.

"History–21st Century." *International Organization for Migration*. IOM. Available at http://www.iom.int/cms/en/sites/iom/home/about-iom-1/history/21st-century.html.

Holborn, Louise W. (1939). "The League of Nations and the Refugee Problem." *Annals of the American Academy of Political and Social Science* 203(May): 124–35.

――――. (1965). "International Organizations for Migration of European Nationals and Refugees." *International Journal* 20.3: 331–49.

Holborn, Louise W., Philip Chartrand, and Rita Chartrand. (1975). *Refugees, a Problem of Our Time: The Work of the United Nations High Commissioner for Refugees, 1951–1972*. Metuchen, NJ: Scarecrow.

Hollifield, James F. (2004). "The Emerging Migration State." *International Migration Review* 38.3: 885–912.

Hollifield, James F. and Caroline B. Brettell, eds. (2008). *Migration Theory: Talking across Disciplines*. New York: Routledge.

Houlihan, Shea. (2011). *Assessment of the Implementation of the Trafficking Protocol by Primary International Stakeholders*. Working paper. Washington, DC: Georgetown University.

Housden, Martyn. (2010). "White Russians Crossing the Black Sea: Fridtjof Nansen, Constantinople and the First Modern Repatriation of Refugees Displaced by Civil Conflict, 1922–23." *The Slavonic and East European Review* 88.3: 495–524.

Hugo, Graeme. (2008). *Migration, Development and Environment*, Migration Research Series No. 35. Geneva: IOM.

Human Rights Watch/Asia. (1995). *Contemporary Forms of Slavery in Pakistan*. New York: Human Rights Watch. Available at http://www.hrw.org/reports/pdfs/c/crd/pakistan957.pdf.

Human Rights Watch. (2007). Human Rights Watch's Statement to the IOM Council, 27–30 November 2007 (94th Session). Available at http://www.hrw.org/news/2007/11/28/human-rights-watch-s-statement-iom-council.

Hune, Shirley. (1987). "Drafting an International Convention on the Protection of the Rights of All Migrants Workers and Their Families." *International Migration Review* 21.1: 123–27.

Hutchinson, Edward P., and Wilbert E. Moore. (1945). "Pressures and Barriers in Future Migration." *Annals of the American Academy of Political and Social Science* 237: 164–71.

Huysmans, Jef. (2000). "The European Union and the Securitization of Migration." *Journal of Common Market Studies* 38.5: 751–77.

Ibrahim, Maggie. (2005). "The Securitization of Migration: A Racial Discourse." *International Migration* 43.5: 163–87.

Icduygu, Ahmet. (2008). *Circular Migration and Turkey: An Overview of the Past and Present-Some Demo-Economic Implications*, CARIM AS (2008/10), Robert Schuman

Centre for Advanced Studies, San Domenico di Fiesole (FI): European University Institute.

ICAO. (2008). *Machine Readable Travel Documents*. Vol. 1: Passports with Machine Readable Data Stored in Optical Character Recognition Form. Montreal: International Civil Aviation Organization. Available at http://www.icao.int/publications/Documents/9303_p3_v1_cons_en.pdf.

ICAT. (2006). Inter-agency coordination meeting on collaborative interventions to counter trafficking in persons, held in Tokyo on 26 and 27 September 2006: Report of the Secretariat. Submitted to the Parties of the United Nations Convention against Transnational Organized Crime, October 10, 2006 (CTOC/COP/2006/CRP.5).

IDMC. (2007). Internal Displacement Monitoring Center. "Internal Displacement: Global Overview of Trends and Developments in 2006." Geneva: IDMC. Available at http://www.internal-displacement.org/8025708F004BE3B1/(httpInfoFiles)/9251510E3E5B6FC3C12572BF0029C267/$file/Global_Overview_2006.pdf.

Immigration Commission. (1911). *Emigration Conditions in Europe. Reports of the Immigration Commission*. Volume 4. Government Printing Office.

IO. "Intergovernmental Committee for European Migration." *International Organization* 7.1 (February 1953): 169–70.

———. "Intergovernmental Committee for European Migration." *International Organization* 8.3 (August 1954): 418–21.

———. "Intergovernmental Committee for European Migration." *International Organization* 9.3 (August 1955): 453.

———. "Intergovernmental Committee for European Migration." *International Organization* 10.2 (May 1956): 347–50.

———. "Intergovernmental Committee for European Migration." *International Organization* 11.2 (Spring 1957): 404–06.

———. "Intergovernmental Committee for European Migration." *International Organization* 12.3 (Summer 1958): 418–19.

———. "Intergovernmental Committee for European Migration." *International Organization* 13.2 (Spring 1959): 355–56.

———. "Intergovernmental Committee for European Migration." *International Organization* 14.3 (Summer 1960): 491.

———. "Intergovernmental Committee for European Migration." *International Organization* 15.3 (Summer 1961): 532–33.

———. "Intergovernmental Committee for European Migration." *International Organization* 15.1 (Winter 1961): 207–08.

———. "Intergovernmental Committee for European Migration." *International Organization* 16.3 (Summer 1962): 663–65.

———. "Intergovernmental Committee for European Migration." *International Organization* 17.3 (Summer 1963): 828–29.

———. "Intergovernmental Committee for European Migration." *International Organization* 18.3 (Summer 1964): 669–70.

Inter-agency Coordination Meeting on Collaborative Interventions to Counter Trafficking in Persons, Held in Tokyo on 26 and 27 September 2006 Report of the Secretariat. Vienna: UN, 2006.

Inter-Agency Standing Committee (IASC), Guidance Note on Using the Cluster Approach to Strengthen Humanitarian Response. November 24, 2006. Available at http://www.humanitarianreform.org/humanitarianreform/Portals/1/Resources&%20tools/IASCGUIDANCENOTECLUSTERAPPROACH.pdf.

International Labor Office. (2004). *Towards a Fair Deal for Migrant Workers in the Global Economy: International Labour Conference, 92nd Session, 2004*. Geneva: International Labor Organization. Available at http://www.ilo.org/wcmsp5/groups/public/---ed_protect/---protrav/---migrant/documents/publication/wcms_204115.pdf.

———. (2005). Human Trafficking and Forced Labour Exploitation: Guidelines for Legislation and Law Enforcement: Geneva: International Labour Office.

———. (2006). *ILO Multilateral Framework on Labour Migration: Non-binding principles and guidelines for a rights-based approach to labour migration*. Geneva: International Labor Organization. Available at http://www.ilo.org/wcmsp5/groups/public/---asia/---ro-bangkok/documents/publication/wcms_146243.pdf.

———. (2006b). *Trafficking for Forced Labour: How to Monitor the Recruitment of Migrant Workers Training Manual*. Geneva: International Labour Office.

———. (2007). Green Jobs: Facing up to an 'inconvenient truth' (World of Work No. 60) Available from http://www.ilo.org/wow/Articles/lang--en/WCMS_083900/index.htm.

———. (2008). *Combating Forced Labour: A Handbook for Employers and Business*. Geneva: International Labour Organization. Available at http://www.ilo.org/sapfl/Informationresources/ILOPublications/WCMS_101171/lang--en/index.htm.

———. (2011). *Programme and budget for the Biennium 2012–13*. Geneva: International Labor Organization. Available at http://www.ilo.org/public/english/bureau/program/download/pdf/12-13/pbfinalweb.pdf.

———. (2012). *ILO 2012 Global Estimate of Forced Labour Executive Summary*. Rep. International Labour Organization.

"International Labor Organization." *International Organization* 3.1 (February 1949): 152–54.

"International Labor Organization." *International Organization* 3.3 (August 1949): 532–36.

"International Labor Organization." *International Organization* 3.4 (November 1949): 712–14.

"International Labor Organization." *International Organization* 4.3 (1950): 488–91.

"International Migrants Bill of Rights." (2010). *Georgetown Immigration Law Journal* 24: 395–506.

"International White Slavery." *Journal of the American Institute of Criminal Law and Criminology* 3.1 (1912): 134–37.

Interpol Fact Sheet: Trafficking in Human Beings. Interpol, 2012 Available at http://www.interpol.int/Crime-areas/Trafficking-in-human-beings/Trafficking-in-human-beings Available at http://www.iom.int/cms/countertrafficking.

IOM. (2003). IOM-UN Relationship: Summary Report of the Working Group on Institutional Arrangements at the Eighty-Sixth Session of the IOM Council. November 10. Available at (2003). IOM – UN Relationship: Summary Report of the Working Group on Institutional Arrangements. Geneva: IOM. Available at http://www.iom.int/jahia/webdav/shared/shared/mainsite/about_iom/en/council/86/MCINF_263.pdf.

———. (2007). "Options for the IOM-UN Relationship: Additional Analysis of Costs and Benefits." Paper presented at the Ninety-Fourth Session of the IOM Council. November 9.

———. (2013). "Constitution." *International Organization for Migration*. Available at http://www.iom.int/files/live/sites/iom/files/About-IOM/docs/iom_constitution_en .pdf.

IPCC. (2007). Intergovernmental Panel on Climate Change. *IPCC Fourth Assessment Report: Working Group II Report "Impacts, Adaptation and Vulnerability."* Appendix 1 "Glossary." Geneva, p. 869. Available at http://www.ipcc.ch/pdf/ assessment-report/ar4/wg2/ar4-wg2-app.pdf.

J. R. (1947). "U.N.R.R.A. 1945–1947: The End of a Chapter." *The World Today* 3.8: 370–74.

Jaeger, Gilbert. (1978). *Status and International Protection of Refugees*. Strasburg: International Institute of Human Rights.

Jandl, Michael. (2007). "Irregular Migration, Human Smuggling, and the Eastern Englargement of the European Union." *International Migration Review* 41.2: 291– 315.

Josephson, Harold. (1974). *James T. Shotwell and the Rise of Internationalism in America*. Rutherford, NJ: Fairleigh Dickinson University Press.

Juels, Ari, David Molnar, and David Wagner. (2005). "Security and Privacy Issues in E-Passports." Published in SECURECOMM '05 Proceedings of the First International Conference on Security and Privacy for Emerging Areas in Communications Networks. Washington, DC: IEEE (pp. 74–88). IEEE Computer Society, Washington, DC.

Kälin, Walter. (2012). "From the Nansen Principles to the Nansen Initiative." *Forced Migration Review* 41: 48–49.

Kaprielian-Churchill, Isabel. (1994). "Rejecting "Misfits: Canada and the Nansen Passport." *International Migration Review* 28.2: 281–306.

Keely, Charles. (1996). "How Nation-States Create and Respond to Refugee Flows," *International Migration Review* 20.4: 1046–66.

Kelley, Ninette, and M. J. Trebilcock. (1998). *The Making of the Mosaic: A History of Canadian Immigration Policy*. Toronto: University of Toronto.

Kniveton, Dominic, Kerstin Schmidt-Verkerk, Christopher Smith, and Richard Black. (2008). *Climate Change and Migration: Improving Methodologies to Estimate Flows*, Migration Research Series No. 33. Geneva: IOM.

Kohler, Jobst. (2011). "What Government Networks do in the Field of Migration." in Randall Hansen, Jobst Kohler and Jeannette Mooney. *Migration, Nation States, and International Cooperation*. New York: Routledge.

Kolmannskog, Vikran. (2009). "Climate Change-related Displacement and the European Response." Paper presented at Society for International Development, Vijverberg Session on Climate Change and Migration. The Hague, January 4.

Koser, Khalid. (2005). *Irregular migration, state security and human security*. Paper prepared for the Policy Analysis and Research Programme of the Global Commission on International Migration.Geneva: GCIM.

———. (2008). "Strengthening Policy Responses to Migrant Smuggling and Human Trafficking," Background paper prepared for Civil Society Roundtable 2.2 at the 2008 Global Forum on Migration and Development. Manila, October 27– 30.

Koslowski, Rey. (2011). *Global Migration Regimes*. New York: Palgrave MacMillan.

Krasner, Stephen D., ed. (1983). *International Regimes*. Ithaca, NY: Cornell University Press.

Kritikos, Georgios. (2005). "The Agricultural Settlement of Refugees: A Source of Productive Work and Stability in Greece, 1923–1930." *Agricultural History* 79.3: 321–46.

Kulischer, Eugene M. (1943). *The Displacement of Population in Europe*. Montreal: International Labour Office.

Kunz, Rahel, Sandra Lavenex, and Marion Panizzon, eds. (2011). *Multilayered Migration Governance: The Promise of Partnership*. New York: Routledge.

Kyle, David and Rey Koslowski, eds. (2001). *Global Human Smuggling: Global Perspectives*. Baltimore: Johns Hopkins University Press.

Laczko, Frank, and Christine Agharzarm. (2009). *Migration, Environment and Climate Change: Assessing the Evidence*. Geneva: IOM.

"Latest Highlights." *United Nations Institute for Training and Research (UNITAR)*. UN. Available at http://www.unitar.org/ny/.

"Law Enforcement Capacity Building in West Africa to Prevent and Combat Smuggling of Migrants." *United Nations Office on Drugs and Crime*. UN. Available at http://www.unodc.org/nigeria/en/law-enforcement-capacity-building-in-west-africa-to-prevent-and-combat-smuggling-of-migrants.html.

League of Nations. (1920). "Conference of Passports, Customs Formalities and Through Tickets." *1 League of Nations Official Journal* 52 1920. Content downloaded/printed from HeinOnline (http://heinonline.org) on June 18, 2012.

———. (1926). "Passport Conference." *7 League of Nations Official Journal* 1088 1926 Content downloaded/printed from HeinOnline (http://heinonline.org) on June 18, 2012.

Lehman, Herbert H. (1945). "Some Problems in International Administration." *Public Administration Review* 5.2: 93–101.

Levmore, Bernard W. (1939). "A Stimulus for American Industry: Nonprofessional Refugees." *Annals of the American Academy of Political and Social Science* 203: 162–67.

Lillich, Richard B. (1984). *The Human Rights of Aliens in Contemporary International Law*. Manchester: Manchester University Press.

Limoncelli, Stephanie A. (2010). *The Politics of Trafficking: The First International Movement to Combat the Sexual Exploitation of Women*. Stanford, CA: Stanford University Press.

Loescher, Gil. (1993). *Beyond Charity: International Cooperation and the Global Refugee Crisis*. New York: Oxford University Press.

———. (2001). *The UNHCR and World Politics: A Perilous Path*. Oxford: Oxford University Press.

Lonnroth, Juhani. (1991). "The International Convention on the Rights of All Migrant Workers and Members of Their Families in the Context of International Migration Policies: An Analysis of Ten Years of Negotiation." *International Migration Review* 25.4: 710–36.

Lowell, B. Lindsay, and Rodolfo O. de la Garza. (2000). *The Developmental Role of Remittances in U.S. Latino Communities and in Latin American Countries*. Washington, DC: InterAmerican Dialogue.

Lowell, Lindsay, and Allan Findlay. (2001). *Migration of Highly Skilled Persons from Developing Countries: Impact and Policy Responses Synthesis Report*. Rep. Geneva: International Labor Organization.

Lynch, Allen. (2002). "Woodrow Wilson and the Principle of "National Self-Determination: A Reconsideration." *Review of International Studies* 28.2: 419–36.

Lyons, Gene M. 1958. "American Policy and the United Nations' Program for Korean Reconstruction." *International Organization* 12.2: 180–192.

Mair, George F. (1950). "The 1950 Meeting of the Population Association." *Population Index* 16.3: 193–99.

Managing International Migration through International Cooperation: The International Agenda for Migration Management Chairman's Summary from the Berne II Conference. Berne, Switzerland. December 16–17, 2004.

Marks, Edward. (1957). "Internationally Assisted Migration: ICEM Rounds Out Five Years of Resettlement." *International Organization* 11.3: 481–94.

Marrus, Michael R. (2002). The Unwanted: European Refugees from the First World War through the Cold War. Philadelphia, PA: Temple University Press.

Martin, Philip. (2010). *Climate Change, Agricultural Development, and Migration.* Washington, DC: German Marshall Fund.

Martin, Philip, and Susan F. Martin. (2006). "Global Commission on International Migration: A New Global Migration Facility." *International Migration* 44/1: 5–12.

Martin, Philip L., Susan F. Martin, and Patrick Weil. (2006). *Managing Migration: The Promise of Cooperation.* Lanham, MD: Lexington Press.

Martin, Philip, Susan Martin, and Sarah Cross. (2007). "High-level Dialogue on Migration and Development." *International Migration* 45/1: 7–25.

Martin, Susan. (2003). Refugee Women: Second Edition. Lanham, MD: Lexington Books.

———. (2004). "Making the UN Work: Forced Migration and Institutional Reform." *Journal of Refugee Studies* 17: 301–318.

———. (2010). "Climate Change, Migration and Governance." *Global Governance* 16.3: 397–414.

———. (2010). "Forced Migration, the Refugee Regime and the Responsibility to Protect." In Sara Ellen Davies and Luke Glanville, eds. *Protecting the Displaced: Deepening the Responsibility to Protect.* Leiden: Martinus Nijhoff, 13–34.

———. (2011). "Human Trafficking and Smuggling (with Amber Callaway)," in *Global Migration Governance*, ed. Alexander Betts. Oxford: Oxford University Press.

———. (2011). "International Cooperation on Migration and the UN System," in *Global Migration Regimes*, ed. Rey Koslowski. New York: Palgrave MacMillan.

———. (2011). "International Migration and International Cooperation: An Overview," *Migration, National States and International Cooperation*, eds. Randall Hansen, Jobst Koehler, and Jeannette Money. New York: Routledge, 128–144.

Martin, Susan, and Abimourched, Rola. (2009). "Migrant Rights: International Law and National Action." *International Migration* 47: 115–138.

"Mauritius Workers Leave for Canada under special migration program," *Net News Publisher*. March 9, 2008. Available at http://www.netnewspublisher.com/mauritius-workers-leave-for-canada-under-special-migration-program.

Massey, Douglas S., Joaquin Arango, Graeme Hugo, Ali Kouaouci, Adela Pellegrino, J. Edward Taylor. (1993). "Theories of International Migration: A Review and Appraisal." *Population and Development Review*, Vol. 19, No. 3 (Sep., 1993), pp. 431–466, "Migration and Climate Change." *International Organization for Migration*. Available at http://www.iom.int/cms/jahia/Jahia/migration-climate-change-environmental-degradation.

Migration Health: Report of Activities 2010. Report. IOM, 2010.

Migration Policy Institute and Brookings Institution. (2005). *Towards a Comprehensive Regime for Refugees and Internally Displaced Persons*. Washington, DC: MPI and Brookings.

Miko, Francis. (2006). "Trafficking in Persons: The U.S. and International Response" Congressional Research Service Report for Congress, Code Order RL30545.

"Mission and Tasks." *Frontex*. Frontex, Accessed October 20, 2012. Available at http://www.frontex.europa.eu/about/mission-and-tasks.

Moens, Bruno, Veronica Zeitlin, Codou Bop, and Rokhaya Gaye. (2004). "Study on the Practice of Trafficking in Persons in Senegal." Development Alternatives, Inc. Report for U.S. Agency for International Development.

Morton, Andrew, Philippe Boncour, and Frank Laczko. (2008). "Human Security Policy Challenges in Climate Change and Displacement." *Forced Migration Review*. Oxford: Refugee Studies Centre, 5–7.

"Movement of Natural Persons." (n.d.). *Services: Sector by Sector*. Geneva: WTO. Available at http://www.wto.org/english/tratop_e/serv_e/mouvement_persons_e/mouvement_persons_e.htm.

Mrazik, Ryan T., and Andrew I. Schoenholtz. (2010). "Protecting and Promoting the Human Right to Respect for Family Life: Treaty-Based Reform and Domestic Advocacy." *Georgetown Immigration Law Journal* 24: 651–84.

Myers, Denys P. (1948). "Liquidation of League of Nations Functions." *The American Journal of International Law* 42.2: 320–54.

Nafziger, James A. R., and Barry C. Bartel. (1991). "The Migrant Workers Convention: Its Place in Human Rights Law." *International Migration Review* 25.4: 771–99.

Nag, Sajal. (2001). "Nationhood and Displacement in Indian Subcontinent." *Economic and Political Weekly* 36.5: 4753–60.

The Nansen Conference: Climate Change and Displacement in the 21st Century. (2011). Report. Oslo: Norwegian Refugee Council.

Nansen, Fridtjof. (1928). "War and Its Aftermath." *Advocate of Peace through Justice* 90.8: 491–98.

"National Adaptation Programmes of Action (NAPAs)." *United Nations Framework Convention on Climate Change*. UN. Available at http://unfccc.int/national_reports/napa/items/2719.php.

National Commission on Terrorist Attacks Upon the United States. (2004). The 9/11 Report. Washington, DC: National Commission. Available at http://www.9-11commission.gov/report/911Report.pdf.

The Next Decade: Promoting Common Priorities and Greater Coherence in the Fight against Human Trafficking. Inter-Agency Coordination Group Against Trafficking in Persons (ICAT), n.d. Available at http://www.ungift.org/doc/knowledgehub/resource-centre/ICAT/ICAT_overview_paper.pdf.

"Nobel Lecture: ILO and the Social Infrastructure of Peace." *International Labour Organization*. The Nobel Foundation. Available at http://www.nobelprize.org/nobel_prizes/peace/laureates/1969/labour-lecture.html.

Oberoi, Pia. (2005). "Indian Partition." in Matthew J. Gibney and Randall Hansen. Immigration and Asylum: From 1900 to the Present. Santa Barbara CA: ABC-CLIO Ltd.

O'Connor, Edward M. (1952). "The Brussels Conference." *Social Service Review* 26.4: 399–404.

Official Bulletin. (1919). Vol. 1. Geneva: International Labour Organization.

Official Bulletin. (1922). Vol. 1. Geneva: International Labour Organization.

OHCHR. (2002). *OHCHR Recommended Principles and Guidelines on Human Rights and Human Trafficking.* Report of the United Nations High Commissioner for Human Rights to the Economic and Social Council. New York: United Nations.

OHCHR. (2010). *OHCHR Recommended Principles and Guidelines on Human Rights and Human Trafficking.* Commentary, Geneva and New York: OHCHR.

————. (2012). "List of Projects Selected at the 16th Session of the Board of Trustees of the UN Voluntary Fund on Contemporary Forms of Slavery." Available at http://www.ohchr.org/Documents/Issues/Slavery/2012Projects.pdf.

Organization of African Unity Convention Governing the Specific Aspects of Refugee Problems in Africa, adopted by the Assembly of Heads of State and Government at its Sixth Ordinary Session. Addis-Ababa, Ethiopia. September 10, 1969.

"Outcome of the Conference." Proceedings of United Nations Conference on Sustainable Development. Rio de Janeiro, Brazil. June 20–22, 2012.

"Overcoming Barriers: Human Mobility and Development." (2009). *Human Development Reports.* Available at http://hdr.undp.org/en/reports/global/hdr2009/.

"Overview." *The World Bank.* Available at http://econ.worldbank.org/external/default/main?menuPK=469435&pagePK=64165236&piPK=64165141&theSitePK=469382.

"Palestine Refugees." *UNRWA.* United Nations Relief and Work Agency for Palestine Refugees in the Near East. Available at http://unrwa.org/etemplate.php?id=86.

Pearson, Elain. (2003). "Study on Trafficking in Women in East Africa; A situational analysis including current NGO and Governmental activities, as well as future opportunities, to address trafficking in women and girls in Ethiopia, Kenya, Tanzania, Uganda, and Nigeria." *Deutsche Gesellschaft fur Technische Zusammenarbeit (GTZ).*

Pecoud, Antoine, and De Guchteneire, Paul. (2007). *Migration without Borders: Essays on the Free Movement of People.* Oxford: Berghahn Books.

Perruchoud, Richard. (1989). "From the Intergovernmental Committee for European Migration to the International Organization for Migration." *International Journal of Refugee Law* 1.4: 501–17.

Phillips, Nicola. (2011). *Migration in the Global Political Economy.* Boulder, CO: Lynne Rienner Publishers.

Physicians for Human Rights. (2002). War-Related Sexual Violence in Sierra Leone: A population-based assessment with the support of UNAMSIL. Boston/Washington, DC.

Picarelli, John. (2002). "Trafficking, Slavery, and Peacekeeping: The Need for a Comprehensive Training Program" Conference Report. Turin: UN Interregional Crime and Justice Research Institute.

PICHÉ, Victor. (2012). "In and Out the Back Door: Canada's Temporary Worker Programs in a Global Perspective" in Martin Geiger and Antoine Pécoud (eds), *The New Politics of International Mobility: Migration Management and Its Discontents,* Osnabrück: IMIS – Beiträge.

Polania, Fanny. "Analysis on the relation between trafficking in humans and drugs in Colombia." Programme Coordinator Trafficking in Persons at IOM Colombia.

Population Reference Bureau. (2012). World Population Data Sheet 2012. Washington, DC: Population Reference Bureau.

"Press Briefing Notes." *International Organization for Migration*. IOM. April 19, 2011. Available at http://ftp.iom.int/jahia/Jahia/media/press-briefing/notes/pbnAF/cache/offonce/lang/en?entryId=29543.

Price, John. (1945). "International Labour Organization." *International Affairs* 21.1: 30–39.

Priore, Michael D. (1979). Birds of Passage: Migrant Labor and Industrial States. Cambridge: Cambridge University Press.

Proceedings of ILO General Conference. (2004). Geneva: ILO.

Proctor, Tammy M. (2010). *Civilians in a World at War: 1914–1918*. New York: New York University Press.

Programme and Budget for the Biennium 2012–13. Rep. 1st ed. Geneva: International Labour Office, 2011.

Public Law 101–649 (Immigration Act of November 29, 1990), Section 302.

Quesada, Patrice. (2009). *Compendium of IOM's Activities in Migration, Climate Change, and the Environment*. Geneva: IOM.

Rahman, Mahbubar, and Willem Van Schendel. (2003). "'I Am Not a Refugee': Rethinking Partition Migration." *Modern Asian Studies* 37.3: 551–84.

Raleigh, Clionadh, Lisa Jordan, and Idean Salehyan. (n.d.). *Assessing the Impact of Climate Change on Migration and Conflict*. Working paper. Washington, DC: World Bank. Available at http://siteresources.worldbank.org/EXTSOCIALDEVELOPMENT/Resources/SDCCWorkingPaper_MigrationandConflict.pdf.

Ratha, Dilip. (2003). "Workers' Remittances: An Important and Stable Source of External Development Finance" in World Bank. *Global Development Finance*. Washington, DC: World Bank.

Recommended Principles and Guidelines on Human Rights and Human Trafficking. Report of the United Nations High Commissioner for Human Rights to the Economic and Social Council at the Substantive Session. New York, July 1–26, 2002.

Refugee Protection and Mixed Migration: A 10-Point Plan of Action. UNHCR, 2007.

Reintegration of Iraqi Nations from Selected European Countries: An Analysis of Polices and Practices. The Hague: IOM, 2010.

Renaud, Fabrice, Janos J. Bogardi, Olivia Dun, and Koko Warner. (2007). *Control, Adapt or Flee?: How to Face Environmental Migration*. Bonn: United Nations University.

Report of Proceedings, Global Forum on Migration and Development. Brussels, 2007: 153. Available at http://gfmd.org/en/gfmd-documents-library/brussels-gfmd-2007/cat_view/934-brussels-gfmd-2007/983-report-of-the-proceedings.html.

Report on the Ninety-Fifth (Special) Session of the Council. Report. Geneva: UN, 2008.

R. H. G. (1912). "International White Slavery." *Journal of the American Institute of Criminal Law and Criminology* 3.1: 134–137.

Richard, Amy. (1999). "International Trafficking in Women to the United States: A Contemporary Manifestation of Slavery and Organized Crime" Intelligence Monograph, DCI Intelligence Analyst Program: 1–87.

Richardson, B. (1950). "The United Nations Relief for Palestine Refugees." *International Organization* 4.1: 44–54.

Richmond, Oliver P. (2002). "States of Sovereignty, Sovereign States, and Ethnic Claims for International Status." *Review of International Studies* 28.2: 381–402.

Robbins, Richard. (1956). "Refugee Status: Challenge and Response." Author(s): *Law and Contemporary Problems* 21. 2: 311–333.

Roosevelt, Theodore. (1907). "Rules Governing the Granting and Issuing of Passports in the United States." *The American Journal of International Law* 1.3: 317–20.

Rucker, Arthur. (1954). "Korea-The Next Stage." *International Affairs* 30.3: 313–319.

Rudolph, Christopher. (2003). "Security and the Political Economy of International Migration." *American Political Science Review* 97.4: 603–20.

Ruhs, Martin, and Philip Martin. (2008). "Numbers vs. Rights: Trade-Offs and Guest Worker Programs." *International Migration Review* 42.1: 249–65.

Salter, Mark B. (2003). *Rights of Passage: The Passport in International Relations.* Boulder, CO: Lynne Rienner.

Saul. Ben. (2006). "The Legal Response of the League of Nations to Terrorism" *Journal of International Criminal Justice* 4.2: 78–102.

Sayre, Katherine. (2007). "India Struggles Against Trafficking: Many women, girls sold into prostitution." *Washington Post.* June 17, 2007: A12.

Schoenholtz, Andrew I. (2005). "Newcomers in Rural America: Hispanic Immigrants in Rogers, Arkansas" in Elzbieta M. Gozdziak and Susan Forbes Martin (eds.), *Beyond the Gateway: Immigrants in a Changing America.* Lanham, MD: Lexington Books.

Schoenholtz, Andrew I., and Jennifer Hojaiban. (2008). *International Migration and Anti-Terrorism Laws and Policies: Balancing Security and Refugee Protection.* Washington, DC: Institute for the Study of International Migration, Walsh School of Foreign Service, Georgetown University.

Secretary-General's High-level Panel on UN System-wide Coherence in the Areas of Development, Humanitarian Assistance, and the Environment. (2006). *Delivering as One.* New York: United Nations. Available at http://www.un.org/events/panel/resources/pdfs/HLP-SWC-FinalReport.pdf.

Sekar, A. "A Study of Granite Export and Bondage of Stone Cutters in Tamilnadu." India: The Association of the Rural Poor.

"Services: Rules for Growth and Investment." *Understanding the WTO.* WTO. Available at http://www.wto.org/english/thewto_e/whatis_e/tif_e/agrm6_e.htm.

Shelley, Louise I. (2010). *Human Trafficking: A Global Perspective.* Cambridge: Cambridge University Press.

Skran, Claudena M. (1995). *Refugees in Inter-war Europe: The Emergence of a Regime.* Oxford: Clarendon.

Solomon, Michael K., and Kerstin Bartsch. (2003). "The Berne Initiative: Toward the Development of an International Policy Framework on Migration." *The Migration Information Source.* April. Available at http://www.migrationinformation.org/feature/display.cfm?ID=114.

"Special Rapporteur on Trafficking." *United Nations Human Rights Office of the High Commissioner for Human Rights.* UN. Available at http://www.ohchr.org/EN/Issues/Trafficking/Pages/TraffickingIndex.aspx.

Sridharan, Swetha. (2008). "Material Support to Terrorism: Consequences for Refugees and Asylum Seekers in the United States" *Migration Information Source,* January. Available at http://www.migrationinformation.org/usfocus/display.cfm?ID=671.

Stadulis, Elizabeth. (1952). "The Resettlement of Displaced Persons in the United Kingdom." *Population Studies* 5.3: 207–37.

Sumberg, Theodore A. (1945). "The Financial Experience of UNRRA." *The American Journal of International Law* 39.4: 698–712.

Summary and Conclusions by the Chair for the International Symposium on Migration. Berne, Switzerland. June 14–15, 2001. The Berne Initiative.

Sumner, B. H. (1924). "The Aims and Working of the International Labor Organization." *International Journal of Ethics* 34.2, 157–74.

"Support for the Sierra Leone Reparations Programme." *International Organization for Migration*. IOM. Available at http://www.iom.int/cms/en/sites/iom/home/what-we-do/reparation-programmes/support-for-the-sierra-leone-reparations.html.

Taylor, Alastair M. (1945). "The Necessity for UNRRA." *World Affairs* 108.1.

Torpey, John. (2000). *The Invention of the Passport: Surveillance, Citizenship, and the State.* Cambridge: Cambridge University Press.

Trachtman, Joel P. (2009). *The International Law of Economic Migration: Toward the Fourth Freedom.* Kalamazoo, MI: W.E. Upjohn Institute.

Trafficking for Forced Labour: How to Monitor the Recruitment of Migrant Workers, Training Manual. International Labour Organization, 2006.

Truman, Harry S. (1945). Statement and Directive by the President on Immigration to the United States of Certain Displaced Persons and Refugees in Europe, December 22. Available at http://trumanlibrary.org/publicpapers/viewpapers.php?pid=515.

UK Foresight. (2011). *Migration and Global Environmental Change: Future Challenges and Opportunities.* London: The Government Office for Science.

UN Convention Against Transnational Organized Crime and the Protocols Thereto, adopted by General Assembly Resolution 55/25. November 15, 2000.

UN Convention Relating to the Status of Refugees, adopted on July 28, 1951 by the United Nations Conference of Plenipotentiaries on the Status of Refugees and Stateless Persons, convened under General Assembly Resolution 429 (V) of December 14, 1950.

UNDESA. Report of the Meeting, Second United Nations Coordination Meeting on International Migration, at the Headquarters of the United Nations in New York, October 15–16, 2003. Available at http://www.un.org/esa/population/meetings/secoord2003/Final_Report.pdf.

UNDP. (2007). Human Development Report 2007/2008: Fighting Climate Change. New York: UNDP.

UN Division for the Advancement of Women. (2004). 2004 World Survey on the Role of Women in Development: Women and International Migration. New York: UN Division for the Advancement of Women.

UNESCO. (2010). *Approved Programme and Budget 2010–2011.* Paris: UNESCO.

UNFCCC. (2010). "Chronological Evolution of LDC work Programme and Concept of NAPAs." Available at http://unfccc.int/cooperation_support/least_developed_countries_portal/ldc_work_programme_and_napa/items/4722.php.

UNFPA. (1995). International Conference on Population and Development (ICPD) Programme of Action and Report of the International Conference on Population and Development. A/CONF.171/13/Rev.1. New York: UNFPA. Available at http://www.unfpa.org/webdav/site/global/shared/documents/publications/2004/icpd_eng.pdf.

UNFPA. (2000). *Replacement Migration: Is It a Solution to Declining and Ageing Populations?* New York: United Nations Population Division.

UNFPA. (2013). *Fertility Levels and Trends as Assessed in the 2012 Revision of World Population Prospects.* New York: United Nations Population Division.

UNFPA and IOM. (2006). *Framework for Operational Cooperation.* New York and Geneva: UNFPA and IOM.

UNHCR. (2000). Internally Displaced Persons: The Role of the United Nations High Commissioner for Refugees. Geneva: UNHCR. Available at http://www.refworld .org/docid/3ae6b33a0.html.

———. (2001). *Addressing Security Concerns without Undermining Refugee Protection: UNHCR's Perspective*. Geneva: UNHCR. Available at http://www.un.org/en/ sc/ctc/specialmeetings/2011/docs/unhcr-security-refugee-protection.pdf.

———. (2006a). *State of the World's Refugees*. Oxford: Oxford University Press.

———. (2006b). *Guidelines on International Protection No. 7: The Application of Article 1A(2) of the 1951 Convention and/or 1967 Protocol Relating to the Status of Refugees to Victims of Trafficking and Persons At Risk of Being Trafficked*. Geneva: UNHCR.

———. (2007a). *Handbook for the Protection of Internally Displaced Persons*. Provisional Release 2007. Available at http://www.unhcr.org/protect/PROTECTION/ 4794b6e72.pdf.

———. (2007b). Policy Framework and Corporate Strategy: UNHCR's Role in Support of an Enhanced Inter-Agency Response to the Protection of Internally Displaced Persons. January. Available at http://www.unhcr.org/excom/EXCOM/45c1ab432.pdf.

———. (2007c). Report of the fifty-eighth session of the Executive Committee of the High Commissioner's Programme, 21. Available at http://www.unhcr.org/excom/ EXCOM/471615cb2.pdf.

———. (2002). Statistical Yearbook. Geneva: UNHCR. Available at http://www.unhcr .org/41206f762.html.

———. (2007d). Statistical Yearbook. Geneva: UNHCR. Available at http://www .unhcr.org/4981b19d2.html.

———. (2008). Climate change, natural disasters and human displacement: a UNHCR perspective. Geneva: UNHCR. Available at http://www.unhcr.org/4901e81a4.html.

——— (2012). Statistical Yearbook. Geneva: UNHCR. Available at http://www.unhcr .org/52a7213b9.html

———. (2011a). *Update on the Humanitarian Situation in Libya and in the Neighbouring Countries*. Geneva: UNHCR.

———. (2011b). *Summary of Deliberations on Climate Change and Displacement*. Report. Bellagio: UNHCR, 2011.

"UNICEF and Migration." *Social and Economic Policy*. UNICEF. Available at http:// www.unicef.org/socialpolicy/index_migration.html.

UN International Strategy for Disaster Reduction (UNISDR). (2009). "Terminology on Disaster Risk Reduction." Available at www.unisdr.org/eng/terminology/ terminology-2009-eng.html.

United Nations. (1996). "Promotion and Protection of the Rights of Children: Impact of Armed Conflict on Children." A note by the Secretary General; Fifty-first session, Item 108 of the provisional agenda.

United Nations. (1946). *Constitution of the International Refugee Organization*, United Nations Treaty Series, vol. 18: 3. Available at: http://www.unhcr.org/refworld/docid/ 3ae6b37810.html.

United Nations. (2008). The Question of Palestine and the United Nations. New York: United Nations. Available at http://unispal.un.org/pdfs/DPI2499.pdf.

United Nations. (2012). The Future We Want: Outcome of the Rio Plus 20 Conference on Sustainable Development, Rio de Janeiro, Brazil, June 20–22, 2012 A/CONF.216/L.1*

"United Nations Action to Counter Terrorism." *UN News Center.* UN. Available at http://www.un.org/terrorism/instruments.shtml.

United Nations Conciliation Commission for Palestine (UNCCP). (1950). *Summary Record of a Meeting between the Conciliation Commission and Delegations of Egypt, the Hashemite Kingdom of the Jordan, Lebanon and Syria,* held at the Palais des Nations, Geneva, on Monday, 12 June 1950, at 4 p.m. Available at http://unispal.un .org/UNISPAL.NSF/0/BFC1325A49D49C4C85257535007A3EC8.

"United Nations Millennium Development Goals." (2013). *UN News Center.* UN. Available at http://www.un.org/millenniumgoals/global.shtml.

UNODC. (2009). *Global Report on Human Trafficking.* Vienna: United Nations Office of Drugs and Transnational Crime.

———. (2010). *Promoting Health, Security and Justice: 2010 Report.* Report. Vienna: UNODC.

———. (2011). *International Framework for Action to Implement the Smuggling of Migrants Protocol.* New York: UNODC.

———. (2012). UNODC's *Comprehensive Strategy to Combat Trafficking in Persons and Smuggling of Migrants.* Vienna: UNODC.

"United Nations Secretariat to the High Level Panel on System-wide Coherence." UN News Center. UN, 2006. Available at http://www.un.org/events/panel/.

UN Resolution Adopted by the General Assembly on 23 December 2005. Resolution 60/227 International Migration and Development.

UN Resolution Adopted by the General Assembly on 13 Oct 2010. Resolution 64/297 The United Nations Global Counter-Terrorism Strategy.United Nations Universal Declaration of Human Rights 1948.

University of British Columbia, Canada. (2005). "Human Security Report 2005: War and Peace in the 21st Century" Human Security Center: Oxford University Press.

UNWomen. (2011). Empowering Women Migrant Workers to Claim Their Rights and Celebrate Their Contribution to Development, Ninth Coordination Meeting On International Migration, Population Division, Department of Economic and Social Affairs, United Nations Secretariat, New York, February 17–18, 2011. Available at https://www.un.org/esa/population/meetings/ninthcoord2011/p13-unwomen.pdf.

U.S. Commission for the Study of International Migration and Cooperative Economic Development. (1990). *Unauthorized Migration: An Economic Development Response.* Washington, DC: Government Printing Office.

U.S. Department of Labor (1924). Annual Report of the Secretary of Labor. Washington, DC: Department of Labor.

US State Department (1943). *Foreign Relations of the United States Diplomatic Papers. Vol. 1.* Washington DC: U.S. Department of State.

U.S. State Department. (2004). Charter and Amendments: Human Smuggling and Trafficking Center (HSTC). July 9. Available at: http://www.state.gov/m/ds/hstcenter/ 41444.htm.

U.S. State Department. (2006). *Country Reports on Human Rights Practices.* Washington, DC: U.S. State Department.

U.S. State Department. (2007). *Trafficking in Persons Report.* Washington, DC: U.S. State Department.

U.S. State Department. (2012). *Trafficking in Persons Report.* Washington, DC: U.S. State Department.

Uy, Robert. (2011). "Blinded by Red Lights: Why Trafficking Discourse Should Shift Away from Sex and the 'Perfect Victim' Paradigm." *Berkeley Journal of Gender, Law & Justice*, 204–19.

van Ginneken, Anique H. M. (2006). *Historical Dictionary of the League of Nations*. Lanham, MD: Scarecrow.

"The Versailles Treaty June 28, 1919." *The Avalon Project: Documents in Law, History and Diplomacy*. Lillian Goldman Law Library, Yale University. Available at http://avalon.law.yale.edu/subject_menus/versailles_menu.asp.

Walker, Christopher J. (2004). "World War I and the Armenian Genocide" in Richard G. Hovannisian (eds.), *The Armenian People From Ancient to Modern Times, Volume II: Foreign Dominion to Statehood: The Fifteenth Century to the Twentieth Century*. New York: Palgrave Macmillan.

Walker, Francis A. (1896). "Restriction of Immigration." *The Atlantic*. Available at http://www.theatlantic.com/magazine/archive/1896/06/restriction-of-immigration/306011/.

Walter, Christian, Silja Vöneky, Volker Röben, and Frank Schorkopf (2004). *Terrorism as a Challenge for National and International Law*. Berlin: Springer.

Webber, Frances. (2011). "How Voluntary Are Voluntary Returns?" *Race and Class: Sage Journals* 52.98: 98–107.

Weiner, Myron. (1990). *Security, Stability, and International Migration*. Cambridge: Massachusetts Institute of Technology Press.

———. (1992–1993). "Security, Stability, and International Migration." *International Security* 17.3: 91–126.

Weiss, Paul. (1954). "The International Protection of Refugees." *The American Journal of International Law* 48.2: 193–221.

Weissbrodt, David. (2002). *Abolishing Slavery and Its Contemporary Forms*. New York & Geneva: United Nations.

White, Gregory. (2011). *Climate Change and Migration: Security and Borders in a Warming World*. Oxford: Oxford University Press.

Williams, Robert C. (1997). "The Emigration" in Edward Acton, Vladimir Cherniaev and William Rosenberg (eds.), *Critical Companion to the Russian Revolution: 1914–1921*. Bloomington: Indiana University Press, 507–14.

Wilson, Woodrow. (1917). *The World Must Be Made Safe for Democracy*. Speech presented to Congress, April 2.

"What Is the GMG?" *Global Migration Group (GMG)*. Available at http://www.globalmigrationgroup.org/en/what-is-the-gmg.

World Bank. (2006). *Global Economic Prospects: Economic Implications of Remittances and Migration*. Washington, DC: World Bank.

———. *Migration and Remittances Factbook 2011*. Washington, DC: World Bank.

Wubnig, Arthur. (1935). "Review of The Origins of the International Labor Organization by James T. Shotwell." *Pacific Affairs* 8.2: 245–47.

Zolberg, Aristide R., Astid Suhrke, and Sergio Aguayo. (1992). *Escape from Violence*. Oxford: Oxford University Press.

Zurcher, Erik-Jan. (2003). *Greek and Turkish Refugees and Deportees 1912–1924* in Turkology Update Leiden Project Working Papers Archive. Universiteit Leiden.

Index

34650642R00198

Made in the USA
Middletown, DE
29 August 2016